Theory and Practice of Writing

APPLIED LINGUISTICS AND LANGUAGE STUDY

General Editor
Professor Christopher N. Candlin, Macquarie University, Sydney

For a complete list of books in this series see pages vii–viii

Theory and Practice of Writing

An Applied Linguistic Perspective

William Grabe
and
Robert B. Kaplan

Longman

London and New York

PE
1404
.G65
1996

Addison Wesley Longman Limited
Edinburgh Gate
Harlow, Essex CM20 2JE, United Kingdom
and Associated Companies through the world.

Published in the United States of America
by Addison Wesley Longman, New York

First Published 1996
Second Impression 1997

First Published 1996

ISBN 0 582 553830 PPR

British Library Cataloguing-in-Publication Data
A catalogue record for this book is
available from the British Library

Library of Congress Cataloging-in-Publication Data
Grabe, William.
Theory and practice of writing: an applied linguistic perspective
/William Grabe and Robert B. Kaplan.
p. cm. – (Applied linguistics and language study)
Includes bibliographical references and index.
ISBN 0-582-55383-0 (ppr)
1. English language–Rhetoric–Study and teaching–Theory, etc.
2. English language–Study and teaching–Foreign speakers.
3. Academic writing–Study and teaching. 4. Applied linguistics.
I. Kaplan, Robert B. II. Title. III. Series.
PE1404.G65 1996
808'. 042'07–DC20   96-24745
                                           CIP

Set by 8H in 10/12pt Baskerville

Produced through Longman Malaysia, CLP

Contents

APPLIED LINGUISTICS AND LANGUAGE STUDY

GENERAL EDITOR

PROFESSOR CHRISTOPHER N. CANDLIN

Macquarie University, Sydney

Error Analysis
Perspectives on second
language acquisition
JACK RICHARDS

**Stylistics and the Teaching of
Literature**
HENRY WIDDOWSON

Constrastive Analysis
CARL JAMES

Language and Communication
JACK R. RICHARDS *and*
RICHARD W. SCHMIDT (EDS)

**Learning to Write: First
Language/Second Language**
AVIVA FREEDMAN, IAN PRINGLE
and JANICE YALDEN (EDS)

**Strategies in Interlanguage
Communication**
CLAUS FAERCH *and* GABRIELE KASPER
(EDS)

Reading in a Foreign Language
J. CHARLES ALDERSON *and*
A.H. URQUHART (EDS)

**An Introduction to Discourse
Analysis**
New Edition
MALCOLM COULTHARD

**Language Awareness in the
Classroom**
CARL JAMES *and* PETER GARRETT

Bilingualism in Education
Aspects of theory, research and
practice
JIM CUMMINS *and* MERRILL SWAIN

Second Language Grammar:
Learning and Teaching
WILLIAM E. RUTHERFORD

**The Classroom and the
Language Learner**
Ethnography and second-language
classroom research
LEO VAN LIER

Vocabulary and Language Teaching
RONALD CARTER *and* MICHAEL
McCARTHY (EDS)

**Observation in the Language
Classroom**
DICK ALLWRIGHT

Listening to Spoken English
Second Edition
GILLIAN BROWN

Listening in Language Learning
MICHAEL ROST

**An Introduction to Second
Language Acquisition Research**
DIANE LARSEN-FREEMAN *and*
MICHAEL H. LONG

Language and Discrimination
A study of communication in
multi-ethnic workplaces
CELIA ROBERTS, TOM JUPP *and*
EVELYN DAVIES

**Translation and Translating:
Theory and Practice**
ROGER T. BELL

**Process and Experience in the
Language Classroom**
MICHAEL LEGUTKE *and*
HOWARD THOMAS

Rediscovering Interlanguage
LARRY SELINKER

**Language as Discourse: Perspectives
for Language Teaching**
MICHAEL MCCARTHY *and*
RONALD CARTER

Foreword

This volume presents an applied linguistics perspective on the theory and practice of writing. An examination of writing and writing instruction from an applied linguistics orientation, however, is a daunting task. First, a comprehensive study of writing in first-language contexts is itself a difficult interdisciplinary undertaking. One must consider perspectives from English, education, linguistics, psychology, and sociology. In addition, there are radically different issues and concerns which emerge when discussing the teaching of writing to children at elementary schools as opposed to tertiary (undergaduate and post-graduate) students.

An applied linguistics perspective complicates the situation further. As an interdisciplinary field in itself, applied linguistics adds new dimensions to the study of writing. The varieties of writing to be accounted for, the increased complexity of purposes for learning to write, and the added cross-cultural variations created by different groups of second-language learners all force the study of writing into a larger framework. We have attempted to survey the nature of writing and the teaching of writing from this larger framework, and, in doing so, have inevitably remained faithful to an applied linguistics inquiry. As applied linguists, we may also have made assumptions about the nature and development of language abilities that may be unfamiliar to some teachers and teacher trainers. We sincerely believe that such potential obstacles to understanding can be rectified with an introductory text in linguistics.

Adopting a broad interdisciplinary orientation, the book discusses major issues in writing research, current directions in the teaching of writing, and the somewhat ill-defined set of connections between theory and practice in many instructional contexts. As applied linguists, we intend this volume to contribute especially to an understanding of those connections between theory and practice in writing and, at the same time, to reveal the many different and complex settings in which such connections must take place. To the extent that these connections are clarified, attendant problems raised, and directions for resolution suggested, the volume will have achieved its primary goal. Of course, it would be unreasonable to think that any volume could be fully successful in achieving this goal. The undertaking of this volume has certainly revealed to us the limitations under which we have laboured, particularly with respect to the demands of an applied linguistics framework.

This volume is expected by its publisher and by its audience to have genuinely international interest; that is, the discussion is expected to contain information that transcends national boundaries and has universal applicability. We believe that in the discussion of theory we have succeeded in providing notions that do indeed transcend the local – that do reflect the cutting edge of research everywhere. However, to the extent that we have dealt with practice, we have had to imagine an idealized classroom, some specific context of teacher/student interaction, and some real characteristics of teachers and students who enter into such an interaction. It is, we believe, impossible to create these idealized situations without starting from some specific context.

We confess to some bias in creating the framework within which our theoretical discussions occur. We, as authors, both work primarily in the USA and, as a consequence, are more familiar with US-based publications and US-based scholars. We primarily attend conferences that are convened in the USA; we exploit the resources of libraries in the USA; we communicate largely with other scholars who share our geographic (and philosophical) constraints, and – because we work in the USA – we have concentrated our individual and collective research on the solutions of applied linguistic problems which derive from, and apply to, conditions in that country.

This is not to suggest that our experience is entirely myopic. We have both, at various times and for various intervals, worked in other environments in other geographical areas and, together, we have had at least some experience in approximately a score of educational systems. But as this exposure is certainly not universal and covers a great many years, our knowledge of other educational systems is often dated.

In compiling this volume we have tried to incorporate a wider international perspective, drawing upon our collective experience of other educational systems, and have looked carefully at the applied linguistics research deriving from other literature that was available to us in international journals and books. On occasion, we have been randomly assisted by colleagues in other countries who have made more local research materials available, and the extent to which we have succeeded in drawing together such international, or perhaps more accurately *multinational*, resources, will determine the broad applicability of this volume and will reflect perspectives from at least those parts of the world in which applied linguistic research is done on the teaching and learning of English.

If we are to any extent guilty of an academic myopia, we apologize to our colleagues and readers. We trust that readers who are interested in any larger issues that have been omitted will bear with us, as we believe that we have covered the various facets of most of our research paradigms fairly and fairly exhaustively. Some of the issues may appear to have pertinence only in the US context, but the linguistic and cultural diversity of that country is so great that notions deriving from that base will certainly have wider implications.

With respect to the matter of practice, many of our ideas and illustrations have admittedly been drawn from a US context, but many of the suggestions we offer will be of use to teachers in any geographic location. Nevertheless, we cannot pretend that all of the suggestions have universal applicability, nor can we pretend that, given our conceptual constraints, we have exhausted the possibilities for practice in all possible contexts. We hope that the readers of this volume understand that we are not offering a perfect set of pedagogical practices – or that our notions of things to do exhaust the possible or the useful – but rather we hope that this volume will be regarded as an ideas supermarket in which readers are welcome to shop.

In closing this foreword, we would like to thank a number of individuals who have been willing to provide us with feedback on various parts of the volume – Angela Barker, Jena Burgess, Ulla

Connor, Tom Miller and Fredricka Stoller. We would also like to thank Chris Candlin and Longman for their guidance and patience as we managed to work through a project that extended us far beyond out initial expectations.

April 1996

William Grabe
Northern Arizona University

Robert B. Kaplan
University of Southern California

This volume is respectfully dedicated to
Kathe Rositzke and Audrey Kaplan

General Editor's Preface

'Good soup needs no salt' strikes one as an apt maxim for General Editors to bear in mind with any volume such as this that seeks to offer an extensive account of a central topic of applied linguistics. The scope of this latest contribution to the *Applied Linguistics & Language Sudy Series* is necessarily so extensive not only because of the obvious pervasiveness of *writing* but because of the signal significance of its plural roles; as a means of measuring cognitive abilities, as a central skill area in the design of educational curricula and in the patterns of their delivery in teaching and assessment, as a way of understanding some of the occupational and social demands of daily communication in living and working, in revealing its key gatekeeping role in enabling or disabling the sheer accessibility of life chances for all in contemporary industrial and post industrial societies, and its ethnographic significance in exploring and explaining cultural variation and relativities. And yet, despite the extensiveness of the treatment here, there is room and a place to highlight why this book is needed now. The reason lies partly in the need to highlight and unpack these ever-differentiating roles and multiple purposes, and, more than that, even in the face of apparently major distinctions of first and second language performances, in so doing to reassert the essential nature of writing and the writing process as overarching, despite that variation and that fragmentation.

Appropriately enough, then, the authors begin with an exploration of the nature of writing, its authorships, their individual ande collective purposes, and the rationales that motivate these writing processes and their varied output texts. They argue that the facets of writing sketched above cannot at one level be treated individually, nor can one facet be asserted as necessarily prime: their discussion of *composing*, for example, is at once cognitive, social, personal and educational. Nor, in their view, can writing be appropriately addressed without reference to its histories. Not only the genesis of writing *per se*, (though that is interesting in itself in just such a complex way) but in the varied histories of writing development in different socio-cultural and socio-political con-texts – the relative conditions of production and reception of writing at different times and in different circumstances – in short, the socially and culturally embedded and contested mul-tiple literacies of writing. Nor again, as they demonstrate, can writing now be usefully discussed as a domain entirely distinct from that of speech. Research on text structure, into the social practices of literacy and oracy in different communities, into the interconnectedness of speech and writing in public discourse, into the intertextuality and interdiscursivity of many if not most con-temporary genres, all point to a needed multidimensionality in the study and practice of writing.

From this point, then, Bill Grabe and Bob Kaplan embark, and provide in their first introductory Chapter a cogent and defining account of writing research in English in first and second lan-guage contexts, drawing on the facets of the writing process identified above, and in the context of varied responses to a plu-rality of writing needs. Such an account permits them a second overlay of interdisciplinarity – that of the methodologies of writing research. Here they show how some asserted distinctions between L1 and L2 writing, already problematic cognitively and also socially in many contexts, similarly blend and become fuzzy in research terms as experimental, linguistic/textual, ethnographic and social psychological techniques form aspects and tools of a common repertoire.

We should, however, be properly cautious in celebrating this unity in diversity. Seen from the point of view of the history of writing practice and writing pedagogy, especially in English, there is now and has been at once much more overt sectarianism and at the same time masked differences of purpose, than one might assume. 'Genre-based', 'process-focused', 'whole language', 'product-orientated' may be less descriptions of academic or educational value than they are manipulated slogans for the credulous, yet they do signify importantly distinguishable positions, if as I say, often exploited. Approaches to textual description are not uncontested, nor are their 'applications' to instructional materials. Teaching strategies ought not to be simply read off from some linguistic analysis, however successful a blend of the formal and functional. Students' writing practices should not be assessable simply as solo performances in terms of a belief that some targetted cognitive strategy can mutate into acceptable linguistic form. Nor in the context of writing development seen as a not too covert recruitment into some disciplinary or professional specialism, should such individual writing performances merely be seen as momentary personal and individual responses to some given instructional task. The value of this book is that while acknowledging this variability, it is still bold enough to assert and document the core issues that writing research and writing practice has addressed and still must address.

It does so in thorough detail in its following chapters. Beginning appropriately enough with the text as product, it locates it, equally convincingly, as a tangible, analysable artefact deriving from two related inferrable processes of discourse: the discourse of the writer and the discourse of the reader. Such discourses are at once cognitive and socially conditioned, personal and functional, to a degree accessible through experimental, ethnographic and social psychological accounting, but always to be seen as mutually influencing through the potentially explanatory evidence of the text. Writing and reading processes are thus interconnected in the text. It is this position which permits the authors to warrant their other characteristic close interconnection in this book, that of research and practice. Indeed, one might see writing and reading as their own research laboratories, their own research methodologies, their own research agendas. After all, what is a writer (or a reader for that matter) doing except to test out theories about the realisation of some mental discursive process within the general and actual constraints of the personally available formal system of the lexicogrammar?

Nonetheless, despite this mutuality, the relationship between theory and practice in writing research and instruction has not been self-evident. In part, as the authors argue, this has been a consequence of a more general separation of powers between the academy and the school (let alone the home or the workplace, one might add, in respect of both). In part this has been due to a lack of clarity within each institution about the range of writing skills, knowledge bases and writing processes and how these may be integrated in a descriptive model of language processing in a manner such as that which Grabe and Kaplan outline in their keystone Chapter 8 'Towards a theory of writing'. In part this has been due to an understandable if perverse unwillingness to grasp fully in either teaching or research practice the verity of writing: that interdependence of writer, reader, text and topic I focus on above.

In the sections of this notable chapter, who writes what, to whom, for what purpose, why, when, where and how is, of course, at one level simply to transpose and extend Fishman's famous dictum about sociolinguistics. At another, it defines the questions and conditions for research and for practice. You could build a curriculum on addressing those questions, and as the authors show in their subsequent chapters, some educators have done so, though few, if any, with all the questions in the air at the same time. The conditions, as Brecht wrote, were not right. In a similar way, you could construct a research agenda from those questions, but here, disappointingly and with less excuse, the need for a concurrent consideration of these mutually influencing questions has also been less evident. One might speculate why. My view is that the particularity of the research response derives from the particularity of applied linguistics training. A focus on text without a focus as well on discourse, a focus on the individual rather than as well on the cultural or institutional collective, a focus on the actual rather than as well on the historically conditioned, a focus on the cognitive in the absence of a focus as well on the social, a focus on the instruction rather than as well on the learning, a focus on the linguistic rather than as well as on the subject-matter, all these particularities work to create the conditions which make such an interdisciplinarity of the questions impossible to conceive for researchers, and thus to turn into relevant and authenticated research practice.

Seen in this way, this book about the theory and practice of writing turns out to have a wider implication. Read this way, it becomes a book about the state of the art of applied linguistics, and how the problem-focused nature of the discipline, identified by the authors at the outset, is shown to be relevant not just for its 'applications' but for the discipline of applied linguistics itself.

Professor Christopher N Candlin
General Editor
Macquarie University,
Sydney, Australia

1

Issues in writing research and instruction

1.1 Introduction

Applied linguistics has concerned itself with the development of writing skills for at least the past 50 years, and that it has done so is entirely appropriate. If one is to take seriously the relatively straightforward definition of applied linguistics as the attempt to resolve real-world language-based problems, then the development of writing abilities, whether for learners of English as a first language (L1), or as a second language (L2), or learners of any other language, surely falls well within the domain of applied linguistics.

There are, however, significant differences between the two groups of learners, since there are wide variations in learner issues within each of these major groups. These differences and their consequences for writing theory and instruction will be explored throughout the book. The treatment of both groups within a single volume is, however, the only logical applied linguistics perspective to adopt since both groups subsume learning and instructional problems which are language-based, and there is significant overlap in their historical evolution over the past 20 years. The decision to ignore English first-language research and practice would not only lead to a badly distorted view of L2 writing approaches, it would also misinterpret the true scope of applied linguistics inquiry with respect to issues in writing development.

This chapter outlines many of the larger issues and problems implicit in the theory and practice of writing instruction, adopting a broad applied linguistics perspective. In exploring issues in writing, basic assumptions about the nature of writing must be considered. For example, *why* do people write? That is to say, *what*

1

different sorts of writing are done by *which different groups* of people, and for *what different purposes*? More fundamentally, one must ask: *What constitutes writing*? Such basic questions cannot be discussed in a vacuum but must also consider the larger issues raised by literacy skills development and literacy demands in various contexts. Literacy, incorporating specific writing issues with a related set of reading issues, highlights the necessary connections between reading and writing as complementary comprehension/production processes. It also introduces the distinctions between spoken and written language forms, and the specific constraints of the written medium. Thus, a brief overview of literacy provides an important background for understanding the recent developments in writing theory and instruction.

Any discussion of basic foundations must necessarily incorporate outlines of research on both writing in English as the first language and writing in a second language. From the L1 perspective, many theoretical issues and concerns in L1 contexts also affect writing approaches in L2 situations. From the L2 perspective, research in L2 writing also highlights differences between the two contexts. The many additional variables introduced in L2 contexts – not only cognitive but also social, cultural and educational – make considerations of writing in a second language substantially different in certain respects.

This chapter also explores the gap between research and instruction and considers how that gap may be bridged. The translation from theory to practice in L1 writing contexts has changed considerably over the past 20 years. Such a translation has also had a profound impact on L2 applications from theory to practice; some of these applications have been appropriate, while others have been much less appropriate, given the distinct L2 context. For example, L2 instruction may:

- place writing demands on EFL students, and for some of them, English may not be perceived as a very important subject;
- place distinct writing demands on English for Special Purposes (ESP) students, or on English for Occupational Purposes (EOP) students – demands which may be very different from those on English for Academic Purposes (EAP) students planning to enter English medium universities;
- include writing demands on adult literacy and immigrant survival English students – both groups experiencing very different demands from those which occur in academic contexts;

- include academic writing demands in which a sophisticated level of writing is not a critical concern.

All of these issues form parts of an overview of writing theory and practice from an applied linguistics perspective.

1.2   On the nature of writing

The need for writing in modern literate societies – societies marked by pervasive print media – is much more extensive than is generally realized. When one examines the everyday world, one finds people engaged in many varieties of writing, some of which may be overlooked as being routine, or commonplace, or unimportant. These varieties, however, all represent the ability to control the written medium of language to some extent. It is fair to say that most people, on a typical day, practice some forms of writing. And virtually everyone in every walk of life completes an enormous number of forms. In addition, many people write for reasons unrelated to their work: letters, diaries, messages, shopping lists, budgets, etc.

Describing the various tasks performed every day by writers offers one way of classifying what people write, but a slightly more abstract taxonomy of writing types will prove more descriptively useful. A list of actual writing tasks does not provide a way to group these tasks according to similar function – a goal in understanding what gets written and why. In fact, many different functional sorts of writing constitute common occurrences. These sorts of writing, depending on the context, task, and audience, may be classified functionally in numerous ways, including writing to identify, to communicate, to call to action, to remember, to satisfy requirements, to introspect, or to create, either in terms of recombining existing information or in terms of aesthetic form. Thus:

- writing down one's name identifies
- writing a shopping list may identify, communicate, and/or remind
- writing a memo may communicate and remind
- writing a student essay may at least satisfy a requirement
- writing a diary may promote introspection
- writing a professional article may communicate, recombine, and allow introspection

- writing a novel or a poem may exemplify what is known as aesthetic creativity.

At yet another development level, one may distinguish writing which involves composing from writing which does not; this distinction is useful because most of what is referred to academically as writing assumes composing. Composing involves the combining of structural sentence units into a more-or-less unique, cohesive and coherent larger structure (as opposed to lists, forms, etc.). A piece of writing which implicates composing contains surface features which connect the discourse and an underlying logic of organization which is more than simply the sum of the meanings of the individual sentences. Figure 1.1 illustrates the composing/non-composing dichotomy in terms of audience. The matrix suggests the possible options that are available for writing with or without composing.

Composing, further, may be divided into writing which is, in essence, telling or retelling and writing which is transforming. Retelling signifies the sort of writing that is, to a large extent, already known to the author, such as narratives and descriptions.

Audience	Writing without composing	Writing with composing	
		For knowledge telling	For knowledge transforming
Self	Shopping list	Personal diary	'Journal' notes
One known other	Note to milkman	Personal letter	
One unknown other		Business letter	
Small group known		Lesson plan sermon	
Small group unknown	Questionnaire	Newsletter item	Proposal
Large group	Tax form Driver's licence application form		Poem, drama novel Short story

Figure 1.1   Patterns of composing with differing audiences

The planning involves recalling and reiterating. Transforming, on the other hand, signifies that sort of writing for which no blueprint is readily available. The planning involves the complex juxtaposition of many pieces of information as well as the weighing of various rhetorical options and constraints (Bereiter and Scardamalia 1987). In this type of writing, the author is not certain of the final product; on the contrary, the writing act constitutes a heuristic through which an information-transfer problem is solved both for the author and for his or her intended audience. This notion of composing is much more comprehensive than the idea of drafting or 'shaping at the point of utterance' (Britton 1983), since it takes in the 'final' product. Many sorts of what traditionally have been labelled expository and argumentative/persuasive texts, as well as 'creative' writing, involve transforming. In Figure 1.1, an attempt has been made to distinguish between retelling and transforming, even though both organizing strategies are available for many sorts of composing.

In most academic settings where students are learning to write, the educational system assumes that students will learn to compose with the ability to transform information. In fact, many students learning to write before they enter the tertiary level have little consistent exposure to writing demands beyond retelling. In some cases, students, both in L1 and L2, have minimal practice even with simple retelling. The problems created by these students as they enter the academic environment certainly deserve the attention of applied linguists. Moreover, writing places constraints on student learning that are distinct from the development of spoken language abilities.

To understand these developmental constraints on students, and the more complex demands made by academic institutions, it will be useful to examine briefly the historical development of writing and the changing writing/literacy expectations which have arisen over the last two centuries.

Writing is a rather recent invention, historically speaking. Unlike spoken language – coterminous with the history of the species – written language has a documented history of little more than 6000 years. And while it is generally accepted by linguists that certain aspects of spoken language may be biologically determined, the same cannot be said of writing. While all normally developing people learn to speak a first language, perhaps half of the world's current population does not know how to read or write to a functionally adequate level, and one-fifth of the world's population is totally non-literate. It seems a bit absurd to suggest that this difference is accidental, due to the inaccessibility of writing instruments or material to read. Nor does it seem appropriate to label this one-fifth of humankind as somehow 'abnormal'.

The distinction between spoken and written media calls attention to a significant constraint on the development of writing abilities. Writing abilities are not naturally acquired; they must be culturally (rather than biologically) transmitted in every generation, whether in schools or in other assisting environments. While there are many distinctions between the two media in terms of lexical and structural use, the acquired/learned distinction deserves particular attention. The logical conclusion to draw from this distinction is that writing is a technology, a set of skills which must be practised and learned through experience. Defining writing in this way helps to explain why writing of the more complex sorts causes great problems for students; the skills required do not come naturally, but rather are gained through conscious effort and much practice. It is also very likely, for this reason, that numbers of students may never develop the more sophisticated composing skills which transform information into new texts.

The crucial notion is not that writing subsumes a set body of techniques to master, as might be claimed, for example, in learning to swim; rather, the crucial notion is that writing is not a natural ability that automatically accompanies maturation (Liberman and Liberman 1990). Writing – particularly the more complex composing skill valued in the academy – involves training, instruction, practice, experience, and purpose. Saying that writing is a technology implies only that the way people learn to write is essentially different from the way they learn to speak, and there is no guarantee that any person will read or write without some assistance.

1.3   Literacy and writing

The history of literacy development supports such a writing-as-technology perspective for the nature of writing. Indeed, a number of literacy scholars have argued for this view strongly; any other definition of literacy does not stand up to the historical evidence (Goody 1987, Graff 1987). Since there are, in fact, many types of literacy which have developed historically under very different contexts and for very different uses, any more complex definition tends not to hold up equally well in all contexts (cf. Cressy 1980, Graff 1987, Houston 1988, Purves 1991). Moreover, the history of literacy demonstrates that reading and writing skills were developed and passed on to following generations only in response to cultural and social contexts; these skills were not maintained when appropriate social and cultural supports were removed.

In fact, the definition of writing-as-technology fits extremely well with historical perspectives on literacy because many literacy movements and developments were little more than the wider dissemination of very basic skills, such as the ability to write one's name or fill out a ledger or a form. Such literacy developments hardly count as the sort of writing-as-composing discussed earlier or as the type that is valued academically; yet, these literacy developments undeniably reflect aspects of writing abilities.

The history of literacy development is both enlightening and commonly misunderstood. It is enlightening because the many and varied literacy movements and contexts of literacy development provide a better understanding of the current use of, and expectations for, students' writing abilities; it is often misunderstood because many assumptions about literacy have been widely promoted and accepted without careful documentation and analysis (cf. Graff 1987). One significant point that the study of literacy has demonstrated, both synchronically and diachronically, is that there are many different sorts of literacy skills just as there are many different sorts of writing abilities. Most students who display writing problems in educational contexts do, in fact, have writing skills; they are just not the skills which educational institutions value (Barton and Ivanic 1991, Street 1993). This is particularly true for L2 students in EAP contexts; they clearly come to higher academic institutions with many different literacy practices and many different views on the purposes of reading and writing.

The history of Western literacy begins (from *c.* 3100 BC) with the early uses of writing for recording events, traditions, and transactions by scribal specialists who were able to translate orally for the masses as was necessary. The powers of priesthood can be attributed to the apparently mystical properties associated with the ability to read and write. The rise of the Greek city-states signalled a greater dissemination of literacy skills among the populace. However, literacy among the classical Greek citizenry was less widespread and less sophisticated than has commonly been assumed. Perhaps only 15–20 per cent of the Greek population consisted of 'citizenry', and oral traditions were still the trusted and preferred means of communicating. Similarly, the Roman period was marked by a limited literacy among the populace; in this context, literacy was due in large part to the rise of public schooling, the need for civil servants to do government business in the far-flung regions of the empire, and the rise of commercial literacy needs. Nevertheless, it was a very small intellectual, political, and religious élite that possessed literacy skills (cf. Goody 1987, Graff 1987).

The decline of Rome saw the role of literacy relegated primarily to the religious infrastructure which emerged across Europe from the fourth to the eighth century. While many schooling traditions of the Roman era persisted throughout Western Europe, most were taken over by the church for the training of priests, clerics, and other functionaries. The development of literacy for other than religious uses began during the eighth to tenth centuries; and contrary to popular belief, the 'Dark Ages' was not a period of complete illiteracy beyond the monastery walls. The tenth and eleventh centuries marked the beginnings of a commercial literacy and set the stage for literacy practices across Europe from the twelfth to the fifteenth century. It is evident from the research of such scholars as Harvey Graff that literacy has a continuous history in Europe from the Greek city-states to the present. What must also be understood is that literacy was still restricted, tied to church, state, or economic necessity, and to particular practices in particular contexts. The mass literacy to which we are accustomed simply did not exist and, during most of this time, the ability to compose was extremely limited.

As noted above, religious institutions played a critical role in the history of Western literacy. It was not until the evolution of Protestantism in the sixteenth century that popular literacy became necessary. Unlike the Roman Catholic church, Protestant theology took the view that personal salvation could be achieved through direct access to the biblical gospels. Protestant sects have contributed importantly to world literacy through missionary activities which supported the translation of the Bible into hundreds of non-Indo-European languages as well as the teaching of literacy in the languages of the missionaries (e.g. English, French,

German, Spanish) for purposes of access to the Bible in European languages (e.g. the work of the Summer Institute of Linguistics and the Wycliff Bible Translators).

The first well-defined popular literacy movement in Europe may arguably be traced to the English revolution and the rise of Oliver Cromwell or to Martin Luther and the Protestant reformation. (The earlier development of Hangul in Korea should not be overlooked, though it is unlikely that literacy beyond the aristocracy was a serious objective.) The clearest early case of a successful mass literacy movement, however, is attributable to the Swedish movement of the seventeenth century to require of all Swedish citizens the ability to read the Bible (Arnove and Graff 1987, Graff 1987). This movement was remarkably successful since reading the Bible was a prerequisite for religious confirmations, and confirmation in the church was a requirement for marriage. For the first time, women as well as men were trained in literacy skills. This literacy campaign, however, as in much of the previous history of literacy, concentrated almost exclusively on reading, and in particular on reading the Bible. The role of writing in common literacy development can only be seen as an innovation of the last 200 or so years. Even rudimentary writing skills (beyond signing and recording) among the populace were unknown until very recently.[1]

In the modern historical era, the rise of popular literacy – including the uses of writing for secular purposes beyond government and business – emerged in the late eighteenth century, primarily in England, France and the USA. As traced by Cook-Gumperz (1986; see also Resnick and Resnick 1977), the rise of modern literacy (including writing skills) can be seen as occurring in three stages. Roughly, the period between 1750 and 1850 can be considered to mark the rise of common literacy (not school-directed or taught). In the mid-nineteenth century, parts of continental Europe, the UK, and the USA supported the rise of schooled literacy along with the beginnings of compulsory education. Literacy then became a means whereby the ruling classes could train the larger populace to be more efficient workers – a tool in support of the status quo, a gateway for upward mobility for a chosen few, and a means to control the spread of information to the larger society. It is also the case that the quantifiable level of skills needed to be considered literate were subject to definition by the élite. As the pressure on the élite increased, in part through the spread of literacy, the élite redefined the degree of literacy necessary for entry – thus, a constantly increasing literacy demand evolved.

In the twentieth century, literacy has undergone at least one profound transformation. The growth of positivism and the belief that scientific progress would resolve all problems led to the use of psychometric testing and evaluation procedures in European and American educational systems. This pervasive influence on educational systems led to gradually increasing expectations of literacy uses in society and of literacy expectations in academic training. It also served to compartmentalize and stratify students at many levels of skills and abilities; finally, it introduced to education the notion of failure and remediation. Students could be classified as deficient in particular skills and the notion that literacy could be a problem rather than an opportunity took hold.

After the Second World War, the increasing demands for professional uses of literacy concomitantly increased demands on reading and writing training. Professional literacy now is the goal of educational systems throughout much of the literate world. The rise of professional literacy has also led to an increasing demand on the sort of writing ability that involved composing (Kaestle *et al.* 1991, Purves 1991, Stedman and Kaestle 1987). It is also through the growth of compulsory schooling during the twentieth century that writing has come to be emphasized both in school and in white-collar employment. It remains to be seen what impact computers will eventually have on the conception of literacy. While there have been a number of extravagant assertions that the computer will transform literacy, and the 'word', it may be quite some time before such a transformation is realized. The Greeks took centuries to make the alphabetic system a tool of wider literacy for its citizenry (Graff 1987), and the printing press (a technological innovation of enormous importance in the increasing dissemination of texts) as an agency of change took centuries to have a major impact on mass literacy (Eisenstein 1979, 1985). It may therefore be generations before the capabilities of the computer cause significant transformation in literacy practices.

The last two centuries in the history of Western literacy are paralleled by changes in the demands and expectations in students' writing abilities. Most school rhetorics in the eighteenth and nineteenth centuries amounted to rudimentary guides to usage and etiquette. At the tertiary level, however, writing instruction and composition became important aspects of a university education as part of rhetorical studies, coinciding with the influential rhetorics of Campbell (1776), Blair (1783), and Priestley (1777). As one outcome of this trend, Freshman Composition courses were initiated at Harvard in 1874 (Berlin 1984); instruction in freshman composition in the USA has never looked back (Berlin 1984, 1987, Crowley 1990, 1995). Why this trend should take hold so strongly in US but not European institutions is a question which deserves study. Whatever the motivations, they led to a rapid institutional growth in composition instruction in the USA which was not paralleled elsewhere. And while the recent history of rhetoric and composition is long and complex, the still accepted 'current traditional' approach to writing instruction has at least a 100-year tradition going back to the inception of freshman composition courses in the USA. Such approaches are recognizable through the emphasis on handbooks, the use of model texts, and theme writing in the various modes of discourse (which, even until 20 years ago, was uniformly popular).

The current academic interest in literacy and writing is readily traceable to the recent historical evolution of professional literacy. Over the past 15–20 years, educators have complained of a 'crisis in the schools' because of the observed decline in national test scores in the USA (and elsewhere in the English-speaking world – e.g. Australia, Canada, New Zealand – as well as in new nations which rely on English as a national or official language – e.g. Hong Kong). In the USA, arguments have been advanced by politicians, educators, and parents that literacy standards have been declining at the time when political and economical skills are in greatest need. These concerns, of more importance to administrators and politicians, do not seem well-founded in the light of a sober history of literacy, nor do they reflect the realities of an ever increasing school population. As more lower socio-economic class and minority students were added to the population taking these tests, it should have been expected that a temporary decline would occur (Coe 1986). It is only symptomatic of the effect of larger numbers of people aspiring to higher education and social mobility; it is not an inevitable sign of cultural decay or of educational literacy failure (cf. Bracey 1995, Stedman 1994).

The current popular concern over literacy has generated a number of theories concerning its nature and its consequences on both the individual and society. The consequences of literacy on society are well attested and quite profound, as literacy is a socially motivated phenomenon; its purposes, uses, and values are determined by the society in which such literacy skills are practised. Literacy is not a universally uniform set of skills, but rather a set of highly contextualized skills, determined by the society in which it functions (Street 1984, 1993). An opposing view focuses more directly on the cognitive influence of literacy on the individual: the theory, commonly referred to as the 'Great Divide' or the 'Great Leap' theory of individual cognitive development, claims great individual cognitive changes as a consequence of the acquisition of literacy (Goody 1977, Olson 1977; cf. Gee 1986, Goody 1987, Olson 1994). In brief, this theory holds that learning to read and write alters the cognitive thought processes of the individual; literacy transforms the way in which the mind functions.

Since the mid-1960s, various scholars have argued for this 'Great Divide' position, primarily on logical rather than historical grounds. The seminal article triggering this view of literacy and its consequences for the individual was published by Goody and Watt ('The consequences of literacy') in 1963. This article argued for the 'Great Divide' theory as a result of the Greek adoption of the alphabetic principle. The alphabetic principle led to mass literacy among the Greek citizenry – a change in Greek society, it was argued, which subsequently led to the (asserted) inventive genius of classical Greek civilization. Goody and Watt argued more generally that the rise of literacy led to a number of dramatic changes (both social and individual):

- the domination of history over myth
- the distinction between the natural and the supernatural
- the ability to store and access greater amounts of knowledge
- the creation of abstract logical deduction
- the ability to analyse language itself as an object
- the awareness of the individual as distinct from the group and consequently the need for private introspection
- the rise of critical scepticism towards previously reified knowledge and beliefs
- the rise of democratic institutions.

This long list of consequences reads remarkably like a set of educational goals in modern Western school systems. Thus, it is easy to see how literacy has come to be equated with the essence of academic education. The 'Great Divide' view has received support from a variety of sources over the last 30 years. Scholars such as Havelock (1976), Olson (1977), Ong (1982), and Vygotsky (1962, 1978) have raised arguments of a similar nature with respect to the acquisition of literacy.

In the last 15 years, a number of strong refutations of this theory of individual cognitive differences have emerged. Even earlier, Gough (1968) compared the rise of literacy in Greece with similar historical evolutions in India and China. Her research indicated that different societies do not necessarily follow the same paths of developments as a result of literacy dissemination among the population. In particular, the notions of history-as-concept, deductive logic, and democratic institutions as consequences of literacy were not supported. Her research led later scholars to qualify early claims for individual differences since she demonstrated that societal contexts play a large role in the uses and consequences of literacy.

The line of reasoning that literacy is a social phenomenon (in service to the social milieu) rather than a universally consistent cognitive phenomenon was strongly supported by the research of Scribner and Cole (1981). In a series of studies on the acquisition of literacy among the Vai people of Liberia, they showed that literacy alone did not account for any generalized cognitive differences among the subjects; rather, they found that specific skill differences among subjects were a consequence of specific skills and tasks emphasized by each type of literacy (Vai, Arabic, or English). Schooled education rather than literacy appeared to predict the sorts of individual cognitive skills – such as abstract deductive reasoning, drawing logical inference, and connecting unrelated information – which are assumed to result from learning to read and write. Rather than literacy being the cause of the cognitive skills valued by academic institutions, it would seem that the skills are inculcated by the institutions, which then attribute to these skills the idea that they represent basic cognitive development.

The cognitive impact that may be attributed to literacy is more probably the result of the gradual extension of specific literacy-related skills learned in particular situations (cf. Goody 1987, Olson 1991, Scholes 1993) which, themselves, are socially embedded. Further support for the socially embedded nature of literacy skills has appeared in a range of educational research (e.g. Boggs 1985, Cook-Gumperz 1986, Heath 1983, 1986b).

This current research, in combination with the historical research of Graff, demonstrates that literacy skills and literacy acquisition do not constitute a single unitary cognitive process across cultures and social groups; rather, there are different sorts of literacy skills which develop to serve the needs of each social/cultural group. School children, when they participate in schools, are typically not literate or illiterate; they bring the practices of their community or social group or family to the classroom (cf. Bernstein 1972a, 1990, Halliday 1978, Hasan 1989, Heath 1983, Wells 1986). Problems occur when the sorts of literacy practices of certain students do not conform to the expected literacy practices of the school community. The central issue in literacy development is not the development of uniform cognitive skills, but the recognition that there are many different literacy practices, of which only a few are likely to be valued by a given educational system. At the same time, it is likely that the availability of the technology of literacy modifies the way in which a society behaves; no specific theory of cognitive change is necessary to support such a notion (cf. Goody 1987, Olson 1991, 1994).

Akin to this history of literacy, the study of writing – its history, uses, purposes, and consequences – must be seen as socially contexted. There is not a unique set of writing skills which universally defines all of writing, apart from particular social contexts. There are many different ways to practise writing, and an educational system typically values one particular set of writing practices, and not every student – particularly not every immigrant student – will come into the educational context having practised that set of writing skills valued by the educational structure.[2] This does not necessarily mean that such students 'don't know how to write' or that they are cognitively deficient; but only that they are not well versed in the practices of writing which are valued institutionally. Following this line of reasoning, it is not enough simply to teach the valued practices of the academic discourse community; it is also necessary for all members of the institution to understand that students may come with sets of writing practices that have been valued and purposeful in other contexts. Such an awareness should change the way in which the teaching of writing and the writing practices of students are approached.[3]

The long history of literacy, and the current debates which beset it, provide critical insights about the nature of writing development, and provide lessons which should be heeded if the simple erroneous assumptions of earlier literacy research are not to be perpetuated.

1.4 Oral and written language

The study of literacy and its relation to writing shows that oral language and written language are not contraries, nor are they exact reflections of each other. The history of literacy has demonstrated that oral and written language coexist in many complex patterns of use. Even when literacy became widespread in European societies, most reading was performed aloud as a social activity; the written form was closely linked with oral presentation. Silent extensive reading as a deviation from oral interaction is only a relatively recent practice. Present-day uses of language often go hand-in-hand with various oral practices such as lecturing, recounting, and debating. Moreover, certain oral practices can either reinforce or obstruct the writing practices that students are expected to master. Recent educational research, for example, demonstrates that methods of oral interaction have a strong influence on the later development of reading and writing skills (Bloome and Green 1992, Cook-Gumperz 1986, Purves 1991, Wells and Chang-Wells 1992).

Throughout the history of modern linguistics, most linguists have taken the position that oral language is primary and written language is simply a reflection of oral language (cf. Biber 1988, Halliday 1989). Most education researchers have taken the opposite position – i.e. the written language is a true representation of the correct forms of language and should be valued and practised. The past ten years have seen these two positions coalesce in sociolinguistic research on the ethnography of education and on register variation in different types of oral and written texts. This research has tried to come to terms with the conflicting assumptions of two major disciplines involved in language and language teaching. Research by Biber (1988, 1994), Chafe (1982, 1985), Halliday (1989), Kress (1989), and Tannen (1982, 1985) has pointed out the various ways in which oral and written language vary and overlap. Findings from this research have greatly extended the knowledge of properties of both media.

The work of these scholars indicates that patterns of variation across oral and written language texts differ on a number of dimensions: structural and organizational differences; different frequencies of use of various language features, different production constraints; and different uses for the varieties of oral and written language texts. Chafe (1985) and Tannen (1982) in particular have argued that any understanding of oral and written text variation cannot be determined along one dimension of variation; rather, they have claimed, texts vary and overlap with other texts along a number of functional dimensions. From this perspective, it is not enough to consider texts as simply oral or written; texts vary in ways that cannot be captured by such a single continuum.

In a recent series of studies, Biber (1988, 1992, 1994, 1995) has clarified the complex set of relationships that hold among various types of oral and written texts. In his research, Biber has developed a multidimensional model of textual variation that compares relations among 23 different genres of spoken and written texts. By incorporating a large number of linguistic features, a large number of texts, and a sophisticated research design, Biber (1988) sought to overcome the difficulties of much of the earlier research on spoken and written textual variation which often led to confusing if not contradictory findings. Text features were analysed by an automated counting program. The resulting frequency counts were then used in factor analyses to determine the co-occurrence patterns among the linguistic features for all of the texts in the corpus (approximately one million words). His factor analysis model identified six interpretable dimensions; that is to say, the linguistic features co-occurred together on six different factors, each of which could be interpreted as a communicative/ functional dimension of textual variation. The communicative interpretations were based on the grouping of linguistic features which have been seen as having compatible discourse functions in previous discourse analysis literature.

The results of his research indicated that three of his six dimensions are related in some way to orate–literate variation (involved versus informational production, explicit versus situation-dependent reference, and abstract versus non-abstract information), though none of the six dimensions interpreted provided an absolute distinction between oral and written genres; that is, no dimension clearly distinguished all types of written texts from all types of spoken texts. Thus, the traditional dichotomy between oral and written texts that is so often assumed does not appear to be represented by any single dimension of textual variation in a strict interpretation of his results. Biber's results also provide strong evidence for the multidimensional nature of textual structure. No small set of feature counts and no single notion of a communicative dimension will offer a satisfactory interpretation of textual variation or textual structure.

A major conclusion to be drawn is that the spoken–written continuum does not exist in any strict sense as *a single dimension* of textual comparison. The implications of this line of research for the study of writing and composition is that all texts are complex multidimensional structures, including texts written by students; claims made in writing research about distinctions between oral and written language, as well as oral features in student composition, are, for the most part, greatly oversimplified, requiring caution with respect to many of the assertions based on these premises.

Many of the issues addressed in the comparison of oral and written language and in the discussion of literacy point to basic assumptions about the nature of written language which should be clarified so that the interpretations of current research on writing are given an appropriate context. It has been argued to this point that:

(1)   the study of writing is an appropriate domain for applied linguistic inquiry (including language-based problems with English L1 and L2 students);

(2)   writing is a technology insofar as it is a culturally transmitted set of practices;

(3)   writing involves many different uses and functions, not all of which are valued academically;

(4)   the study of literacy demonstrates that writing should be viewed as a set of practices which are socially contextualized – academic writing is simply one valued set of practices appropriate to that context – rather than as a single universal set of cognitive skills;

(5)   academically valued writing requires composing skills which transform information or transform the language itself;

(6)   the uses of oral and written language interact and reinforce each other as sets of practices that serve social functions;

(7)   research on spoken and written language demonstrates that

all texts are highly complex multidimensional structures, and the actual linguistic-functional nature of many of these dimensions is just beginning to be explored;

(8) oral and written language variation points out that different types of written texts vary greatly according to task, audience, and purpose;

(9) assertions about sweeping differences between oral and written language made by composition theorists must be regarded with some scepticism based on recent sociolinguistic research.

These and other related assumptions guide the following discussion of research in writing, both in L1 and L2 contexts.

1.5   Research on writing in English L1 contexts

Generally speaking, writing research in L1 contexts has been conducted along four distinct but interacting dimensions which can be represented, though only somewhat loosely, by four respective disciplines: education, psychology, linguistics, and rhetoric/composition. While there are a number of analyses of writing research which divide the territory somewhat differently (cf. Hillocks 1986, North 1987, Phelps 1988, Witte 1992), this particular synthesis is not meant to be definitive but only to provide an organizing guide to the somewhat confusing array of extant research. The first of these research strands is the study of literacy development or the acquisition of writing, particularly at the early stages. Researchers in education, applied sociolinguistics, and educational psychology explore ways in which children learn to write, as well as why some students experience difficulties in learning to write.

Educationists and educational psychologists have been primarily concerned with the socio-educational contexts for learning to write, the need to express meaning in writing, the need for students to view writing as a purposeful activity, and the various stages of learning through which young writers are nurtured. Much of this research has centred on case studies of individual children, learning experience approaches (LEA) and whole-language approaches (Calkins 1986, Dyson 1989, 1993, Graves 1983, 1984). Many of the practical approaches are also in line with Vygotskean perspectives on literacy development (Moll 1990,

Tharp and Gallimore 1988, Vygotsky 1983, Wertsch 1985, 1991). In addition, current research in Australia addresses the role of language form and genre knowledge as critical aspects of learning to write from early grades (Christie 1992, Cope and Kalantzis 1993).

The research is also paralleled by the ethnographic research in educational contexts undertaken by sociolinguists. The ethnography of education explores ways in which children from divergent social and linguistic backgrounds learn in educational contexts that are designed for mainstream students. Such research has examined different groups of high-risk students and the differences between school expectations and home environment (Boggs 1985, Heath 1986b, Philips 1983, Poole 1991, Snow *et al.* 1991), the impact of conversational style and interactional discourse on learning (Bloome and Green 1992, Cazden 1988, Cook-Gumperz 1986, Wells and Chang-Wells 1992), and the attitudes of students and teachers in the classroom context (Williams 1976). In particular, researchers have found that exposure to literacy events, attitudes towards school literacy, and the teaching of meaningful literacy tasks are important conditions for writing development.

A second strand of research involves study of the cognitive aspects of writing. Researchers in cognitive psychology, education, and composition represent those interested in modelling and explaining the mental processes used in the act of writing. Much of the research is empirical in nature. While earlier cognitive research on writing principally studied the written products and used experimental research on text recall (Britton and Black 1985b, van Dijk and Kintsch 1983), more recent research on cognitive processes has included studies of the actual process of writing on-task (that is, as it is occurring in real time), as well as protocol analyses, and task intervention (e.g. Bereiter and Scardamalia 1987, Flower 1994, Flower *et al.* 1990, Hillocks 1986, Kellogg 1994, Smagorinsky 1994).

Other approaches involve the use of retrospective case studies and observational research as ways to examine qualitatively the nature of the composing processes and their development. Important results from this research include the findings that writers constantly shift among pre-writing, writing, and revising tasks. Writing is not a linear process; instead, it involves the complex combination of content information, rhetorical demands, and reader interpretation. Good writers and poor writers also appear to make use of processing skills in different ways.

A third strand of research is the study of the text itself, or text construction. This research typically falls under the heading of 'text linguistics' or 'discourse analysis'. Researchers in cognitive psychology, linguistics, applied linguistics, and rhetoric/composition are interested in how texts are constructed and organized in ways which allow appropriate reader interpretation. Central topics for this research field are the study of contributing lexico-grammatical structures, cohesion, coherence, inferences-making processes, and text modelling (Coulthard 1994, Halliday and Hasan 1989, Hoey 1991, Mann and Thompson 1992, Singer 1990, van Dijk and Kintsch 1983).

Research on these topics is both quantitative and qualitative. Much work relating to main-idea comprehension and recall, and comparing good and poor writers, involves the counting of surface features, propositional units, or inference chains together with appropriate statistical analyses of the resulting data (Beck *et al.* 1991, Cox *et al.* 1990, 1991, Speigel and Fitzgerald 1991). Other research exploring the coherence of texts has focused on macro-structures (or text themes), logical relations among clauses and text units, and information structuring in texts (given–new information, topic–comment, theme–rheme, focus–presupposition structures; Singer 1990, vande Kopple 1986, 1990). All three sub-sets of coherence notions have proved important for research on writing as well as for writing instruction.

The fourth and final strand of research on writing is the rhetorical study of writing. Researchers from rhetoric, composition, applied linguistics, and literary criticism examine variation in writing skill or writing interpretation as a function of writing purpose, topic, genre, audience, intertextuality, and the social construction of writing, as well as the larger sociopolitical, historical, and educational contexts. Rhetorical research traces its origins back to the five canons of Aristotle: invention, arrangement, style, memory, and delivery (Corbett 1971, Horner 1983). Modern rhetorical research, after a long history of declines and emergences, comprises three branches of inquiry: historical, philosophical, and critical/hermeneutic research (North 1987). While many rhetoricians may object to this classification and indeed combine research in the three areas, this tripartite scheme provides a useful way to encompass rhetorical inquiry.

Current research on both classical and nineteenth–twentieth-century rhetorical history, rhetorical criticism of (literary) texts, and social and political contexts of intertextuality represent important concerns. The revival of rhetoric in the 1970s and 1980s in US universities has led to a much greater influence of rhetoric on composition studies and, in general, on the teaching of composition in educational institutions, particularly at secondary and tertiary levels. Perhaps the most enduring influence of the modern rhetorical revival will be the increasing emphasis on discourse communities and the role of social construction in writing, both of which are having a significant impact on theories of writing and writing instruction, particularly in academic and professional contexts. Writing instruction across the curriculum as well as content-based writing instruction have also been influenced by these rhetorical developments.

In general, research on writing in L1 contexts has greatly changed writing instruction at almost all levels – from elementary to post-university professional contexts. While it is true that conservative instruction (the term used in the literature is 'current-traditional') still exists and dominates in some institutions, the ongoing research on writing in all four research strands has changed writing instruction for the better. These research strands have also had a strong impact on writing assessment and evaluation, though the demands of testing theory and the institutional requirements for grading impose conservative constraints on changes in assessment.

A new area in writing research which also stands to benefit from research is computer-assisted writing instruction, with computers being used both as a research tool and as an instructional resource (Bangert-Drowns 1993, Cochran-Smith 1991, Pennington 1993, Snyder 1993). At present, most computer-assisted instruction has simply transferred the more traditional writing instruction to a new medium. This particular field will make significant contributions when it learns to use the capacities of the computer in innovative ways beyond current conceptions of its utility for writing (Bruce *et al.* 1993, Bruce and Rubin 1993, Selfe and Hilligoss 1994, Tuman 1992)

This review of L1 writing research is dominated by research in the American educational context, but the work of Britton, Carter, and Wells in England, of Bereiter, Freedman and Jones in Canada, and of Christie, Halliday, Hasan, and Martin in Australia all point to important changes in writing theory and instruction. Overall, however, the contributions of these researchers have not yet greatly altered the picture of writing research as it has developed in the USA. Perhaps the fact that the USA is the only country with uniformly compulsory freshman composition requirements at the tertiary level helps to explain differences in focus.

The visibility of US L1 writing research has also not been matched in research on second language writing theory and instruction. Reasons for this difference are readily explicable:

1. The US composition research community is insulated from much of the rest of world in terms of other students' writing development, writing contexts, and writing needs in educational institutions.
2. The ethnocentric attitudes among US composition researchers towards English as the only language worthy of study meant that, for many years, immigrant students and international students were not given any consideration with respect to their unique backgrounds and needs. There was an unspoken assumption that the research on L1 writers would apply equally to these second language learners.
3. The 'crisis' in writing instruction in the USA has allowed researchers to focus their interests on secondary and tertiary L1 student writing problems to the exclusion of other learners.
4. The large amounts of grant funding, the lucrative textbook markets, and the likelihood of professional advancement biased research in the USA, until very recently, towards mainstream composition research.
5. The discipline most open to the concerns and problems of L2 learners – i.e. applied linguistics – emerged from linguistics and foreign language departments rather than from English departments. This situation greatly reduced interchange between applied linguists and composition researchers (many with literary studies backgrounds) as well as between applied linguists and language arts education researchers.
6. The concerns and problems encountered by the various L2 learners needing to improve their writing abilities has only recently received the attention it deserves. This concern is primarily due to the growing awareness of the needs of language minority populations within the USA rather than a concern for English uses in international contexts.
7. Research on writing for L2 students has been pursued more vigorously in other English-speaking countries than in the USA.

All of these factors have contributed to a much later emergence of research on L2 writing abilities and writing instruction, particularly in the USA. This network of causes is reflective, as well, of social attitudes in some multilingual nations. Obviously, while the seven points raised above are true and do explain the failure of L2 research to emerge earlier in a more powerful form, they evade the major issue that such distinctions as ESL/EFL or as L1/L2 inevitably break down. The educational systems of such countries as Australia and the USA must deal with all students in their multilinguality. Socially, there should be continuity, rather than polarity, which tends to create second-class citizenship for some group(s) of children.

This later development of L2 writing research in the USA has not been paralleled in the UK or Australia. Perhaps the greater awareness of immigrant and international student needs, coupled with a greater awareness of English language needs in other countries, created more interest in writing in a second language. At the same time, however, recent work in the USA in L2 writing research is again emerging as significant, due to the large and ever-increasing numbers of international students entering US education – particularly tertiary education – and to efforts to support language minority students' learning needs in elementary and secondary schools. Increased federal funding to support research on language minority student problems has also assisted this change in US educational research on writing.

The emergence of interest in the USA in the writing problems and needs of L2 learners has led to an awareness that these students cannot be judged according to the same research assumptions guiding L1 writing instruction. While there are similarities between L1 and L2 students of writing, there are also differences which must be recognized if research implications and practical instruction are to be most appropriate for the needs of L2 learners (Leki 1992, Silva 1993).

1.6   Second language student needs and writing instruction

Any discussion of L2 students' writing needs must first take into account the wide diversity among L2 learners as distinct groups each with its own uses of, and needs for, writing. The broadest distinction that can be drawn is a two-part division between English as a Foreign Language (EFL) and English as a Second Language (ESL) learners. More reasonably, the two lie at opposite ends of a single continuum but are treated separately for non-linguistic (administrative/budgetary) reasons. EFL courses include those students who need to learn English (or in this case need to learn to *write* in English), who live in countries in which English is not regularly spoken or written as a language of the community (e.g. the People's Republic of China, Indonesia, France). ESL courses include those students needing to learn English who live in countries where English is a language, or *the* language, of the community.

This division between ESL and EFL includes more-specific variations: students in countries where English shares a role as an official language (e.g. Singapore, India, Nigeria), students in countries where English is an important educational language though not recognized officially (e.g. Malaysia, Malta), students in countries where English is a major language of the community (the USA, the UK, Canada, Australia, New Zealand). Students in these latter countries may be subdivided further into students who reside permanently and students who will remain only for the duration of their academic and/or professional training. Students who reside permanently in an English dominant community may be divided into those groups which seek to learn English from an early age, typically in the public school system, and those groups who are adults needing writing skills for survival literacy or job training (English for Occupational Purposes [EOP]). Students in the public school systems may be further divided into students who have recently arrived, or whose parents have recently arrived, in the community, as opposed to those students who are indigenous to the community (in the USA: Native Americans, Puerto Ricans, Cubans, Indochinese, New Mexico Spanish speakers, Cajun speakers, New England French speakers). All of these students share a common designation in US public schools as Limited English Proficiency (LEP) students. Additional issues in writing instruction also depend on whether these student are studying at the elementary or secondary levels.

This wide array of L2 student groups requiring writing proficiency to varying degrees creates a set of research and instructional issues that are not fully responded to by research focusing on L1 students of writing. The various L2 groups will differ markedly in terms of the need for writing abilities. Students in

EFL contexts will need English writing skills ranging from simple paragraph writing and summary skills to the ability to write essays and professional articles (depending on students' educational levels, academic majors, and institutional demands). Even within an EFL country, it is not possible to generalize beyond local educational institutional expectations. Kachru (1985, 1992) has looked at the uses of English as an alternative language for speakers of various other languages in South Asia and Africa and has shown that English may serve literary and social functions even where it is not a majority language. Such variation in these countries makes textbooks and appropriate advice on writing instruction difficult to provide.

In ESL contexts the range of writing needs is equally diverse, although the needs will, for the most part, be more academically oriented. Survival literacy and low-level occupational needs for writing are typically handled not by writing specialists but by basic adult education teachers, and they may not stress writing as composing.

The reticulated structure created by different student groups and different student writing needs is only at the margin of the set of factors which make L2 writing theory and practice so complex. Any appropriate instruction must take into account the influence from students' various L1 life and cultural experiences. The need for this information is amply illustrated by the recent research on the ethnography of education and the sociolinguistics of literacy. Students from different backgrounds approach educational tasks in ways at variance with the approach adopted by students from the mainstream culture. It has further been found that educational instruction that has been modified so as to be more compatible with, or simply to account for, students' L1 socialization practices leads students to higher literacy rates in the classroom (Au and Jordan 1981, Heath 1986b, 1993, Tharp and Gallimore 1988).

In addition to the L1 experiences of these students, researchers and practitioners need to consider the level and types of language interference that may influence learning as well as students' educational experiences in, and attitudes towards, their L1. Problems related to language transfer and interlanguage development are well known to applied linguists and are central to second language acquisition research. The problems created by this phenomenon for L2 writing instruction are less well defined overall, though a major thrust of research in this area is the study of contrastive rhetoric. On the level of the social contexts of language use, serious if typically unexplored issues include:

- Careful study of students' educational attainment in their L1 educational system (and what it means to have reached different levels of education in various school systems – in other words, the ways in which literacy is defined in their L1 communities).
- Study of students' reading motivations and abilities in their first language.
- Study of students' writing motivations and abilities in their first language.
- Study of students' attitudes towards their first language and literacy in that language.
- Study of students' attitudes towards English and English literacy.

In addition, processing issues beyond language interference and language transfer include such issues as the impact of learning through two languages; i.e. how processing information in one language affects vocabulary development in a second language. This issue also influences curriculum design choices in situations in which two languages are provided in the curriculum, and the various ways in which each of the two languages might be accounted for instructionally:

- Bilingual transition programmes
- Bilingual maintenance programmes
- L2 immersion programmes
- L2 submersion
- SL pull-out classes
- Some other option.

Thus, there are a number of factors relating to the theory and practice of writing instruction in a second language which go well beyond the concerns and issues central to writing practices in L1 contexts. Given an imperfect understanding of many of these factors, it is not surprising that L2 writing research has generally not advanced beyond the practices of L1 writing research, even if the actual instructional practices are more informed about the L2 student than L1 research might suggest. It should be clear from this review of L2 students and factors affecting their learning that a wholesale borrowing of research and practice from L1 contexts will not be entirely appropriate. At the same time, L2 researchers studying writing have examined and adapted many of the research projects and instructional practices first investigated with L1 students. In the following overview of writing research on L2 students, it is important not only to be aware that parallels with L1 research exist, but also to recognize the very different learning circumstances of many L2 students.

1.7   Research on writing in a second language

Research in L2 writing began in the late 1960s and early 1970s in the USA and the UK, accompanying the increasing numbers of international L2 students coming to tertiary-level academic institutions and an increasing awareness of domestic second language students who are failing in the public educational system. Writing in second language contexts in countries where English is not dominant has received relatively little research treatment. This may be more a case of research neglect than of any lack of educational difficulties to address.

The pattern of research on writing in a second language does not follow exactly the pattern of research in L1 writing. In the L2 research, applied linguistics has been the academic discipline giving most attention to the writing needs and problems of students. Applied linguists have drawn on the work of cognitive psychologists and linguists on the one hand to study the organization of discourse and text construction processes, and on the work of sociolinguists and ethnomethodologists on the other to study the social contexts in which students learn to write. The research effort in L2 writing is quite recent. Apart from work in contrastive rhetoric and ESP, relatively little research on writing was undertaken before 1980. Most professional articles which appeared prior to 1980 centred on techniques for teaching writing rather than on the nature of writing in various contexts.

In addition to applied linguistics, research on L2 writing has emerged recently in education and in composition studies. In education, the concern for language minority students and other high-risk language arts students in elementary education has led to greater interest in and awareness of writing in the public school in the USA and Australia. The education research in the USA has drawn extensively on Goodman's whole language philosophy and on ethnographic classroom research for ways to develop students' writing abilities (Edelsky *et al.* 1991, Freeman and Freeman 1992, Goldman and Trueba 1987, Hudelson 1989a, 1989b). Research arising from composition studies has followed recently from L1 composition research, employing similar composition research approaches on groups of L2 students (Kroll 1990, Johnson and Roen 1989, Raimes 1991, Reid 1993). Many L2 researchers, although they may specialize in child writing development or composition studies, consider themselves as belonging to the applied linguistics community as much, if not more, than to the related discipline in which they are working.

Writing research in applied linguistics first centred around the study of rhetorical variation noticed in the writing of L2 students from various L1 origins (Kaplan 1966, 1972). This line of research, commonly referred to as *contrastive rhetoric*, drew on discourse analysis and textlinguistic research to explore how student writing could be analysed at the discourse level as a way to understand the varying patterns of organizational preferences in student writing. Work still continues and has contributed to a more general expansion of discourse analysis studies on L2 student writing. Since the appearance of Kaplan's original work, a number of applied linguists have drawn on research in cognitive psychology, text linguistics, and discourse analysis to explore ways in which L2 texts are constructed, how these texts differ from texts constructed by L1 students, and how and why these texts differ among L2 students representing different linguistic communities. Recent research along these lines includes the study of cohesion and coherence, the macrostructure of texts, the arrangement of information, using propositional analysis, discourse bloc analysis, inferencing and schema theory, story structure, the comparative study of text corpora, and the textual co-occurrence patterns of lexico-syntactic features (cf. Chapter 2).

One of the larger subspecializations to have grown out of the developments of discourse analysis and text linguistics in applied linguistics is the study of the special writing needs of various groups of students. The best known of these research directions is the study of the writing needs of English for Special Purposes (ESP) students. Following the early research in contrastive rhetoric, this field was the most active area of writing research through the 1970s, and it has continued to be popular to the present time. Other special-purpose groups who need writing skills of a special sort include future doctors, lawyers, civil service workers, etc. (Hutchinson and Waters 1987, Johns and Dudley-Evans 1991, Maher and Rokosz 1992, Swales 1990, Trimble 1985; see the extended discussion in Chapter 6).

Research in the L2 writing of students in the public education sector owes its beginnings to the concerns of informed language-arts and bilingual-education teachers that language minority students were facing serious difficulties developing expected literacy skills. Drawing on many of the findings of whole language research, L2 specialists have explored the applications of many new language-arts approaches to writing instruction for children (Enright and McCloskey 1988, Faltis 1992, Peregoy and Boyle 1993). Results of this recent research are now emerging and should affect considerably the literacy instruction of younger children. The needs of L2 students in secondary education have yet, however, to emerge as an area of L2 writing research (cf. Wald 1987). One can only hope that researchers will turn to this area and study the writing problems of L2 adolescents (e.g. Montaño-Harmon 1991).

Research on writing in a second language in contexts other than the USA, Australia, Canada, and the UK is minimal. It is clear that different countries will have different needs and expectations for students learning to write in English. It is not clear what research has been carried out in various countries to establish these needs and expectations, or to explore the successful instructional implementation of these expectations (see Kaplan 1995). Certainly countries such as Japan, Hong Kong, India, Malaysia, etc., which send many students to the USA and the UK for tertiary education, give some consideration to the writing needs of these students. In some cases, the needs are being addressed by the development of US university programmes in-country which claim to provide the equivalent of the first two years of tertiary-level academic credit (Japan, Malaysia). It remains to be seen how successful these programmes will prove to be.

The current emphasis in English L2 writing research strongly follows English L1 writing research. There are, however, certain criticisms which question the apparently extensive adaptation of L1 research into L2 contexts that is so prevalent today. It is important, in this regard, to distinguish research methods from interpretations of research results. It is intuitively reasonable that research methods useful in L1 contexts should also be applicable to L2 contexts. In this respect, distinctions in L1 and L2 writing research have become much fuzzier in the past ten years; e.g. both L1 and L2 writing research includes studies employing experimental treatments, text analyses, protocol analyses, ethnographic observations, etc. This situation does not, as we argue, mean that L2 writing research is purely derivative; indeed, it addresses some very different questions about some very different students.

1.8   Moving from theory to practice

While research on writing in L1 and L2 contexts has developed remarkably over the last 20 years, the teaching of writing is only now beginning to reap the benefits of this research. In the 1950s and 1960s, most teachers of writing, whether for L1 or L2 students, felt that writing instruction had a well-established and effective methodology. This methodology centred around what is now termed a 'current traditional' approach. As described by Britton (1983: 2):

> There had arisen that very limited tradition of composition teaching which is so familiar to all of us in first *and* second-language situations, with its emphasis on 'correct usage, correct grammar, and correct spelling,' and its focus on the topic sentence, the various methods of developing the paragraph ... and the holy trinity of unity, coherence, and emphasis ... Richard Young (1978) calls this tradition 'current-traditional rhetoric' and he argues that its practitioners' emphases and pedagogical techniques were all determined by certain tacit but shared assumptions concerning the nature of the composing process. Chief among these was the Romantic conviction that the creative aspects of the process are mysterious, inscrutable, and hence unteachable. What can be taught and discussed are the lesser matters of style, organization, and usage.

Similar accounts of writing practices are presented in Berlin (1984, 1987), acknowledging a long twentieth-century tradition of writing instruction. The parallel tradition in L2 contexts, to the extent that it was emphasized, was reinforced by a feeling that L2 students needed to focus on correct grammar, spelling, and usage to the point at which they were then ready for the same 'current traditional' writing instruction that L1 students were given (Raimes 1983a, 1991). The mid-1960s constituted the turning point in writing instruction. Dissatisfaction with (a) the slow devel-

opment of students' writing abilities, and (b) the increasing numbers of international and domestic L2 minority students in
academic institutions, led to new theories of writing instruction
based on more successful teaching practices. Many of these new
approaches to writing instruction were less informed by as yet
undeveloped or underdeveloped theoretical research than by
'techniques that worked' (North 1987).

Raimes (1983a) noted that L2 writing instruction was typically
uninformed by writing theory through most of the 1970s, providing, for the most part, 'proven' techniques for teaching writing. As
Raimes (1983a: 261–2) states:

> ... we have stressed the ESL part of ESL composition at the expense
> of the composition part, and we have done so because we have
> thought that students need mastery over the sentence before pro-
> ceeding to the paragraph, and mastery over the paragraph before
> proceeding to the essay. So we have provided controls and limits
> which make the task easier for us ... Many of our students ... cry out
> for rules, for something concrete to monitor their writing perfor-
> mance with. So we give them grammatical Band-Aids and doses of
> paragraph models. We must then realize that we are teaching edit-
> ing and imitation. We're not teaching composing.

Raimes goes on to assert the importance of grammar for ESL writers but not at the expense of composing practice.

The emerging theories of writing of the late 1970s, drawing on
cognitive psychology, sociolinguistics, educational ethnography,
whole-language education, and applied linguistics, began to
spread so that there were powerful competing theories of writing
by the 1980s. These theories have finally begun to change writing
instruction. At the same time, it must be said that most writing
instruction is still oriented around 'current traditional'
approaches. Many ESL classrooms still rely on writing textbooks
which stress paragraph models, grammar and usage rules, and
vocabulary development as their entire curriculum. The large
majority of these textbooks, while advertised as process oriented,
do not typically emphasize purposeful writing activities. 'Current
traditional' approaches are also alive and well in L1 writing
instruction, particularly in secondary and university level classes.
In many elementary classes, students still do little writing of any
kind beyond occasional paragraphs, short-answer seat work, and
taking objective question examinations (Applebee 1981).

Despite this state of affairs – in which many teachers appear to be immune to, or unaware of, current writing research – writing instruction is improving in a number of contexts. In elementary schooling, whole-language approaches to literacy are having an increasing effect on the amount of writing done and the methods by which writing is taught. While the evangelical overtones of whole-language advocates can be disturbing, more teachers are adapting certain whole-language teaching practices in their own classroom routines. Many teachers now stress early composing practice for children, encouraging students to express themselves in writing that is both meaningful and purposeful. In these contexts, the translation from theory to practice is just beginning to take hold in a large number of classrooms. Its applications to the teaching of language minority children appears to be as successful as it is in the teaching of L1 elementary school children (Dyson 1993, Faltis 1992, Peregoy and Boyle 1993).

Research on the composing process is now having a strong influence on the teaching of writing in US tertiary institutions and pre-tertiary programmes. More composition curricula are adopting instructional approaches which emphasize relevant topics, class discussion, brainstorming (invention), multiple drafting/revision, peer feedback, and realistic tasks. Many writing textbooks have been rewritten to stress a 'process approach', though how successful such textbooks are in developing students' writing practices is still an open question. Writing process research has also often been combined with Freirean notions of liberatory literacy practices and with the philosophy of stressing meaningful communication to focus more attention on the content of writing courses. Gradually, composition programmes have been moving towards content-centredness, maintaining a consistent and coherent theme or set of themes about which students have personal knowledge and in which they can invest their time meaningfully (Bartholomae and Petrosky 1986). In L2 contexts, similar efforts are underway in some places with content-centred courses and sheltered classes (Brinton *et al.* 1989, Crandall 1993, Krueger and Ryan 1993, Short 1994). Writing across the curriculum movements – a major issue in public education in the UK – constitute another manifestation of this trend; more programmes are seeking to add more writing to the content courses rather than more content to the writing courses.

Research on the nature of texts and on text construction has also had an impact on writing practices, though many of these changes are only now being disseminated to classrooms and teachers. Research on the various aspects of textual organization – such as topic progression, information structuring, discourse mode variation, logical relations among discourse units, the role of inferencing, and patterns of lexico-syntactic usage – has led to increasingly productive instructional practices.

Perhaps the major obstacle to the translation from theory to practice in the case of text-linguistic research is that there is no one overarching linguistic perspective on the application of the research; unlike whole-language and composing-process research, many researchers in text linguistics come from disciplines as separate as psychology, linguistics, applied linguistics, artificial intelligence, educational psychology, communication, and rhetoric/criticism. A fair amount of the research is considered basic rather than applied, and little consistent attention has been given to the implications for instruction (cf. Christie 1992, Halliday 1993b, Martin 1993, Miller 1995). Applied linguists, however, have been seeking to combine this research into an overarching research perspective which is relevant to instructional practices. Work to create an underlying synthesis of textual coherence is leading to effective instructional practices particularly with L2 students (Cerniglia *et al.* 1990, Grabe and Kaplan 1989, Johns 1986, Reid 1993).

The overall picture emerging from the various research approaches and their different translations into writing practice is that there is some disagreement as to what will be the most appropriate curriculum for writing instruction. When the research-influenced approaches to writing instruction are mixed with the practices of many teachers who still espouse some form of 'current traditional' instruction, the resulting confusion is understandable. A large problem lies in the earlier (and persistent) assumption that *one* standard method can be developed which will be appropriate to all students in all settings.

It is, however, possible to sort out the different instructional practices and, in the case of the recent trends, formulate coherent rationales that recognize and exploit the strength of each perspective, identify the different student populations most likely to benefit from each perspective, and, most importantly, combine those perspectives into a coherent theory of writing instruction which bypasses many of the apparent tensions among the perspectives (Leki 1992, Raimes 1991, Reid 1993). The most notable of these tensions is the overstated distinction designated 'process versus product', a strawman which has been created by some composition researchers (cf. Kaplan 1988, Raimes 1991).

On a practical level, the goal of writing research is to move beyond simple dichotomies and gain a better understanding of at least the following issues comprising a comprehensive theory of writing and writing development:

- the nature of coherent written discourse which is appropriate to the task, topic, genre, and audience;
- the set of processes which are called into play to generate the discourse;
- the social contexts and attitudes which influence the writing (and the writer); and
- the nature of the various learning processes that coalesce to support the development of student writers.

From this point of view, writing is a matter of combining complementary perspectives rather than oppositions, and it is the goal of any theory of writing to account for these various factors in one manner or another (see, for example, Flower 1994, Witte 1992).

In the following chapters the many issues associated with theories of writing as well as instructional practices, will be explored in greater depth. The combination of theoretical discussions are synthesized into a coherent framework for writing theory. The latter chapters then focus on the transition from theory to practice, various instructional approaches for different groups of students, and issues in feedback on writing and writing assessment. The extended discussion in the following chapters build upon the many insights noted in this chapter and explore issues and practices that should promote more informed discussion and lead to improved writing instruction.

Notes

1. This pre-modern history is admittedly Eurocentric. Literacy in Arabic, Chinese, Japanese, and other languages was also limited to an élite or used for special purposes (e.g. Koranic literacy). Dealing with literacy development in non-European languages is an undertaking beyond the scope of this book, and we apologize for the admittedly Eurocentric limitations to this history of literacy.

2. In the USA, the term 'immigrant student' is being used to include not only recent immigrants but also refugees, permanent resident aliens, political asylum holders, and other categories of individuals part or all of whose education has occurred in another culture and who do not speak English as a first language.

3. Arguments have been put forward that teaching socially and culturally diverse students to 'buy into' the literacy practices of the dominant group is assimilationist and prevents alternative voices from being heard. The same post-structural and social-constructivist supports for this argument, however, would also argue that the contributions of new individuals necessarily alter the existing social structure at the same time that the social structure influences these new individuals (e.g. Wells 1994).

2

Textlinguistic research

2.1 Introduction

Informed instruction presupposes theories of the arrays of knowledge required (what one needs to know), the sets of skills which may be brought to bear upon successful learning (what one needs to be able to do), and an account of the social contexts influencing instruction (the factors influencing what one needs to be able to do). Writing instruction, as of yet, lacks clear consensus in all three of these contexts. What is more, much current research in writing presupposes these issues without actually coming to terms with them.

A more successful counterpart, reading instruction, has, in the past 15 years, become the focal point of much theory construction, and, more recently, the locus of attempts to translate theory into practice. Reasons for this development are not hard to find. In large part, reading has always been strongly related to the cognitive activities of comprehension and understanding, a central concern of cognitive psychology and artificial intelligence. As such, research on comprehension, understanding, mental representations, memory, information retrieval, and learning have all tended to devise experimental research with reading as the language task involved (Adams 1989, Oakhill and Garnham 1988, Rayner and Pollatsek 1989, Rieben and Perfetti 1991, Stanovich 1992).

The result of such activity in reading research has provided both theorists and practitioners in reading instruction with models of the fluent reading process, with factors which influence the process, and with extensive studies of individual differences in reading. Following the wider acceptance of more recent interactive models of reading, the implications for instructional design, and the motivation for practical instructional concerns (i.e. how to teach reading) have increased substantially. Reading instruction has lost some of its mystery and such slogans as 'reading is learned by reading' have been recognized as oversimplifications, even if partly correct, as the result of insightful theory construction and research in theoretically grounded instruction.

2.2 Writing research needs

The analogous situation for writing demonstrates much less evidence of progress, despite the equally well-articulated concern about the difficulties students have in learning to write. There is, in fact, a fair amount of research on the writing process, as well as on successful writing instruction. However, writing has yet to enjoy the same input from cognitive psychologists generally, who, perhaps justifiably, feel that research on production models first requires a strong comprehension model. While many rhetoricians and composition researchers are developing theories of writing, and simultaneously exploring the implications of such theories for instruction, little consensus has emerged which would allow for significant advances in writing instruction parallel to the achievements in reading instruction.

The range of research on writing theory and practice is diverse, reflecting a wide range of theoretical interests as well as student constituencies. What emerges from this diversity is a field of research and instruction based on individual preference, subjective study, tradition, and, for practical purposes, on notions of pragmatic issues – i.e. of what seems to work. North (1987) comes to a similar conclusion from the perspective of composition instruction.

More complex models of writing are needed – ones that not only appeal to both process- and product-oriented perspectives on writing, but also account for audience and social context concerns. In the past, too much discussion has been given to debates over process versus product. It should be clear from analogous interactive reading models that a study of the text product alone will not lead to the kinds of models of fluent writing necessary to support improvements in writing instruction. At the same time, theories of the writing process do not, of themselves, form a comprehensive interpretation of the written text.

As a way to break free from past attempts to formulate theories of writing, it is necessary to return to basic questions. A first stage in moving towards a theory of writing abilities, then, lies in addressing anew questions such as the following:

1. What is a text?
2. How may texts be examined as product?
3. How may texts be analysed as process?
4. How may product and process be viewed as reflecting an interactive model of writing?
5. How do process and product issues embed themselves within a coherent interpretation of wider social contexts for writing?
6. What types of texts do we want learners to produce?
7. What do these issues suggest for writing instruction in the classroom?

What is being proposed here is a set of essential criteria for establishing a theory of writing (supported by textlinguistics, cognitive psychology, rhetoric, and composition research). In this and the following chapters, essential elements of such a theory will be sketched. These issues may be seen as definitional in the sense that any adequate model must begin with a definition of the phenomenon supported by research findings. It is not suggested that the present work constitutes a comprehensive model of the writing skill; however, responses to the questions posed above will lead at least to a preliminary statement.

2.3   On the nature of written text

The analysis of written text is in many respects a relatively new research area. Text analysis has grown rapidly over the past twenty years in quantity and variety with contributions from sociolinguistics, psycholinguistics, applied linguistics, cognitive psychology, and artificial intelligence research. It is also important to recognize a number of ongoing traditions for their contributions to text analysis.

One of the earliest of these traditions is hermeneutics (Eagleton 1983, Ong 1982). Originally intended to serve biblical interpretation, the discipline has grown in the last century to involve the interpretation of all literary forms, though its focus is on historically validated text. While of central importance to literary criticism, this tradition also has implications for text analysis (Britton and Black 1985a, Rabin 1986). Britton and Black, for example, note that biblical interpretation was related to Bible translation, and translation requires the analysis of discourse, rather than grammar, if the translation is to be comprehensible and not merely trivial. A second tradition, the rhetorical, again easily pre-dating modern text research, goes back to Aristotle and other classical Greek scholars. The rhetorical tradition is having a greater impact on recent discourse analysis and text analysis (Berlin 1984, 1987, Neel 1988, Phelps 1988, Young 1987). A third tradition, possibly also pre-dating modern linguistics, is that of modern literary criticism and stylistics (Comprone 1987, Crowley 1989, Eagleton 1983, Fowler 1986). While this kind of research seldom generates specific methodologies for modern discourse analysis, it raises fundamental questions about the nature of texts – questions which must regularly be reconsidered.

These three traditions, combined with recent developments in linguistics, form the historical base for the rise of text analysis as a field of study; de Beaugrande and Dressler (1981) and Tate (1987) provide good summaries of these developments. Although text analysis has been perceived as an important discipline in Europe, the same cannot be said for text analysis in North America. The developments in linguistic theory in the USA over the past 30 years have, for the most part, hindered the development of text analysis. Functional linguists, some working with sociolinguists and some from a non-generativist background, have focused considerable attention on discourse analysis, both spoken and written (see, e.g., Brown and Yule 1983, Grabe 1992). Work by Coulthard (1994), Givon (1983), Halliday (1994), Halliday and Hasan (1976, 1989), Mann and Thompson (1988, 1992), van Dijk (1985) and others has explored aspects of discourse structure, and from this research has come both a better understanding of text and a set of techniques for examining the nature of text.

The range of research influencing text analysis requires the view that text is a multidimensional construct; that is, no unidimensional analysis of text can offer an adequate interpretation of the nature of text. As Hudson (1980: 131) notes:

The most obvious fact about discourse structure is that many different kinds of structure run through discourse, and any attempt to reduce them to a single type is bound to fail.

Biber has demonstrated this assertion convincingly in his research on textual variation in spoken and written genres. As Biber (1988: 22) notes:

> Linguistic variation in any language is too complex to be analyzed in terms of any single dimension. The simple fact that such a large number of distinctions have been proposed by researchers indicates that no single dimension is adequate in itself. In addition to the distinctions ... such as restricted versus elaborated and formal versus informal, linguistic features vary across age, sex, social class, occupation, social role, politeness, purpose, topic, etc. From a theoretical point of view, we thus have every expectation that the description of linguistic variation in a given language will be multidimensional.

Many previous efforts have assumed, however, that textual variation could be discussed along single overarching continua which would capture the essence of the variation. Only recently, however, have researchers been willing to entertain the notion of multidimensional constructs and what such constructs might mean (Biber 1988, Schiffrin 1987). Once it is recognized that text is a multidimensional construct, it becomes clear that no simple definition can possibly suffice; however, it is possible to provide a working definition that will serve as a reasonable heuristic for determining what is *not* a text.

A text is a structural equivalent of language in real use which conveys meaning in all four senses of Hymes's (1972) communicative competence (whether a text is: possible, feasible, appropriate, and performed), and which suggests a topic of discourse (however minimal). Further, As Halliday (1978) argues, a text should not be solely defined as having formal opening or closure, as text is seamless, with predictable structure. The beginning and end of texts are more likely to be determined socially and semantically from the context, rather than from a set of formal structural patterns of organization. Taking into consideration the above constraints, text may be defined simply as follows:

> A text occurs when the discourse segment is identified as possible, feasible, appropriate, and performed, and has a topic.

This definition amounts to a textual version of the previously discussed notion of writing as composing. (See also Brown and Yule 1983.)

2.4   The Text as communication

Language, it is assumed, is primarily for communication, as communication is broadly interpreted (see Widdowson 1980). For this reason, writing may be said to represent an attempt to communicate with the reader (Widdowson 1980; see also Raimes 1983b). The writer has certain intentions and purposes, as well as certain information to convey. Writing will, therefore, be structured to communicate information within certain accepted linguistic, psychological, and sociological principles; e.g.:

1. Gricean maxims – the need to be informative, factually correct, relevant, and clear; and the systematically interpretable violations of these maxims (cf. Empson 1961, Steiner 1978).
2. Conventions for conveying status, situation, intent and attitude.
3. Mechanisms for indicating newness of information, rate of information flow, and probability of information.
4. Predictability of cognitive structures which anticipate larger patterns of organization: schemata, scripts, frames, goals, etc.

Any theory of how a text is constructed will have to consider how these principles influence the organization and structure of writing. However written texts are examined, it is necessary to recognize that theoretical assumptions must include influences beyond low-level linguistic descriptions. Text analysis will have to be relational and depend on the context within which the text was written. The following extracts should illustrate this point.

> Nearly eight decades ago, for instance, a South African zoologist named J.E. Duerden published his observations on the decorator crab, a species widely distributed across the Indian and Pacific Oceans. Its tools, living sea anemones. While conducting his study, Duerden discovered that the crab removes two anemones from the ocean floor and grasps one in each of its front claws. Then, holding its living 'tools' out in front of itself, the crab moves along the ocean bottom in search of food. As the anemone's fingerlike tentacles, or polyps, reach out into the currents, they gather tiny food particles, which the crab then removes from the anemones with its second set of claws. Moreover, the anemones serve another purpose. If any part of the crab is touched in front it automatically extends its stinging tools in that direction. 'It would be impossible,'

> Duerden wrote, 'for any marine animal of moderate size to molest
> the crab in front without touching the polyps.' The decorator crab
> has an effective tool of defense. Perhaps because more scientists are
> spending more time these days studying invertebrates, they are
> finding more and more such examples of tool use among the primi-
> tive creatures.
>
> (Abrahamson 1985: 25–6)

In this first text the author is addressing a general audience; he
does not presuppose specialist knowledge. The attitude of the
author is one of equal status with the readers, though the author
is definitely the expert. The topic is carefully elaborated with clear
examples.

> Jobs that you wish to run under batch processing should be submit-
> ted at the Input window. Each job that you submit must have a valid
> pre-punched UCC Job Card as the first card of the deck. After your
> cards have been read through the card reader, the right side of the
> job card is torn off and kept by the operator and your deck is
> returned in the job deck return bins (immediately to the right of the
> Input window) according to the first letter of the jobname (printed
> in the upper left hand corner of your job card).
>
> (USC UCC USM AAO2 1985: 8)

This text, by contrast, is terse; the author presupposes a great deal
of information and assumes a specific audience in a specific situation. The rate of information flow is more rapid because of the
presupposed shared knowledge. The writer takes a position of
authority with respect to the reader, as indicated by the numerous
second person pronouns.

These two texts clearly illustrate how larger organizing principles play a role in text construction. These examples show that
texts convey information to the reader on many different levels.
Any theory of writing will, therefore, have to provide explanations about such multilevel communication; that is, understanding
and producing texts will not only require knowledge of the surface structuring of texts but also of the underlying textual
structuring.

The final section of this chapter will review in detail a number
of research approaches which attempt to explore these various levels of structuring at the surface syntactic level. The following
chapter will extend the analysis to considerations of the underlying textual level.

2.5   Research on the surface/sentence level

2.5.1   *Syntactic analyses*

The Chomskyan enterprise of the 1950s and 1960s generated an interest in examining the writing of students in order to determine syntactic features which would indicate writing development. Basing their analyses on Chomsky's notions of kernel sentences and transformations, Hunt (1983) and others (Loban 1976, O'Hare 1973) developed the concept of the T-unit as a central structure of student writing. Discourse, for them, was viewed as a series of structural T-units (defined as a main clause and all dependent modifying clauses). The large majority of this work was aimed at efforts to explore the output of student compositions. Hunt's well-known study (1965), 'Grammatical structures at three grade levels', demonstrated a consistent increase in the syntactic complexity of student writing at grades 4, 8, and 12. From the basic T-unit, Hunt created a number of measures claimed to demonstrate writing development. Most popular among these have been:

Number of words per T-unit
Number of T-units per sentence
Number of clauses per T-unit
Number of words per clause.

Despite numerous criticisms of the T-unit approach to writing research, Hunt's findings have since been replicated sufficiently to warrant some reliability for his measures (at least for L1 contexts; Hillocks 1986; cf. de Beaugrande 1984, 1985 for L1 criticism; Gaies 1980 and Larsen-Freeman 1978 and for L2 discussion and criticism). The best results using this methodology have been with measuring writing differences across clearly distinct age/grade cohorts. Its effectiveness is more debatable when the compared groups are less obviously distinct. Overall, his methodology has been the source for innumerable studies and dissertations as well as the instructional methodology known as sentence combining (see Daiker *et al.* 1985 for a review of L1 sentence combining research).

While the theoretical grounds supporting sentence combining have been strongly criticized, there is evidence that sentence combining does lead to writing improvement to some extent; the instructional approach has achieved some measure of success and cannot be labelled a failure. Both de Beaugrande (1984) and Hillocks (1986) provide a number of suggestions why this would be the case. Included among these factors are that sentence combining:

- brings to conscious attention syntactic formats;
- provides an orderly tactic for revision;
- promotes student confidence;
- increases familiarity with syntactic patterns;
- improves fluency and frequency of sentence writing;
- promotes sentence variety;
- allows for denser informational load in sentences;
- aids the controlling of chunking in discourse; and
- integrates syntax with other levels of discourse processing.

Certainly sentence combining offers a way to raise student awareness of various construction types and their combinatorial possibilities. In the larger sense, however, a basic difficulty remains; that is, there is no real evidence that either 'syntactic complexity' or 'syntactic maturity' is a major reason for improvement in writing ability. Every L2 teacher has encountered students who can write perfectly correct syntactic structures (or can parse an isolated sentence accurately) but cannot generate written text. Some degree of syntactic maturity seems to be a prerequisite to discourse ability, but the precise relationship is not well understood.

In addition to T-unit research and the development of sentence combining, other syntactically based findings from composition researchers and developmental psychologists provide results similar to T-unit analysis. In particular, the following gross developmental changes can be seen in 'more successful' written text (see Hillocks 1986, Perera 1984, Witte and Cherry 1986):

- increased use of adjectives
- increased nominal complexity
- increased use of free modifiers
- increased use of sentence adverbials
- increased use of relative clauses
- increased use of finite adverbial clauses
- increased use of stylistic word-order variation

- increased use of passives
- increased use of complex NP subjects
- increased range of tense and modal usage, and
- decreased use of unmodified NPs.

Based on the research to date on syntactic features (including T-unit analyses), there are a number of measures which differentiate among a range of grade levels. It is uncontroversial to say that a mature writing style would contain more of these features in an equivalent task comparison. The more interesting and more controversial question is the extent to which any of these features is genuinely a 'marker' of a mature writing style (as opposed to being, for example, a marker of register variation). For many of these features, this question remains open; further, it is not clear that a similar general developmental progression occurs in the writing of L2 students. Perhaps, more importantly, it is not clear that one can assume the reverse – that promoting or teaching these features in instruction will lead to better writing quality. The finding from L1 sentence combining research is suggestive for the teaching of complex syntax to L2 students. This use of sentence combining, however, should not be confused with the development of writing.

Perhaps most serious as a criticism of surface-feature research is the inability to demonstrate a clear relation between syntactic complexity measures and judgements of improved writing quality. While T-units and other similar measures distinguish broadly defined grade differences, there has been no clear connection between these measures of syntactic complexity or fluency, and writing quality as judged by measures of coherence and/or by rater evaluation (Hillocks 1986). Thus, one of the most serious problems of the T-unit approach is the ambiguous relationship between control of sentence level complexity and overall writing quality. And while some significant gains have been made in understanding a writer's growing syntactic development, the relation to overall writing development is not well established. Research by Faigley (1979), Nold and Freedman (1977), and Stewart and Grobe (1979) has provided little correlation between complexity and quality. Hillocks (1986) suggests that sentence combining promotes 'syntactic facility' rather than syntactic complexity, and the effect of facility on overall writing quality remains, at this point, an open question. Hillocks does note, however, that on the basis of experimental research, sentence combining appears to be more effective than a number of other instructional strategies such as free writing and model presentation.

Although syntactic analysis of compositions continues today, and provides important insights into the students' text products, it omits much information on the nature of text construction; if writing were simply the stringing together of complex clauses, the problems currently evident in student writing would be relatively easy to diagnose, predict, and cure. A second syntactic-based approach to text analysis, current textlinguistic corpora research, promises to provide additional insights by employing a more sophisticated methodology and by stressing the discourse-functional basis of groups of surface structural features. While many of these studies began as stylistic analyses, recent developments in corpora research suggest that new insights into text construction, as presented in the next section, are emerging from this line of research.

2.5.2   Corpora research

The general dilemma facing most projects on corpus research is the lack of a theoretical foundation for the interpretation of the results prior to the analysis. Thus, most corpus research has been of a post-hoc nature, looking at the frequency counts and deciding what can be said about these results (cf. Sinclair 1994, who argues for minimizing the effect of theory in corpus analysis). This is true not only for stylistic studies of literary works, but also for more recent text analysis studies which seek to find patterns in the results rather than employ a theory to interpret the results (Sinclair 1991, 1994). It is widely recognized that texts are multidimensional constructs; however, this claim seldom appears to be accounted for in corpora research in ways that will allow for the discovery of these dimensions.

Perhaps the best effort to overcome these limitations in corpora research lies in the work of Biber (1988, 1992, 1995). As described in Chapter 1, Biber's research examines textual variation among spoken and written texts. In his early major study (1988), he argued for the existence of at least six identifiable textual dimensions of variation. His research procedures were similar to those in a number of other corpora analyses using multivariate statistics, and some might argue that his approach is little different from other similar efforts. Indeed, his findings are the result of interpreting a factor analysis of many lexico-syntactic features, and he had no prior indication of the number of textual factors he would create. The major differences lie in the fact that:

- he used many more texts than most corpora studies have previously examined;
- he measured more lexico-syntactic features, each of which was included because it had been discussed in the linguistic literature as having certain functional characteristics in discourse; and
- because he was able to define functional interpretations for each feature, he was able to establish plausible overall interpretations for clusters of features as they co-occurred in the factor analysis.

Biber has since established the validity of his textual dimensions by using a number of confirmatory statistical procedures, and by replicating his results with a number of independent corpora.

A major finding of Biber's research is that text genres may be identified by the co-occurrence patterns of groups of surface linguistic features. Surface structure reflects discourse variation and, by inference, discourse structure, though the way in which surface structure reflects discourse function does not rely on the real or notional relationship between individual features and specific textual genres. As an illustration, Biber's fourth dimension, 'Overt Expression of Persuasion', comprises necessity modals (e.g. *must, should*), prediction modals (e.g. *will, shall*), suasive verbs (e.g. *agree, arrange, ask, beg, pledge, propose, request, suggest, urge*), infinitives (e.g. *to go, to change the rule*), and markers of conditional subordination (e.g. *if ... , unless ...*). These features individually may do little to define a textual pattern. Taken as an aggregate, however, they appear to coalesce into a textual dimension which is only definable in the aggregate. These textual dimensions can then be used as barometers to see which textual genres, defined functionally, appear high or low on these dimensions.

Grabe (1987) applied Biber's approach to varieties of expository prose as a way to define textual variation within this larger category. One hundred and fifty texts of 15 functionally defined types were analysed in terms of 31 syntactic, lexical, and cohesion variables. Using Biber's programme for counting the linguistic

features, Grabe employed factor analysis and also derived six interpretable factors. The first four factors proved to be highly reliable
and were used to examine different patterns among expository
prose text types. The textual/functional interpretations were
based on the important co-occurrence patterns of linguistic features for each factor. Following Biber's situational and
communicative interpretations for the linguistic features in the
study, the four important dimensions were labelled as follows:

1. Non-narrative versus Narrative Context (Immediacy of Context)
2. Interactional versus Informational Orientation
3. Abstract/Logical versus Situation Information
4. Objective versus Expressive Style.

These four dimensions served to define three types of expository
prose among the 15 text genres used in the study. The importance
of this research is that it demonstrated textual structure in the surface linguistic features of a text, and it suggested a way to explore
variation in student-written texts which would have greater
explanatory power than simple counts of individual surface features and their correlations to writing development. One such
study explored the general nature of freshman student writing at
an American university.

Grabe and Biber (1987) performed a pilot study using 40 final
essay exams from the University of Southern California Freshman
Writing Program. The goal was to see how freshman student writing compared with a variety of edited prose types from Biber's
major corpus. The essays were entered into the larger corpus of
spoken and written texts used by Biber. The 40 texts showed no
significant differences among themselves though they comprised
ten high non-native English speakers, ten high native English
speakers, ten low non-native speaker essays, and ten low native-
speaker essays. The 40 texts were therefore treated as a group and
compared along five textual dimensions. Results of this pilot study
showed that freshman compositions were most similar to
Humanities Academic Prose on three of the five dimensions
('Narrative versus Non-narrative Concerns', 'Elaborated versus
Situation Dependent Reference', and 'Abstract versus Non-
abstract Style'). It would seem, therefore, that for three of the five
dimensions, student writing is following genre expectations.

On two other dimensions, however, student writing differs from
the pattern. On dimension one ('Involved versus Information

Production'), student essays were unlike any professional expository type but similar to general fiction, having many more markers of involved style than do other categories of expository prose texts. On dimension four ('Overt Expression of Persuasion'), the student essays are unlike any of the professional genres, being extremely marked in their use of overtly persuasive features. Overall, the student essays did not match any of the professional genres along all five dimensions. Rather, freshman essays, at least as demonstrated in the final examinations in a writing course, appear to constitute a hybrid form of writing which combines salient features of a number of text genres. Composition writing may be a somewhat unique genre form, raising certain questions about its usefulness as a learning experience, at least as it is currently taught.

2.5.3 Functional sentence perspective: informational structure

A third area where the study of syntactic level phenomena leads to insights about the structuring of texts and writing development has emerged from the early work of the Prague School of Linguistics (Firbas 1986). Vande Kopple (1986: 72–3) describes their orientation as follows:

> As their name indicates, Functional Sentence Perspectivists take a functional approach to language. … They … investigate what language does, how people use it in various ways to achieve various purposes. Thus, their focus is primarily on connected texts, not on isolated or randomly connected sentences, since people rarely use the latter for communicative purposes. And in much of their work they proceed by examining the relationships between the structure and the meaning of a text, the extralinguistic situation the text exists in and for, the communicative function the text apparently has, and the writer's or speaker's apparent assumptions about the state of his or her addressee's motivation, knowledge, and consciousness.

2.5.3.1 Sorting the terminology

There are, in fact, a number of overlapping notions in the research on information structuring. These are commonly referred to as given–new relations, topic–comment relations, and theme–rheme relations. While each describes the functional arrangement of information in texts, they are at times defined somewhat differently, depending upon the researcher. It is useful to point out these distinctions briefly so that the reader may recognize possible incompatibilities when reviewing other research. A few examples will highlight these potential differences.

In a *given–new* analysis, the researcher defines given as information that has already been mentioned.

1. *Most people* realize that *wolves* have to kill deer, moose caribou, elk and other large animals to survive. *The predators* live in family groups called *packs*, usually containing 6–12 members, and it takes a lot of meat to feed them. *The* pack is well organized. ...

The first sentence begins with an indefinite general noun phrase (*most people*), indicating that new information is likely to follow. This new information is not likely to be closely related to the topic just discussed. In the second sentence, the term *predators* is used to refer back to *wolves* (signalled by the definite article, *the*). The first occurrence of *pack* is introduced as new information and then defined. In the next main clause, the term becomes part of the given information signalled by the use of the definite article, *the*.

Many researchers conflate a *theme–rheme* analysis with a *topic–comment* analysis. When theme–rheme structure is treated differently, the theme is typically assumed to be the first-mentioned phrase in the main clause unit; usually this coincides with the agent/subject/topic of a sentence. In the passage above the themes would be, respectively, 'most people', 'the predators', 'it', and 'the pack'. The change of perspective that this type of analysis offers may be found in the following examples:

2. *In the late 1960s and early 1970s,* I witnessed fluctuations caused by adverse conditions. ...

3. *Curtailed in the area,* he stated that, 'everyone knows the wolves will wipe out the deer'.

In example 2, the theme of the clause is the temporal setting rather than the agent subject. In example 3, the theme is a fronted participle which sets the background (ungrammatically) for the quotation to follow.

Theme–rheme is now most commonly associated with the work of Halliday (1985, 1994) and systemic text analysis rather than with the Prague School directly (e.g. the work of Danes 1974, Firbas 1986, and Vachek 1966). For Halliday, theme–rheme structure in texts is treated as an independent concept. In his systemic analyses, the notion of *theme* represents the point of departure in a structure; in contrast, the rheme represents the move away from the speaker's starting point. This concept works together with given–new relations, though they are not the same concept. The distinction is that the given–new relationship is based on the perspective of the hearer/reader (and based on the intonation unit of information), while the theme–rheme relationship is based on the perspectives of the speaker/writer (and based on constituent sequence). Fries (1994) and Martin (1992) suggest, further, that thematic structure represents the text's method of development; that is, the sequences of clause themes across a text point to the development of the major ideas (or macro-themes) in the text. Systemic linguistics, following Halliday, has contributed to this line of work from a variety of perspectives (Benson and Greaves 1985, Coulthard 1994, Couture 1986, Halliday 1985, Halliday and Hasan 1989).

Topic–comment structures are, when treated differently from the above categorizations, seen as defining 'what the sentence is about'. This designation requires somewhat more interpretation and intuition, though the work by Lauttimatti, discussed below, uses this criterion in her analyses. In examples 1 and 3 above, wolves are the topic of all the sentences, the 'comment' is what is said about the wolves in each case. In example 2, the topic is 'I'.

Finally, there is another set of terms which are sometimes discussed, and are sometimes confused with the previous sets: *focus–presupposition*. This pair of terms refers to the information that is highlighted or focused (and usually contrasted in some unexpected way), and to the information which is backgrounded (and is often treated as presupposed, or assumed, knowledge). Two examples illustrate this relationship:

4. *It* has been my good fortune *to have spent most of my career researching such details of the wolf's life.*

5. It is *this type of stability* that is often referred to as the 'balance of nature'.

In example 4, the *it* subject stands in the place of the understood infinitive clause beginning with 'to have spent ...'. This construction highlights the author's 'good fortune'. In example 5 the use of the cleft construction similarly highlights 'this type of stability' as the focus of the sentence. *Focus* is often treated as synonymous with *new* information and *presupposed* as synonymous with *given* information. However, it is possible to have information in focus which is given, or is the topic of a sentence; it is also possible to have presupposed information actually introduced in the text for the first time. Despite all of these potential confusions, there is much important research on information structuring and, for the most part, the blurring of distinctions does not seem to invalidate the findings.

2.5.3.2   Topical sentence structure

A second major line of research on information structuring is represented by topical sentence structure, as developed by Lautamatti (1987); in this case, using topic–comment analysis to examine written text and discourse simplification. Her theory of topical development in discourse examines the relations between the topic of discourse, the topical subject of a sentence, the syntactic subject, and the initial sentence element. Noting that the latter three notions do not always overlap, she explores the various possible patterns in written texts. Her goal is to isolate the topical subject of a sentence and then to examine the patterns of progression which the topical subjects form in a text. Her approach is important for a number of reasons.

1. She provides a functionally based taxonomy of topical and non-topical linguistic material in a sentence; the categories explain what each segment is expected to do in the sentence.
2. The specification of topical subject is presented in a way which indicates that topic for Lauttimatti is not simply given, as opposed to new, information.
3. She applies her analyses to written discourse to show that certain patterns of topical progression may be more readable than others (i.e. those texts which have fewer competing subtopics, fewer complex sequential progression (A–B, B–C, C–D), and more series of parallel topic progressions (A–B, A–C, A–D) appear to be more readable). This suggestion seems to be well supported by the work of vande Kopple (1986).

Lautamatti's approach to topical development should be applicable to the analysis of student writing. In particular, it may provide specific teaching suggestions for students who appear to be writing texts with deviant, and probably less readable, topical organization. This latter application is investigated by Cerniglia *et al.* (1990).

2.5.3.3 Topic continuity

A third line of research, focusing on the function of topic development in discourse, involves the work of Givon (1983, 1985) on topic continuity. In his research, Givon treats topics as noun phrases (NPs) which receive continuous mention in the ongoing discourse. He does not distinguish topic–comment from given–new information, conflating the two concepts. In fact, his work is more in line with the work on given–new chaining in discourse in that it requires specific prior mention to count something as a topic under analysis.

Beginning from the functional perspective that topic structuring is essential to the continuity of discourse, Givon has proposed that a NP which becomes a topic is restated in the ongoing discourse in different ways depending on:

- how far back in the text the last previous mention occurs;
- the number of potential competing NP referents in the immediate discourse; and
- the strength of its persistence in the oncoming discourse.

These quantifiable measures provide a means to account for the different ways topics are encoded in the structure of the grammar and suggest the writer's decisions in regulating/signalling the flow of information. In a sense, this approach amounts to a type of cohesion analysis. The difference is that his measures relate to the degree of difficulty of maintaining or recovering the topic of discourse with increasingly more marked grammatical forms. Specifically, Givon (1983: 17) suggests that the following scale of topic realization is generally applicable to English:

Most continuous/accessible topic:

1. Zero anaphora (I went to the store and *0* bought some cheese)
2. Unstressed/bound pronouns or grammatical agreement [Does not apply to English]
3. Stressed/independent pronouns (*He* went to the store by himself)

4. R-dislocated DEF-NP's (*It's* on the desk, *the book you want*)
5. Neutral ordered DEF-NP's – definite article initiates search for antecedent match (*The man* came back again)
6. L-dislocated DEF-NP's (*The book you found,* we left *it* on the bus)
7. Y-moved NP's (*The dictionary,* I found yesterday)
8. Cleft/focus constructions (It's *the dictionary* that I found yesterday)
9. Referential indefinite NP's (*A dictionary* was found yesterday)

Most discontinuous/inaccessible topic.

Givon (1985) has since revised his approach into a more complex set of continua which are appropriate to cross-linguistic research. The importance of this line of research is that it provides a specific agenda for examining how information continues and how topics are maintained. It becomes possible to explore the difficulty readers should have in processing a particular text depending on the deviation of topic marking based on the expected continuum. For writers, this continuum indicates the importance of knowing when it is not necessary to stress the topic and when it is important to mark it strongly for easy recovery.

2.5.3.4   Topical structure analysis

Drawing on the work of Daneš and Lautamatti, a fourth line of research in sentence-based functional discourse analysis centers again around a conflation of topic and given information. Witte (1983a, 1983b – see also Connor 1987, vande Kopple 1986) developed a topical structure analysis to study differences in high- and low-quality writing and differences in revision strategies. Looking for topical and sequential chaining patterns in student essays, Witte (1983b) found that low-rated essays did not provide enough appropriate given information and forced the reader to make too many inferences. The texts were not reader-friendly. Witte further found that low-rated essays used fewer sequential chaining patterns, making it harder for the reader to perceive main topics in the essay. Overall, differing patterns of topical structure analysis appeared to provide good predictors of student writing quality.

In a series of related studies, Connor (1987) has applied topical structure analysis to writing instruction to see if students could be brought to recognize the information structuring patterns in their writing. She reports positive results from teaching students to determine the main topics and subtopics, as well as the progression of supporting information. As Connor (1987: 685) states:

> Student responses have been positive, and we have seen improvement in student writing, specifically in regard to clearer focus and better development of subtopics. We feel that topical structure analysis is a useful check of coherence in writing.

2.5.3.5 Given and new information

A fifth research approach in information structuring is the specific examination of given and new information in texts. This approach differentiates given information from topic on the basis that given information must appear in the prior discourse (whereas topic of discourse does not have to appear in prior discourse), and given information does not have to be limited only to the discourse topic. Research by vande Kopple (1982, 1983, 1986) using a variety of patterns of information structure has shown that, generally speaking, the organization of given information before new information makes texts more readable and memorable. His research on information structures and their cognitive correlates suggests that further complex patterns of informational progression probably exist, that students can be taught to identify these patterns of organization in their texts, and that researchers may be able to examine differences among text genres, authors, or writing purposes on the basis of information structuring.

Vande Kopple (1986) also discusses other recent advances in the theory of given–new relations. In particular, the work by Prince (1981, 1992) suggests that given and new relations may not be a two-part division. Instead, she proposes seven categories of new, inferred, and given information for a more refined analysis of information structuring in texts (see also Brown and Yule 1983). Under 'new' information, Prince distinguishes information which is *unused* (readily recognized by the reader when introduced), and *brand new*; the brand-new entities may be either anchored or unanchored depending on whether they contribute to the ongoing discourse or are never repeated. An intermediate category comprises two types of 'inferences': *inferables* and *containing inferables. Inferable* entities refer to information that can be presumed from the information presented in prior discourse (e.g.

'a camera … the lens'). *Containing inferables* refer to entities which are recoverable as parts of a collective reference (e.g. 'one of the eggs'). The 'given' entities can be *evoked* in two ways; either explicitly by the prior text, or by reference to the situation (e.g. '*you* should understand what this means'; what Halliday would term exophoric reference). While this taxonomy of relations in texts is relatively new, it could be used to examine variations among many different types of texts.

2.5.4 Cohesion in texts

Cohesion is the means available in the surface forms of the text to signal relationships that exist between sentences or clausal units in the text. A few of the signalling systems have been indicated above, particularly in the work of Givon on topic continuity. Cohesion research (Halliday and Hasan 1976, 1989) focuses on a comprehensive examination of systematic devices used to connect the surface form of texts. It is the surface manifestation of the underlying relations that bind a text. While cohesion does not provide a full account of the textual interpretation of a text, it is an important indicator.

There are various means by which cohesion operates, principally including reference, substitution, ellipsis, conjunction, and the lexical relationships of repetition, inclusion, synonymy/antonymy, and collocation (Brown and Yule 1983, Halliday and Hasan 1976, 1989, Hoey 1991). There is, as might be expected, considerable controversy over the specific uses, specific domains, and specific forms that cohesion encompasses. The seminal work, *Cohesion in English* (Halliday and Hasan 1976), though most commonly cited, does not represent the totality of cohesion as it will eventually be defined (e.g. Halliday and Hasan 1989, Hoey 1991). Nevertheless, Halliday and Hasan's earlier research is, by any account, the place to begin. The basic categories they define are illustrated briefly below in the following four text segments (6)–(9).

(6) Barber (Samuel) managed to reverse the process; *his* last movement, a driving moto perpetuo, fully realizes the traditional function of a concerto as a showpiece. *It* seethes and stomps with unrelenting fury, *and it* ends in a satisfying climax.
(Goldberg 1985: V, 1)

This text includes a number of cohesive devices. A good example of pronominal cohesion is the use of *his* and *it* to refer across clauses. The text also makes use of the conjunction *and*. Lexical cohesion occurs in this text in two forms: inclusion relations are indicated by *Barber, concerto,* and *movement; concertos* are one form of music composed by *Barber,* and *movements* are basic parts of *concertos.* Lexical collocation is also represented in this text. *Process* collocates with a series of actions: *driving, moto perpetuo, seethes, stomps, unrelenting fury,* and *ends.*

(7) Scientific doubt about using tool behavior as evidence of advanced intelligence is indeed a fairly recent phenomenon. *One reason for this* is the fact that for many years, the majority of the research on the subject was conducted on more evolved species. ... Perhaps *the most dramatic* example *was first reported by behaviorist Jane Goodall* in the mid-1960's, when she discovered that chimpanzees sometimes use small twigs to probe into termite mounds. *Other scientists* have found that some fifteen species of birds exhibit tool use behavior.

(Abrahamson 1985: 25)

Text (7) contains instances of demonstrative and comparative reference, as well as a full range of lexical cohesion devices. A demonstrative connection occurs with *one reason for this,* where *this* refers back to the previous sentence. Comparative cohesion is indicated by *most dramatic example* and by *other scientists.* Lexical cohesion forms represented here include repetition, inclusion, and collocation. Repetition occurs with *using tool behavior: tool-use behavior, species: species, scientific: scientists,* and *behavior: behaviorists.* Inclusion is found in the forms *evolved species: chimpanzees,* and *scientist: behaviorist.* Collocation is extensive throughout this segment: Animal collocation is indicated by *chimpanzees, termites, birds,* and *species.* Science collocation is indicated by *scientific, evidence, phenomenon, research, subject, example, reported, behaviorist, discovered, species,* and *exhibit.*

(8) Another way of putting it is to say that they treat their forests *much as* we in America ravished our woodlands a hundred years ago. *This reference* to *our* own forest history is Myers', *and it* is not a casual *one.*

(Wild 1985: 134)

Text (8) offers a nice example of substitution, where *one* refers back to *reference.* In addition, this text uses conjunction (*and*), demonstrative (*this*), pronoun (*our, it*), repetition (*forests*), and synonymy (*woodlands*) as markers of cohesion.

(9) 'I hope I will not trouble you again,' the former prisoner of conscience said, '*but* there is a strong possibility that *I may*.'
(Amnesty Action Newsletter, Dec. 1984: 1)

Text (9) provides an example of ellipsis, as well as uses of pronominal and conjunctive cohesion. Ellipsis occurs when *may* is not followed by a predicate; the ellipsis refers back to 'trouble you again'. *But* and *I* are the other cohesive devices in this text segment.

All of these operations provide means for linking the surface text structure. As such, they reflect both the communicative intentions and the choices made by the author in the structures used and in the linear ordering of the texts. The concept of cohesion has created a certain amount of controversy, particularly over whether it provides appropriate measures of textual or comprehension development, and whether it represents a complete description of textual relations. The next chapter argues that cohesion is only part of the organizational structuring of texts. As to the former controversy, Brown and Yule (1983) argue that Halliday and Hasan's theory of cohesion offers a taxonomic inventory of textual resources. It is not clear, however, that Halliday and Hasan (1989) would accept the taxonomic limitations which Brown and Yule ascribe to their theory.

Hasan (Halliday and Hasan 1989) has recently revised her description of lexical cohesion by limiting its function in research to specific categories which are more easily replicable. Recognizing that collocation (though critical to the texture of a text) could not readily be verified reliably among researchers, Hasan now employs the lexical categories of synonymy, antonymy, hyponymy (superordinate–subordinate class), meronymy (part–whole), and repetition as types of coextension (lexical cohesion) in texts (cf. Hoey 1991).

Cohesion research on texts and on student composition has been extensive. In particular, research by Cox *et al.* (1990, 1991), Spiegel and Fitzgerald (1991), Tierney and Mosenthal (1983), and Witte and Faigley (1981) presents a complex set of research results. Cohesion research does not appear to be a complete answer to understanding writing development; at the same time, cohesion analyses do provide certain useful insights. Witte and

Faigley, for example, note that cohesion is a reasonable predictor of writing quality across grade levels. They also contend that cohesion is a useful indicator of differences in students' invention skills.

Halliday and Hasan (1989) have more recently extended cohesion analysis into a theory of cohesive harmony. Recognizing criticisms that cohesion quantification, in and of itself, did not distinguish coherent from non-coherent texts, they have proposed an analytic approach which creates chains of identity or 'similarity' cohesion ties. Further, the manner in which the chain elements interlink across chains represents the central elements producing the coherence of a text. Thus, the cohesive elements which form chains, and which interlink with other chains, are the quantifiable features of cohesion which indicate differential coherence in texts. (See also, Singer 1990 for supporting arguments from cognitive psychology research.) At present, some amount of research has been performed using cohesive harmony (Cox *et al.* 1990, 1991, Spiegel and Fitzgerald 1991; cf. Hoey 1991).

The connection between cohesion and coherence is an issue that has been raised numerous times: To what extent does the surface form contribute to the perception of underlying coherence of a text? For Halliday and Hasan, taking a functional perspective on the constructive use of language, the surface structure must make a considerable contribution (see also Christie 1992, Martin 1989, 1992, 1993). Other researchers have argued that an analysis of the logical coherence of a text for comprehension must be augmented by using procedures not specifically marked by surface forms. These procedures are the subject of the next chapter.

3

Towards a model of text construction

3.1 Introduction

The development of text analysis over the past 15 years has been, at least in part, an attempt to develop a model of text construction, a description of how the text structure is assembled, taking into account the message, the writer's purpose, the topic, and the expectations of the audience (cf. Bereiter and Scardamalia 1987, Halliday and Hasan 1989, Martin 1992). As the review of research on text linguistics indicates (Chapter 2), the effort to create a comprehensive model of text construction is a complex task. A model will have to account for the research of psychologists on text structure, the research of engineers and linguists on artificial intelligence, the research of linguists and applied linguists on discourse analysis and text genres in both synchronic and diachronic modes, the findings from studies of writing development, and the insights from rhetoric and critical studies.

It may well be that an explicit model of text construction is beyond current research capacity. Nevertheless, an understanding of how texts are constructed is an essential part of understanding the nature of writing and writing development. Over the past 15 years, efforts to develop a description of text construction have been undertaken by de Beaugrande (1980, 1984), de Beaugrande and Dressler (1981), Brown and Yule (1983), Dillon (1981), Halliday and Hasan (1989), and Martin (1992). In each case, the description stresses certain aspects of text analysis in favour of others. In this chapter, a descriptive model of text construction which is appropriate for a wide range of research on writing and writing development is proposed. This model, in turn, represents one component of a larger theory of writing that incorporates knowledge of text construction.

In order to develop the model, it is first necessary to review the important hypotheses and findings which such a model should address. Among the most important hypotheses that appear to be supported by research are:

1. Written language is distinct from oral language along a number of textual dimensions, and the construction of written language must be studied according to its own structural and rhetorical emphases.
2. Texts have hierarchical structure, most likely constituted as a set of logical relations among assertions, or as elements in a discourse matrix, or as cohesive harmony.
3. Different types of texts will have varying larger structuring because of requirements of purpose, audience, status, author, and information load.
4. Texts have a top-level structure which appears to vary with different text types, purposes, and audiences.
5. A discernable top-level of text structure is related to better comprehension, recall, and coherence assessment.
6. Systems for analysing text structure can be used for research even if each system in current use has particular strengths and weaknesses.
7. A theory of text type variation is possible and is needed for comprehension, production, and assessment research.
8. A theory of coherence is important to any model of text construction.
9. Any theory of coherence must incorporate an analysis of information structure – given–new, topic–comment, etc.
10. The surface form of texts plays a more important role in text construction than previously predicted.
11. Learning to write requires the manipulation of many complex structural and rhetorical dimensions, with greater complexity occurring in expository/argumentative writing.

While the concept of coherence, which is central to many of the points noted above, may be controversial for some researchers – who assume all of coherence to be a construction of the reader – there is now considerable evidence that the structure of the text itself contributes to, or interferes with, the coherence that is perceived by the reader (e.g. Beck *et al.* 1991, Britton and Gulgoz 1991, Martin 1992, Singer 1990). In addition, the notion that a text is a multidimensional construct is now well accepted, as are the many ancillary assumptions that are natural extensions of the basic assertion.

From the various research areas present in the literature (and previously reviewed above), it seems that a descriptive model of text construction requires at least seven basic components which must somehow coalesce as multiple interacting strands.

1. Syntactic structures.
2. Semantic senses and mappings.
3. Cohesion signalling.
4. Genre and organizational structuring to support coherence interpretations.
5. Lexical forms and relations.
6. Stylistic and register dimensions of text structure.
7. Non-linguistic knowledge bases, including 'world knowledge'.

Within each of the components are numerous subcomponents, interacting among themselves as well as with other components and subcomponents, rather like the atoms in chemical molecules. In the following discussion, the components of a text construction model are presented in four parts:

1. The elements of text structure
2. A theory of coherence
3. The functional-use dimensions of texts
4. The non-linguistic resources interacting with the elements and functional use dimensions.

3.2   Elements of text structure

In text structure, four potentially independent components exist on two levels: two on a sentential level and two on a textual (or intersentential) level (Figure 3.1). There is also a major division at both levels between surface structure and underlying structure. This division may be seen generally as constituting a form-meaning distinction. A fifth component – the lexicon – is a diffuse component underlying the other four. Together, these five components comprise the elements of text structure – the fundamental building blocks from which all texts are constructed.

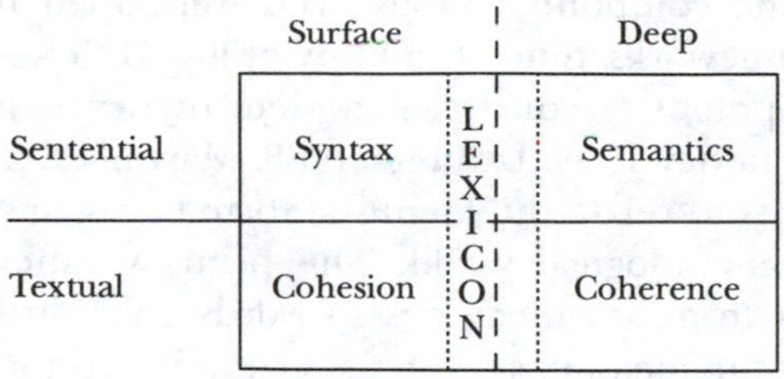

	Surface		Deep
Sentential	Syntax	L E X I	Semantics
Textual	Cohesion	C O N	Coherence

Figure 3.1 Elements of text structure

3.2.1 *The sentential level*

At the sentential level, syntax and semantics are conceived as they are normally understood in linguistic theory. They operate within the structural level of the written clause, representing systems of surface structure and underlying interpretation (senses and mappings from word meanings to sentential meanings). The syntactic component involves types of phrasings, types of clause constructions and clausal combinations, and the ordering of the phrases and words within the sentence.[1] For example, one might want to examine the number and types of passive structures, the types of phrases that appear sentence initially, the number and types of prepositional phrase groupings, or the number of rhetorical questions (cf. Biber 1988, Perera 1984). A researcher would want to adopt or propose a syntax component that describes adequately all the syntactic devices available in the language (e.g. Quirk *et al.* 1985).

Perhaps in the future, as linguistic research continues to advance, the preferred syntactic description would be a matter of empirical research (Sinclair 1991, 1994; see, e.g., the 'grammar' developed in the Collins COBUILD series, based on the analysis of a massive corpus of written English). For the moment, researchers must accept the syntactic approach most compatible with their interests and training. Syntactic analyses, most commonly, will involve the counting of various constructions and categories, and their co-occurrence in various combinations, typically as described in Chapter 2.

The semantic component is also relatively open to workable alternative frameworks. Since the study of linguistic semantics is a recent development, a concise, complete theory is not yet well established (Frawley 1993, Ladusaw 1988, Martin 1992). Semantic theory attempts to relate the linguistic form to objects and events in the phenomenological world. The primary function of this component is to assign meanings to words and phrases, and to interpret how the meanings of phrases combine to form meaning interpretations of entire clauses or clausal combinations. The semantic component also interprets the meaning of certain lexical classes of words within the clause. Included in such classes are pronouns, reflexives, modal verbs, as well as verb groups which are accompanied by particular semantic or syntactic constraints (i.e. factive verbs, perceptual verbs, aspectual verbs, suasive verbs, public verbs). The semantic component will also account for facts of scope interpretation and other semantic issues which can operate within the level of the sentence (Frawley 1993, Jackendoff 1972). For example, in the two sentences below, the negative marker changes its scope of interpretation from the lower clause in (1) to the entire clause in (2).

(1) I regret that Tom *doesn't* like me.
(2) I *don't* regret that Tom likes me.

These and other features of semantic interpretation are often addressed under the term 'sentential semantics' (as opposed to more microstructural 'lexical semantics' on one hand, and more macrostructural 'pragmatics' on the other).

3.2.2   *The lexicon*

The lexicon (our mental word list) pervades all four of the other components, in both surface form and underlying organization. It both affects, and is affected by, each of the other four components. The lexical entries used in text construction provide the basic meaning and inference signalling from which syntactic structures, semantic senses, and pragmatic interpretations are produced. The lexicon assists the syntactic component by providing sets of syntactically useful forms such as prepositions, articles, existential 'there', etc. Further, the lexical entries of specific words include syntactic information for the generation of the syntactic structure of the sentence. The verb *put* requires that a direct object and a locational prepositional phrase follow, while the verb *sit* will not allow a direct object but may require a locational prepositional phrase; e.g.

1. The boy *put the book* **on the desk**. [*put* what where?]
2. The boy *sat* **on the chair**. [*sat* where?]

The lexicon also provides the semantic forms which represent the ideational content of a text. The lexical forms themselves are most likely organized according to semantic criteria (as well as syntactic criteria) such as objects related by schema structures or scripts, or more abstractly as, for example, mental verbs, verbs of perception, psychological verbs, public verbs, verbs of motion, etc., or adverbs of manner, location, time, evaluation, etc.

At the level of text structure above the clause, lexical forms signal textual information in terms of cohesion. The lexicon provides the units for this purpose, including, for example, pronouns, demonstratives, ellipsis markers (e.g. *x* does too), and substitution markers (e.g. one). These, and other forms, may all signal aspects of cohesion. Finally, coherence structures may be lexically motivated in that necessary inferences, rhetorical predicates, and logical relations among assertions can be readily interpreted from specific lexical forms. As a simple example, a first clause using the word 'problem' usually indicates the beginning of a problem–solution discourse (cf. Hoey 1986, 1994, Tadros 1994). Viewing the lexicon as central to a theory of text construction is not a radical departure; a number of researchers argue that lexical cohesion may be the most important aspect of cohesion (Halliday and Hasan 1989, Hoey 1991, Witte and Faigley 1981). Stylists have also long been concerned with the importance of diction in conveying exact meaning and attitude.

3.2.3 The textual level

The two components of the sentential level are rather straightforward, as is the lexicon, in so far as most researchers will accept them as essential to language research. The components on the textual level are, however, somewhat more controversial. Cohesion and coherence parallel syntax and semantics on a 'greater than the clause' level as surface and underlying textual structure. The 'structure' at this level must be different since it is not possible to predict accurately that any sentence will determine the form or the interpretation of later sentences, though it is likely to influ-ence later sentences (unlike words in a sentence which may directly predict the words or structures to follow). The structure at this second, larger level is paradigmatic. This means that it is pos-sible to choose certain sentence forms in lieu of other sentence forms. The range of options available for a given clause position represents the limits of its paradigmatic structure.

Paradigmatic structure can be demonstrated in the following manner. It is possible to begin a paragraph with any of the three sentences below. They all represent viable options as paragraph initial constructions:

3. What led to the change in perspective was the different angles of the sun's rays throughout the day.
4. The different angles of the sun's ray throughout the day led to the change in perspective.
5. A change of perspective was created by the different angles of the sun's rays throughout the day.

The texts following sentence 3 would probably involve a discus-sion of 'what leads to the change in perspective'; the text following 4 would probably involve a discussion of 'different angles,' and that following 5 would probably involve a discussion of 'a change in perspective'. By the same token, the determination of the opening structure and the ensuing environment creates a probability for the immediately following structure; e.g.

6. It was Mary's birthday. _____ . And her mother gave her some perfume.
   (a) I gave her a rose.
   (b) A rose was given to her by me.
   (c) A rose was my gift to her.
   (d) She received a rose from me.
   (e) Giving her a rose was my contribution to the day.

Technically, any one of the five options is possible in the blank space in text 6, but there is a strong probability that native speak-ers of English would choose option (a) because the text creates a probability for a list of gifts Mary received for her birthday and because option (a) is grammatically parallel to the final structure in the text. For example, there seems to be no logical reason to choose a passive construction, and the other options seem to change the focus of the structure. In fact, in actual trials with native and near native speakers, in excess of 80 per cent of subjects chose option (a).

There is less than consistent agreement on the nature and relative contributions of cohesion or coherence to the overall construction of texts. Moreover, there is little consensus on the matter of an overall definition of coherence (cf. Brown and Yule 1983, Johns 1986, Phelps 1988, Singer 1990). The features defining cohesion are generally accepted, though the recent changes in lexical cohesion outlined by Hasan (Halliday and Hasan 1989) make this important area of cohesion more amenable to serious research uses. These issues concerning cohesion have been discussed in Chapter 2. The concern here is to explore the relation between cohesion and coherence, the definitional nature of coherence, and the role of coherence in a text construction model.

3.3   A theory of coherence

The concept of coherence in writing has traditionally been accepted as a component of writing research and writing instruction (e.g. Bamberg 1983, de Beaugrande and Dressler 1981). In the last 20 years, however, researchers in psychology, linguistics, and applied linguistics have begun to explore this notion in an effort to understand how readers interpret a text as coherent and how writers control language structure to convey a sense of coherence.

At the same time, research in pragmatics and conversational analysis has suggested that at least some part of coherence is constructed by the reader's interpretive systems regardless of the text structure itself. Garnham has pointed out that readers make a number of *bridging* inferences which appear to be controlled largely by the reader's efforts to assemble a text-model representation of a text into long-term memory (Garnham 1985, Oakhill and Garnham 1988). An understanding of the extent to which these bridging–inferencing processes (as opposed to *elaborative* inferencing) reflect processing of a specifically linguistic nature as opposed to general cognitive processing, might determine whether these processes are part of the linguistic system or have their origin elsewhere in the cognitive processing model. If they are largely linguistic in nature, then the argument can be made that textual form is the trigger for these inferencing mechanisms (cf. Barsalou 1992, Rayner and Pollatsek 1989, Singer 1990).

A second potentially non-linguistic source of coherence interpretation is discussed by Brown and Yule (1983). They suggest, following Widdowson (1978) and others, that coherence is the result of conventionalized knowledge and sequences which a hearer (reader) will be able to call upon to impose a coherent frame onto a message. These sources are typically referred to as scripts, frames, and/or schemas for organizing knowledge of the world. Assuming these external knowledge sources, Brown and Yule argue that coherence is essentially the creation of the reader rather than a product of the text. Drawing upon a general principle of analogy, the reader looks for similarities between the message and the knowledge he or she already has and, as a consequence, the reader is compelled to make connections. As they state (1983: 65–6):

> The imperative '*need* to *find* regularities' which Popper speaks of, coupled with Bartlett's 'effort after meaning,' constitute a powerful expectation in human beings that what is said or written will make sense in the context in which it appears. ... The natural reaction of man appears to be to make sense of any sign resembling language, resembling an effort to communicate. ... The natural effort of hearers and readers alike is to attribute relevance and coherence to the text they encounter until they are forced not to. ... It is not the sequence of sentences which represents 'coherent discourse.' Rather it is the reader, driven by the principles of analogy and local interpretation, who assumes that [a sequence] describes a series of connected events and interprets the linguistic cues under that assumption.

A third version of the non-linguistic basis of coherence may be seen in the more recent theory of *Relevance* proposed by Sperber and Wilson (1986). In this pragmatic interpretation of language use, the principle of relevance determines how coherent a message is to be taken. The basis of the theory assumes a general cognitive processing principle that human beings are designed to seek relevance in texts by comparing the text to other information resulting in the creation of new information, the contradiction of old information, and/or the confirmation of one's commitment concerning something (Smith 1989). The theory would not specifically state that relevance = coherence; indeed, a text may be coherent and meet none of the three criteria for relevance.

However, the cognitive principle is very similar to that stated above by Brown and Yule and is suggestive of a non-linguistic basis for a theory of coherence.

There is likely to be a fair amount of truth in the perspectives on coherence presented above. At the same time, arguments of this nature are a bit like saying that the printed page is unimportant in the reading process. While advances in discourse analysis and pragmatics have opened new research perspectives on text comprehension and interpretation, the basis for these interpretations nonetheless rests first with the text message itself. Ignoring this fact leads to an unbalanced overemphasis on top-down processing; ignoring the constraints on interpretation imposed by the text leads to the logical conclusion that the text may be altogether irrelevant. However, the vast majority of people, receiving a letter, will decide to read it rather than merely assume that they know the information in the letter and not open it (except perhaps in the instance of unsolicited advertising). The very act of reading a text implies that the text will influence the coherence interpretation constructed by the reader. For this reason, it is reasonable to assume that the text itself has a considerable role to play in the construction of textual coherence.

More recent research on coherence in texts, in fact, suggests that much of the coherence-building information is not simply imposed on the text by the reader, particularly in the cases of more mundane everyday texts. It is currently popular to cite reader response theories and constructivist views on comprehension and coherence in text. Unfortunately, their arguments rest primarily on relatively abstract logic and the illustrative literary examples to argue the matter. In contrast, cognitive psychology research now provides strong evidence for the impact of text structuring itself as a prime contributor to coherence in texts. Certain aspect of coherence are directly traceable to the text structure itself, and other aspects are best seen as an interaction effect of the reader and the text information together. Examples of research which support this view may be found in Anderson (1990), Beck *et al.* (1991), Britton and Gulgoz (1991), Singer (1990) and van Dijk and Kintsch (1983).

In addition, over the past two decades, in contrast to accepting a non-linguistic perspective on coherence, many text linguists have explored the structuring of text to determine how text may be said to be coherent. One early effort to examine this potential property of texts was the theory of cohesion of Halliday and Hasan (1976). A number of responses in the 1980s argued that cohesion was not equivalent to coherence (Brown and Yule 1983, Carrell 1982, Mosenthal and Tierney 1984, Widdowson 1979). However, Halliday and Hasan's more recent (1989) theory of cohesive harmony agrees much more closely with research on information structuring and the influence of local clausal relations in building text coherence.

While it is fair to say that cohesion represents the formal signalling.features of texts beyond the limits of the sentence, and that coherence is probably more than this, it is also likely that writers, in using this surface signalling, are guiding readers to achieve the preferred coherent interpretation intended by the writer. In this respect, the many linguistic signals and markers of cohesion that appear in a text provide a framework within which to establish the coherent logic of the textual information. To assert otherwise would be to argue that the many signalling mechanisms in texts are essentially arbitrary and meaningless bits of convention and stylistic options. The research of cognitive psychology and educational psychology on text comprehension clearly does not support the arbitrariness of structural signalling in text.

The controversies that have arisen over the nature of coherence point to the fact that surface structure in texts does not provide a perfect match with the organizational logic of the text. First, a certain amount of ambiguity is inherent in language and in texts. Second, no set of linguistic signalling will provide all the information needed to construct the text logic completely. Finally, writers will employ the formal resources for signalling text organization to differing degrees depending on their familiarity with intended readers and their knowledge of the topic and genre, the goals of the writer, and the proficiency of the writer in the written medium. These factors together suggest that, while it is relatively easy to explore the surface forms of cohesion, the nature of coherence is much more difficult to discern.

Beyond the surface form, text is organized by the writer's relation to it, to the reader's assumed knowledge, and to the subject matter. Coherence as a theoretical construct in text structure refers to the underlying relations that hold between assertions (or propositions) and how these assertions contribute to the overall discourse theme (or macrostructure) (e.g. Beck *et al.* 1991, Britton *et al.* 1993). This set of relations assumes that coherent texts will be unified by one overarching theme, whether stated or implicit (Britton and Gulgoz 1991, Kaplan *et al.* 1983, Singer 1990). It is the coherence in text structure which allows the reader to build, at least in part, a mental model of comprehension (Garnham 1985, Singer 1990).

Various approaches of coherence structure have been proposed (e.g. Mann and Thompson 1988, 1992, Martin 1992, Meyer 1975, 1985, Sperber and Wilson 1986, van Dijk and Kintsch 1983). In the majority of models, coherence is defined (implicitly or explicitly) as:

- having a discourse theme (overall topic of discourse);
- comprising a set of relevant assertions relating logically among themselves by means of subordination (cause, condition, comparison, specification), coordination (addition, restatement), and/or superordination, from the level of the sentence to the top-level structuring of a text, and
- being organized by information structure imposed on assertions most effectively to guide the reader in understanding the theme or the intent of the author (topic–comment, theme–rheme, given–new, focus–presupposition).

The crucial issue for this textual component seems to be how the relationships between logical assertions and information structure work within the framework of the topic of discourse.

Of the three subcomponents of coherence, discussions of the topic of discourse and of logical relations among assertions are relatively straightforward. Within the subcomponent of topic of discourse there must be some attempt to account for the relations and interactions among clausal units, larger organizing notions and macrostructure (Hoey 1991, Kaplan 1972, Mann and Thompson 1988, Meyer 1987, Singer 1990, van Dijk and Kintsch 1983). These notions can be illustrated in the following problem–solution text:

How delicate is the balance of nature?

1. During two decades of wolf research, conducting studies in northern Minnesota and on Isle Royale in Michigan, I have learned that, far from always being 'balanced,' ratios of wolves and prey animals can fluctuate wildly – and sometimes catastrophically. Wolves may actually starve after killing off almost all the moose and deer in an area. This explains why wolf-control programs may sometimes

ensure greater and more stable numbers of both wolves and the animals they hunt.

2. Most people realize that wolves have to kill deer, moose, caribou, elk and other large animals in order to survive. The predators live in family groups called packs, usually containing 6 to 12 members, and it takes a lot of meat to feed them. The pack is well organized, with each wolf occupying its own place in the social ladder. Each pack possesses a territory large enough to encompass hundreds of prey animals and delineates that territory with urine marks and howling.

3. It has been my good fortune to have spent most of my career researching such details of the wolf's life and of the creature's interactions with its prey. One of my studies that helped fix the balance-of-nature idea in the public mind was the Isle Royale wolf–moose research that I conducted as a doctoral candidate from 1958 through 1962. Flying over the snow-covered, 210-square-mile national park in Lake Superior each winter in a small ski-plane, I learned that there were 20 to 25 wolves on the island and approximately 600 moose. The wolves were harvesting the old and sick moose and the surplus calves, and both predator and prey numbers seemed stable.

4. It is this type of stability that is often referred to as the 'balance of nature.' Prey animals are superbly adapted for escaping wolves, and wolves are well suited for catching prey, and the result is a rough balance between the two. Unfortunately, it doesn't always work so smoothly over the short run. Human interference, unusual weather, or other 'outside' factors can cause disruptions in the predator-prey relationship. For this reason, scientists are increasingly hesitant to use the word 'balance.' Many of us now prefer the phrase 'dynamic equilibrium,' which better describes the phenomenon.

5. In the late 1960's and early 1970's I witnessed fluctuations caused by adverse conditions: a series of severe winters that struck across North America. My students and I were studying wolves and deer in northeastern Minnesota at the time, using aerial radio-tracking. One of my bush pilots wondered why we were doing the study. Noting that wolf-control programs had generally been curtailed in the area, he stated that, 'Everyone knows the wolves will wipe out the deer.'

6. It looked like he was right. Year after year, we watched the wolves decimate an overwintering herd of white-tailed deer throughout a 1,500-square-mile region. Almost all the deer were inaccessible during the hunting season, so wolves caused most of their mortality….

7. But the wolves had help from the severe winter weather. Winter severity played a dual role in the deer decline. First, the deep snow made adult deer easier to kill. Thus in winter 1968–1969,

wolves even took more deer than they were able to consume. Each time we found a wolf kill, we would land our plane on a nearby frozen lake and snowshoe to the carcass. We saw several that had been killed and left with little or nothing eaten. That meant fewer deer the following summer to produce new fawns.

8. Secondly, the fawns that were produced that summer were in trouble from the start....

9. Any prey population can safely sustain intermittent fawn or calf crop loss. However, our herd in northern Minnesota was hit with a series of seven severe winters, from 1966 to 1972, while wolf numbers were high....

10. Initially, during this deer decline, wolf numbers actually increased – a fact I couldn't account for until I realized that they were cashing in on the increased vulnerability of the deer....

11. Wolves, therefore, were suddenly faced with a severe food shortage....

12. The same severe winters battered Isle Royale, which only lies 20 miles from Minnesota....

16. However, there is little disputing the results of a recent well-controlled experiment in central Alaska. Some 38 to 60 per cent of the wolves were removed each year from a test area while wolves were not controlled in several adjoining areas. Moose and caribou calves and yearlings increased two- and four-fold where wolves had been taken compared with their numbers before wolf control and were consistently higher than in the areas with no wolf removal. Actual moose and caribou herd sizes followed the same trend.

17. What would have happened if wolves had not been controlled? Because the herds had been declining before the experiment, I expect that they either would have continued to decrease, would have remained stable but low, or might have increased only slowly. Meanwhile, from what I saw in northern Minnesota, wolf pups would have starved to death, wolf productivity would have declined, and adult wolves would have killed each other. Control programs allowed recovery of both prey and wolves so that more of each could live over a longer period. It is something I am reminded of every time I fly over my Minnesota study area and look at lakeshores that were speckled with deer and wolves in the late 1960s, and that now lie empty.

18. When prey herds are low for whatever reason, wolf control is often proposed as a ready means of relieving pressure on them. The non-hunting public then usually responds with cries of indignation. It looks like wolves are being used as scapegoats. Because many of these people view wolf-prey systems as constantly in balance, they fail to understand how wolf control can aid prey recovery.

(Mech 1985: 57–8)

This text contains larger discourse patterns of organization which can be examined in terms of subordinate, coordinate and superordinate units. Paragraph 1 introduces the topic of discourse and the intentions of the author (wolves, and the balance of nature). This topic is presented as a *problem* (ratios of wolves and prey animals can fluctuate wildly – and sometimes catastrophically). Paragraph 2 is coordinated with 1 in that it provides additive information – appropriate background information on wolves. The third paragraph is also additive information, being parallel to 2 and coordinate with 1. It provides appropriate background information on the author. As such, it legitimizes the authority of the writer to speak on this issue. The final sentence of paragraph 3 refers back to the 'stability' in paragraph 1 as a transition device to continue the hierarchical 'problem' organization of the text.

Paragraph 4 expands and quantifies the notion of 'stability' (the balance of nature) of paragraph 3, and also of 1; as such, it is subordinate to 1. Paragraph 5 is an example of 'imbalance' or loss of 'dynamic equilibrium'; it is subordinate to paragraph 4. Paragraph 6 provides apparent support for the generalization at the end of paragraph 5, but with signals that this view is simplistic. This unit constitutes a transitional paragraph to a more complex 'problem' re-analysis. Paragraphs 7, 8, and 9 develop a second line of analysis where a second cause of imbalance (severe winter weather) is examined. The discussion in these paragraphs refers primarily back to paragraph 4, where the principle of 'dynamic equilibrium' was first introduced. Paragraph 7 is parallel to 5 in providing a second factor responsible for an imbalance, both factors having been initially mentioned in paragraph 4.

Paragraph 10 reaffirms the problem, and paragraph 11 reaffirms the immediate cause. Paragraphs 12 through 15 describe parallel events in another location. Paragraph 16 suggests the *solution* to the problem. These paragraphs reaffirm the description in paragraphs 7–9. The text continues until paragraph 18, where the author once again states his intention to re-examine the notion of 'balance of nature'. Here the author reaffirms the topic of discourse. This paragraph, then, is superordinate to all but the first three paragraphs of the text.

This text exemplifies some of the logical patterns of textual organization which form a part of the text's coherence. The paragraph relations could be graphed using a discourse bloc analysis, a clause relational analysis, a rhetorical structure analysis, or a propositional analysis to examine the different relations operating in this text (cf. Britton and Gulgoz 1991, Hoey 1991, 1994, Kaplan 1972, Mann and Thompson 1988, 1992). Alternatively, the text could be diagrammed in terms of the cohesive relations linking the surface forms with those which support coherence relations.

The third major subcomponent, information structure (see Chapter 2), is not as clearly recognized as a part of coherence. In particular, research on information structure is confused by the wide-ranging sets of definitions for the assorted terminology.

Information structure appears, however, to be centrally involved in the creation of coherent texts. Information structure implicates the issue of how linearized texts signal rate of information flow, amount of information, and the relations involved in the ongoing flow of information. At issue are questions concerning:

- how more important thematic information is highlighted in texts;
- how given (old) and new information are signalled;
- how particular aspects of information may be presupposed in relation to what is expressed; and
- how too little new information or too much new information (which can only be defined with respect to some intended/ assumed audience) affects the coherence of texts.

All of these issues of information structuring are constrained by the linear ordering of texts as well as by how rapidly the author wants to present any given body of information, and from what perspective. A careful discussion of the linearity of texts is found in de Beaugrande (1984).

Finally, the role given to inferencing systems in the construction of text coherence needs to be considered. While these are not specifically aspects of the text itself, such systems interact with textual structure to constrain the writer/reader in determining the limits on interpretation of text meaning. These systems, in their turn, must be constrained by the mechanisms of text structure if appropriate inferences are to be made. For example, a common distinction made in text inferences is between *bridging* and *elaborative* inferences in comprehension of texts. Many researchers now assume that most inferences are elaborative and are not part of the basic comprehension cues directly signalled by texts. Some inferences, however, are required to create connections between the new information and the information already stored. This sort of inference, a bridging inference, is assumed to be produced and stored as part of the basic text analysis (Oakhill and Garnham 1988, Rayner and Pollatsek 1989). These findings would suggest that inferencing, as a coherence-creating mechanism, is strongly constrained by the structure of the text, and defining the concept of coherence in some manageable way seems to be crucial to any understanding of how texts are constructed.

3.4   Functional-use dimensions of texts

There must be a component of text construction which identifies the dimensions along which text elements are functionally organized to create the text. This dimension may be construed as the *interpersonal* level of text construction, though more may be involved (see, e.g., Halliday 1985). The functional/style level explores the correlates of the writer's attitudes to the reader, to the subject matter, to the situation, to world knowledge, and perhaps, reflexively, to himself. This level of analysis also implicates the parameters of appropriateness within the text; e.g. which structural elements match which textual contexts – after all, one does not expect to find direct speech structures in a technical manual. This level of analysis should not simply be considered a matter of style, though it may be closely related to style. Style reflects the personality of the writer. The components discussed here represent the language parameters a writer uses to manipulate the text for various purposes; such manipulations, in and of themselves, may not represent all of a writer's personality, nor is writer's personality all that such manipulations represent.

Unlike the first five text-construction components, this component is not concerned with elements of text structure, but rather is concerned with how the elements are combined to form particular texts. A contribution to textual-dimensions from the field of rhetorical studies has been the establishment of a traditional classification system for the logical organization of texts. More recently, linguists have been exploring ways to examine texts for textual dimensions which organize the text without presuming traditional top-down patterns of text classification. Dillon (1983) suggested that the interpersonal dimension of texts could be understood in terms of five dimensions of stance, representing the relation of writer to the text and to the reader:

- personal–impersonal
- distance–solidarity
- superior–equal
- oblique–confronted
- formal–informal.

While these five parameters represent simply one attempt to define interpersonal dimensions in text construction, most have an empirical reflection in the other research (see, e.g., Biber 1988, Scollon and Scollon 1983). It should be noted that the superior/equal dimension is more commonly discussed in terms of parameters of equal/unequal or politeness/power.

Dillon does not intend this set of parameters to be interpreted as style options, as in Joos (1967), but rather as a set of basic components defining any text (see *alignment* in Tierney and Pearson 1983: 572–6). Dillon refers to the parameters as the 'social signalling functions in a text'. The real issue is how to use these parameters to establish measurable aspects of text structure.

Chafe (1982), in an early attempt to address this issue and define dimensions of text structure, suggested that texts may be classified according to how they vary along two dimensions of text construction: text involvement/detachment and text integration/fragmentation (see Tannen 1987, 1989). More recent research by Biber and his colleagues (Biber 1988, 1989, 1992, 1995, Biber and Finegan 1988, 1989, Grabe 1987) suggests that a number of textual dimensions are constructed from the complex co-occurrence patterns of lexico-syntactic elements. Biber (1988), in his most comprehensive study, defines seven textual dimensions underlying spoken and written texts. From this research, he has proposed that a theory of text types must account for these dimensions: types that are empirically identifiable, rather than determined *a priori*. Following this line of research, the text construction model proposed here includes a component of stylistic use – the textual uses of linguistic structures to create communicative dimensions of text structure. Nine such dimensions of text structure, each of which receives support from text analysis research, are proposed:

1. *Rhetorical intention* reflects that dimension of text construction whereby texts are constrained by the top-level logical structuring of texts (Meyer 1984, 1987).
2. *Interactivity* is a textual dimension which combines various

features to convey relative interaction/involvement between writer and reader through the text (Biber 1988, Grabe 1987).

3. *Referentiality* describes the degree and type (logical, text-internal reference or reference to situation) of referring which takes place in texts and can be related to the 'endophoric versus exophoric reference' distinction of Halliday and Hasan (1976, 1989).

4. *Immediacy of context* reflects the relative use of different temporal signalling to define text information – it typically delineates primarily narrative texts from other text types (Biber 1988, Grabe 1987).

5. *Suasion* refers to the use of features which signal a writer's attempts to persuade the reader, most typically indicated by modals and certain subclasses of verbs (Biber 1988).

6. *Abstractness* reflects the relative degree of neutrality or objectivity appearing in a text; texts are marked for technical and formal styles versus other types of textual style (Biber 1988, Grabe 1987).

7. *Elaboration* refers to the degrees and types of elaboration which occur in different types of texts; it can be equated with the notion of constraints on planned versus unplanned discourse (Biber 1988, Ochs 1979, Reppen and Grabe 1993).

8. *Evidentiality* refers to the need for writers, in careful professional prose, to indicate their degree of commitment to the factuality of what is being stated (Biber 1988, Chafe and Nichols 1986).

9. *Text type (genre)* refers to the variation to be found, more generally, among different text types and the ways that textual features combine to define these types (Biber 1989, Dudley-Evans 1989, Martin 1985, 1992, Swales 1990).

Each of these dimensions (and there may be others as well) represents ways that texts are shaped and constrained according to the various purposes of the writer and the demands of the context. A model of text construction needs to account for these dimensions operating on the creation of texts.

3.5   Non-linguistic knowledge

The final component of the text construction model provides the world/background knowledge for appropriate interpretation and production of text. Certain aspects of this knowledge will be encoded in the lexicon though there is also much more information of a non-linguistic nature that must be accessible as well. There are a number of non-linguistic factors which must be included in a model of text construction:

- reference
- world background knowledge (and intertextuality)
- memory
- emotion
- perception
- intention
- logical arrangement (deduction, etc.)
- situation.

All of the members of this set have powerful influences on aspects of texts but are essentially independent of the linguistic domain of the text model. *Reference,* for example, is the set of abilities functioning to connect cognition to the real world – an activity that can be carried on in the absence of verbal language. The fact that one of its typical manifestations is linguistic does not make the entire notion linguistic. Similar arguments can be made for *emotion, perception,* and *intention. World background knowledge* and *memory,* and *situation* (which perhaps cover the same territory), are sets of schemata or frames for organizing content and context, and are not dependent on language; it would appear reasonable to imagine a set of knowledge in the absence of language, and there is considerable psychological support for such a perception (Cohen 1983, Johnson-Laird 1983, Paivio 1986).

3.6 The overall text model

The components for a text model outlined above should not be seen as an accurate, fully formed model, nor even as a formal attempt at psychologically valid model building; that would require specific processing mechanisms and an explanation of exactly how the pieces interact in the way they do. Such an explicit model is beyond current understanding of text construction. Rather, what has been provided is a descriptive model of the written text which attempts (1) to include what must be considered in a theory of text construction, (2) to explain the reasons why the various components are important, and (3) to suggest ways in which future research might explore component interaction in texts.

With this goal in mind, theories of text construction would seek to explain what is involved in the linguistic-production aspects of a cognitive model of the writing process (e.g. de Beaugrande 1984, Martin 1992). The model by Flower and Hayes of the writing process does not provide a specification of *what* is involved in text construction, but it would require such a specification if it were to define specific text-construction research questions. By the same token, any text-construction model would also need to be complemented by a processing model for a larger theory of writing. Such a processing mechanism would describe *how* the various components of text production are combined in the creation of text. For the moment, however, the model described here does not need to specify *how* text information is combined and created; its main concerns are *what* is combined for *which* purposes. The text-comprehension description by Garnham (1985, also Oakhill and Garnham 1988) and/or the processing models of Bereiter and Scardamalia (1987), and Flower and Hayes (1981a, 1981b) provide appealing descriptions which are compatible with, though distinct from, the text-construction model presented in this chapter. This conception of text is represented as Figure 3.2.

The seven components represented in the figure (syntax, semantics, lexicon, cohesion, coherence, functional dimensions, and non-linguistic resources) form the basis of the text-construction model. Each component should represent a significant aspect of text structure or of text-structure constraints in its own right. Whether this may be so can eventually be tested by quantitative methods. This first model also strongly suggests that earlier research, depending on only one or two components of text, evokes the tale of the seven blind men and the elephant. At the same time, it is important to recognize the basic nature of texts as interactive, rather than simply componential in nature; that is, the whole is greater than the sum of its parts in isolation. That is why a componential approach (like that used in sentence-level analyses) is insufficient. One cannot simply assemble the pieces and thereby create the whole text.

There is an emergent quality to texts that does not allow for the simple adding of the parts (Bateson 1979, Dillon 1981). An analogous situation may well be represented by the chess board; that is,

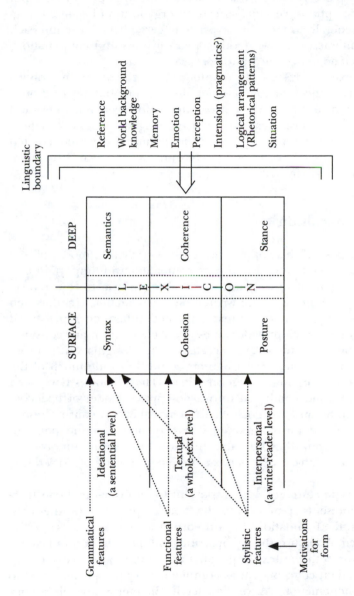

Figure 3.2 A model of text construction

the text can be conceived as a chess board on which the force field of each piece is visible. Many pieces have multiple, though not limitless, options; certain patterns of organization become recognized generally as more appropriate in certain contexts, and each piece interacts with every other piece in ways and combinations that do tend to become limitless.

For texts, the results of the interacting elements are not only a number of one-to-one effects but also of combinations of groups in relation to any one, etc., forming unforeseen relations (and creating real 'covert' categories in the language; see, e.g., Whorf 1941). The text is a multifactored, multidimensional field, created out of identifiable components, but not fully reducible to them. Perhaps this is why writing is so much a practised art.

3.7   Conclusion

The purpose of this chapter has been to present a model of text construction – one that would be compatible with important current research on writing and would also conform to research on prose comprehension and written discourse analysis. In all, seven components of a model of text construction have been presented in Figure 3.2. Each provides an essential element for any consideration of how texts are created. The insights into prose organization discussed in Chapters 2 and 3 provide much of the support for the model presented here. These notions have been elaborated and combined into a descriptive model of text construction. Because the goal of such a model of text construction is to understand the components of text, and at some point to understand how they interact, this model fits within a more general research objective which is to define properties of written text in real use.

At this juncture, it is also important to recall that text construction represents a model of the text as product. In the next chapter, the foundations for a theory of writing as process will be explored. A mature theory of writing will have to account, minimally, for both the text as product and writing as process, not as independent concepts but as complementary perspectives on the same phenomenon. As we shall see in Chapter 8, a viable theory of writing will also have to incorporate an interpretation of social contexts and their effects on writing.

Note

1. It must be understood that the grammatical model which is adopted for research will determine the structures available to be analysed; that is, grammatical theories produce models which are, in Kuhn's sense, self-defining. For example, if one adopts an early transformational generative grammar – one utilizing kernel sentences and a phrase-structure grammar – the kernal structures will define *what can be examined*, as they do in Hunt's T-unit analyses (see Chapter 2). At the same time, the model taken as the standard will also define the means of analysis; that is, to the extent that certain grammatical functions are foregrounded in the model and others are marginalized, the model will define *how various structures can be examined*. The point is simply that the choice of a grammatical model is not a neutral choice.

4

Writing process approaches

4.1 Introduction

At the close of Chapter 1, the issue of the writing product versus the writing process in composition research and instruction was mentioned as perhaps the controversy of the 1980s. The development of the writing process approach is now widely recognized as the major impetus for the emerging field of composition research and also for composition studies as a graduate field of study.

Such a development – with its emphasis on tertiary-level composition – may be unique to the USA, as most research on writing in other English-speaking countries has focused primarily on elementary and secondary students (e.g. Boomer 1985, Britton *et al.* 1975, Christie *et al.* 1989, Wells 1986, Wells and Chang-Wells 1992). It should also be noted at the outset that much current research on writing in a L2 is based directly on theoretical and instructional trends in writing-as-a-process theory. In fact, current perspectives on writing-as-a-process in L2 contexts can only be understood properly when seen as an outgrowth of the process movement more generally (Hudelson 1989b, Johnson and Roen 1989, Kroll 1990, Leki 1992, Raimes 1991, Zamel 1987).

Up to just past mid-century, writing instruction in the USA was approached in a rather uniform way. Students, who often did very little writing (see, e.g., Applebee 1981), would learn to outline and write 'themes' based on the four major 'rhetorical' distinctions – description, narration, exposition, and argumentation – and often framed in a three- or five-paragraph format. Through expository assignments, students were taught such patterns of logical arrangement as definition, classification, comparison and contrast, etc., and told to write an essay imitating (or approximating) a given pattern. Essays were written in one draft, and errors were corrected by keying to a writing handbook, these in turn primarily providing answers and exercises on various aspects of surface grammar. Ideas for writing topics were extrapolated from literary source books and 'readers', containing models for analysis and imitation or from lectures delivered by the writing instructor. Even research writing was organized around published sets of selected primary materials. Generally, the focus in writing classes was on the form of the written product rather than on how the learner should approach the process of writing.

In the 1960s, a number of factors coalesced to generate a strong reaction to this instructional profile:

1. US tertiary institutions, during the 1960s, underwent a period of extraordinary expansion, and as a result of a liberalizing movement many schools adopted a policy of 'open enrolment'; that is, they admitted any student who applied, and, in many cases, used 'gatekeeping' courses – such as composition – to eliminate students from the institution.

2. As a result of open enrolment policies and equal-educational-opportunity demands, many more minority student were admitted into tertiary institutions; the minority students were often eventually those who were screened out.

3. The concern among some tertiary institutions over the high minority drop-out rate, as well as the growth in the number of two-year community colleges throughout the USA, led to an increasing focus on remedial/basic writing classes for high-risk students. Many institutions began to test students' writing abilities on arrival and to place lower-ability students in remedial writing classes before permitting them to enrol in the required 'normal' first-year composition classes.

4. Teachers in remedial writing and freshman composition classes became dissatisfied with traditional approaches to writing instruction, recognizing that the conventional approaches may have been acceptable in a system of education designed for the culturally homogenous élite and middle class but were now essentially irrelevant for students with vastly different life experiences. Instructors in tertiary-level institutions began to move away from a focus on purely expository essay writing and literary criticism as the content (or non-content) of writing courses.

5. Tertiary-level institutions moved to become open forums for inquiry rather than bastions of authoritative knowledge.
6. At the same time, researchers noted a downward trend in nationwide test scores which were believed to index literacy levels; that slide in standardized test scores fuelled a general concern in the 1980s over the perceived erosion of literacy skills among students.
7. In the 1960s the psychological and philosophical foundations of human skills research began a major shift in the direction of what is now defined as cognitive psychology (Gardner 1985); its major underlying assumptions – (i) that the inner workings of the mind can be studied, (ii) that complex skills are made up of interacting components working together in complex processes, and (iii) that learners are creative hypothesis generators – led researchers to view language skills, particularly reading and writing abilities, as legitimate domains for theoretical research.

All of these trends, together, have led teachers, researchers, and evaluators to reassess the nature of writing and the written medium, and the ways in which writing is learned and taught. While the outcomes of this reassessment are many, the focus here is specifically on the rise of what has been popularly designated the *writing-as-a-process movement.*

As a liberating concept, writing-as-a-process did much to change the general perceptions of writing instruction and of the ways students learn to write. An obvious sign that this major change has become well established is the instantiation of this innovation in the textbook market.[1]

The writing-as-a-process approach, as a reaction to earlier instruction, freed instruction from:

- the three- or five-paragraph model;
- simplistic assumptions about the organization and ordering of information;
- the typical one-draft writing assignment;
- the assumption that each student should be working alone, or only with the instructor on summative feedback;
- reliance on grammar/usage handbooks and lectures;
- the linear composing model based on outlining, writing, and editing;

and it freed instructors from imposed, artificial topics for writing.

In the place of these previous practices, the process approach encourages:

- self-discovery and authorial 'voice';
- meaningful writing on topics of importance (or at least of interest) to the writer;
- the need to plan out writing as a goal-oriented, contextualized activity;
- invention and pre-writing tasks, and multiple drafting with feedback between drafts;
- a variety of feedback options from real audiences, whether from peers, small groups, and/or the teacher, through conferencing, or through other formative evaluation;
- free writing and journal writing as alternative means of generating writing and developing written expression, overcoming writer's block;
- content information and personal expression as more important than final product grammar and usage;
- the idea that writing is multiply recursive rather than linear as a process – tasks are repeated alternatively as often as necessary; and
- students' awareness of the writing process and of notions such as audience, voice, plans, etc.

The process approach is frequently discussed as a wholly positive innovation allowing teachers and students more meaningful interaction and more purposeful writing.

In fact, writing-as-a-process has become so popular that some researchers (e.g. Hairston 1982) claimed a paradigm shift (as explicated in Kuhn 1970) in writing theory and instruction (thus requiring an independent theoretical foundation). The fact that this movement has developed so strongly and remains so popular testifies to the fact that the writing process perspective has captured certain important truths about language. Like any movement in education which asserts itself as the new truth, the writing process approach has been the object of careful scrutiny in recent years, leading to serious criticism, much of it well justified.

By the 1980s, the first critiques of this new orthodoxy began to emerge and many of the writing process claims have now been seriously questioned or qualified. At the center of much criticism is the assertion that the writing process approach is an instructional notion without a strong theoretical foundation, a foundation which it has claimed to have as it attempted to revolutionize writing (see, e.g., Hairston 1982, North 1987). In retrospect, it is evident that the writing-process approach fares about as well as most other new perspectives; it offers significant insights, but it claims to offer much more (cf. Applebee *et al.* 1994). An understanding of writing-as-a-process is best achieved by reviewing the major developments in the movement over the past 30 years. In this way, the excesses may be separated from the genuine strengths and insights.

The history of writing process approaches can be divided into a rough set of four stages from the 1960s to the present. First proposed in the mid-1980s (Faigley 1986), this perspective remains an effective analytic scheme: Each stage represents new insights and responds to difficulties identified in the preceding stage. These stages can be outlined as follows:

1. The expressive stage
2. The cognitive stage
3. The social stage
4. The discourse community stage.

It is important to note that these stages do not represent general historical transitions for all practitioners; in fact, many researchers and instructors still prefer to use an expressive approach to writing instruction. Others, for example, still prefer a cognitive approach without serious consideration of social-context factors in their instruction.[2]

4.2   The expressive approach to the writing process

The expressive stage of the writing process can be traced back, in recent times (cf. Myer [1985] for an historical review of process claims asserted more than 50 years ago), to the 1960s and the arguments put forth by Elbow (1973, 1981), Macrorie (1970, 1980), Murray (1968, 1980, 1985) and others, urging that writers look for their authentic voices and be able to express themselves freely. The goal, a romantic one, as both Berlin (1987) and Faigley (1986) note, was to produce writing that was fresh and spontaneous and had integrity. Writers should say what they really thought; they should be creative and take chances. Writers should let their natural voices speak out.

North (1987) refers to the leading figures of this expressive movement as writing practitioners guided primarily by pragmatic insights into the nature of good writing and writing instruction. In essence, their advice amounts to recounting what worked for them as good writers and what should, consequently, work for others in the classroom. As North notes, this approach to writing, either as theory or as practice, had no guiding theoretical foundation which could differentiate lesser insights from better insights or determine how, when, or why pragmatic advice on writing instruction would transfer to other contexts and other teachers. Relatively little attention was given to *why* these insights were appropriate as opposed to *what* to do in a classroom, and *how* to do it.

Elbow, in his influential books on writing, added a touch of biology – writing was to be seen as an organic, if not mysterious, process, springing from a creative source; it was the writer's vehicle for self-expression.

However, despite the mysterious, romantic underpinnings of the expressive movement, it should also be noted that the practical lore on writing instruction devised during this period proposed great changes from the more traditional approaches to writing. Many of the writing-as-a-process concepts explored in later research have their origins in practical advice given to writing instructors by these expert practitioners.

The major problem with such an approach to writing is that it assumed that the writer already has all the intellectual resources he or she would need and was merely looking for an appropriate outlet for expressions. It essentially ignored the context of writing and the social context in which writing is performed in the real world. Perhaps, more importantly, it assumed that the cognitive processing of immature writers and expert writers during the writing process operate in the same manner, though to different degrees of refinement (see, e.g., Bereiter and Scardamalia 1987, Moffett 1968). Nevertheless, the neo-romantic assumptions of this expressive view, combined with its weak theoretical methodology, served at least to open the door to more scientific approaches to writing-as-a-process.

4.3   The cognitive approach to the writing process

In the early 1970s, a competing process approach to writing – psychologically based – arose out of research in cognitive psychology.

Janet Emig's (1971, 1983) pioneering efforts at case study research and protocol analysis represented a breakthrough for writing research – a more scientific way to study the writing process, and to see what writers were actually doing, at least on the surface, when they were writing. She legitimized the case study approach, the think-aloud methodology, the study of pauses, the role of re-reading in revision, and the amount and type of revision among writers (Faigley 1986: 532). On a more practical level, her research led to a view of writing as recursive rather than linear; she called attention to the importance of pre-planning and editing as ongoing activities, and to the importance of writer's errors as a source of data (cf. critique by North 1987). As such, she was a precursor to a range of studies classifiable as clinical research (North 1987), particularly the influential case study research of Perl (1979), Selfe (1981, 1984), and Sommer (1980), and the study of writer errors by Shaughnessy (1977). At the same time, new interest in the composing of elementary and secondary students, led by Calkins (1986), Graves (1983, 1984), and others, opened up research using case study approaches but also, more generally, ethnographic research methods. From the work of Emig and other earlier researchers using the case study approach, a theoretical dilemma arose. What Emig had not provided was a theoretical foundation for the sort of research she had developed (Hillocks 1986, North 1987). To fill this theoretical lacuna, writing researchers turned to cognitive development/Piagetian theory, audience awareness theory, and real-writing situations.

Researchers began to see writers as developing from egocentric stages of writing, initially composing writer-based, rather than reader-based, text (Calkins 1983, Graves 1984, Kroll 1981, Moffett 1968). Given that writing is an exceedingly complex task, and given the voluminous research findings that have appeared in the literature, it became clear that some attempt should be made to provide a coherent framework – a model that would account for the data reported, and would explain conflicting findings and interpretations. The goal was to draw together findings from many types of research and from many kinds of evidence, using perspectives from many disciplines. During this time, two teams of researchers who had figured prominently in the 1980s, began to publish results of experimental research on the writing process, developing cognitive models of the writing process: Flower and Hayes (from 1977 on), and Bereiter and Scardamalia (e.g. 1987).

Beginning in the late 1970s, Flower and Hayes (1977, 1980a, 1980b, 1981a, 1981b, 1984) developed a cognitive model of the writing process which attempts to provide a synthesis of research, and which has been dominant for the past 15 years in composition research. Strongly influencing the writing-as-a-process movement, Flower and Hayes have asserted that:

■ composing processes are interactive, intermingling, and potentially simultaneous;
■ composing is a goal-directed activity;
■ expert writers compose differently than novice writers.

These three hypotheses have become basic premises of a theory of the writing process. The research methodology proposed by Flower and Hayes has been based on protocol analysis, drawing legitimacy from the protocol analysis methods of Herbert Simon and colleagues (Ericsson and Simon 1984, Newell and Simon 1972), a major research approach in cognitive psychology for examining goal-directed behaviour. By collecting and examining protocols, transcripts, and videotapes of students talking aloud while they are writing, Flower and Hayes presented data which supported their perspectives on composing. (For explanation and discussion of protocol analysis in research, see Hayes and Flower 1983, Lauer and Asher 1988, Smagorinsky 1994.) From their earlier efforts, they subsequently developed a model of the composing process (e.g. 1981a), a processing model based on their protocol research and fashioned closely after the Artificial Intelligence (AI) processing models created by Simon and others to explain problem-solving routines.

Figure 4.1 displays their model as it is most commonly represented. The model divides the composing processes of a writer into three major components: *the composing processor, the task environment,* and *the writer's long-term memory.* Within the composing processor, three operational processes generate the written text: *planning, translating,* and *reviewing.* The three processes are managed by an executive control called *a monitor.* Finally, in the planning process, there are three subcomponents – *generating ideas, organizing information,* and *setting goals.* In the actual generation of text, the ideas in planning are translated into language on the page, which is then reviewed and revised. This model of writing has remained essentially unchanged since it was first proposed in the late 1970s (cf. Flower 1994).

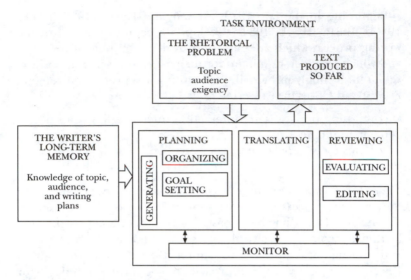

Figure 4.1   The Flower and Hayes writing process model

This theory of the writing process has generated much excitement and research using protocol analysis. It has also generated criticism on a number of levels. Some researchers have noted that writers are not likely to be uniform with respect to their processing preferences and cognitive abilities. Rather, writing involves numerous processing-model options, and different writers will approach the task employing different processing strategies.

Further criticism of their influential model has centred on the elaboration of the model itself. North (1987) argues that the model as proposed by Flower and Hayes is much too vague to satisfy criteria for formal model building; specifically, he notes that the translation from the model to people actually writing is barely explained. For example, there is virtually no specification of how the text material might be constructed and what linguistic constraints might be imposed on this construction (see Chapter 3 of this volume).

A final critique of the Flower and Hayes model is methodological, and therefore one that strikes at the heart of their theory. Essentially, it is argued that a protocol analysis approach may not be a valid primary methodology for the study of the writing process to the extent that Flower and Hayes claim (Dobrin 1986; cf. Smagorinsky 1994). A more moderate perspective is that protocol analysis can reveal certain important things about what writers do, but it cannot be the primary source of evidence for a theory of the writing process. A balanced discussion of this issue is provided by Bereiter and Scardamalia (1987: 42–4, 195–6) who point out that evidence from any source must be controlled, reliable, and convergent with findings from other experimental sources if it is to be persuasive (Scardamalia and Bereiter 1986: 724).

Despite the many criticism the writing process model developed by Flower and Hayes must be credited with important findings resulting from their research program:

1. They have raised a new range of issues for public debate.
2. They have raised understanding of recursion in writing to a new level, and provided a perspective which is not presently controversial. Essentially, they have brought to writing the notion of interaction among processes in parallel, echoing recent developments in reading research (see, e.g., Grabe 1988a, Stanovich 1980, 1986, 1992).
3. They have attempted to model writing processes, and thereby have opened writing research up to more explicit claims, more explicit and testable hypotheses (even if not by protocol analysis), and more carefully defined research methods.

Following the work of Flower and Hayes, other efforts to synthesize research findings into a coherent model have benefited from their efforts, though not all have attempted the same sort of synthesis. A model by Cooper and Matsuhashi, appearing in 1983, drew extensively from research on the text product to infer the processes required for expert text production. Their model represented an ideal, and rather informal, description of the composing process – one which relied more heavily on findings and research in rhetoric and text linguistics than it did on observational studies of writers composing.

A third processing model, which draws together a wide array of information, is the model devised by de Beaugrande (1982, 1984). He proposed a descriptive account of the features that must be included in a model of the writing process. His analysis draws heavily from research in cognitive psychology, particularly the research on memory, attention, and reading. His model provides a coherent global argument for what expert writers do, and extrapolates from the actions of children and poor writers, much as Flower and Hayes have done. Although de Beaugrande's model is highly detailed and well supported by research in cognitive psychology, it is still essentially a descriptive global model. It is not an operational model making specific falsifiable predictions.

While the various models of composing all appear to have limitations, they have all moved the debate on writing research forward and have led to more refined analyses (cf. discussion of more recent research by Flower and Hayes in Chapter 5). The gradual development of model construction for composing processes has led to the more current powerful model proposed by Bereiter and Scardamalia (1987); their theory represents a major advance in the understanding of what writers do when they write and why different writers write in different ways. They provide a more explicit theory which accounts for many different research perspectives and sources of evidence in a coherent explanation. Their theory accounts for what children and beginning writers do, for what poor writers do, and for what expert writers do. It also makes explicit predictions as to why writing differs from person to person – predictions which can be confirmed or refuted. In this sense, then, their model is not merely descriptive, but rather explanatory to the extent that it is more easily verifiable by experimental evidence.

4.4   A social-context approach to the writing process

Beginning in the 1980s, socially oriented views of writing developed from a number of different sources, among them sociolinguistics, Hallidayan functional linguistics, elementary education research, socially based rhetoric, and the sociology of science. These perspectives on literacy, knowledge, and writing found a receptive audience among writing researchers who were troubled by the educational status quo, Piagetian developmental psychology, and the limitations of protocol analysis. Rather, the new groups of researchers have proposed that a writing-as-a-process approach has little meaning outside of the social context which defines the particular writing purpose, a notion as applicable in the classroom as it is in the real world (e.g. a Vygotskyan perspective). The essential point, as argued by Cooper (1989), Faigley (1986), and Witte (1992), is that writing can only be understood from the perspective of a social context and not as a product of a single individual.

This general trend in writing research is a product of recent years and is, understandably, not yet well formed in terms of a consistent theory of the writing process (cf. Flower 1994). In fact, there are a number of distinct perspectives within a social view of the writing process: one from the perspective of educational ethnography (being more educationally oriented), a second from the perspective of sociological linguistics (more sociolinguistically oriented), and a third from the perspective of discourse communities (more theoretically oriented). Yet another perspective is that from the sociology of science, treating the production of writing as also being creative of a social context. This latter perspective will be treated in Chapter 6 on writing in specialized contexts.

4.4.1 *Ethnography in educational contexts*

Ethnographic research in education, and particularly in the study of writing, has emerged in the past 20 years, largely from the ethnomethodology and participant-observation research in sociology, sociolinguistics, and anthropology (e.g. Cazden 1988, Heath 1983, 1986a, Spindler and Spindler 1987b). A researcher assuming this methodological orientation eschews theoretical preconditions and observes what is actually occurring without imposing an *a priori* framework on the observations. The observer participates in the community over a period of time so that the community becomes familiar to the researcher. The ethnographic approach makes an effort not to be biased by self-fulfilling theoretical models which may distort the observed reality, and to collect naturally occurring data in its social context rather than to create and control data artificially.

From an ethnographic perspective, writing, much like speaking, loses its purpose outside of its naturally occurring context. To know how and why people write, it is necessary to see how they perform under normal, natural conditions; and to see how children and basic writers develop writing skills, it is necessary to observe them in the process of their development without interfering (Graves 1984, North 1987). The importance of this perspective cannot be overestimated; too often, theoretical models emerge before there is adequate data on the range of phenomena for which the theory can account.

Ethnography applied to educational contexts and literacy instruction:

(1) recognizes and studies the social contexts in which language occurs;

(2) assumes that different language uses occur in different contexts; and

(3) attempts to interpret/bridge the uses of different languages in their contexts, including the usually rigid demands imposed on all students by the formal educational system (e.g. Boggs 1985, Tharp and Gallimore 1988), and it investigates language in terms of these assumptions.

In educational settings, the first group of ethnographic studies focuses specifically on the writing tasks of students in classes as they occur during the course of the day. Researchers such as Calkins (1986), Graves (1983, 1984), and Harste *et al.* (1984) are all representative of this line of investigation. Because these studies are more in line with case studies and task intervention approaches, they should be seen as distinct from more mainstream ethnographic approaches, represented by the second group of studies discussed in section 4.3.

4.4.2   *Writing research by Graves and his colleagues*

Graves (1984) first developed the use of ethnographic case studies to study writing in classrooms in his 1973 dissertation on the writing of 7-year-old children. Since then, he and his colleagues have studied the writing of children in Europe, the USA, Canada, and Australia. Based on observational research projects of students' writing typically extending a year or more, he has argued that children are able to, and want to, write from the day they enter the classroom. It is the educational system which alters this natural tendency by providing little positive assistance to take advantage of students' desires. Rather, in most schools, writing is given very little time, and students are not encouraged to write. Teachers, for their part, typically do not know how to teach writing and seldom write anything themselves; even less frequently do teachers model writing in the classroom, and then share the writing with students for their comments and feedback. Educational funding in the USA has also, until recently, ignored writing issues. Graves (1984), in particular, notes that there is a striking disparity in funding for research on writing as opposed to research on reading at the primary school level.

Finally, many of the traditional uses of writing in school have negative associations for most children: writing tasks are used for disciplinary purposes, for testing and evaluation, for busywork – artificial assignments with little relevance for students; and when writing is produced, it is returned with teacher feedback in the form of extensive correction of surface features. This disheartening picture of writing, particularly in US elementary school classes, has led Calkins (1983, 1986), Graves (1983, 1984), and others to develop participatory ethnographic-research approaches to elementary school writing. From the results of these research studies they have proposed a number of directions for instruction:

1. Writing is a process of discovery; its development progresses as a problem-solving activity.
2. Drawing and talking are means for pre-writing and rehearsal.
3. Students learn to internalize their conversations to the point where they do not simply write down what they say – they learn to rehearse better.
4. Students learn to move from writing for themselves to writing for others.
5. Students learn that they need to spend time on planning, pre-writing, and rehearsal activities to improve their writing.
6. Students learn that they are capable of serious revision by themselves, even at lower levels of ability, particularly by conferencing with teachers about their writing.
7. Students learn that they need to have control over their writing.
8. Since schools do not create student motivation and involvement, teachers need to generate a commitment to writing; students need to be involved and motivated to write, and teachers also need to practise writing in class and to share their writing with children.
9. Teachers need to have control over their classrooms and become active teacher/researchers with respect to their own practice.

These findings have had a strong influence on the teaching of early writing in Australia (Walshe 1981a, 1981b). They also parallel similar research by Clay (1975) for New Zealand and are consistent with the Bullock Report (1975) in Great Britain leading to the 'Language across the Curriculum' movement (Marland 1977). In the USA, these findings, as well as a range of other early literacy research, have had a strong influence on the promotion and development across the country of National Writing Centers, the purpose of which is to promote the teaching of the writing process. Teachers from different area schools in the USA come to summer workshops to learn how to teach writing effectively. In return, these teachers must hold workshops on teaching writing for other teachers in their school. Thus, every year, more and more teachers become involved in writing and devote more time to writing in their classes.

It is inevitable that a research approach which has made numerous claims would come under close scrutiny as others scholars have time to reflect upon the work gradually appearing in publication. In particular, Bereiter and Scardamalia (1987), Hillocks (1986), Lauer and Asher (1988), and North (1987) have commented to some extent on the work of Graves and his colleagues. The five criticisms which follow represent the general arguments against this particular groups' use of ethnographic research.

1. Graves' research perhaps should not be considered ethnographic. There is very little description given of the overall classroom contexts in which these observations have taken place; rather, the studies only focus on the time spent writing during the observations (cf. Heath 1983). This criticism is a common one directed at many writing research studies which claim to be ethnographic but which are, in fact, types of case studies.

2. Naturalistic data, such as that which has been collected, may not be a valid source for making larger generalizations. The goal of ethnography is to tell a particular story, to provide a detailed description of what goes on at a particular place and at a particular time, and to provide such information as it occurs with those particular students. Such a methodology does not permit 'averaging' across case studies (cf. Spindler and Spindler 1987a, Wells 1986).

3. Graves and others have made a number of causal statements on the basis of relations between two co-occurring behaviours or objects of investigation. They give power to one variable as causal of the other. However, Graves does not appear to use any systematic control across observation subjects, which is minimally necessary for cause and effect assertions (Hillocks 1986, North 1987).

4. Graves and his colleagues present quite minimal data in the range of their published writings. It is difficult to verify their claims and impossible to assess the depth of insight they derive from their data; perhaps other researchers faced with a larger segment of the data might arrive at different conclusions (Hillocks 1986).

5. Nowhere in the research publications in question is the issue of researcher intrusion given careful attention. However, it clearly is an issue when researchers are intruding into the 'natural' classroom setting. Graves, for example, in his early research, sat directly in front of particular students when they appeared to be ready to write. He copied down the students' words, coded the students' behaviours, and asked students questions about what/why they were writing (Hillocks 1986, Lauer and Asher 1988, North 1987).

As damaging as these criticisms are – and they do raise serious questions – it is also important not to underestimate this line of research which constituted a pioneering effort in the study of early student writing, and which has generated a number of important hypotheses.

1. It has confirmed notions advanced by other researchers (e.g. by Flower and Hayes).

2. It has generated many new research questions which remain to be answered.

3. It has had a beneficial effect on the teaching of writing in US elementary schools, though the extent of the benefit has yet to be documented.

4. It has influenced and reinforced the more general language arts approach known as the *whole-language* approach (Goodman 1986).

5. It has stimulated discussion which can only lead to improved research in the future.

Hillocks (1986: 60–1), in a carefully balanced commentary, has this to say about the research of Graves and his colleagues:

> Research on composing has developed many important ideas, most of which must still be regarded as hypotheses – but hypotheses worthy of further exploration and testing. Ideas developed by Graves, Calkins, ... and their colleagues are fascinating examples. In their work we see children beginning to write very early in the first year of

school by using invented spellings, learning to use the space on the paper, sharing work with other youngsters and the teacher, shifting from externalized to internalized behavior in revising, moving from egocentric to sociocentric, and so forth. Researchers should examine these ideas as rigorously as possible, presenting rules for the analysis of the events observed, displaying data across cases, and using controls to account for alternative explanations.

A considerable amount of space has been devoted to a review of the work of Graves and his colleagues because of the widespread influence this work has had both on other researchers and on teachers.

4.4.3   Sociolinguistic research in the ethnography of writing

The second ethnographic line of research might be described as a more 'regular' approach to the study of writing. Its impact on the writing process can be traced to studies of social communities designed to observe the match between (a) literacy at home and literacy expected in schools, and (b) studies of classroom interaction designed to observe teacher–student and student–student language uses. Major studies of the match or, more often, the mismatch, between home and school begin with Bernstein's sociological research exploring the influence of socialization processes on the language registers used by different groups of students, and how these register uses match the demands of educational language (Bernstein 1972a, 1972b, 1990). Based on his research in the 1950s and 1960s, Bernstein argued that children who are failing in the school system do not have adequate control of the registers used and demanded by the educational system – not because they are incapable of such uses but because they are neither encouraged nor expected to use these registers in their home socialization environment (Cope and Kalantzis 1993, Freebody and Welch 1993, Hasan 1989, Lareau 1989, Wells 1986, 1994). His research opened the way for ethnographic research on the educational mismatch between home community/culture and the demands of the formal educational system (see also Halliday 1978, Stubbs 1980, Wells 1986).

Other research following in this direction includes at least work by the following: Boggs (1985), studying Hawaiian children; Cazden (1988), studying variation in classroom discourse; Cook-

Gumperz (1986), studying patterns of oral discourse interactions on later literacy development; Heath (1983, 1986a, 1986b, 1993, Heath and Mangiola 1991), studying variation in home and school language uses in numerous contexts ; Philips (1983), studying variation in home and school language use among Warm Springs Indian students; Scollon and Scollon (1981), studying variation in home and school language use among Athabaskan Indian students; and Tharp and Gallimore (1988), studying the applications of a Vygotskyan approach to literacy development with Hawaiian and Navajo elementary school students.

A consistent axiom running through all this research is to find out what students do, how they do it, and why, both in the formal educational environment and in the community outside the school. Only when these issues are understood can some decision be made about how writing develops differentially, how the writing process works, and why and when it works appropriately (e.g. Heath 1983). On the basis of this research foundation, a writing-as-a-process approach can be proposed which takes into account: (i) the context in which writing occurs, (ii) the possible instructional contexts which have ecological validity, and (iii) contexts which have the power to guide more effective writing instruction.

Perhaps most influential in this line of research is the work of Heath (1982, 1983, 1986b, 1993). In her major study (1983), she examined the writing of three groups of students from different communities in North Carolina enabling her to suggest, by the study of different language uses in different home contexts, that the language of the educational system would be accepted and used in very different ways, and would lead to systematic differences in educational success and failure.

Similar discontinuities between home and school uses of language have been studied in a variety of other contexts. In Boggs' (1985) study of the socialization practices among Hawaiian children, he found that the children were socialized to learn one set of language practices at home and a very different, conflicting set of practices at school. One early outcome of this research by Boggs and his colleagues has been the development of literacy lessons which incorporate aspects of Hawaiian socialization practices (Au and Jordan 1981, Au *et al.* 1986). Phillips (1983) and Scollon and Scollon (1981) explored the mismatch in language socialization practices between Native American communities and the

Anglo educational system. Great differences in socialization practices between home and school are seen as a major contributing factor to the high Native American student failure rate.

Heath (1986b), in a study of three ethnic groups in California (Chinese-American, Mexican-American, and Southeast Asian-Americans), compared their home socialization practices with the literacy practices expected in schools. She found that Chinese-American students were more successful in schools, in part because the home socialization practices for Chinese-American children most closely resemble the school literacy practices in the US educational system, and in part because the Chinese–American children had greater exposure to public language use in the community outside the home. Wells (1986), in a ten-year study of children in Bristol (UK), compared various student groups in their use of written and oral language in both the home and at school. He found that socialization practices in language use by parents affected student success in early grades (see also Christie 1992, Hasan 1989, Lareau 1989, Wells 1994).

The comparison of home–school literacy practices has also been, in turn, a resource for writing process instruction, asking students to be active ethnomethodologists (Heath 1985, Heath and Branscombe 1985, Heath and Mangiola 1991). Students become real field workers in collaboration with the teacher and an outside researcher, collecting language data, and writing up their results for real researchers to use, respond to, and question. The result of such an ongoing activity is that students:

- observe language uses
- become aware of language metalinguistically in order to talk about their 'research' findings
- develop new ways to express their ideas about what they have observed, and
- write for a real and rewarding purpose to a real audience.

For students, the experience thus becomes a purposeful writing-as-a-process learning activity.

A growing body of research is demonstrating that oral language practices in schools have a profound effects on children's literacy development (Bloome and Green 1992). How a child interacts verbally with the teacher and with other students will determine to a significant extent how that student is evaluated by the teacher, and more importantly, how the child will learn to read and write.

4.4.4   Halliday's social semiotic approach to literacy

M.A.K. Halliday has probably been more influential in the current changes in writing instruction in many countries than some researchers and teachers realize. To the extent that his linguistic-sociological approach (Halliday 1978: 38–9) to language provides a theoretical linguistic foundation for *whole language* instructional theories, his views of language and of the development of writing are permeating US, Australian, New Zealand, and British educational systems. Over the past 20 years, Halliday (1973, 1975, 1978, 1985, 1993b) has developed a socially contextualized approach to linguistics which stresses functional use of language. In the early 1970s, as an integral part of his overall linguistic theory, he articulated a theory of language development which has since become very influential among early-literacy development researchers. In particular, his ideas – that language is primarily used to serve functional purposes, and that patterns of language development depend on the needs of the child to express meaningful communication – have been a major source of *whole language* philosophy in the USA (Edelsky *et al.* 1991, Goodman 1986, Jagger and Smith-Burke 1985).

Halliday proposes that all language use serves social-functional purposes. Children learn language initially by recognizing that language serves the purpose of activities of which the children are in need. To quote Halliday (1978: 57):

> ... what is learning to read and to write? Fundamentally it is an extension of the functional potential of language. Those children who don't learn to read and write, by and large, are children to whom it doesn't make sense; to whom the functional extension that these media provide has not been made clear, or does not match up with their own expectations of what language is for. Hence if the child has not been oriented towards the types of meaning which the teacher sees as those which are proper to the writing system, then the learning of writing and reading would be out of context, because fundamentally, as in the history of the human race, reading and writing are an extension of the functions of language. This is what they must be for the child equally well.

This notion of writing as a functional extension of oral language, one which can be mastered when the child sees the purpose for its use, is basic to the *whole-language* instructional philosophy. Elsewhere Halliday expands upon this perspective in relation to the educational context.

> [Education] starts from what children can do with language, which is already a great deal by the time they come to school; and from what they cannot do yet but are learning to do with language, as well as what they will need to learn to do with it in order to succeed in school and in life.... The impetus for reading and writing is a functional one, just as was the impetus for learning to speak and listen in the first place. We learn to speak because we want to do things that we cannot do otherwise; and we learn to read and write for the same reason.   (1978: 205)

> What are the functions for which [a student] is now beginning to need the *written* language, and writing as a medium? ... Will learning to read and write make sense to him, matching his experience of what language is and what it is for, so that he sees it as a means of enlarging that experience; or will it seem to be a meaningless exercise which is unrelated to any of his own uses of language?
>   (1978: 213)

> The key question, perhaps, is this: to the extent that the school is a new culture into which the child has been socialized (and, as we have seen, this makes greater demands on some children than it does on others), is the actual pattern of language use in the daily life of the school adequate to the socializing task? If it is not – what can be done to remedy this situation.
>   (1978: 215)

The three quotations above raise questions which have been taken up as a challenge by the founders of the *whole-language* movement – a movement which refers to Hallidayan functional linguistics for theoretical support.

Leaders in the *whole-language* movement – e.g. Edelsky, *et al.* (1991), K. Goodman (1986), Y. Goodman (1985), and Harste *et al.* (1984) – have taken Halliday's questioning of the educational system as the key to literacy learning. From their perspective, 'the actual pattern of daily language use in the schools' is not adequate to the socializing task. Children find that learning to read and write is difficult because the school system makes it difficult. As K. Goodman (1986: 20) notes:

> Schools frequently isolate language from its meaningful functional use. Then they change language into non-language. Only in the social context of language usage does it have a meaning potential for the learner, and only in such a context is it language and easy to learn.

The response of these various scholars to the reality of the school environment is to reassert the Hallidayan notion that children learn language by 'learning how to mean', and they learn to read and write much more successfully when the reading and writing is, similarly, a meaningful (or *whole*) activity.

Perhaps most important for the idea of learning to mean, all language skills are practised together to convey meaningful communication rather than in isolation so that students learn one language skill, reading for example, separate from other language skills (see also Enright and McCloskey 1988). As Goodman (1986: 30) notes:

> Speaking, listening, writing, and reading are all happening in context of the exploration of the world of things, events, ideas, and experiences. The content curriculum draws on the interest and experiences children have outside of school, and thus incorporates the full range of oral and written language functions. It becomes a broad, rich curriculum that starts where learners are in language and knowledge and builds outward from there.... Integration becomes the central motif in a whole language curriculum.

Other researchers concerned with the writing development of children have tended to confirm a number of the observational claims of the *whole-language* perspective. As early as 1970, Chomsky argued that learning to write by students did not have to wait until they were well developed in their language arts (see also Clay 1975, Feitelson 1988, Gaskins 1994, S. Stahl 1994). Rather, the exploration of language through the process of early writing and the creativity of invented spelling tended to have a beneficial effect on both later writing and reading development (see also Adams 1989). Since that pioneering research, other scholars have found evidence to support those claims. In addition to the findings of Graves and his colleagues, Bissex (1980), Clay (1975), and Hudelson (1984, 1989a) have all provided significant supporting research perspectives on early writing development.

While the *whole-language* approach to early literacy development has a strong logical appeal, it must be recognized that much of the evidence in support of the whole language approach is in the form of observation, case study, and teacher testimonial. There has, in fact, been little empirical research demonstrating the superiority of this approach over other instructional approaches (Gaskins 1994, McKenna *et al.* 1993, 1994, S. Stahl 1994, Stahl and Miller 1989).

4.4.5   Post-secondary writing and discourse communities

Given the widespread appeal of ethnographic research in grade
school settings and the considerable changes taking place in elementary school language arts instruction, it is somewhat
surprising that there is very little ethnographic research on writing at post-secondary levels. Instead, the discussion at tertiary
levels focuses more broadly upon reasons why standard research
does not translate well into writing instruction and why students
do not seem to transfer what they learn in writing classes to writing in other classes or in the workplace.

In the 1980s, Cooper (1986), Miller (1984) and Reither (1985)
all argued for an approach which sees writing as occurring within
the social-rhetorical situation. Recognizing that writing is
produced, read, and interpreted in social contexts, Cooper
argued that a model of writing guided primarily by 'writing as
thinking' is an inadequate representation of the writing process.
Writing cannot be seen as isolated from the social world of inter—
action. Rather, 'writing is a social activity, dependent on social
structures ... ' (Cooper 1986: 366), and

> writing and what writers do during writing cannot be artificially sep-
> arated from the social rhetorical situation in which writing gets
> done, from the conditions that enable writers to do what they do,
> and from the motives writers have for doing what they do.
>
> (Reither 1985: 621)

This perspective on writing research has been extended further in
recent work by Berkenkotter and Huckin (1995), Flower (1994),
Freedman and Medway (1994), and Witte (1992).

Writers, much like speakers, take on roles that are defined by
social structures. And by writing within socially recognized conventions and expectations, writers can also alter the situation (or
reconstruct a new version of interaction); thus, writing reflects
ecology – the totality of relations between organisms and their
environment. For Cooper, an ecological model of writing 'is an
activity through which a person is continually engaged with a variety of socially constituted systems' (1986: 367).

Taking such a notion one step further opens a set of basic issues
now discussed regularly; these discussions centre on socio-cognitive approaches to writing, on audience, and on genre and
discourse communities. The gradual merging of social and cognitive perspectives has been discussed over the past decade in

various L1 writing contexts. It has been raised by Langer (1987) for elementary and secondary school contexts (see also Davis *et al.* 1994, Needels and Knapp 1994), and, more recently, Flower (1994) has proposed a social-cognitive theory of writing that addresses more advanced writers. In these approaches, the essential argument is that a comprehensive theory of writing needs to recognize the various social factors which influence writing; but at the same time, recognition must also be given to the idea that writing itself is produced through the cognitive activities of the writer. In this way, a theory of writing which disregards either major component – cognition or social context – will be necessarily inadequate. (Cf. Berkenkotter and Huckin 1995, Freedman and Medway 1994, Nystrand 1989 and Witte 1992.)

Over the past 20 years, considerable interest has been directed at the issue of audience as a major social-context factor, owing its inception to the increasing rhetorical influence over composition in the 1970s (Ede and Lunsford 1984, Kroll 1984, Park 1982). While many perspectives have been promoted in attempting to define audience (the precursor to the social context of writing), the concept has remained elusive (cf. the discussion of audience in Chapter 8).

A more recent perspective on the social context defined by readers has been the emergence of the notion of discourse community (Bazerman 1988, Swales 1990, 1993). The notion of discourse community includes writers, readers, texts, and social contexts in their natural interaction, rather than artificially highlighted and separated relations between writer and reader based on other considerations (Rafoth 1988).

At post-secondary levels of writing instruction, these views have led to a number of developments which may change the nature of tertiary-level writing instruction in the future. One issue lies in the move to introduce students to 'discourse communities' so that their writing becomes purposeful in the academic setting. Another related issue is the expanded role that disciplinary awareness creates for writing across the curriculum; writing is not a skill that can be taught in isolation, but is the entire faculty's instructional responsibilities. Still another issue raised involves the development of content-based writing courses which teach writing as the means to interact with the material and with other students. This approach is compatible with the whole language approach, but at the tertiary level (cf. Bartholomae and Petrosky 1986, Brinton *et al.* 1989, Shih 1986).

The notion of discourse community is appealing, and must be explored if it is to be useful in the expansion of writing theory. The idea underlying the academic discourse community is that students need to initiate themselves into the academic discourse community they wish to join. The discourse community in this case is the community of scholars who both discuss and write about ideas and information relevant to their professional interests.

Recently, a number of reservations and concerns have been raised about the notion of discourse community. One is a definitional concern: what exactly is a discourse community? This question, raised by Cooper (1989), is not easily answered (see also criticisms by Nystrand 1990). Citing a conference paper delivered by John Swales in 1987 (cf. Swales 1990), Cooper suggests that his explanation provides a satisfactory working definition from an institutional perspective (1989: 212–16), though the criteria also are open to criticism on exclusionary grounds. Swales (1990: 23–7), in his later book, *Genre analysis*, outlines six criteria for identifying a discourse community:

1. A discourse community shares common public goals, even if the private goals of individual members are distinct. Stating public goals of groups serves a real function: 'it creates the illusion of agreement by allowing members to interpret the stated goals in their own way' (Cooper 1989: 212).
2. The discourse community is a forum for discussion and debate; discourse communities must have interaction among their members. These mechanisms may include meetings, correspondence, newsletters, etc.
3. Discourse communities will provide feedback and information to members through various participatory mechanisms. A major function of newsletters, journals, conferences is to support members with useful resources which match their interests and needs.
4. Discourse communities, as they interact, will develop discourse expectations and discourse genres as norms by which interchange regularly occurs. These genres will become norms for the community and may also become conservative in nature.
5. The discourse community develops along with a regularized set of genre expectations a specific set of terminology and specialized vocabulary. Community specific abbreviations, acronyms, and references will become commonly used.

6. The discourse community must have enough members to discuss matters of importance to a wider group and to generate content expertise and the regularized exchange of this information.

Recent work by Fairclough (1992a, 1992b) from the emerging perspective of critical linguistics is also pertinent with respect to defining the shape of the discourse community.

A central issue raised by Cooper is not simply whether or not a discourse community can be defined, but whether it is a structure into which student writers should be initiated (see also Bizzell 1993). As Cooper (1989: 216–19) argues:

> Knowledge, power, success are seen to flow from the community automatically to those who before their apprenticeship lacked any relevant cognitive or social abilities.... We may wish to see the writing classroom in a foundational way, as a stable discourse community, one that validates our interests, our values, our status, our way of life, automatically. But we are also concerned that our students – all of our students – become effective writers, learn how to enter into discourses, which may not be the same thing as the foundational notion of joining a discourse community as a neophyte.... Claiming that a foundational notion of discourse communities should guide our teaching of writing can only be seen as cynical and self-serving. And it is far from clear that students want to – or should want to – join any of these communities we are creating for ourselves.... If we insist that students adopt what we see as the values of our community (our values), we will effectively withhold power within academic discourse from all students who come from a different generation, a different ethnic background, a different race, a different sex, a different economic class.

Cooper is not merely defining discourse community, but is also examining the possible weakness of the notion as theory and as guide for writing instruction (see also Fairclough 1992a, 1992b).

From the beginning, the discourse community perspective has raised such concerns. Both Bartholomae (1985) and Bizzell (1986a, 1993) have asked how someone becomes initiated into a discourse community and what it takes to become accepted in that community. Bartholomae notes that apprenticeship in the academic community may not be easy to achieve. Bizzell goes one step further and asks whether it is desirable for students to become members of the academic discourse community. As Cooper notes (above), discourse communities can quickly assume a foundation of rightness (righteousness) that appears to exceed the actual collective will of the group. The community decides what not to accept and who not to accept as if guided by some sort of absolute knowledge rather than by the political/subjective decisions of authority figures in the community.

If the notion of discourse community becomes defined as a community of élite members, then the discourse community does not represent an exchange of knowledge or a discussion of differing views; instead, it reifies itself into a body of information to be absorbed much as pieces of cultural literacy are to be learned without question (see, e.g., Hirsh 1987; cf. Nystrand 1990).

One approach to writing which appears to have made use of this notion of discourse community without silencing the voices of the student-initiates has been the adaptation of a Freirean approach to literacy to the tertiary-level writing class. A Freirean approach, perhaps oversimplified, requires the group to become aware of its condition and to learn how to change its condition through dialogue, confrontation, and literacy development (Freire 1985, 1994, Freire and Macedo 1987, Giroux 1988, Shor 1987).

Recently, Bartholomae and Petrosky (1986) reported on a long sequence of curricular projects to develop a tertiary-level first-year writing programme at the University of Pittsburgh based on the notion of developing a discourse community within the writing class. Special composition classes consisting of 12 students, an instructor, and a writing lab assistant were set up; each such class met six hours a week throughout the semester (six credit hours). Students, all high-risk, were asked to read 12 books and produce 24 writing assignments. The essential features of the course which made it unique were:

(1) the content theme of the course ('growth and change in adolescence');

(2) the requirement that all students participate in extended discussions of the readings and the writing assignments – dialogue and exchange being seen as a crucial part of community building;

(3) the requirement that all assignments be done on time and all classes attended – with the penalty that delinquent students would be dropped from the class;

(4) the expectation that each student had something to contribute to the group since all students have experienced growth

and change in adolescence and therefore have 'expert' knowledge;

(5) the sequence of assignments, which moved from a personal awareness to an understanding of how academic communities undertake research on the same topic;

(6) a low student-to-teacher ratio.

The goal of the curriculum in this class was not simply to create a content-based instructional setting, but to confront students with issues that should force awareness of their condition in three ways: (1) in relation to the content of the course, (2) in relation to their status as students, and (3) in relation to the expectations of the academic institution. At the same time, the small class size, six hours per week with the same instructor, and the extensive additional use of a writing laboratory assistant were all meant to provide support for struggling students who were willing to commit themselves to the course.

This use of the discourse community to create awareness of the social-context of writing represents one of a number of approaches to writing that have developed recently as a result of the move in writing research from a cognitive emphasis to a social emphasis, and finally to a socio-cognitive emphasis.

Drawing on post-structuralist literary criticism, Faigley (1986) notes the impact of reader–response theory (e.g. Fish, Eco), to the effect that any effort to write about reality, or self, or author always demands reference to prior text (intertextuality). Further, it is impossible to say in the abstract what constitutes expertise (knowledge) because it is defined by a community of writers. Finally, for some writers, continuing problems may well be due to ignorance of the privileged language of the academic community. Most importantly, Faigley discusses recent sociology of science research. Texts, particularly science texts, are not autonomous presentations of information; rather they are 'social tools (used) in the complex interaction of the research community'. How this is so will be a major focus of the next chapter.

Notes

1. Since most textbooks trail research innovations by 5–10 years, only the more powerful changes manifest themselves quickly in a textbook industry.

2. This chapter has drawn upon four useful sources of information for reviewing the historical antecedents of current writing-as-a-process theory and practice, as well as competing perspectives: Berlin (1987), Faigley (1986), Hillocks (1986), and North (1987).

5

Writing process research and recent extensions

5.1 Introduction

The previous chapter presented an overview of writing process approaches, as commonly interpreted. The present chapter will explore research into the cognitive processes involved in writing in three ways. First, it addresses the more current research on the well-known Flower and Hayes model of the writing process; it then discusses alternative approaches suggested by Bereiter and Scardamalia, and by researchers concerned with the nature and development of expertise. Second, the discussion is extended to recent research and instructional practices which explore a Hallidayan approach to language, and particularly to the emphasis on genre form in writing research and instruction. This extension reasserts the balance between linguistic form and cognitive processing in writing; it also moves the chapter away from cognitive research on the writing process and towards a consideration of the varying social contexts in which writing is practised. Finally, the influence of the process approach on L2 contexts for writing research and instruction will be discussed. Increasingly, writing instruction which is informed by process approaches is being employed in contexts involving L2 students. However, it is important to establish the extent to which the contexts for L2 writing differ from writing in the L1, and the extent to which such differences may suggest different instructional practices.

5.2 Theories of the writing process

A careful account of the more recent research on the writing process in the past decade is important because that research has greatly refined our understanding of writing; it has incorporated into its concerns a greater awareness of the complexity of writing; it makes strong connections with the developing theory of genre for writing, and it has placed a number of very strong claims about writing into a more balanced perspective. In particular, the more recent research of Flower and Hayes and of Bereiter and Scardamalia has provided important insights into the development of writing abilities. In order to place these recent developments in proper perspective, we shall first summarize recent research on the well-known Flower and Hayes model of the writing process. Given this background, it will then be possible to situate the work of Bereiter and Scardamalia (1987; Scardamalia and Bereiter 1987), highlighting the importance of their theory as a synthesis for a wide range of writing research. The theory they propose also provides a strong foundation for designing a more principled and effective writing curriculum in academic settings.

5.2.1   The writing process: the Flower and Hayes model of writing

In Chapter 4, we reviewed carefully a number of ideas which have evolved out of research on the writing process, particularly with respect to the earlier work of Flower and Hayes. Much of the work of Flower and Hayes in the past ten years has been directed towards building more explicit definitions of the various subcomponents of their model (Flower 1988, 1989, Flower *et al.* 1990, Haas and Flower 1988, Hayes *et al.* 1987). For example, beginning in 1980, Flower and Hayes (1980a) developed the notion of the *rhetorical problem* in the *task-based component* of their model (Chapter 4) as a part of the process of discovery in writing. They presented a model of the rhetorical problem, the major elements involved, and showed how expert and novice writers differed in their application of this model. For Flower and Hayes, the rhetorical problem breaks into two major units: the rhetorical situation (audience, topic, assignment), and the writer's own goals (involving the reader, the writer's persona, the construction of meaning, the production of the formal text). In short, the model is intended to show the range of potential writing problems which a writer could face during the composing process. This notion of 'problem' in writing is extended in Hayes *et al.* (1987) through the discussion of problem solving in a theory of revision. In this case, problem solving centres on responding to the text and developing processes for detecting and diagnosing problems, then developing strategies for resolving the identified problems.

The theory of revision presented in Hayes *et al.* (1987) also constitutes an effort to explore the subcomponent of *reviewing* in their general model. In their theory of revision, there are four basic processes: (a) task definition, (b) evaluation, (c) strategy selection, and (d) modification of text in the writing plan. The goal of this subcomponent model is to explain, from their protocol research and from earlier research findings, how writers revise, why it is often difficult to revise globally (e.g. change organization or plans, restructure information), and how expert and novice writers differ in their revision processes.

In another set of studies (Flower *et al.* 1990), the relationship between the major components *task environment* and *writing processes* is examined. In particular, Flower analyses the academic task of reading-to-write. These studies explore how students read in order to perform a writing task, how different students represent the task (and its influence on reading) differently, and how task representation and reading influence the writing processes. The studies also examine students' own views on writing in the context of a particular task. The combined study of teacher perspective, student perspective, students in the process of writing, and the written text together created a complex set of factors which argue that students primarily need to develop strategic knowledge – having strategies to determine appropriate writing goals, having awareness of the writing-task goals, and having strategies for carrying out the goals set. The overall theme in this research is to establish the interaction of context and cognition in the carrying out of a particular writing task: writing is to be seen as both a cognitive activity and a contextually constrained activity. In cases in which the context might impose limiting constraints (e.g. a complex writing assignment), the goal of writing instruction would be to have students develop strategic knowledge and be able to transform their knowledge rather than rely on simpler strategies such as knowledge telling.

For Flower, the major transition which writers have difficulty learning is not how to acquire new writing skills but how to apply already-practised writing skills in new ways for new purposes. As she argues:

For the student, ... the classroom content, the teacher's concern with content, and the role of the paper as a tool in the grading process ... are likely to fit a familiar schema for theme writing. But what is important in college is not the apparent genre or conventions, but the goals. The goals of self-directed critical inquiry, of using writing to think through genuine problems and issues, and of writing to an imagined community of peers with a personal rhetorical purpose – these distinguish academic writing from a more limited comprehension and response

(Flower *et al.* 1990: 251)

Thus, a major outcome of this particular study, as well as many of their earlier studies, is to see the growth of writing ability as the development of strategies for appropriate goal-formation – constrained by task environment and content knowledge (i.e. constructing a 'rhetorically-bounded purpose', Flower 1989: 292), and the concomitant expert strategies for carrying out the goals through the writing process.

Results of their research on this model argue that good writers consider many more aspects of the rhetorical problem, and to a much greater depth. Good writers also can respond to a unique rhetorical problem with a fully developed representation of the problem. Finally, good writers are able to reassess their goals (*vis-à-vis* audience, persona, meaning, text production) in the light of rhetorical problems which arise in the course of writing; that is, good writers are able to alter their goals appropriately. Overall, Flower and Hayes derive two major implications from their model. First, good writers have a richer sense of what they want to do when they write, and have a fully developed image of the rhetorical problem. Good writers are, in effect, creative in their problem finding and in their problem solving. Second, recognizing and exploring the rhetorical problem is a teachable process.

Flower and Hayes's emphasis on students' strategic knowledge and the ability of students to transform information (and difficulties students have in doing this) to meet rhetorically constrained purposes is echoed in a number of other studies (e.g. Bereiter 1990, Bereiter and Scardamalia 1987, Brown and Palincsar 1989, M. Carter 1990, Collins *et al.* 1989) and opens the way for writing instruction which tries to teach students to be more strategically aware of their goals and of ways to carry out their goals in writing.

At the same time that this influential theory has evolved into a more elaborated and socially contexted approach to writing, it has also been limited in its assumption that there is a single writing process which is essentially the same for all writers; that is, expert writers would appear to do the same thing as novice writers, but do it much better. In their model, skilled and less-skilled writers exist on a single continuum. While Flower and Hayes devote considerable effort to comparing skilled and less-skilled writers, their model seeks to describe features that are common to all writers. A different perspective is proposed by Bereiter and Scardamalia (1987), who have argued that expert writers appear to go through a different sort of writing process, which allows these writers to transform information through an additional set of strategic processes.

5.2.2 The Bereiter and Scardamalia model of the writing process

Bereiter and Scardamalia's theory proposes that 'the writing process' cannot assume a single processing model, but should consider different processing models at different developmental stages of writing. They argue that the writing process of a young student and that of a mature skilled writer cannot be the same: the skilled writer does *not* perform the same processing, but many times more efficiently. Instead, the skilled writer performs a different kind of writing process (when necessary) – one which the unskilled writer is not (yet) capable of performing. Rather than debate the polemical question of how many such models might exist, it is enough, for their purposes, to demonstrate that a theory proposing two models of writing processes accounts for the range of accumulated research findings better than a theory proposing a single processing model.

Since Bereiter and Scardamalia focus more on describing why and how skilled and less-skilled writers compose differently, rather than on describing the common features of all writers, they consider a wider range of research. Their theory accounts for these research findings coherently and allows for the generation of a number of testable hypotheses as a primary means for elaborating and extending their theory. (Flower and Hayes, in contrast, often argue that they are exploring data to develop their theories of writing, leaving others to test the various aspects of their model.)

In particular, Bereiter and Scardamalia are concerned with accounting for the following important questions:

1. How does a processing model distinguish skilled writing from less-skilled writing?
2. How do audience and genre differences create distinct writing difficulties, and why do some genres appear more difficult to master, and some audiences more difficult to address?
3. Why are some writing tasks easy and others more difficult (not only genre and audience, but also purpose, topic, and language variation)?
4. Why do writing skills in one writing task or genre not transfer to other writing tasks or genres?
5. Why do some writers have more difficulty than others on some writing tasks yet appear to be at the same general proficiency level?
6. Why do some children find writing easy and natural, yet skilled writers often find it difficult and painful?
7. Why is advanced writing instruction particularly difficult and often ineffective?
8. Why do some writers never seem to develop mature composing skills in spite of much practice and long educational experience?
9. Why do expert writers revise differently from less-skilled writers?
10. How can the writing process account for the notion of 'shaping at the point of utterance' (cf. Britton 1983)?

The essential mechanism which Bereiter and Scardamalia use to explore these issues is the notion that mature, skilled composing is based on a sophisticated interplay of problem recognition and solution – a process that must be different for skilled writers of complex prose than it is for children and less-skilled older writers. The basic difference is captured in their two models of the writing process: the *knowledge-telling* model and the *knowledge-transforming* model. They draw the basic rationale for such a two-model theory from research findings which point to very different types of composing behaviour among skilled and less-skilled writers. In particular, they present evidence that less-skilled writers begin to write on a given assignment much sooner (less time for initial planning):

  (i) less-skilled writers produce much less elaborated or abstract sets of pre-writing notes;

(ii) less-skilled writers primarily concern themselves with gen-
    erating content during composing, rather than also
    considering goals, plans, and problems;
(iii) less-skilled writers are seemingly incapable of making
    major revisions which would involve reorganization of the
    content;
(iv) less-skilled writers use less complex routes (no references
    to goals, organizational strategies, etc.) for recalling ideas
    used in their writing; and
(v) less-skilled writers do not make use of main ideas in their
    writing as guides for planning and integrating information.
                                    (Scardamalia and Bereiter 1987)

These findings, argue Bereiter and Scardamalia, suggest not simply a more efficient use of a writing process for more skilled
writers, but a qualitatively different kind of writing process for
skilled writers.

The *knowledge-telling* model of writing used by less-skilled writers
provides a streamlined set of procedures which allow writers to
bypass the sorts of complex problem-solving activities often seen
in the composing of skilled writers. When children and less-expe-
rienced writers begin to compose texts, they need to keep the task
relatively uncomplicated if they are to be successful. In order to
do this, they must solve the most basic problem, converting oral
language experiences into written form, without having to worry
about issues that will confound the process. In particular, they
have to shift from engaging in dialogues and responding to topics
initiated by a partner, to a monologue in which they can only
imagine the dialogue as a way to retrieve and create information
that will be used for writing. Thus, their primary problem is that
of generating enough useful information from their own internal
resources. The primary goal becomes to *tell* what they have
retrieved.

In order to simplify the retrieval procedure it appears that
beginning writers rely on a few specific strategies:

- They consider the topic of the assignment and ask themselves
  what they know.
- They consider the genre of the assignment and ask themselves
  what they know.
- They read what they have just written and use this to generate
  additional information.

These strategies work well for writing about personal experiences or feelings, writing in journals and diaries, and for telling narratives – recounts of specific events and stories. These topics, as writing assignments, are typical of early writing instruction (see Applebee 1984, Graves 1983, Martin 1989). Teachers have learned from their teaching experience that students can accomplish those assignments and practise basic writing skills without great confusion or a lack of 'something to say'. A further advantage of these assignment types is that 'coherence', however it might be defined theoretically, tends to take care of itself through the basic process of simple content generation on a topic and possibly through the simple device of chronological ordering of details and events.

A description of the task facing a young inexperienced writer will explain the operation of the *knowledge-telling* model.

Starting from an example writing assignment such as

'What did you do during the holiday weekend?'

the writer will look for things to write about by looking at the question, seeing the words 'holiday weekend', and thinking about what he or she did that weekend. He or she can also think about what people normally do on weekends that is worth writing about as another way to generate content. The writer also knows that he or she has to recount events, since that is the genre being called for, typically within a simple time order. Because of the assignment, almost everything that is retrieved will be associated with the topic, and thus be coherent by association with the topic and probably will be unified by simple chronology. Abstract logical organization is not a major concern. As the student writes, the prior written text also becomes a stimulus to activate and retrieve additional information from memory. The result of this process is a written text:

- for which it is easy to find sufficient information,
- which does not overburden the writer with too many cognitive tasks (and so is relatively easy), and
- which tends to organize itself coherently by simple association to the topic and to time.

This general writing process is presented in Figure 5.1.

In this model, information is generated from the assignment, the topic, the genre, and any terms or lexical items in the assignment. Idea identifiers are retrieved and memory is searched for relevant

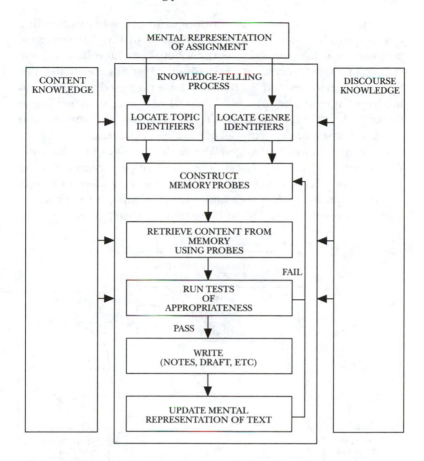

Figure 5.1 Structure of the knowledge-telling process

information. If retrieved information seems appropriate to the topic, the information should be written down and used (together with material retrieved through the previously identified strategies) to search memory for more things to say. The processing demands are fairly simple in this model, as are the retrieval and evaluation demands. The *knowledge-telling* model accounts for a manageable solution to composing which then becomes an efficient means for writing.[1] However, the model does not account for writing tasks which demand more complex processing, in which considerations of information ordering, of relative salience of information, of audience expectations, and of logical patterns of argument organization will determine the effectiveness of the writing. This sort of writing task is typically expected in more advanced writing for academic purposes, and the *knowledge-telling* model sheds little light on the task complexity involved in such advanced writing demands. For this reason, Bereiter and Scardamalia have proposed that a second model of the writing process be invoked when such writing is demanded, and performed, by the writers. They have named this the *knowledge-transforming* model of the writing process.

In Figure 5.2, the *knowledge-telling* model becomes just one component of a different process. The larger model represents the reflective problem-solving nature of expert writing when task complexity requires such processing. In particular, problems are solved by conscious resolution in either the *content problem space* or

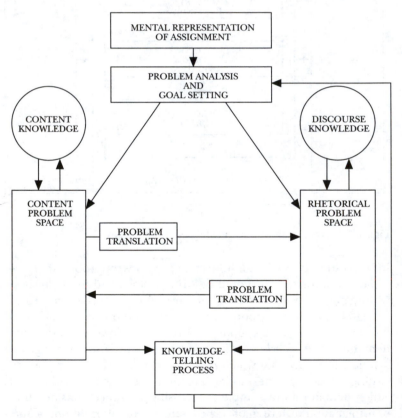

Figure 5.2 Structure of the knowledge-transforming process

the *rhetorical-problem space* – the output of one becomes the input of the other.

In this model, the writing task leads directly to problem analysis and goal setting. The resulting goals and problem anticipation lead to plans for the resolution of the perceived problems, whether they be problems of content generation, content integration, audience expectation, writer intention, genre form, linguistic style, organizational logic, etc. The resolution of one problem may create another. Thus, generating additional content (solving a content problem) may lead to a new rhetorical problem of how to organize the new information best in light of the previously presented information. As problems become resolved they feed to the knowledge-telling component which generates the writing. As writing is generated, it also contributes sets of problems which must then go through the problem-solving processes.

As an example of this writing process, suppose that in writing about the development of students' reading skills the writer has been using the term *decoding skills* to explain how words are identified rapidly, but, on reflection, realizes (a problem) that some readers in the audience (rhetorical problem space) would have a different understanding of the term *decoding*. For some readers, the term means only the mental translation from letters to sounds; for others it can mean word recognition. The writer goes to the content problem space and searches for a better term in content knowledge. The term *word recognition skills* fits the intended meaning without the misinterpretation potentially caused by the other term. This new term, along with its connotations and connections, is taken back to the rhetorical problem space to see how it will fit into the organization of the text. Rhetorical problems will include:

- where in the prior text to introduce the term
- how carefully to explain the term
- whether or not the new term will create some other types of confusion for the readers
- whether or not additional information will be needed elsewhere in the text because of the change of terms.

The latter two concerns may move the writer back to the content problem space to find supporting content information. If there are potential confusions arising from the new term or if additional information is needed, the writer will have to consider also whether or not the organizational framework of the text will need to be adjusted (back to rhetorical problem space). Such an interplay may continue for all the problems raised by goal setting, problem anticipation, or problem recognition from the generated text.

The two writing processes, *knowledge telling* and *knowledge transforming*, represent two different ways that writers compose, and many writers seem never to master the *knowledge-transforming* process. The *knowledge-telling* process provides adequate support for less-skilled writers to generate sufficient on-topic material while keeping cognitive complexity at a manageable level. The *knowledge-transforming* process represents writing with reflection on the complexity of the task, and leads the writer to find an appropriate way to address the complexities. A good writer, in many cases, may depend solely on a *knowledge-telling* process because the information has been through a *knowledge-transforming* process from an earlier similar writing task, or because the writer can satisfy the task requirements from a sophisticated use of the *knowledge-telling* process. Thus, it is possible that even genres which may be viewed as expository in nature can be generated by a skilled writer who relies primarily on a knowledge-telling process, generating sophisticated content with minimal problem solving required. For students, the five-paragraph model often fills the role of making an essay topic an exercise in knowledge telling.

The evidence which Bereiter and Scardamalia draw upon to support this theory is in two forms. Their own research program over the past 15 years has explored many of the issues argued for by their theory and, in combination with a wide array of other research findings, strongly supports this theory. In addition, their two-model theory provides a powerful explanation for many of the differences noted in the novice–expert writing research, thereby accounting parsimoniously for many research findings. In particular, their theory accounts for the research questions raised earlier.

5.2.3   *Accounting for skilled and less-skilled writing performance*

The two-process theory provides an explicit account of how children can write well and not find writing to be overly difficult (knowledge telling), yet skilled writers often find writing (knowledge transforming) to be difficult and complex. Similarly, writing tasks will vary in difficulty depending on how complex the information management demand becomes, and this will vary from person to person depending on background knowledge of the topic and the extent to which the particular topic has been practised previously by a writer. The more information that has to be addressed in the problem spaces of the *knowledge-transforming* model, the more complex the composing demand and the more difficult the writing task for a particular writer. In this way, the theory accounts for different performance on particular writing tasks by equally skilled writers.

The *knowledge-transforming* model allows for the elaboration of explicit hypotheses relating audience and genre differences to writing task difficulties. It suggests that writers who have practised one genre or writing task will not necessarily transfer their skilful performance to other genres or tasks until they have had practice resolving the sorts of complex writing problems which are typically created by such new tasks and genres. The difficulties encountered by advanced-level instruction can also be explained. If students seldom practise the sorts of writing tasks which develop *knowledge-transforming* skills, they are not likely to be able to perform those skills easily. Bereiter and Scardamalia (Scardamalia and Bereiter 1987) have argued that the combined effort to resolve both content and rhetorical problems through the movement between these problem spaces invokes a dialectical process for reflection, a process which is excluded in simpler writing tasks. In this way, simpler writing tasks (typically narrative recounts, and personal expressive writing) which do not require such a dialectical process, do not prepare writers for situations in which the dialectical process is essential.

Evidence in Australia, Canada, England, and the USA indicates that many English-speaking students do not receive serious instruction or practice in cognitively demanding writing tasks (Applebee 1981, R. Carter 1990, Christie 1989, Martin 1989). The problem of writing process transfer across tasks and genres is one which has received relatively little attention (except in Australia; see Section 5.3 below), but which constitutes a serious issue for writing development. For example, Peyton *et al.* (1990) argued that dialogue journal writing is a better approach to writing instruction because students write more in dialogue journals than in an essay assignment. Following Bereiter and Scardamalia (and the Australian genre-based theories), such a result ensues because dialogue journal writing is *knowledge telling* and is easier; it is also practised daily.

Both the work of Bereiter and Scardamalia and that of Hayes *et al.* (1987) demonstrate that, also in revision, skilled writers are capable of performing in ways that less-skilled writers do not seem to be able to master, even with training and assistance. This difference is seen even at the tertiary academic level. The clearly different behaviour is a strong argument for a two-process rather than a single-process theory.

All skilled writers have experienced the phenomenon in which they discover what they really want to say only after they put their initial thoughts on paper, or as they reflect on what they have just written. This discovery or transforming of what one has to say is the result of recognizing problems explicitly which then need to be resolved in the writing as it evolves. The act of writing becomes a heuristic process.

At present, it would seem that Bereiter and Scardamalia's two-process theory of writing provides a good account of major research findings on the writing process and on differences in composing between expert and novice writers. At the same time, it should be recognized that recent research by Flower and Hayes has greatly refined their process model. Given the greater elaboration now available for the subcomponents of the Flower and Hayes model (exploring in greater details the components of planning, problem solving, revising, and interactions with task context), it is tempting to argue that their model is sufficient for the many research questions raised earlier. However, the two-process model has certain advantages which cannot be ignored.

First, the non-occurrence of certain writing process abilities among less-skilled writers would not support a model in which a continuous development would be predicted. If less-skilled writers had the same general processing model but were able to employ a less-refined version of it, one would expect them to perform like skilled writers, but not as well. However, the less-skilled writers actually perform in ways which suggest that they are doing something different.

Second, the two-process model focuses on differences rather than similarities. Consequently, it provides a more direct account of the many results deriving from comparisons of skilled and less-skilled writers.

Third, the two-process model provides an account of how more complex writing tasks create problems that are beyond the abilities of less-skilled writers but can be handled by skilled writers; it more directly addresses the problem-solving nature of more complex writing tasks.

5.2.4 Limitations of the Bereiter and Scardamalia theory

It must be recognized, however, that the Bereiter and Scardamalia theory of writing processes also has a number of difficulties which need to be addressed if it is to become the strong hypothesis-generating theory that the creators assume it to be. It will be necessary to account for the influence of context on the writing process, as has been argued recently by Flower (1989, 1994, Flower *et al.* 1990). This becomes possible by elaborating on specific model components: the problem spaces, the organization of content knowledge, and the organization of rhetorical knowledge; and the ways the elaborated sources of information and problem representations are connected.

A second problem concerns the ways in which a writer develops a *knowledge-transforming* model of the writing process. It is not clear, from the evidence Bereiter and Scardamalia have presented to date, how – or when – a writer makes this cognitive transition (cf. Bereiter and Scardamalia 1993). A related question is whether or not it is possible to speak of a stage in which a writer has a partially developed *knowledge-transforming* ability. If it is possible, how can it be recognized, and how generalized is its applicability (e.g. to what extent will it be context dependent)? Yet another related question is whether or not the more complex writing process is limited only to certain individuals and not equally accessible to all who would want to become expert writers. For example, many studies of L1 students in grades 4–8 indicate that, even with prompting and training, students have difficulty carrying out more expert approaches to writing and revision.

Bereiter and Scardamalia have argued that a major impediment to learning this more complex strategy for composing is the non-challenging nature of writing demands in school curricula. According to Bereiter and Scardamalia (1985), among the ways inert knowledge is promoted in schools include:

- pre-writing activities when they are not needed for content generation
- the extensive use of expressive 'turn-on' topics
- acceptance of 'tell what you know' strategies – even when not called for by the task

- a willingness by teachers to put up with recognized weaknesses in structure and content – even when students admit the existence of these weaknesses but make little effort towards improvement
- the use of conversational ploys to avoid rhetorical problems in the writing (see also Scardamalia and Bereiter 1986).

More recently, Bereiter and Scardamalia have argued that the development of school-based generalized learning skills, and (*knowledge-transforming*) writing in particular, is possible by promoting students' capacities for 'intending to learn' (Bereiter and Scardamalia 1989). This perspective on school-based learning is that students create a 'contextual module' (Bereiter 1990) in the course of their dealing with school activities and requirements.

A contextual module constitutes an acquired complex of knowledge which combines and integrates procedural knowledge, declarative knowledge, goal structures, problem models, affect, persona, and a code of conduct. As Bereiter (1990: 613) states:

> A contextual module consists of this entire complex of knowledge, skills, goals, and feelings. So long as all these components are separately represented in the mind, however, there is little reason to talk about them as a unit, even though they are interrelated. Acquired modularity implies that over time these separate components come to form a more organic whole.

In the 'schoolwork' module that Bereiter and Scardamalia describe, students perform school tasks as though these tasks were a job, and a student's goal is to find the most efficient way to get the job done. The 'intending-to-learn' module, in contrast, refers to breaking out of the simpler efficiency-driven 'schoolwork' contextual module and learning a second, self-driven learning module – the intentional learning-module. In the second learning module, students set learning goals which go beyond the school task requirements and reflect a willingness both to understand knowledge and processes in terms of problem-solving activities, and to confront learning problems, all of which points to a learning system as an active goal-seeking process.

5.2.5 *Expertise, cognitive-strategy training, and the problem of ill-defined knowledge*

Approaches related to the notion of intentional learning are suggested by cognitive research on expertise. Applied to the educational context, such approaches would explore how students make the transition to a goal-setting and problem-solving orientation in writing. Bereiter and Scardamalia (1993) have recently explored the nature of expertise, drawing on their work in writing and synthesizing it with much of the recent work on developing expertise. A number of other researchers have explored the growing field of expertise and applied this research to writing development. Michael Carter (1990), for example, has pointed out that the research on 'expertise' has debated the importance of general learning strategies versus applications of local knowledge. From the studies he reviewed, it appears that experts turn to general problem-solving strategies only when they are faced with unusual problems. In such a situation, experts can transfer skills, but usually only with assistance, practice, and explanations. Results suggest that the best way to transfer skills and strategies is through consistent practice in a variety of similar contexts to the point of proceduralization or automaticity. At the same time, Carter notes that the influence of local knowledge on expert performance has been similarly overestimated. The importance of local, context-specific knowledge tends to become greater for learners as they are asked to perform in specific contexts such as those in graduate school or in professional work environments. As Carter notes, 'experts become experts because they possess very highly organized schemata, developed over a long time, that are related to a specific skill' (1990: 272). Novices, by contrast, lack the specific knowledge which comes from practise in the organizational abilities, content information, and genres required by a context.

Many less-skilled student writers would appear to approach writing tasks with few resources in either local knowledge or general strategies. Among the research studies developed to create such resources, Bereiter and Scardamalia (1987) explored a general strategy-training approach involving the use of procedural facilitation and goal concretization. The steps that they recommend are:

- Define a self-regulatory system which students should learn to control.
- Design a way of cuing the type of expert processing in which student should be trained.
- Set up a teachable routine which externalizes the process and allows students to learn it.

One example involved giving sixth-grade students a set of cards with strategy prompts for writing. For example, when students arrived at a block, they would draw from a pile a card suggesting a possible further direction; e.g.

'an even better idea is ...'
'an example of this ...'
'I'm getting off topic so ...'
'my purpose...'.

There were approximately 30 cards with instructions (for each genre) and they were randomly ordered. The point was to provide students with a cue that would foster their reflective thinking about their writing, and would interrupt the knowledge-telling flow. A similar training strategy was used to develop skills in revision. Students would examine a set of guidelines for comparing their text with their composing goals. If a problem was seen in the comparison stage, for example, a set of guidelines was available to the students to suggest a revision strategy for fixing the problem. The goal was to make students aware of revision processes and to encourage them to practise appropriate strategies. In general, results showed that students could learn to use these strategies in their essay writing; the limitation was that these strategies did not seem to transfer readily to other writing tasks which were not supported by the cues.

This limitation is typical of many strategy-training approaches for writing. (See also Pressley *et al.* 1994 for procedural training involving reading strategies.) Students must:

- first become aware of the limits of their performance;
- then become aware of specific ways in which their performance is limited (some means for comparison);
- then learn ways to resolve the problems in their performance (guided by some technique);
- then learn to transfer their improved performance to tasks not directly supported by assisting cues.

Many strategy-training studies have demonstrated success in teaching students specific techniques and strategies, but few have demonstrated that the techniques can be transferred to contexts beyond the specific training environment, or that the training has an effect on performance in post-training tasks (Pressley *et al.* 1992).

The general goal of having students become aware of different performance criteria, having them learn to use these different performance criteria, and then having them transfer these criteria independently to other contexts has been the purpose of much work under the name of metacognitive strategy research. Following Bruner's (1983) notion of scaffolded instruction, and Vygotsky's (1978) notion of the 'zone of proximal development', researchers such as Brown (1994), Collins *et al.* (1989), Newman *et al.* (1989), Palincsar and Brown (1984), and Pressley *et al.* (1991, 1992, 1994), and have sought to move students through to independent use of new strategies by having them become co-constructors of knowledge and co-users of more expert strategies.

A major problem with the application of problem-solving training procedures to writing instruction is that writing itself tends to be what some researchers call 'ill-defined problem solving'; that is, situations in which there are no single well-defined solutions. Spiro *et al.* (1987) argued that notions such as 'cognitive flexibility' and 'cognitive transfer' are not well understood for ill-defined problem-oriented tasks such as writing. In ill-defined contexts of cognitive strategy use, it is not clear just what skills are transferable to new contexts, or how this transfer can be accomplished.

Based on a review of research, Spiro *et al.* (1987) argued that, for ill-defined knowledge to be transformed, students need to be exposed to a variety of related situations in which they must assemble a new schema structure rather than rely on established schema structures (see also Bereiter and Scardamalia 1993, McGinley and Tierney 1989). The best approach for developing this ability lies in exposure to many variations of a content domain; that is, students are presented with many related cases and contexts, all bearing some relationship to each other. Spiro *et al.* suggest that students will learn to handle ill-structured tasks best when first introduced to a content via the presentation of a task with an intermediate degree of ill-structuredness. (For example, a situation may suggest more than one good solution, yet each solution can be demonstrated as reasonably effective.)

5.2.6 *Balancing process and form*

As suggested by Spiro *et al.* (1987), one of the major issues which appears repeatedly in strategy research lies in the need for students to be aware of the constraints of the type of writing they are being asked to perform. Bereiter and Scardamalia (1987) point out the different requirements of narrative and expository writing and the need for students to write for different purposes to develop problem-solving skills. Carter (1990), in his discussion of writing expertise, points out the importance of extensive practice in a wide variety of writing tasks which will require different strategy use. Similarly, Swales (1990) has pointed out the need for genre knowledge as an important part of students' knowledge about writing if they are to be academically successful. In the next section, the notion of genre as it applies to writing development is explored. Genres represent ways that groups of writers have managed to solve problems in writing which conform to general expectations, which facilitate communication for both the writer and the reader, and which provide students with frames suited to communication about different sorts of knowledge and different ways of addressing the reader.

The renewed emphasis on genre also represents a corrective reaction to an earlier emphasis on process as a simple set of procedures for all writing tasks. Applebee (1986), Bereiter and Scardamalia (1985), Christie (1985), and Martin (1989) have all addressed the difficulties involved in the typically oversimple application of a process approach – an approach which has led to sometimes disappointing results despite strongly affirmative statements (cf. Applebee *et al.* 1994). All argue that the disregard for formal aspects of writing and the problem-solving required by different genres of writing, seriously limit students' writing abilities. They argue, rather, that it is necessary to recognize the wide array of tasks which will extend students' cognitive abilities.

The work of applied linguists and educational researchers in Australia has extended this argument to a recognition that language form, as it reflects genre and writing purpose, is also a critical component in writing development – one which has been ignored in the false dichotomy between skills and content instruction (Cope and Kalantzis 1993; see also Coe 1994). These scholars do not downplay the important role that writing processes play in writing research and instruction, but they do see the notion of the writing process, as currently interpreted in instruction, as a severely limiting view (Christie 1985, Maclean 1989). Instead, they propose that the incorporation of form should lead to a balance between form and process in a functional approach to writing development. Through a focus on the functions of language use, the goal is to account for the cognitive and social influences on writing as realized through the genre form. In the next section, this perspective will be examined, and it will be argued that the development of genre knowledge, in Halliday's functional sense, plays a particularly important role in a student's writing development beyond the knowledge-telling stage. The Australian perspective on writing development is particularly important as an argument for student empowerment through writing – a notion which has yet to be given careful consideration outside Australia .

5.3   Genre-based approaches to writing development

5.3.1   A Hallidayan view of language as function

A view of language which is important to any understanding of writing development is that derived from Halliday's functional theory of language. In this approach to language, grammar develops out of the need for speakers and writers to interact for functional purposes; that is, language development evolves out of a child's 'learning to mean' (Christie 1989). In this view, language is not separable from content or context, but varies systematically with content and context, and is the medium through which meaning is realized. Halliday's emphasis on meaningful use of language in educational contexts is a perspective adopted by whole-language theorists in the USA. However, a Hallidayan orientation to meaningful language use in context extends further to include the ways in which language *form* gives structure to meaningful communication. As Christie states, 'Success in mastering a content area is actually a matter of mastering the necessary linguistic resources with which to deal with that content – this implies knowing how one's discourse is to be structured' (1989: 167).

Unlike the assumptions of American generative grammarians – in which language form is seen as independent of language use – Halliday sees language form and meaning-making as an integrated system. For Halliday, language form is functional in nature; it is meant to serve functional purposes. As Painter (1989: 21) notes,

Language is a functional resource in that the language system as a whole can be viewed as having the form it does because of what it is called upon to do – the needs of language learners have shaped the linguistic system itself.

Children's first language abilities develop out of the growing need to communicate, first with parents, then with the expanding world of human contacts. As children learn to interact and manipulate their environment through language, language forms expand to meet new functional needs. In this way, children are engaged in making meaning, and they do so through language forms which serve children's abilities to make meaning.

Students learning to interact orally and in writing need to come to understand how language form and generic text structure provide resources for presenting information and interacting with others. They learn to choose linguistic patterns which are appropriate to the meanings they are trying to make. One of the goals of school, then, is to help students to recognize and use those linguistic patterns. As Christie (1989: 198) states:

> Knowledge is created in patterns of discourse, and successful mastery of a 'body of knowledge' like the associated development of various mental skills of reasoning, speculation, and inquiry, is entirely dependent upon mastery of linguistic resources necessary for these to come into being. It is for this reason, contrary to prevailing custom, that good teaching practices should always have an overt and explicit interest in the nature of the language students must learn to use.

Making meaning is the production of discourse and of texts. The extension of this perspective is that students in school situations also make meaning – and learn – through their use of discourse and their construction of texts. Such a view argues that writing and attention to form, as part of content exploration, is critical for learning. This perspective is argued for forcefully by Halliday (1993b) and Martin (1989), an argument which will be the subject of the next section.

5.3.2   *Extending language use to genre knowledge*

Martin (1989), examining the causes for success and failure in elementary school literacy development, posits an argument for extensive instruction in factual writing, and, in particular, expository writing – writing which explores how the world works. He contrasts this view directly against writing instruction which focuses almost entirely on expressive and narrative writing – writing which describes how the world looks (see also Bereiter and Scardamalia 1987). This argument does not discount the importance of narrative and expressive writing as a way to provide scaffolding for students as they make the transition from spoken to written language use. Indeed, the utility of familiar genres for learning to write is well recognized. Rather, the issue is whether or not early school curricula recognize that students must practise a range of genre forms in writing.

Assuming a functional view of language following Halliday, Martin argues that school and teachers tend to reinforce the status quo of success and failure by ignoring the connection between language use and social purpose, and by disregarding any specific analysis of language form which would result from children's efforts to work with information, whether through speech or through writing. Learning how to use writing for understanding the world offers, instead, the possibility (but not the guarantee) for change and for student success.

Martin (1989) sees the learning of factual writing skills through content studies as a way of giving students power over their own learning. Students who can infer the requirements of controlling information, in part because they have experienced a larger socialization process which will allow them to do so, will succeed; but other students who are less familiar with the expected genres and their functional purposes will continue to fail in schools. By this reasoning, the goals of school should include explicit instruction in those forms of language which many students will not be able to infer indirectly. Students learn to control the information presented in school by solving problems in integrating language, content, and context, and by practising the types of writing which demand this integration, not by writing practice in other genres which do not.

In order to explain the notion of factual writing and the importance of genre for students' writing development, Martin has developed a framework for factual writing. In this framework, writing genres are identified which relate to functional goals of knowledge presentation (see D'Angelo 1987, de Beaugrande 1984: 100). For Martin (1989), types of factual writing in which elementary students should engage include:

Recounts (a specific event-related presentation);
Procedures (a general event-related presentation);
Descriptions (a specific object-related presentation);
Reports (a general object-related presentation);
Explanations (a specific argument on an issue, event, or object);
Exposition (a complex sequence of multiple explanations).

In a similar classification of factual genres which should be incorporated into a curriculum, Derewianka (1990) suggests a slightly different set of options:

Recount (What we did?/What took place?)
Instructions (How something is done)
Narrative (Recounts with a twist)
Information report (What an entire class of things is like)
Explanation (Why is it so?/How does it work?)
Argument (Stating your case).

In both frameworks, the stress is on children learning how language functions to present content in ways which are most appropriate to a writer's purpose. Neither framework refers to matters of grammar practice or style exercises which might be divorced from working with meaningful curriculum content (Collerson 1990). Rather, *in the process of exploring content,* students learn how to present the content through effective language use and genre form. The critical point is that some notion of student support from the teacher – either through such notions as language apprenticeship (Collins *et al.* 1989), scaffolding (Bruner 1983), or the practice of reciprocal teaching (Brown and Palincsar 1989) – should be extended to include the functional role of language form as text (Christie 1989).

5.3.3   The importance of genre

To understand how a focus on language is not a matter of attention to arbitrary form, but is central to meaning-making, it is necessary to pick up the argument presented in subsection 5.3.1 above – the argument that language and content are integrated in the sense that language serves the needs of the writer to make meaning. Kress (1989) develops the important role of genre as an essential factor in language use by noting that all language use is a matter of making discourse. The making of discourse depends on differences between speaker and listener, or writer and reader. As certain discourses become more deeply embedded in the social functioning of groups, these discourses become conventionalized; they become recognized as genres which serve functional purposes in communication.

Students in school contexts are expected to make use of genres for learning information to the extent that they see how such genres serve functional purposes, and to the extent that genre-structures are made apparent to students. Assuming a close relationship between language use and learning purposes – as a Hallidayan approach would – students need to be taught to work effectively with the language medium appropriate to the learning task and informational content. When this does not happen, as posited by Kress (1989) and Martin (1989), learning purposes are obscured for those students who do not have the advantage of socialization which reflects school-based expectations (see also Heath 1986b, Painter 1989).

An argument has been raised at times that teaching students genres will degenerate into teaching arbitrary models and textual organization with little connection to a student's learning purposes (e.g. Freedman 1993, Silva 1990). While this can in fact occur – e.g. in such pedagogical procedures as the teaching of the three- or five-paragraph model – it is not the argument being presented here. Genre is not being presented as an end for instruction, but rather as a means to understanding meaningful content. Genres must be taught, understood, and critiqued in terms of the potential they provide for working with informational content and learning context. Since genres also reflect a cultural ideology, the study of genre additionally opens for students an awareness of the assumptions of groups who use specific genres for specific ends, allowing students to critique not only the types of knowledge they learn but also the ways in which knowledge is valued and in which it reflects covert assumptions.

To be successful, then, students must learn how language works to convey content through school-valued genres. In a sense, they must learn the schemas for organizing different types of knowledge, as well as those for presenting different types of information (Cope and Kalantzis 1993, Mohan 1986). This is only likely to happen in contexts in which students get consistent practice with different types of writing tasks, and in which teachers can point to the language structuring in different genres for highlighting different ways of making meaning. Spiro *et al.* (1987) suggest that practice of this type would provide sufficient training in dealing with relatively ill-defined problem-solving tasks. A slightly different perspective is suggested by the various Australian researchers who would agree with the need for extensive practice, but would argue that explicit instruction is also needed to show how language serves meaningful communication.

5.3.4   *Extending genre use to academic contexts*

Looking at the opposite end of the writing development spec-
trum, Swales (1990) also argues for the importance of genre as
having functional purposes in advanced writing development. He
similarly points to a knowledge of genre as an important way to
give students power over their learning. Taking as a starting point
the notion that genres serve meaningful purposes and provide
frames for various academic schema-based sets of knowledge, he
contends that the ability to use genre structure effectively will
transform students' abilities to learn and function successfully in
academic contexts. Swales, referring to Martin and Rothery (1986;
see also Martin 1985), points out that genres provide ways to constrain information in socially recognized forms (e.g. a letter of
regret is not a good genre for inviting a person to a party). These
genre forms are intimately tied to cultures and discourse communities. Thus, as Swales states, 'genres comprise a system for
accomplishing social purposes by verbal means' (1990: 41). For
students to gain power over particular knowledge, and to gain
recognition in particular discourse communities, the ability to use
genre forms effectively is critical (see also Coe 1994).

Throughout this discussion of genre, it is important to recognize the connections to all levels of writing development and
instruction. It is also important to see the relationships to research
on: the cognitive psychology of writing, cognitive strategy development and student difficulties in literacy developments. If genre is
the locus of local cultural assumptions, of language structure, of
writer's purpose, of informational content, and of register contexts, then it is evident that genre is a key notion in writing
development, and in learning through writing. As students learn
to control genre, they concomitantly learn to control language,
writing purpose, content, and context.

5.3.5   *Knowledge of generalized genres from rhetoric*

A natural tendency is to look for superordinate categories for various possible genres; this is a tendency which apparently has deep
historical roots as attested by the field of rhetoric. In the twentieth
century, such tendencies have led to a general educational recognition of categories such as narrative, exposition, argumentation,
description, etc. This rhetorical perspective assumes that there are

different types of discourse which have systematic formal features and reflect ways of organizing thought.[2] The use of organizing principles to guide discourse and teach patterns of arrangement has been in existence since Aristotle. Much more recently, in the eighteenth and nineteenth centuries, these principles were presented as representative of basic aims of rhetorical organization, leading to Bain's widely recognized classification: description, narration, exposition, and argumentation (Berlin 1984, Crowley 1990, D'Angelo 1987).

Among the currently discussed theories of discourse arrangement, those of Britton *et al.* (1975), D'Angelo (1975, 1987), Kinneavy (1971, 1983), and Moffett (1968) are the most prominent. All propose conceptual theories for kinds of discourse and functions of discourse arrangements, though there are enough distinctions among the theories to make a synthesis difficult (see, e.g., D'Angelo 1987, Kinneavy 1983). In all cases, however, the theories conceive of writing as influenced by the functional roles of the writer, the reader, the text, and the world (as opposed to the traditional genres of Bain which were not functionally motivated). Kinneavy, for example, translates these roles into four basic types of written discourse: expressive, persuasive, literary, and referential. These basic types are supported by modes of written discourse: description, narration, classification, and evaluation.

These theories of discourse types have had a powerful impact not only on research issues relating to formal features of discourse but also on writing pedagogy. In the USA, most English writing textbooks (ranging from elementary language-arts texts to tertiary-level writing textbooks), in both L1 and L2 contexts, base their design on some set of discourse types (the resulting pedagogy often referred to disparagingly as 'current-traditional' method [Berlin 1987, Silva 1990]). The specific relevance of these rhetorical theories is that they provide general classification heuristics for formal organizational patterns which are intuitively appealing even if they oversimplify or ignore the importance of purpose, audience, attitudes, and topic in shaping discourse.

There is some evidence for the larger and more abstract classification of genres (or rather, meta-genres) – e.g. expository, argumentative, and narrative, depending on the context in which these terms are applied. A considerable amount of research, conducted in educational contexts, has demonstrated repeatedly that students work with texts, defined as distinct by this classification system, in quite different ways (e.g. Crowhurst 1987; 1990, Meyer 1987, Richgels *et al.* 1987, Spiro and Taylor 1987). It has also been demonstrated that careful linguistic analyses of such meta-genres reveal significant and consistent differences in the ways that linguistic features co-occur and define these genres. Whether or not such general classification is as useful as the strictly functional genre schemes of Martin or Derewianka, or the advanced academic genres addressed by Bhatia (1993), Swales (1990), and others, is an open question.

5.4   Research on second language writing

In the English-speaking countries of the world, increasing numbers of students find themselves in an educational system that does not provide them with extensive support as L2 learners. In the USA, for example, by the year 2000, there will be over 5 million English L2 speakers in the school systems (Bernhardt 1994). Yet relatively little effort is made to distinguish these students from English L1 students for purposes of instruction, or to recognize different student needs. In the area of writing research in particular, L2 writers have only recently been discussed (Leki 1992, Silva 1993). However, with so many students writers of English being L2 students, it is essential that their situations and their needs be given specific consideration. This section considers the research issues that have been investigated with L2 students.

5.4.1   Support from, and for, L1 research

Throughout much of this chapter (and elsewhere), the discussion has not focused specifically on learning to write in a second language. The primary goal has been to assemble the various strands which define the nature of writing in general. At various points in this discussion, L2 research which supports and corroborates the findings of L1 research has been cited. It is important, however, to address:

- the ways in which L2 contexts create unique concerns;
- the possible forms of these concerns; and
- the research that has been done to address these concerns.

Until quite recently, L2 research on writing has been closely dependent on L1 research. Perhaps only in three areas – con-

trastive rhetoric, English for Specific Purposes, and writing assessment – has L2 research followed independent paths. (The first
two are addressed in Chapters 6 and 7; and writing assessment will
be discussed in Chapter 13 [see also Hamp-Lyons 1990, 1991d].)
One of the major catalysts for the rapid emergence of research on
L2 writing has been the growing numbers of foreign and language-minority students entering English-speaking tertiary-level
institutions. Perhaps because of the ubiquitous freshman composition requirements at US colleges and universities, L2 writing
research has been quite prominent in that country. Also, in the
USA and in Australia, a secondary emphasis on the difficulties facing language-minority students has become more evident. These
two contexts for research have generated a large proportion of L2
writing research; not surprisingly, most of this research stresses the
similarities rather than the potential differences between L1 and
L2 learners.

Relying predominantly on case studies with small groups of writers, research on composing processes and on revision strategies
has shown that L2 students often behave rather like less-skilled L1
writers, as described in the L1 research. In research on composing
processes, it appears that L2 writers make use of the same sets of
composing processes but, for various reasons, many L2 writers
apply these composing processes with less ability than is shown by
L1 writers (Raimes 1985, Zamel 1983, 1985). Raimes (1985)
argues that writing difficulties for ESL students typically are
largely the result of difficulties with composing skills than with linguistic skills. A second similarity, pointed out by Raimes (1985),
lies in the fact that L2 students may be driven by the need to generate content and write it as they initiate it (see also Bereiter and
Scardamalia 1987). Edelsky (1986), Gaskill (1986), and Jones and
Tetroe (1987) have also argued that L1 writing processes transfer
to L2 writing. In addition, it has been argued that process-
oriented instruction has led to similar student progress, whether
learners are working in first or second language, particularly at
the elementary grades (Hudelson 1989b, Urzua 1987). In large
measure, the strong claims made for close similarities between L1
and L2 writers centre on research on composing processes (see
Krapels 1990 for an overview). This research orientation may
reveal important similarities; and this line of inquiry may also
mask evidence that would show L2 writing to differ more from L1
writing than has been suggested in writing process research.

5.4.2   *Writing differences: L1 vs L2*

Apart from the clear differences in L2 writing illustrated by research in contrastive rhetoric and ESP, and by assessment research, a number of specific findings from recent research suggest that L2 writing has a great many differences from L1 writing – more, perhaps, than it has similarities.

First, it is not clear that L2 writers who write at greater length or with greater frequency typically write better; unlike the generalization about L1 writers, there is evidence which argues that weaker L2 writers sometimes write more (Reppen 1995, Reppen and Grabe 1993). This is a topic that needs further investigation since a connection between writing quantity and writing quality is often assumed in certain research studies (e.g. Carlisle 1989, Ferris 1994).

Second, it is widely recognized that L1 students have some implicit knowledge of rhetorical plans, organizational logic, and genre form in their native language; it is not at all clear that students have the same implicit knowledge with respect to L2, as is indicated in the contrastive rhetoric research. This distinction may actually be greater for research which assumes that writing naturally emerges from students and cannot be taught directly (e.g. Jones 1985, Krashen 1984). A Hallidayan perspective, by contrast, would argue that many L1 students may not be so different from L2 students in the sense that many L1 students have an inadequate knowledge of textual structuring and need the same sorts of direct instruction on written discourse form that are required by L2 students.

A third difference between L1 and L2 students emerges in studies of revision. While L1 research suggests that most revision has little effect on writing improvement (Hillocks 1986; cf. Freedman 1987), feedback of various kinds (on form, on content, on both) appears to be useful for improving the essays of certain L2 students (Fathman and Whalley 1990). It has also been found that teachers' general comments referring to content and organization seem to be useful to L2 learners. Similarly, Raimes (1985) found that L2 students were less inhibited by teacher-editing and feedback. In effect, L2 learners appear to expect and accept greater intervention, and to make greater improvements when they get such feedback (Radecki and Swales 1988). Because there is not sufficient L2 research to explore potential differences between L1 and L2 learners in revision strategies and the influence of feedback, this is an area that needs additional careful study (e.g. Cohen and Cavalcanti 1990, Fathman and Whalley 1990, Ferris 1995, Leki 1990).

A fourth area of difference between L1 and L2 students lies in the impact and influence of the L1 on writing in the L2. Clearly, this is an added factor for L2 writing which is not present in L1 writing. Apart from the potentially positive influence of strategy and process transfer from the L1, the L2 learner also faces constraints deriving from potentially limited linguistic abilities in the L2. It is clear that limited knowledge of vocabulary, language structure, and content constrains a L2 writer's performance. The entire question of the impact of level of language proficiency on writing in the L2 has yet to be examined in careful detail (see, e.g., Carson *et al.* 1990, Silva 1993). While Charney and Carlson (1995), Hillocks (1986), and Smagorinsky (1992) all make a case for the use of models and modelling in L1 writing instruction, as do the Australian proponents of genre-based curricula, the limited linguistic abilities of the L2 writer may also account for the finding that writing models can have a beneficial effect for L2 students in particular.

5.4.3 Towards a model of L2 writing

The results to date in L2 writing research suggest that:

- there are many contradictory findings;
- many results and interpretations of research reflect expected findings and conform to L1 research results;
- L2 research must be developed more fully through carefully developed studies and research designs, and in more carefully controlled research situations.

Silva (1992, 1993) forcefully makes the argument for more controlled research specifically addressed to L2 writing contexts. In particular, he argues that theories of L1 writing will not be adequate for advances in L2 writing. Moreover, current L2 research is primarily exploratory, limited in numbers of participants, uneven in quality, and not accounting for the full range of factors which influence the L2 context. These limitations on research are reflected by a limited view of L2 writing theory. It is necessary to develop a theory of L2 writing, making use of L1 research when such research is relevant, but incorporating the unique features of L2 writing.

For Silva (1990: 19), such a model of L2 writing,

> is one that ..., at a minimum, regards writing as an interactive activity; is reasonably comprehensive and internally consistent; reflects an understanding of historical developments in the field; is informed by current work in relevant disciplines; and is sensitive to the cultural, linguistic, and experiential differences of individuals and societies.

Silva (1990: 19) suggests that a model of L2 writing must incorporate the following five components:

  (i) L2 writing theory,
  (ii) research on the nature of L2 writing,
 (iii) research on L2 writing instruction,
 (iv) L2 writing instruction theory (approach), and
  (v) L2 writing practice.

The extent of interaction among these components constitutes an open questions, as does the sort of research which is capable of supporting each of the five components. A second way to develop a theory of L2 writing may lie in a reconsideration of the ethnography of writing to be described in Chapter 8, and in the way in which ethnographic information can be used to explore differences between L1 and L2 writing, as well as the extent to which such ethnographic data can generate testable hypotheses.

A model of L2 writing based on an 'ethnography of writing' approach would ask what is known about the various major components of the writing situation:

the writer;	the writing;
the reader;	the content and form of the text;
the purpose;	the writer's underlying intention;
the location;	the processes of writing.

One possible outcome of such an undertaking would be an argument that L2 writing is so varied and distinct from situation to situation that a general theory of L2 writing may not be possible (e.g. Cohen and Cavalcanti 1990), at least not with the current state of knowledge. Exactly how a descriptive theory of L2 writing would differ from a descriptive theory of L1 writing is an issue going beyond the scope of this work, though we believe that an effort of this type would be a step towards the generation of a theory of L2 writing.

5.5   Moving from the cognitive to the contextual

This chapter has sought to bring together more current perspectives on cognitive approaches to writing processes and, at the same time, extend the current research in two directions that are not typically discussed in much writing research. The notion that the text form itself is re-emerging as an important component in the study of writing follows from cognitive research on expertise as well as from Bereiter and Scardamalia's discussions of the resources required to transform knowledge. It is also important to recognize that many students learning to write in different contexts around the world are L2 students.[3] Current L1 writing research gives minimal attention to these students, but there are important research issues to consider, primary among them being whether students learning to write in a second language have different skills, resources, needs, and expectations (see, in particular, Kachru 1992, Sridhar 1994). Research on L2 students is needed to assess the generality of claims made in the current L1 writing literature. Moreover, to the extent that L2 students reveal differences from L1 students, research must explore these differences and their implications for both first and second language instruction.

In the domain of cognitive research on writing in the L1, researchers are increasingly recognizing the importance of different contextual variables in understanding writing development. In particular, the recent work of Flower (1989, 1994) demonstrates a strong movement to consider the social contexts for writing that operate in conjunction with the cognitive efforts of the writer. This trend is an important corrective to the earlier discussions of the Flower and Hayes model. Any appropriate descriptive theory of writing will have to account for the many social contexts that influence writing in various ways. This trend is also seen in recent discussions of writing theory by Cope and Kalantzis (1993), Dyson (1993), Kress (1994), and Witte (1992).

In the field of L2 writing and applied linguistics, there are two additional contexts for writing which do not commonly receive treatment in L1 writing discussions. These are the areas of English for Specific Purposes (ESP) and contrastive rhetoric. In both cases, the interests of applied linguists are obvious and, perhaps, the relative disinterest of L1 writing research is understandable. The clearest parallel for L1 research is the growing interest in writing in advanced academic settings and in non-academic settings. Current research is exploring how these contexts alter the needs for writing, change patterns of use, and suggest different options for writing instruction. In the next two chapters, these areas – writing in special-purpose contexts and contrastive rhetoric – will be explored in detail and their contexts examined for the additional dimensions they bring to our understanding of writing.

Notes

1. The knowledge-telling model of writing is also used by mature skilled writers when it is sufficient to perform the task required (e.g. writing a common memo many times).
2. It should also be noted that many contemporary rhetoricians object to this assumption.
3. This is, they are learning to write in any (national/official) language other than their first language; e.g. native speakers of Cebuano and Illocano in the Philippines learning to write in Filipino (Pilipino/Tagalog), or native speakers of Tamil or Gugarati in India learning to write in Hindi. The L2 is not necessarily English, and the issue is that little is known about the ways in which such teaching is actually conducted or the ways in which learning is accomplished.

6

Writing for professional purposes

6.1 Introduction

From the discussion of the previous chapters, it would be easy to
get the impression that writing only occurs in school, or is only
used for schooling purposes. In the past 15 years, however,
researchers concerned with writing and literacy have now recognized that most uses of writing are tied to situations which extend
well beyond the educational context. Writing is now studied in
many professional and technical contexts, as well as in the workplace. The general goal of such research is to understand the
sorts of writing that are actually used in contexts outside of
school, to examine the connection between writing in the school
context and in other contexts, and to determine whether the
relation between school writing and writing in other contexts is
productive – that is, are students being trained in writing so that
they will be able to write effectively in other contexts once they
leave school?

This chapter will explore these questions by examining in some
detail four areas of writing specialization:

- technical writing as taught in post-secondary courses;
- writing actually performed in non-school contexts and its comparison with writing in school contexts;
- writing approaches in English for Special Purposes (ESP);
- a social constructionist view of writing in professional contexts.

These issues also raise such important concerns as the role of
English in professional communication world-wide and the need
to incorporate significant audience, topic, and purpose variation
in instructional approaches.

6.2   The teaching of technical writing

In the USA, at the tertiary level, technical writing is taught to students studying certain technical or pre-professional fields. These courses are sometimes taught in English departments by technical writing specialists; sometimes the courses are taught by the respective departments wanting their students to become familiar with format and genre norms of that technical/professional/business discipline. In each case, the basic assumption is that students need to learn special ways to write (e.g. letters, memoranda, reports) which are not taught in more general writing courses. It is also often suggested that students are taught to break the bad writing habits of secondary and tertiary instruction, inculcated by teachers who do not understand how to be clear, objective, and concise. In order to understand this seeming prejudice in writing instruction, it is necessary to review certain guiding assumptions in technical writing instruction.

It is first important to introduce a number of distinctions. The first of these is the distinction between writing as a technology and writing for scientific and technological purposes. Often one finds the assumption being made that writing can be reduced to a template – to a set of techniques, or a set of simple step-by-step procedures which will guarantee 'correct' and objective language (see, e.g., Dobrin 1989, Winsor 1990). This notion of writing as technology is not the same as the notion advanced in Chapter 1, where writing was described as a technology in the sense that it is a learned skill rather than a biologically conditioned one transmitted through the human genetic system. Language-as-technology, as it is introduced and discussed in this chapter, refers to an assumed set of guidelines, a general 'discovery procedure' for writing 'objective' prose.

A second distinction that must be made concerns the use of writing in scientific and technical fields versus the preparation of documents to be used in instructions, letters, manuals, and other explanatory material. In the former case, there is a lower percentage of routine writing tasks and more opportunities for planning, collaborative revision, oral interaction, and presentation. In the latter cases, technical writing involves the use of certain formats and rules of usage which may or may not be as effective as the technical writing textbooks would lead one to believe. This latter approach to technical writing would cover such conventional uses of writing as:

- memos for business purposes
- business reports
- guidelines for the use of heading, tables, and other illustrative material
- professional letter-writing conventions: salutations, formats, closings
- effective grammatical usage rules.

In fact, much of technical writing, as taught in the USA, involves the sort of instruction that provides students with templates for various non-academic genres. In essence, these courses constitute training in document design and bureaucratic usage, and less emphasis is placed on the actual uses of writing that scientists and technical researchers employ as they work in their professional environments. While it is important to fashion texts into standard formats perceived as reader friendly in particular environments, it is still necessary to solve rhetorical problems central to the content rather than the forms of various types of technical texts (MacKinnon 1993). The more formulary approach of much discipline-related writing instruction assumes relatively simple form-function equations which have not been established and in fact are not likely to be possible.

While there is a certain amount of *pro forma* discussion of scientific and technical writing – typically the laboratory report, the scientific method paper, and the grant proposal – relatively little time is given to the study of what professional scientists and technical researchers do when they write. Nor is much consideration given to research on writing in the commercial workplace (cf. Reither 1993, Reynolds *et al.* 1995, Spilka 1993a). This chapter, in contrast, will be much more concerned with the writing that is actually done in professional contexts outside of school, and will essentially ignore document design issues and the constraints of bureaucratic text production.

A third distinction lies in writing for research and publication purposes versus writing in other professional contexts. For the purposes of this discussion, the creative use of writing for the dissemination of research information will be treated as more important than the uses of writing which appear to be more programmatic and which reflect the day-to-day invocations of a similar set format such as the business memo, the rejection letter, the insurance claim, the police arrest report, etc. (cf. Matalene 1995).

Questions of information access and information transfer – important issues in applied linguistics – centre to a greater extent on research reports, grants, and professional publications than they do on the day-to-day programmatic types of writing in non-academic contexts. In particular, the focus on the presentation of research findings for wider dissemination has the status of a different type of writing than do other kinds of writing that typically occur in work or school contexts. Although professional research writing also is assumed to conform to certain conventions for objective reporting, it will be argued that scientific writing does not simply follow a set of mechanical writing procedures for reporting results, though the articles which represent such research typically appear to conform to a set of writing procedures. Rather, scientific writing is as subjective and as rhetorically conscious as other forms of writing, and may be even more rhetorically sensitive in many situations (Geisler 1994, Kaplan and Grabe 1991). At the same time, research on the full range of writing done in non-academic contexts provides important insights for instruction; this matter will be considered in the next section.

Each of the three distinctions noted above influences the critique of writing instruction in tertiary courses. The teaching of technical writing in tertiary-level courses, in general, seeks to address certain uses of writing for technical and scientific purposes. Such courses teach basic formats and writing conventions which are widely recognized as marking writing in technical subject areas and genres. The courses stress the careful definition of terms, the avoidance of ambiguous terminology, and an impersonal/objective style of writing ('neutral' with respect to the attitudes of the writer). On a relatively abstract level, such criteria seem to be appropriate goals, though recent research would argue that technically oriented writing may be much more complex than these generalizations suggest (Spilka 1993b). Much technical writing instruction assumes that:

- information may be 'transferred' from the writer to the reader (in the sense that fresh produce is 'transferred' from the grower to the consumer – a situation in which 'treatment' is minimal and packaging is critical);
- the reader can understand information better if it is broken down into small, step-by-step, incremental explanations – if it is, in a naive way, 'programmed';

- information exists 'out there', apart from the writer or the reader, independent of interpretive background knowledge;
- writing should follow an outline;
- paragraphs have a structural shape, invariably introduced by a topic sentence.

In a critique of this perspective, Dobrin (1989) examined the fundamental assumptions guiding much technical writing instruction and concluded that many of these assumptions do not explain how technical writing in the workplace is actually done; or, when technical writing does follow this line of instructional training, why it is done badly (cf. Reynolds *et al.* 1995). Dobrin sees the technical writing approaches practised in schools as making a number of assumptions about writing which can also be traced to cognitive writing models such as those following Flower and Hayes, particularly the assumption that writing is a straightforward problem-solving activity. As noted in Chapter 4, such an assumption may ignore much of the social context in which writing – any writing – occurs. For this reason, Dobrin argues that the notion of technical writing as technology or technique is misguided. Further, the notions of purely *objective* writing, unambiguous terminology, and clear definition are impossible without bringing in the situational intentions of the writer and the interpretive assumptions of who the reader may be. Dobrin also argues that the notion of information transfer, when applied to the technical writing process, is inappropriate because it suggests that writing can be reduced to a mechanical translating procedure; research on writing in the workplace, however, demonstrates that there is considerable 'noise' from (1) the writer's background, (2) the intention of the message, and (3) the lexico-syntactic choices made.

From his perspective, Dobrin suggests that technical writing is distinct from other sorts of writing, but that certain features of technical writing cannot be mechanically isolated as critical defining signals of the genre or subject matter. Rather, technical writing is as difficult to understand and teach as any other type of writing; its understanding and productive skill derive from knowledge and experience, from steady practice, and from frequent failure. One should not look to technical writing instruction as some sort of panacea that has somehow escaped other writing teachers and researchers (see also Anderson 1985, Doheny-Farina 1986, MacKinnon 1993, Odell 1985).

A better understanding of writing in non-educational contexts involves examining the actual writing and, where possible, studying the writing processes being used by writers in these contexts.

6.3   Writing in non-academic contexts

In the 1980s, a number of writing researchers recognized the need to understand how well, or how badly, US tertiary students were being prepared for the writing they would have to do in professional/business careers after graduation. It was widely perceived that general tertiary-level composition courses were not, by themselves, an adequate preparation, nor were technical writing classes a sufficient response. One approach introduced at the tertiary level of instruction consisted of proposing 'writing across the curriculum', a notion which required that all tertiary-level courses and departments – regardless of their technical content – jointly take responsibility for students' writing abilities (Ackerman 1993, Kaufer and Young 1993, Kinneavy 1987). Such an approach to writing, it was argued, would guarantee a greater quantity of writing practice, more specialized assignments related to a student's primary field of study, and an awareness that writing development is the responsibility of all tertiary-level faculty (see Chapter 4). A second approach was to study the writing tasks, attitudes, and expectations of people on the job – to determine what were in fact the writing demands placed on tertiary-level graduates in non-academic settings. This latter research approach has demonstrated that writing in the professional and business contexts is both highly valued and complex (Couture and Rymer 1993, Odell and Goswami 1985, Reynolds *et al.* 1995).

In a comprehensive study and review of other survey research on writing in the workplace, Anderson (1985) presented a picture of writing needs in non-academic contexts which could not be addressed simply by the kinds of technical writing courses critiqued by Dobrin (1989; see also MacKinnon 1993). He found that writing in professional contexts involved many factors which could not be reduced to simple pedagogical solutions. Anderson (1985) carried out a survey of university graduates (7 different fields of study, 841 respondents) to answer the following questions:

1. How important is writing in the workplace?
2. What sort of writing is actually done?
3. How much writing is typically done, by whom?
4. To whom do people write most?
5. Why do they write – that is, what is their purpose?
6. Does length of employment change the amount of writing?

Writing turned out to be very important in the workplace – 93 per cent of respondents in his survey said that writing is of some importance and 57 per cent stated that writing is of great/critical importance. In general, writing is seen as an integral part of most professional employment. While a few surveys have indicated that certain job categories require less writing (e.g. retail and whole-sale trades, and blue-collar manufacturing jobs), most job categories have been found to be consistent with the finding that writing is basic to most types of employment.

Writing on the job varies to a considerable degree across a number of variables. Questions of audience, purpose, and topic all shape writing. It is true that a number of writing formats predominate: letters, memos, forms, and instructions are frequently recurring genres in workplaces. Less common, though important, genres include: internal reports, progress reports, and project proposals. Only a small number of employees are requested to publish articles (though for this minority, such activity is extremely important). One consequence of this finding is that technical writing in schools is perceived as useful; it does assist students with practice in a number of standard genres such as letters, memos, and instructions. The standard forms of these genres are seen as important in the workplace because they provide a quick and clear cognitive frame for information transfer, and thus are functionally useful for effective and efficient communication. The importance of audience is stressed in all surveys. Writers in the workplace always emphasize that audience selection strongly influences their writing – depending on whether the writing is intended to be read by a subordinate, a colleague, a superior, a customer, or a company-external official.

Most respondents to Anderson's (1985) survey said that they spent a substantial amount of time writing in the workplace:

69 per cent claim to write more than 10 per cent of the time,
38 per cent wrote more than 20 per cent of the time,
15 per cent wrote more than 40 per cent of the time.

Thus, almost 40 per cent stated that they spent at least the equivalent of one full day of work during the work-week doing some sort of writing. These findings have been amply supported by other subsequent research.

It was also found that writers in the workplace write to persons within the organization much more frequently than they do to persons external to the place of work. Paradis *et al.* (1985) found that internal written communication was clearly the most important use of writing in the workplace, particularly in the professional research context, and they found that writing served many different functions. Other surveys were divided on the percentage of writing sent to superiors, colleagues, or subordinates. The general conclusion to be drawn is that there is broad variation in the intended audience.

The purposes for writing are:

- to distribute information
- to give instructions or orders
- to respond to memos and letters
- to complete forms for record keeping
- to propose new alternatives and options.

Most of this writing is done in the major genre formats: letters, memos, and forms. Ethnographic research on this question has brought out a number of other purposes for writing in the professional context which are not normally presented as functions for writing, though their roles in the workplace are crucial (Faigley 1985, Spilka 1993b). Paradis *et al.* (1985) state that these roles – which define, and are defined by, the social context of the workplace – include:

- establishing cooperative research networks
- verifying work progress
- allowing self-promotion
- stimulating ideas
- educating colleagues.

In general, writers on the job felt that their own writing skills were good, though writing skills in the workplace overall were perceived to be weak. Newer employees tended to overstate their writing skills more than older workers. Most workers thought that the writing courses in college were important, particularly those in technical writing and business communication.

Odell (1985), in ethnographic research on writing in the bureaucratic context, pointed out two additional factors to consider. Much writing involves collaboration, checking with colleagues about facts, relevant background information, identification of possible additional readers of the document, etc. In addition, audience concepts are not necessarily determined by knowing specifically who will be reading the document; rather, much of the sense of audience develops from past experiences with writing and feedback received from supervisors. Thus, collaboration and prior experience with very specific contexts play important roles in writing in the workplace (see also Reynolds *et al.* 1995).

Research on writing in the workplace points to a number of issues for writing instruction. Anderson (1985) includes the following four general suggestions:

- explaining the importance of writing in these contexts;
- attending to general writing skills for clear, concise and well-organized prose;
- addressing a variety of audiences;
- practising a variety of writing tasks and types.

Odell (1985) suggests, in addition, that general frameworks for organizing writing may be less useful than tasks involving very specific background and social context information typical of the workplace environment (see also Reynolds *et al.* 1995).

6.4 English for Special Purposes and advanced writing instruction

A first concern for ESL/EFL contexts is whether writing is sufficiently important for students that it needs to be taught explicitly, to a high level of sophistication, and on a large scale. It would seem that in many EFL contexts, the great majority of students (particularly those learning basic English skills to complete secondary school requirements, to sit national examinations, or to seek improved employment opportunities), do not need extensive writing instruction. The extent to which they might be called upon to practise sophisticated writing in English is extremely limited. Instead, the focus of writing instruction in EFL contexts may more profitably be placed on the training of skilled professionals

who are more likely to interact with English-speaking professionals, whether for job-related purposes, for scientific research, or for
professional/academic exchanges. Until recently, it was rare for
an EFL curriculum to require such high levels of writing sophistication.

It is now well established that English is the primary world language of science and technology. A number of researchers have
provided consistent evidence of this fact. Large (1983) was among
the first to present the arguments by examining the language distribution of scientific publications. After looking at language of
publication and language of article citation from a number of
indexes and abstracting sources, he concluded that the use of
English for scientific and technical publications is enormous and
growing (e.g. for biological abstracts, 77 per cent [1965], 87 per
cent [1977], 88 per cent [1980]; for medicine abstracts, 51 per
cent [1965], 76 per cent [1978]; for physics, 73 per cent [1965],
87 per cent [1977]). Similar results from a number of other
sources confirm this overall trend (Baldauf 1986, Baldauf and
Jernudd 1983, 1987, Grabe 1988b, Kaplan 1993, Laponce 1987,
Maher 1987, Medgyes and Kaplan 1992). The dominant role of
English in these fields creates serious potential problems for information access and retrieval in places where English is not a
commonly used/learned language. This situation arose as a result
of three historical phenomena that occurred within a relatively
short timespan.

First, the nature of scientific research changed in certain directions. The present century is often described as a technological
age; but all ages before the present century have also been technological ages as the human species has always been involved with
technology. Indeed, the presence of technology is a defining characteristic of the species. What is different about the current time is
the *speed* of technological change rather than the character of
such change, making the management of, and access to, information a major enterprise.

Second, at the conclusion of the Second World War, the United
States was the only major industrialized nation with its educational
and technological infrastructure fully in place. Following the war,
the scientific influence of the USA advanced, and the USA
became both the largest contributor to the pool of scientific information and the greatest user of such information. Consequently,
the USA succeeded to the control of this information (Grabe and

Kaplan 1986, Kaplan 1992, van Naersson and Kaplan 1987), and control of the system also meant control of the definition of the categories through which the system was organized. Thus, the underlying infrastructure now relies upon an English-based sociology of knowledge.

Third, the great automated information storage and retrieval networks which have gradually evolved over the past half-century are based on the capacity of the computer to deal with huge quantities of information. Because the inception of information network development coincided with the end of the Second World War, the Allies played a significant role in determining how those systems would be structured and, by political agreement, virtually all information entered into the great networks must be either written in or abstracted in English, French, German, or Russian. Furthermore, there has been little requirement for Western scientists to worry about learning other languages, and there has been little pressure on system managers to hurry the development of the capacity to deal with non-Roman scripts (Large 1983).

The coincidence of these three factors implies that nations which do not have access to either English or the information systems are limited by their inability to cope with information or to modify the information to make it locally useful. The transfer and adaptation of information is not only a problem of technical content but also a problem of language, of language variety, of cultural bias, and of intercultural understanding (Shuchman 1981). The developing nation is, in this sense, a dependent on the advanced country's information storage and access sophistication. As a consequence, English has become the language of science and technology, and the teaching of this language has become a world-wide activity (cf. Phillipson 1992).

Given this scenario, most developing countries have found it necessary to train enough translators and researchers to a sufficient level of English language proficiency to be able to access scientific and technical information. In many cases, the advanced language skills have been combined with professional training – a strategy accomplished by sending students to the USA or the UK for university and professional studies/research.

There have been two primary responses to the ESL/EFL science and technology focus. In ESL contexts, the primary response has been to prepare students for all the academic language skills required for tertiary study (English for Academic Purposes [EAP]). Defined in many cases as pre-academic study at the tertiary level, this training then is intended to prepare students for the ubiquitous composition course requirement, at least for most US tertiary level institutions. The EAP curricular sequence leads international students through the same writing instruction and writing problems faced by English L1 students. Thus, at advanced levels of study, many of the issues raised for writing in L1 contexts apply equally to ESL students. In EFL contexts, a major response on the part of applied linguists has been to provide various types of English for Specific Purposes (ESP) programmes, and, in particular, English for Science and Technology (EST) courses. English for Specific Purposes syllabi have been the source of considerable controversy when applied to situations for training advanced level students in sophisticated English language skills (as opposed to short-term occupational training).

The history of ESP is primarily UK-oriented, ESP being an instructional approach for students who needed some English language skills, usually a reading ability, and who only had limited time in their training to learn English amid all their other academic requirements. A brief review of this history is essential to understanding the research directions which grew out of ESP as well as the criticisms and ultimate limitations of this approach for advanced level language learning (including writing).

In two major sources which trace the development of ESP up to the 1980s, Robinson (1992) and Swales (1985) examine:

- its pragmatic origins,
- its early emphasis on register analysis and morphosyntactic frequency studies,
- its use of discourse analysis for the study of rhetorical structuring in scientific texts, and
- the stress on communicative language use for teaching.

(See also Johns and Dudley-Evans 1991, van Naerssen and Kaplan 1987.)

These trends have continued through the 1980s and the early 1990s with additional questions being raised about the effectiveness of ESP as a separate entity, distinct from more general academic-oriented instruction (i.e. EAP).

In the 1960s, pragmatic questions about the need to train students in English in technical contexts led applied linguists to look for those formal features which distinguish technical and scientific writing from other types of writing. This approach provided a number of insights into register variation, discourse analysis, and, more recently, genre analysis. Barber (1962, in Swales 1985), in one of the first studies of scientific writing, identified a number of formal features of this register, many of which are now generally taken as received knowledge:

> long sentence length (words/sentence); many complex noun and adjective phrases; many non-finite subordinate phrases and clauses; many infinitive clauses; many occurrences of the verb BE (in all conjugations); many conditional structures; a relatively greater number of passive structures; a relatively greater number of relative clauses; a relatively greater proportion of simple present tense verbs; a relatively greater number of past participles; a smaller number of progressive tense forms; a smaller number of past tense verbs; few questions; and few contractions.

Later research on the formal features of register analysis has added other features (e.g. a greater number of lexical repetitions, few pronouns, a greater number of prepositional phrases), and combined these features with functional interpretations explaining *why* certain features of text would appear and, in the overall structure of the text, *when* they are most likely to appear (e.g. Lackstrom *et al.* 1973 for tense shifts; Tarone *et al.* 1981 for passive voice uses).

In the 1970s, the study of scientific texts shifted from specific formal features to the organization of the overall discourse. Rhetorical analyses of texts and the application of patterns of arrangement in the discourse became a major research focus (e.g. Trimble 1985), and this line of study continues to the present in research on genre analysis and text type variation, particularly among functional/systemic/Hallidayan linguists (Bhatia 1993, Dudley-Evans 1989, Halliday and Martin 1993, Hoey 1983, 1994, Martin 1985, 1992, Martin and Rothery 1986, Swales 1981, 1991).

The debate over the importance of ESP is focused on the question of whether scientific and technical language is sufficiently distinguishable from more general academic language to merit separate instruction. Hutchinson and Waters (1987) and Widdowson (1983) argue for an approach to ESP which does not require a strong separation for more general language training of an EAP orientation. While Widdowson makes the case that scientific and technical prose is identifiable as a distinct genre type, he argues that many of the skills and strategies for more general language learning transfer directly to the study of technical information; therefore, a larger EAP orientation to language learning provides a good foundation for students in technical fields of study. This is a position which is now popular, particularly among applied linguists who have become disillusioned by the promises of earlier ESP training curricula. Hutchinson and Waters take the somewhat more extreme position that scientific and technical prose is really not different from other prose text types (a somewhat dubious view, given the large volume of current research on text types and genre variation). For them, then, whether one employs a general curriculum, or a curriculum including technical material makes little difference in language teaching.

Whichever position is more accurate matters less than the more general observation that advanced language instruction for academic/professional purposes may now be viewed as more closely related to discussions of academic – and writing – instruction which centres on English L1 contexts. Both are concerned with the general preparation of students to write successfully in academic contexts, principally at tertiary level institutions in the USA and the UK.

Swales (1990) suggests that the above debate, in some respects, misses the primary issue for ESP instruction. The debate is perhaps not whether students should receive training in general academic English for special purposes; rather, the issue concerns *when* students should receive general academic English training and *when* they should specialize in discipline-specific English-language training. For Swales, the answer is that ESP instruction, at least at academic institutions, should represent one aspect of advanced training, and in particular, involve specialized writing instruction. The argument is that learning to write in sophisticated discipline-specific genres is time-consuming and is only essential as students move into advanced training. In advanced learning contexts, then, students need to be trained in the genre structures that are valued by a given discipline; in such cases, the considerable time invested in this training is worth the effort. Of course, it is also at this point that many native-English students need specialized training in specific genres such as proposal writing, grant writing, letters of enquiry, letters of application, and the natural sciences research articles, etc.

Thus, the history of ESP has come full circle for advanced language learners. The primary locus of training for these students is in advanced tertiary – undergraduate and post-graduate – institutions, where the ability to write well becomes a critical skill. This writing skill, in advanced professional and academic contexts, is shown to be more than a matter of knowing various language structures and discourse strategies. The problem is that scientists and technicians communicate within their own networks based in various professional communities (see the discussion of discourse communities in Chapter 4).

A physical phenomenon may be studied from a variety of backgrounds by many scientists who may arrive at the same basic result, but individual scientists – and individual disciplines – may approach the problem quite differently. These differences may be the result of various ways of thinking, which are in turn shaped by cultural phenomena including educational, rhetorical, political, and philosophical systems. While there is no question that physics is physics, regardless of where in the world it is performed – and it is quite clear that there is no 'Chinese physics' as distinct from 'English physics' – the fact remains that the application of physics varies enormously from place to place and from time to time. The most obvious cases of this variation occur across cultures, but significant variation also occurs within cultures across time (see Atkinson 1993) and even within professional discourse communities. This variation is often the product of groups of individuals who decide, consciously or unconsciously, what is legitimate knowledge, and how to construct their disciplines. The basis for such a view of science and scientific knowledge is known as social construction, and that view now plays a significant role in both knowledge theory and writing theory.

6.5   Writing in professional/research contexts

The social construction of scientific information is, then, a final area of research on specialized writing for scientific or technical publication. This research direction has become especially important for a number of reasons: first, it provides a very different view of the text construction features of scientific texts; second, it confirms the importance for writing research on the social and rhetorical contexts of writing; and, third, it creates a locus where applied linguists and rhetoricians converge in the study of writing in a real-world context. The central issue concerns the nature of scientific writing as it occurs in specific contexts – in particular, in the context of the research laboratory.

Science writing, as seen through the finished text, appears to conform to certain well-documented generalizations said to represent the scientific 'style' of writing. The underlying assumption concerning this style is that it faithfully and accurately reflects the experimental process that occurred in the laboratory. In fact, however, research in the sociology of science indicates that the relationship between the experimental method of the laboratory and the text in which it is reported is anything but straightforward. The shaping of a written text by a writer reflects deeply embedded cultural and rhetorical assumptions about what materials may be presented, how those materials are to be organized, and how they may be represented in a maximally acceptable way – not necessarily in a way that is objectively most transparent. Such writing may, then, be seen not only as constituting a social act, but as constituting an act falling within a total social construct (Bazerman 1988, 1993, Geisler 1994). To put it a slightly different way, writing is both context constrained and context creating; not only is writing a response to some need to express, but it is also simultaneously contributing to, reinforcing, and redefining notions of what may be construed as part of the knowledge-canon and of what may be construed as 'writable'.

It is frequently claimed, with considerable validity, that science is cumulative – that is, that the discoveries of a given scientist depend in no small degree upon the work of previous scientists, and that the new discoveries as a matter of course will, then, become part of the scientific canon available to ensuing generations of scientists. In fact, the situation is probably much more complex (see Bazerman 1983, 1988). Scientists seeking to publish, or to have grant requests favourably reviewed, are constrained because they are impacted not only by the passive weight of previous science defined as a knowledge canon, but also by the ascendant 'knowledge matrix', including the dominant paradigm and the view of the most respected researchers currently being published and/or funded.

The ascendant knowledge matrix influences strongly what can be defined as science:

- what may be observed
- how it can be reported
- what is considered evidence
- how is evidence arranged
- how is scholarly argument conducted so that it becomes acceptable to the scientific community.

The notion of scientific writing as pure objective reporting is a myth promulgated by the science community itself. Objective fact is only what the dominant group says it is (except for what Bazerman (1983, 1991) calls *passive resistance* – a set of incontrovertible facts derived from the past); and the reporting of objective knowledge becomes the means by which the myth is maintained.

Scientific writing is also substantiated through the concept of replicability; in principle, any experiment reported in the scientific literature can be replicated by other scientists and, through such replication, verified. In reality, few experimental descriptions, as they appear in the published literature, provide adequate information to permit independent replication. Thus, the criterion of replication from description becomes, similarly, a myth (see Collins 1985, Gilbert and Mulkay 1984, Mulkay 1979).

The examination of science writing – indeed, of any writing – normally should occur at three levels:

- the surface structure level,
- the rhetorical level, and
- the level of assumption – in this case, scientific assumptions, and their potential instability.

In the past, much research has occurred at the surface structure level; some (though not a great deal) has occurred at the rhetorical (or functional) level (see Bhatia 1993, Biber 1988, Grabe 1987, Kaplan 1987, Swales 1990, Swales and Najjar 1987, Trimble 1985); and perhaps less has occurred at the level of the sociology of science (which may be considered the *genuine* rhetorical level), though a considerable output has occurred at this level over the past ten years.

In order to understand how the genres of science writing are produced, it is necessary to take into account all three levels (or layers, or courses) of their construction (or organization). Should any of the levels be disregarded, the understanding of science

genres will necessarily be distorted. Differences among various
genres, then, can be investigated through the surface structural
form, through the functional and organizational logic of the text,
and through the rhetorical features (including aims) which cir-
cumscribe the text as a whole.

The third level of research into science text – the level of
assumptions and aims – requires some preliminary discussion of
the sociology of science as it applies to writing (specifically to text
organization). However, before discussing science genres in this
context, a brief digression dealing with rhetorical and composition theory may be appropriate. It is through such theory that the
role of the sociology of science in science writing can be understood and interpreted. Faigley (1986), in a review of process
theories of composition, argues that contemporary theories of
writing are turning increasingly towards considerations of the writing context and are drawing on the recent research in writing in
scientific communities to illustrate how the assumptions of a particular discipline impact both the reading and the writing of text.
At the heart of his review is the important notion that writing
occurs within a structure of power, and, consequently, that the
structure of power must be taken into consideration in any analysis of writing.

Similarly, research on social construction and on the sociology
of knowledge are introduced by Bruffee (1986) into the context
of studies on rhetoric and composing. He shows how such considerations determine the subject matter, the audience expectation,
and the rhetorical organization of text. Drawing on the important
work of Bakhtin (1981), Geertz (1973, 1983), Kuhn (1970), and
Rorty (1979), Bruffee defines social construction as the creation
of 'reality, knowledge, thought, facts, texts, selves, and so on ... as
generated by communities of like-minded peers' (1986: 774). This
conceptualization is in contrast to the cognitive view of knowledge
and language – a view that is widely held among scientists and
laypersons. The social constructionist view, instead, perceives reality as constructed out of social relations within the research
community. This co-constructed reality maintains the coherence
and the power structure of the research community (through,
perhaps less so, sets of well-established physical facts). According
to Bruffee, there is, in this theoretical view, no tension between
objective and subjective; everything is subjective. In sum, individuals use writing (and language more generally) (a) to help them

become members of communities, (b) to cement relations with a community, and (c) to determine and define who they are and what they believe within a discourse community of peers.

Bizzell (1982, 1986a, 1986b, 1993) concurs with this view that discourse communities are central as the locus of power and as a source of acceptance for the writer functioning as a scholar contributing to a given discipline. Similarly, Atkinson (1993), in a study of the rhetorical development of the *Philosophical Transactions* of the Royal Society from 1695 to 1975, has shown the ways in which the preferred structure of scientific articles has changed under the pressure of changing views of science and of the collective personae of scientists (see also Bazerman 1993, Berkenkotter and Huckin 1993, Olsen 1993, Rafoth 1990).

The importance of social construction as an ongoing force in composition is reinforced by the research of rhetoricians and sociologists who have analysed scientific discourse from the perspective of social construction and/or from the perspective of the sociology of science. Beginning with Kuhn (1970 – a benchmark analysis), researchers have shown through careful participant observation how scientific knowledge is constructed. As Bruffee notes, scientific knowledge is a social construct, not a discovery of 'what is out there' (1986: 779). The clearest indication of the validity of this conceptualization occurs when knowledge ceases to be knowledge: this phenomenon occurs when a scientific community disbands, or when its members simply die off – as, for example, in the cases of American structural linguistics, and later Generative Semantic – two theoretical linguistics movements which faded in the 1960s and late 1970s, respectively (cf. Langacker 1995).

Bazerman (1988, 1993), Collins (1985), Gilbert and Mulkay (1984), Latour (1987), Latour and Woolgar (1979), Lynch (1985), and Myers (1985, 1990) have all observed and analysed scientists at work, tracing the progression from experiment to description to publication in a journal (or grant submission). All of this research shows quite clearly that writing for publication (and/or grant submission) is not a matter of reporting findings objectively; rather, it involves the interpretation and modification of information, the citation of appropriate 'authoritative' literature, and the imitation of appropriate models in order to be accepted, and, in turn, to become part of the authoritative establishment and its literature. As Gilbert and Mulkay point out, the seriously difficult part of scientific journal writing is that part of the process in which key questions are asked is refined rhetorically so that it will be acceptable to the peer community. These issues are discussed extensively by Bazerman, perhaps the most productive rhetorician/researcher of writing in scientific communities from a sociology-of-science perspective (e.g. 1988, 1993). His arguments, because they are germane to the discussion throughout this chapter, are outlined here in detail. In an early (1983) study, Bazerman comments on the difficulty involved in the study of scientific writing:

1. Published articles in science do not reflect what actually happens in a laboratory; they omit false starts, digressions, and failed procedures. They also omit those factors initially underlying the choice of problem as well as factors motivating the research design used to investigate the problem.

2. Published reports seldom supply adequate information to permit other independent researchers to replicate the experiment.

3. Reader research among the readership of scientific papers suggests that the acceptance of claims made in scientific papers is dependent on factors other than the proof actually offered in the paper itself.

On the basis of these observations, Bazerman (1983: 158) raises an important question:

> If a scientific paper is not a complete account of a scientist's observations and doings, nor a tightly reasoned deductive proof of claims, nor an unproblematic conveyor of claims to be evaluated fairly and promptly, what indeed is the scientific paper communicating, and to whom?

Bazerman answers the question by proposing that scientific writing is the result of a writer's effort to be placed into an accepted research programme deriving from (and defined by) currently accepted theory.

> Each scientific contribution is to be understood against the background of the existing research program, the problems the program proposes, and the evolution of the program in response to new findings. Consequently, in order to communicate the point and value of new work, the scientific writer would be well advised to understand how his or her new contribution fits within the continuity of the problems of the relevant research program....

> More concretely from the writer's point of view, the writer must
> know the problems of the field, the ideals and ethos of the field, the
> accepted justificatory arguments, the institutional structure in which
> the knowledge is to be communicated, and the criteria of adequacy
> by which the innovative work will be judged.
>
> (Bazerman 1983: 160–1)

It is certainly true that scientific writing builds upon the work of
prior researchers – that scientific research is a cumulative process;
but this trend implicates more than the objective impartial development of science. A researcher ignoring the major accepted
views runs the risk of being ignored once in print, attacked on
irrelevant grounds, or simply not published at all. Escape from
this pressure is difficult and is rarely achieved. Major shifts in paradigm – in theory, in possible research questions, or in permissible
research designs – are not often the result of singular reported
research; rather, such shifts come about through the gradual
accretion of dissatisfaction or difficulty with the accepted
approaches. When two distinctly different research matrices com-
pete for acceptance, the tenor of scientific writing changes to
become more persuasive, as appeals and arguments are mar-
shalled to reassert the value of individual pieces of the matrix.

All of this is not to claim that the social nature of scientific
research is capricious; even in the most turbulent periods, as
Bazerman points out, competing approaches must take into
account what has been called 'passive constraint' (Fleck 1935) –
observations about nature that have been collected and measured
and are so widely accepted as basic that they must be accounted
for in any theory. Scientific research is constrained by facts too
widely accepted to be ignored (cf. Gilbert and Mulkay 1984). This,
then, is the background for any discussion of scientific writing as a
social act within a social context – the social construction of scientific reality.

Bazerman (1983, 1988) suggests that there are four main areas
which collectively illustrate the social co-construction of science:

- the writing process
- the textual form
- the dissemination process
- the audience response.

It is important to note that the writing process and the research
activity appear to be co-extensive. The pre-writing stage is

coincident with the beginnings of the research activity and usually extends over a considerable time period; by contrast, the actual writing of the results often occurs over a very brief period. During the extended pre-writing phase, the scientific paper acquires its shape. Laboratory research regularly involves tinkering – moment by moment rethinking and adjusting as the research progresses – to the point at which the specific problem and its possible analysis crystallizes; and this process is recursive, continuing throughout the research phase. In laboratory research, the choice of problem or question to be addressed is selective; that is, the researcher is led towards certain questions and away from others by the constraints imposed within the dominant research matrix. To some extent, research questions are defined by available instrumentation; that is, a paradigm defines the instruments needed to evaluate it. To some extent research questions are economically defined; the available economic resources, the potential for achieving recognition, and the state of experimental resources all constrain funding support. In sum, the development of scientific research is dependent upon a range of decisions which are social and strategic.

With respect to textual form, the rhetorical level plays a greater shaping role than the surface structural level. Scientific writing, if it is to achieve acceptability, must appear to be more universally applicable than the confines of any particular research laboratory. As a consequence, a significant amount of persuasion is required to establish new criteria for evaluating research and to lend credibility to the results being reported (including the judicious use of appropriate citations); the published report is a persuasive document whose purpose is to increase the value of the researcher's ideas (and the persona of the researcher) within a particular market. As Bazerman (1983: 169) notes:

> The paper must first reconstruct the market, define the needs of the market, and identify the research being reported as the proper vehicle for the satisfaction of those needs. The paper must then fulfill the mandate it has constructed by demonstrating that its solution to the market needs was in fact achieved in the laboratory.

In short, the textual form of a scientific paper is less objective and more persuasive than would normally be assumed.

With respect to research papers, two primary modes of dissemination are available – the informal and the formal. The informal mode represents what might be termed 'word-of-mouth' communication, through conference presentations and the circulation of draft manuscripts. This mode may provide the best means for the maintenance of stable research areas and for the replication of results (Gilbert and Mulkay 1984).

The formal mode occurs through the publication of papers in journals, invoking the referee system. Journals reflect the concerns of referees as representatives of the larger audience which a paper is intended to reach. As research fields achieve greater consensus with reference to what constitutes important research issues, the likelihood of acceptance of a paper which conforms to the expectations of referees is great; by the same token, the acceptability of a paper which does not clearly conform to those expectations diminishes. Thus, scientific writing arises within a social context wherein the writing is responsive to the accumulated writing of others, and where the author is able to manipulate what actually appears in text, within the established limits of 'passive constraints' (Bazerman 1983). The long-term accumulation of evidence and argument provides a continuum in research acting as a corrective to the excesses of any particular research programme or theory; thus, mistaken findings and misunderstandings are corrected.

The social co-construction of science requires salesmanship as an essential characteristic of scientific writing (Czubaroff 1989, Prelly 1989); if other scientists can be persuaded and intrigued, the greater will be the number of scientists working on similar problems and reporting findings of a similar nature (Bazerman 1985). Myers (1985), examining the work of two particular biologists, found, as Bazerman had, that the biologists were required to account for the interests of their peer audience, for the domain of knowledge which constituted the accepted canon, for the need to sell their product on the open market, and for the rhetorical significance of their own writing. Looking specifically at grant proposal writing, Myers (1985: 220) notes:

> Most researchers would grant that proposal writing is a rhetorical activity in which the writer seeks a strategy for persuading a reluctant audience. There is a paradox here because the proposal format, with its standard questions about background goals and budget, and the scientific report style, with its passives and impersonality, do not allow for most types of rhetorical appeals; one must persuade without seeming to persuade. Yet almost every sentence is charged with

rhetorical significance. In classical rhetorical terms, the forms of the appeal in the proposal are ethical and pathetic as well as logical; one shows that one is able to do the work, that the work is potentially interesting to one's audience of other researchers, as well as showing that one is right.

Myers takes the view that this demand on scientific writing is essential to the health of scientific inquiry because it reinforces the consensus-building process which is necessary to the ongoing discovery of scientific knowledge, even if the formal writing act itself contributes only a small part of that necessary consensus-building. Thus, scientific knowledge is a socially constructed belief system, explainable in relation to historical and social forces. The objective façade of science masks the intense rhetorical manipulation within the restrictions imposed by the surface form of the research report. In the short run, empirical fact may not always carry the day; rather, the most successful persuader – the writer with the most appealing argument – often triumphs (Myers 1986). Thus, there is the need for the kind of consensus-building which both Myers and Bazerman refer to as the corrective for temporary misunderstanding or error.

Of particular interest in Myer's review is his effort to relate the sociology of science to writing research and writing instruction. He notes that the view of writing available through social construction makes possible a top-down analysis, beginning with the social forces which shape the underlying assumptions of the writing act. This contrasts sharply with the more linguistically oriented analyses of science writing, which are bottom-up structured, and which examine local surface forms to determine the constraints of particular text genres. Myers suggests that neither approach is, in itself, sufficient; he believes it to be essential for researchers to understand the discourse community in order to unravel the structure and purpose of text.

> The major lesson for writing researchers is that we cannot limit our studies to written texts, or to the controlled observations of individuals developed by cognitive researchers, but must get out into the field and enter into the flow of language and work. Again and again I realized what (perhaps necessary) limitations I was making in considering just texts, even draft after draft of revision.
>
> (Myers 1986: 606)

The understanding of scientific text genres, the constraints on their creation, the forces shaping the (published) product, and the persuasive intent masked within the ostensibly objective format collectively require a perspective on scientific writing which goes beyond, though it does not exclude, traditional applied linguistic approaches to research on scientific text. In precisely the same way that it is difficult to penetrate the differences between texts in two different linguistic systems, it is difficult to penetrate the differences between scientific texts and other types of text within the same linguistic system (cf. Hutchinson and Waters 1987). The latter difficulty may result from the fact that scientific text belongs less to a particular linguistic system than it does to an international interdisciplinary community unique to science writing (e.g. Merton 1973).

Whatever the cause of this difficulty, there are central questions to be asked about the construction of science genre and the available resources to teach such writing skills to anyone; it is particularly difficult to teach scientific writing skills to individuals who are primary participants in language systems other than English and who may simultaneously be participants in communities in which literacy is recent and non-intensive. When such students enter traditional language programmes to learn to write science text, or when they enter special-purpose language instruction, they are, in fact, being asked to understand not only the lexical, syntactic, and rhetorical systems of the target language, but also the assumptions underlying science writing and the requirements implicit in science publication.

In sum, science writing constitutes a value-laden rhetorical activity. Science writers – particularly if they are writing in English (generally accepted as the international language of science and technology), and particularly if English is not their first language – need to possess a complex set of skills which are only partially definable in linguistic terms. They need to:

- have a highly sophisticated sense of appropriate areas of research, of proper research questions, and of acceptable research designs;
- be cognizant of intertextuality – that is, have a clear sense of what others have had to say on the topic and know how to incorporate that material into their text;
- be able to align their own work with the recognized leadership in the field so that the leadership will (seem to) legitimize their work;

- have a highly sophisticated sense of audience; that is, be aware of what will influence peer reviewers and the general readership in the discipline;
- be able to convey the necessary (and necessarily) rhetorically charged information through appropriate mechanisms of persuasion within the constraints of a formal objective format.

This listing of requisite skills illustrates the problem of most language instruction:

First, the continuing insistence on the substitution of grammatical instruction for discourse instruction, or the equation of the two, simply prevents attention from being directed to the problem site.

Second, the persistence of the view that external reality can be objectively represented means that productive rhetorical forms in the creation of science text will be undervalued; this trend is powerful even in those instructional programmes that have recognized the importance of rhetorical instruction,

Third, the absence of any attention in the teaching of discourse to epistemological issues forces the focus in such courses to fall on secondary issues; that is, courses ignore the fact that science writing can only be understood in terms of the contemporary sociology of science and in terms of the whole pre-existing body of science texts. Further, when the learner is a member of a discourse community alien to all of these considerations, the problem is vastly more complicated. It is in part complicated by a universalist tendency to claim that there is no significant difference between texts in various languages, or to claim that, if any differences exist, they only occur at the surface level.

That these difficulties persist in instructional programmes should be no surprise since the same issues beset research in discourse analysis. Researchers in the discourse of science do not yet know what it is necessary to know in order to understand the rhetoric of science text, whether in the form of the published report or the grant proposal, the introductory science text, or the popular science article (cf. Bazerman 1993, Bhatia 1993, Lemke 1995, Swales 1990).

Contrastive rhetoric may offer one informative approach to scientific text from a discourse perspective; that is, it provides both motivation and mechanisms for text analysis, though it needs to adopt the sociology-of-science orientation to be useful for text analysis within particular languages. In the final analysis, however, it is far more important to broaden pedagogical bases so that language learners can in fact become aware of the complex reticulated systems of constraints that exist in text.

It remains highly unlikely that the unmodified 'process approach' to teaching composition will prove to be sufficient. The kinds of knowledge that a writer is expected to have in science writing – in addition to a thorough grasp of the lexical, syntactic, semantic, and rhetorical systems of the language – is not likely to be acquired through exercises in keeping a journal or in composing narrative or descriptive texts of a far more general type. It will be necessary to rethink writing instruction, and in that rethinking to recognize that there is more to the composing of texts than is normally assumed in the linguistic system; traditional linguistic knowledge is necessary but not sufficient. To the extent that science texts are about science, epistemological issues must be addressed; indeed, to the extent that any text has a content carried through its linguistic and rhetorical structure, epistemological questions need to be addressed.

It is possible that the constraints on science writing are special; but it is also possible that similar types of constraints apply to all writing intended for any but the most general audiences. For example, though the preceding discussion has focused on scientific and technical text, similar problems are involved in the teaching of writing in law. Legal text has not been submitted to quite as much scrutiny as scientific text. On the other hand, law schools often provide special courses in legal writing. Such courses tend to suffer from the same kinds of concerns for convention that occur in virtually all technical/specialist writing instruction. However, because it is clear that the law is a linguistic construct – in that sense rather different from science – much more attention is given to the kind of formal logic which operates in writing about the law (Conley and O'Barr 1990, O'Barr 1982, Paradis 1991, Shuy 1987, 1991, Stygall 1991).

6.6 Specialized writing contexts and the teaching of writing

In the preceding sections of this chapter, a number of specialized contexts for the study of writing – each providing a somewhat different perspective – have been reviewed. The technical writing perspective, while criticized, nevertheless represents a general movement to respond to student needs as they leave tertiary education and enter the workplace and the professional environment. Technical writing courses provide students with extensive practice in the use of common formats such as letters, memoranda, and reports; they also stress the importance of form and the need for clarity, concision, and logical organization. These basic skills were perceived to be very important by writers in non-academic contexts when researchers actually explored writing in non-academic organizations.

Specialized writing skills are important for students whose native language is not English, whether in the UK, the USA, Canada, Australia, or in their own countries. As argued above, the need for sophisticated English language skills, including writing, constitutes a critical skill for some percentage of the professional and academic population of any country. This need explains the rise of English for Specific Purposes and, in particular, of English for Science and Technology courses.

The final extension of research on writing in specialized contexts has followed from research by rhetoricians and sociologists of science. In this approach, researchers have examined the uses of writing in advanced research contexts, primarily in academic laboratory settings, and a number of rather startling insights have emerged:

1. This research suggests that much science writing, assumed to be objective, disinterested, and factual, is in fact highly rhetorical and value-laden in nature.
2. This research supports social construction theories of knowledge wherein all knowledge is understood to be the creation of discourse communities rather than to exist 'out there in the world'.
3. This research demonstrates the importance of recognizing audience, establishing the intertextuality of ideas, and being persuasive without appearing to be so.

It is important to stress that the elimination of the 'objective' ground from beneath knowledge does not mean that knowledge is less important, only that knowledge is something that is negotiated; students need to understand the nature of such negotiation, the rules for engaging in this negotiation, and the translation of the rules deriving from negotiation of meaning into written discourse. Thus, rhetoric returns to writing instruction as a foundational discipline which informs all types of writing, scientific writing being just one of many domains in which the impact of rhetorical principles may be explored. One of these extensions of rhetorical principles involves the study of contrastive rhetoric. Research in this field has been evolving over the past 30 years and is now providing useful insights into both the writing product and the writing process. This, however, is the subject of the next chapter.

7

Writing across cultures:
contrastive rhetoric

7.1 Introduction

There have, historically, been two quite different ways of looking
at the nature of language, and each has led to a different theoretical posture. On the one hand, in what has been called 'general'
linguistics (also 'formal' or 'autonomous' linguistics), the object
of inquiry has traditionally been seen as an independent language
system composed of unique and invariant structural and semantic
rules. In contemporary linguistic thinking, this system is seen as
innate to human beings – a species-specific phenomenon
encoded into the genetic structure; given this biological explanation of its ontogeny, it is perfectly logical to investigate language as
a separate entity because it has an independent existence unrelated to human production or use. The relationship between that
system and the investigator is straightforward and unproblematic
– *subject–object*. The object of formal inquiry is a system description
in 'neutral' scientific language quite separate from the value-laden
characteristics of everyday language. Such description is thought
to give rise to rational predictions about the internal operations of
the system and about its future directions and development.

This view derives from the traditions of logical positivism and
scientific realism, and holds the promise of a parsimonious and
invariant description – a notion that has captured the imagination
of some linguists and has now extended into work in artificial
intelligence. Without doubt, this enterprise has produced useful
information and has discovered certain cognitive-linguistic structures that appear invariant, but it has fallen increasingly under
attack from scholars holding alternative views.

These alternative views are not to be conceived of as a single powerful theoretical thrust, though they do hold in common certain basic assumptions. Here, language is perceived not as an independent system, but rather as a human product and a social tool. The perception in this view is that, while the physical sciences deal with inanimate objects outside the human sphere, language is the product of the human mind and is therefore inseparable from that mind and all its attendant subjectivity, value-orientation, and emotion. The investigator is simultaneously both the subject and the object of inquiry; the study of language is the study of human beings; and the relationship can be described as *subject–subject*. Such a perception challenges, on logical grounds, the notion of the existence and objectification of language as well as the possibility of devising an invariant abstract model.

Given the complexity of language, the fact that language changes over time, and the fact that language exists within various cultural systems, it would be impossible to discover invariant laws as in physical sciences; thus, the study of language, at certain levels, must be descriptive rather than predictive and explanatory. In addition, it would be impossible to describe language in a context-free, neutral scientific language because there is constant movement between the parts and the whole with no absolute beginning and ending points. Contrastive rhetoric derives its origins from such a view.

Discourse study in general constitutes one member of this group of views. Discourse analysis recognizes the significance of social (and perhaps physical) *context* and, most importantly, of *prior text* in constituting meaning. And it has insisted on 'grounded' research. The recognition of *context* and *prior text*, however, increases the tension between an interpretive stance and an empirical one – a tension not yet satisfactorily addressed in discourse analysis and one which, in turn, exacerbates the rift between *quantitative* and *qualitative* research. Quantitative researchers preserve and often reify the language system's independent existence in at least some of its aspects, emphasizing certain structural continuities and regularities (on the basis of which empirical research can be undertaken), and showing that the system does have predictable structural properties which, appropriately defined, can be quantified and employed to build an abstract model (cf. Biber 1988, 1995, Biber and Finegan 1989, Grabe 1987).

At the same time, there is an increasing awareness that quantitative research needs to be augmented by some theory of the linguistic object that can account for its dynamism – by some integration between the characteristics of a particular corpus and both *contexts* and *prior texts*. Thus, there is a need to reach an understanding of the linguistic system before attempting structural and quantitative descriptions of it, and there is a need to acknowledge that such an understanding can probably only be achieved through interdisciplinary approaches.

One particular problem associated with the quantitative approach has been what is known as the 'disappearance of the phenomenon'. In scientific realism, the objective of empirical research is to capture an invariant objective reality through repeated testing of hypothetical correspondences that occur between models and observed phenomena (but, as has been observed elsewhere, such repeated, consistent testing is very difficult because published methods tends to limit consistent repetition). In the alternative view, deriving from the notions of Husserl, that sort of empiricism was conceived as an error traceable back to Galilean systematization because the notion *hypothesis–test–verification* is based on an assumption of the constancy of any given phenomenon. Such an assumption ignores the practical problems inherent in setting up a consistent measurement system, or an experiment which always does what it is supposed to do, or a survey employing a team of assistants; it is not a question of sound methodology, but rather of practical organization, and the result is the potential disappearance of the phenomenon. The need for objectivity, consistency across investigators, and so on, led to the replacement of the phenomenon by the artefacts of the methodology (e.g. data runs, variables, statistically derived factors, and so on).

To avoid this problem and to permit analysis of the phenomenon, a different, interpretive, empiricism developed, leading to the extraordinarily detailed analyses of texts, but the problem of replacing the text with artefacts of the method has not been completely solved. The concern with this problem has led to two alternative strategies: one deriving from the work of Sachs and his colleagues and gradually enlarging into the whole ethnomethodological enterprise (Schiffrin 1991, 1994), the other giving rise to the various techniques being employed in written discourse analysis (cf. Cooper and Greenbaum 1986, Coulthard 1994, Purves 1988, van Dijk 1985).

Another problem lies in the fact that both subject–object and subject–subject notions of the relationship between the investigator and the object of analysis are perceived as ahistorical. The interest in history in the context of text analysis is a very recent phenomenon. It became possible only when the notion of language as an invariant structure independent of human activity was abandoned; as long as language is perceived as genetically conditioned and independent of human agency, history is irrelevant. As soon as language is seen as a product of the human mind and as a tool, its continuing existence over time constitutes a theoretical problem which can only be approached from the historical perspective. But these opposing views also bring into focus an older dualism between structure and action (function) and the question of the impact of larger social structures on individual behaviour (cf. Kress 1991). The question of individual behaviour raises, in turn, the question of learning (acculturation, socialization) and the difficulty of modelling learning behaviour.

Contrastive rhetoric has its origins in notions of language structure, learning, and use which are not strongly autonomous, and its goal is to describe ways in which written texts operate in larger cultural contexts. It has sought to arrive at some understanding of the ways in which written language operates and the ways in which written language diverges from spoken language. It is interested in questions relating to the description of various genres – the question of whether or not these genres occur in various languages, and the questions of what constitutes evidence and what is the best arrangement for such evidence in various genres as they occur in different languages. It frankly derives some, but not all, of its orientation from the weak version of the Whorf/Sapir Hypothesis – a notion reintroduced into both linguistic and literary study by the French structuralist and post-structuralist writers (see also Berman and Slobin 1994, Hunt and Agnoli 1991, Lucy 1992, Slobin 1990).

7.2 The question of genres

Elsewhere in this volume, it has been noted that there are not only differences between genres of the same language but important differences also exist between similar genres in different languages (Berkenkotter and Huckin 1993, Biber 1988, 1995, Kachru 1987, Purves 1988, Swales 1991). While certain scientific and technological genres have taken on global, translanguage features, important differences still remain in the nature of evidence, the means of organizing evidence, and even the matter of what can be discussed in writing as opposed to speech (cf. Taylor and Chen 1991). It has been clear for some time that such differences are not merely manifestations of varying surface features across languages but are caused by important underlying cultural and historical differences, which contrastive rhetoric has consistently sought to understand.

7.3   Spoken and written language

In Chapter 1, the notion that writing is a late-added technology different from spoken language, was discussed in the context of literacy. To recapitulate very briefly, while spoken language seems to have been a part of the human genetic baggage for at least 100,000 years, written language represents rather distinct post-biological evolutionary changes that have occurred, in terms of species time, over quite a short period.

At the present time, many of the functions served by written language are not duplicative of the functions of oral language though a fuzzy overlap does exist. That overlap is based on the existence of genres which straddle oral and written forms; e.g. sermons written out but delivered orally, or academic lectures, or the nightly television news.

Evidence has shown that written and oral language developed separately. Written language developed differentially among those populations that have it, but is neither universally distributed across the species nor even universally distributed in societies that possess it. Written language is not merely transcribed oral language; on the contrary, over time, written language has acquired a number of unique functions not shared with oral language (Olson 1994).

7.4   Written language across cultures

Because written language is not universally distributed but has developed differentially, it has come to serve somewhat different purposes in different languages. To a minor degree, these differences may reflect surface variations between discrete languages.

In English, for example, *knowledge* is not countable as it is in Japanese; this difference suggests that the concept would be differently managed in discourse structure. But such obvious factors as the placement of modifiers pre- and post-nominally will result in differing discourse manifestations. The way in which verb systems are actualized (e.g. the presence or absence of tense, aspect, mode, etc., in the verbal system; or the relative richness of distinctions which they engender) will produce different discourse treatments. By the same token, other surface structure features will likely result in somewhat different discourse treatments (e.g. forms and uses of passives in English and Chinese). But the more essential questions deal with semantic and logical issues as those issues are encoded in a language system. The questions raised earlier:

- What can be encoded in written language (as opposed to spoken language and as opposed to not being discussable at all)?
- What is evidence?
- How is evidence arranged to produce the most effective, persuasive, attractive text?

are the key questions that must be addressed if contrastive rhetoric is to serve its purpose (see also Connor 1995).

It is also important to point out that contrastive rhetoric is responsive to cultural-use preferences, and not simply to differences in language structures and their frequencies of use. While it is true that culture and language influences may appear to be disassociated in certain situations, such as when a Chinese scientist writing in English chooses a rhetorically Chinese approach, the explanations for such choices may nevertheless reflect both cultural and linguistic preferences (cf. Taylor and Chen 1991).

7.5   The historical development of contrastive rhetoric

The notion of contrastive rhetoric[1] emerged in the middle 1960s from an essentially pedagogical impetus. As the population of international students grew at US tertiary institutions over the decades of the 1950s and 1960s – a period when the audio-lingual method was widely used for teaching English to speakers of other languages – and as it became evident that the approaches being used did not offer a means for teaching connected writing to those students, it became clear that a need existed for a better approach to the teaching of writing. In early research reported in Kaplan (1966, 1972, 1988), a large number of international student compositions were examined by hand and a number of patterns emerged from those examinations. It seemed clear that the writing in English of students whose native languages were Arabic, Chinese, French, Japanese, Russian, etc., was systematically different from the writing of comparable students who were native speakers of English. The purpose of the research was intended to understand those differences and to suggest pedagogical strategies to assist students to bridge those differences.

Contrastive rhetoric does not primarily concern itself with such matters as the basic placement of modifiers or with basic word-order questions or with superficial differences in tense, aspect, or mode. Rather, it is concerned with matters relating to topicalization, to the various ways of achieving cohesion (as, for example discussed in Halliday and Hasan 1989), to the combination of surface linguistic features which reflect identifiable discourse functions, and to the mechanisms through which coherence is achieved.

For example, in English, the following structure appears nonsensical:

> *Last week, my brother and I went fishing. We didn't catch a thing; the largest was only a foot long.*

The implication is, on the one hand, that *no* fish were caught, and, on the other, that fish were caught but none over one-foot in linear length. On the face of it, this is a contradiction; it is impossible to catch *no* fish and yet to catch *some* fish (regardless of their size). But it is necessary to place the utterance in a context. If the speaker is a fisher of sailfish, the utterance is non-contradictory; that is, the implication is that *no sailfish* were caught even though some 'junk' fish, all relatively small, were caught. Thus, an utterance which seems to lack coherence in isolation may acquire coherence in a specific context.

The interesting question, of course, is how such coherence-making contexts operate in languages other than English. Would it be possible, for example, to provide a comparable utterance in a comparable context in Mandarin, or would the discourse constraints on Mandarin require a different way of encoding the implications of the utterance? The interesting questions, then, do not lie in the syntactic structure of the utterance itself (which, in Chinese, would necessarily be different because past-time is differently signalled), but in the way in which implicature is encoded in coherent text.

Consider the two following utterances:

1. *The two men were talking on the platform.*
2. *On the platform, the two men were talking.*

Utterance 1 observes normal English word order, with the locative prepositional phrase at the end of the utterance; utterance 2 dislocates the locative prepositional phrase to the front of the utterance. In purely syntactic terms, there is no significant difference between the two utterances; the only difference is that in one case an additional moving rule has been applied. But in discourse terms the difference is important. Assuming that these two utterances stand, respectively, at the beginning of a text, the text that follows utterance 1 may be about the two men, perhaps about the subject of their conversation, but not about events on the platform; on the other hand, the text following utterance 2 is likely to be about events on the platform, and may not be about the two men or the subject of their conversation (e.g. a setting in fiction narrative, a police recall of a crime scene).

Of course, these discourse rules are fairly flexible, and it is impossible to make categorical statements about the context of the continuing text. To illustrate, the text below suggests the sort of coherence normally expected to follow utterance 1:

> The two men were talking on the platform. They met there daily in the course of their commuting routine. Each day, they reviewed the state of their lives, the condition of their marriages, the health and achievement of their children and their wives. They were friends, and the mundanity of the conversation only served to strengthen the tie of friendship – of commonality – between them.

The second text suggests the sort of coherence normally expected to follow utterance 2:

> On the platform, the two men were talking. The rain fell gently, and the twilight was encroaching on the scene. The last train from the city had arrived, and the platform was quiet, deserted by the hordes of daily commuters, settling into the silence normally associated with isolation and decay. In the morning, with the return of the commuters, the platform would spring into renewed life, the cycle of the seasons, of death and resurrection, repeated in a diurnal chain.

It appears that topicalization can be accomplished in English, at least in some environments, by leftward dislocation of sentence elements in the initial text sentence. A question of considerable interest is the extent to which similar dislocation serves topicalization in other languages.

The fact remains that there are observable differences among the rhetorical structures of different languages though those differences are not necessarily manifested at the surface level.

7.6   External research evidence for contrastive rhetoric

Supporting evidence for contrastive rhetoric from other disciplinary studies includes cross-linguistic language development research in the past decade (Berman and Slobin 1994, Choi and Bowerman 1991, Demuth 1990, Slobin 1990, Slobin and Bocaz 1988). In this line of research, Slobin and others have noted how children acquiring different languages will sometimes exhibit preferences for different sorts of linguistic structures (e.g. early Spanish speakers make greater use of tense and aspect distinctions than do English speakers). Slobin and Bocaz (1988), noting differences in the use of prepositional phrases to present the setting for the narrative, state (p. 21):

> Spanish-speaking children ... tend to devote more effort in their narratives to establishing the static locations of objects and participants in scenes, as if sensing that it is difficult to independently specify trajectories. English-speaking children, by contrast, devote less attention to static description, attending more to the elaboration of trajectories, and leaving much of the arrangement of objects and participants to be inferred....
>
> All of these language-specific characteristics of the encoding of states and processes, scenes and trajectories, seem to have consequences for the eventual construction of narrative discourse in two types of language.

The structural differences uncovered do not argue for a strong form of the Whorfian Hypothesis, but for the recognition of cultural preferences which make greater use of certain options among the linguistic possibilities.

Sociolinguistics and the study of literacy have provided further evidence of variation in discourse which can only be understood in terms of the sociocultural contexts; that is, patterns of discourse use are socially and culturally shaped. The literacy research of Gee (1990), Heath (1983, 1986a, 1986b), Scollon and Scollon (1981), and Street (1984, 1993) provide extensive evidence to support this line of argument.

Outside of the specific context of literacy, the sociolinguistic exploration of language socialization, and its influence on patterns of language use, supports a contrastive rhetoric perspective (Clancy 1986, Ochs 1988, Philips 1983, Schieffelin and Ochs 1986, Spindler and Spindler 1987b). Different cultures have different ways of doing things with language. These different uses are culturally/socially shaped and they have reflexes in the preferential organization of discourse. It would seem natural, therefore, to suggest that the same socially contexted language use preferences in oral discourse would influence written discourse.

The development of social construction theory and its influence on rhetoric as discussed by Bazerman (1988, 1991), Bruffee (1986), Kaplan and Grabe (1991), and Myers (1986, 1990) provide yet another source of evidence for a contrastive rhetoric perspective. In particular, the study of scientific discourse in the last decade has demonstrated how even the most 'objective' and universal of discourse genres is, in fact, a product of rhetorical socialization and preferred conventionalizations accepted by the scientific community (see Chapter 6). For example scientists do not write objective value-neutral articles; rather, they respond to the current trends in theory making and shape their reporting accordingly (much as this chapter is doing). A particularly interesting analysis of this rhetorical shaping in linguistics is Czubaroff's study of Chomsky's review of B.F. Skinner in *Language* (1989).

A final area supporting the notion of contrastive rhetoric can be found in rhetoric with the emergence of post-structural approaches to the critical study of text and their emphases on the socio-historical forces which shape our writing and our reading of any text (Crowley 1989, Neel 1988, Shapiro 1987). Following this line of argument, any text is a product of multiple forces, all of which are in some way contextual. The notion that any text could be objective, free from contextual shaping, does not appear logically valid.

Given this diverse array of supporting evidence for the general notion of contrastive rhetoric, it would seem appropriate to acknowledge contrastive rhetoric's broad theoretical appeal (see also Leki 1991). At the same time, it is important to consider the range of evidence emerging specifically from the direct study of contrastive rhetoric across many languages. There is considerable evidence from this line of research, discussed in the next section, which converges with the arguments from other disciplines.[2]

7.7   Text-based research evidence

A typical criticism of research in contrastive rhetoric is that it has not been able to control sufficiently the many confounding variables that enter into any comparison between writing in two languages or in the writing of L2 learners in the second language. There is no doubt that the ability to control many confounding variables has been a problem in contrastive rhetoric research, and will continue to be a difficulty in future research. However, research in all areas of L2 learning have equal difficulties to overcome, and more recent research in contrastive rhetoric has taken this issue into account much more effectively than it had in the past. In fact, the difficulty in exploring contrastive rhetoric, as well as the general growing maturity in research methods in all of applied linguistics, has led to increasingly more sophisticated research and more creative discourse approaches (Connor 1995).

This evolution is first indicated by the increasing stress on the comparison of texts in two different languages (Bickner and Peyasantiwong 1988, Clyne 1983, 1991, Eggington 1987, Hinds 1987, 1990, Indrasutra 1988, Y. Kachru 1983, 1988, Lux and Grabe 1991, Montaño-Harmon 1991, and Ventola and Mauranen 1991). In these more recent studies, the focus is on direct comparison of discourse features in the texts of both languages. Second, the growing body of discourse-based research has led to the study of syntactic/textual features central to the structuring of discourse (e.g. Biber 1988, 1995, Indrasutra 1988, Reid 1988, Reppen and Grabe 1993). These discoveries have been incorporated into more recent research on contrastive rhetoric.

Third, recent research in discourse analysis has extended the study of text to include analyses which assume larger divisions in the organization of text. Earlier efforts have included Kaplan's (1972), Discourse Bloc framework (see also Ostler 1987). More recent approaches include units of persuasive discourse (Connor and Lauer 1988), storygraph analysis (Soter 1988), topical structure analysis (Cerniglia *et al.* 1990, Connor and Farmer 1990,

Lautamatti 1987), and content structure analysis (Connor and McCagg 1987). Finally, discourse research has begun to focus on textual analysis which examines co-occurring linguistic features of texts (Besnier 1988, Biber 1995, Grabe 1987, Lux and Grabe 1991). Some of the more important and striking research in contrastive rhetoric will be reviewed to illustrate these developments and also to suggest the strong array of research evidence directly supporting the notion of contrastive rhetoric (see Connor 1995 for additional research).

7.7.1   German

In a set of studies examining the differences between German and English, Clyne (1983, 1985, 1987, 1991) has argued that there are indeed clearly different preferences for the organization of written discourse. In particular, he notes (1985) that the role of syntactic structures in German 'learned' prose is the major distinguisher from informal prose, whereas, for English, the role of diction in distinguishing 'learned' from informal prose is more important. Clyne also notes that essay writing in the educational system is much more prevalent in English contexts than in German contexts. In German contexts, the role of content is much more important than formal style and organization in writing. As he notes:

> Digressions from a linear structure are tolerated much more in German-language countries, as are repetitions. The less linear and less formal structure of German (academic) discourse also is evidenced in books and articles in fields such as linguistics and sociology (Clyne 1981). There one finds digressions, and digressions from digressions – which entail recapitulation and repetitions to stress the *main* line of argument.
>
> (Clyne 1985: 116)

A main source of evidence for these claims is the difficulty English readers have with close translations of German academic works. Clyne (1981) notes that a key difference lies in the non-linear writing style typical in German academic prose. In particular, the translation of Norbert Dittmar's *Soziolinguistik* has been described by Americans as haphazard in organization and even chaotic. No German or other continental European reviewer has made such critical statements about the book.

Clyne (1991) replicates many of his earlier findings and provides further evidence for differences in written texts in terms of textual symmetry, text hierarchy, argument continuity, data integration, definition giving, use of advance organizers, and hedging and modal verb use. He also finds many of the same German writing patterns in the English writing of German scholars. A major consequence of these distinctions is that German scholars view English academic writing as superficial; in contrast, English scholars view German academic writing as pretentious and badly organized.

7.7.2   Japanese

One of the more fruitful demonstrations of contrastive rhetoric has been the study of major Asian languages in contrast to English. Recent research has argued that Japanese, Korean, Chinese, Thai, and Vietnamese all provide useful contrasts with the discourse practices of American English. Hinds (1983a, 1987, 1990) has devoted considerable time to the study of discourse organization in Japanese texts in contrast with English texts. In particular, Hinds has argued that a major alternative rhetorical pattern in Japanese writing is the organization of texts according to a *Ki–Shoo–Ten–Ketsu* framework, a framework with origins in classical Chinese poetry. The major contrast with English writing expectations is the third element of the development, *Ten*, which develops a subtheme in a manner that would be considered off-topic in English. As Hinds (1983b: 188) notes, 'it is the intrusion of the unexpected element into an otherwise normal progression of ideas'. The final element, *Ketsu*, represents the conclusion, but that label is misleading in terms of English writing expectations. In this Japanese writing format, the conclusions may only ask a question, indicate a doubt, or reach an indecisive endpoint. By English standards, such a conclusion appears almost incoherent.

7.7.3   Korean

Eggington (1987) has made a similar argument for an alternative rhetorical pattern in Korean writing, one which would seem to derive from the same source as the Japanese framework. The Korean rhetorical structure, *Ki–Sung–Chon–Kyul*, follows a pattern of (1) introduction and loose development, (2) a statement of the main idea, (3) concepts indirectly connected with the argument, and (4) a conclusion of the main theme. Eggington argues that Koreans prefer this pattern if they are neither bilingual in English and Korean, nor have been extensively exposed to English prose.

7.7.4   Chinese

A similar pattern has been noted in Chinese by Cheng (1985), who argues that a Chinese rhetorical style consists of a four-part pattern similar to the four-part patterns noted above for Korean and Japanese. This pattern is, again, believed to have originated historically in Chinese poetry. Such sources may also explain the extensive use of allusions and historical references noted in Chinese writing (Tsao 1983). The four-part pattern may also have a historical relation to the Confucian eight-legged essay (Scollon 1991). While the concept of the eight-legged essay has been a controversial issue in Chinese-English contrastive rhetoric, Scollon (1991: 7–8) makes the following argument in support of its influence:

> Kaplan (1966) ... introduced the notion that the 'eight-legged essay' was of structural significance in understanding contemporary Chinese writing in English. Others have taken exception to the use of this essay for comparison ... [and] ... have argued that most contemporary Chinese have little or no knowledge of the 'eight-legged essay' and, therefore, are not likely to be influenced by its structure. This argument is comparable to saying that most contemporary American writers have never read Aristotle and, therefore, the study of Aristotle's rhetoric will shed no light on Western composition practices.

While these issues will continue to be debated, the study of Chinese-English rhetorical contrasts remains an important area of research, both for contrastive rhetoric and for second language writing more generally.

7.7.5   A quasi-inductive style and reader responsibility

In a more recent article, Hinds (1990) suggested that the above Asian rhetorical frameworks are really all variants of a general organizational strategy in writing which he terms *quasi-inductive*. The major premise of this argument is that English writers (and readers) are familiar with strictly deductive and inductive frameworks, but not with a quasi-inductive framework.

Looking at Japanese in this way, Hinds notes that the thesis statement is often buried in the passage. Japanese readers do not expect a thesis to be explained to them at the outset. Instead, Japanese readers are better at contextualizing a text than are English readers. He notes a similar preference in Korean, citing Eggington. In Korean, often no thesis statement is given; rather, there is a list of points revolving around an unstated central theme. Chinese, Hinds argues, also makes use of quasi-inductive organization. In general, Hinds argues that there is an Oriental style (though not the only style) involving a delayed introduction of purpose.

This argument for a quasi-inductive style, with the topic implied but not stated, and with subtheme development, may be a manifestation of Hind's assertion that Japanese is a reader-responsible language; that is, readers are expected to work to fill information and transitions, and a writer who does all the work for the reader is not as highly valued. In contrast, a writer-responsible language places the burden on the writer to make relationships, purposes, and main messages as transparent as possible within the conventions of the text type. Reid (1988) argues that reader-responsible preferences in Chinese may explain consistent findings for shorter sentence length in the English writing by Chinese students, this feature being a reflex of brevity and 'reading between the lines' in Chinese writing. Similar arguments are given by Matalene (1985) and Ostler (1987).

Jenkins and Hinds (1987) also explored the issue of reader or writer responsibility as a major dimension in comparing business letter writing in French, English, and Japanese. They found that French conventions for letter writing were strongly writer responsible. The writer is strongly constrained to follow expected conventions of politeness and formal letter writing, and the writer does not take into account the reader's point of view. English letters were seen as much more reader responsible; that is, the writer is obliged to view the rhetorical situation from the reader's perspective. Japanese letter writing was seen as oriented to the space between the writer and the reader in that the form of the letter took precedence over either the writer's or the reader's perspective. In Japanese business letters, writers will often search guide books for set expressions to use.

7.7.6 Thai

Analysing rhetorical contrasts between English and Th
somewhat different perspective, Bickner and Peyas
(1988) examined sets of students writing on the same task
found that Thai writers used more repetition, made extensive
of lists, and often did not use conclusions. They also noted th
Thai student writing tended to be more impersonal, perhap
through a lack of speculation or a lack of future oriented conclusions; this may be due in part to the absence of counterfactual
statements in Thai writing (cf. Kaplan 1987).

In a similar study, Indrasutra (1988) examined English and
Thai students' narrative writing. American students wrote essays in
English, and Thai student wrote essays both in English and in
Thai. While structure and cohesive measures did not indicate
important differences, there were clear differences in the preferential structure of the narratives. According to Indrasutra, Thai
narratives preferred analogy for narrative descriptions, making
more use of figurative language such as metaphor, simile, and per-
sonification. She argues that this distinction may be due to the
different role narratives play in Thai culture; narratives are an
important means for exposition and instruction – a practice
unlike that in the American educational context. Thai students
did not create stories to entertain or generate interest; rather,
their stories were taken only from real life and were intended to
explain or instruct. With respect to the Thai students writing in
English, Indrasatra (1988: 221) notes:

> 'transfer' occurs when the Thai students convey a pattern or model
> of writing in Thai into writing in English as in the following cases.
> The use of nouns instead of pronouns according to the degree of
> formality shows transfer of Thai conventional style into writing in
> English. In addition, transfer of conventional discourse structure is
> shown when the Thai students wrote in the same way as they wrote
> in Thai; examples are frequencies of mental states and descriptions
> of mental states. Overall, the Thai students' written compositions in
> English are more similar to the Thai compositions than they are to
> the American compositions.

7.7.7 Vietnamese

Other evidence for distinct rhetorical patterning by Asian students
is argued for in Soter (1988). Examining the narratives of

 ...dents writing in English in Australia, she noted that
  students focused less effort on the plot development
    effort on the attributional features of the characters. As
   988: 198–9) states:

> ...ous Vietnamese narratives drawn on for the study reveal ... that
> ...e Vietnamese stories appear to be less goal-oriented and hence
> less focused on plot than the typical English story.... A greater
> emphasis appears to be placed on relationships among the partici-
> pants in the telling of the story situation and on the inner states of
> characters within the story. The Vietnamese students in particular
> also drew more heavily on *dialogue* in their stories and the dialogue
> information did not include information that, in general, forwarded
> the action of the story but was reflective or attributive in nature.

7.7.8 Hindi

Evidence for culturally distinct rhetorical preferences has also been
argued for in a series of studies by Y. Kachru (1983, 1987, 1988)
with respect to Hindi. In analyses of Hindi and English texts, she
has pointed out that syntactic and cohesive features differ in the two
languages as a consequence of distinct rhetorical preferences in the
organization of discourse. In one study of expository prose (1983),
she has argued that Hindi expository prose organization is sometimes spiral rather than linear, reflecting circular patterns of
organization in traditional Hindi culture and religion. She further
argued that traditional organizational patterns are also found in
Indian–English writing. Similar arguments have been made for
Marathi, another Indo-Aryan language (Pandharipande 1983).

In a more recent study, Y. Kachru (1988) notes that while certain Hindi expository prose essays follow linear patterns of
organization and obey English conventions of paragraph unity,
topic statement, and support for an argument following the claim,
other expository prose writing disregards these conventions. It is
important to note that she does not claim that all English expository prose necessarily follows the above conventions, but that they
represent conventional reader expectations in English.

7.7.9 Arabic

The study of Arabic-English differences has been an interesting
source of contention through much of the history of contrastive

rhetoric. In Kaplan's (1966) early discussions of contrastive rhetoric, Arab students who were writing in English were seen as writing in a pattern characterized by repetition and elaborate parallelism rather than in a linear pattern.[3] Ostler (1987), in an effort to explore Kaplan's generalizations more carefully, argued that Arabic ESL writers are heavily influenced by classical Arabic, a language which is more reflective of oral traditions in language use. As a result, she argues, the writing patterns of the Arab ESL students reveal greater uses of coordination and apposition than subordination as well as greater uses of parallelism and symmetry in and across clauses. While her corpus was not large and the comparison problematic, the study did demonstrate an empirical approach to exploring Arabic–English contrasts.

This study has been criticized in particular because it did not examine Arab students writing in Arabic and because the text analysis ignored a number of other possible interpretations. While not directly countering the results of Ostler, Sa'Adeddin (1989) reinterprets the many textually oral features in Arabic texts as representing one rhetorical option in written Arabic, though one which is typically preferred – an 'aural' mode of writing. This mode is preferred because it indicates solidarity and shared cultural beliefs. Its salient features will include a loose pattern of organization, overemphasis, repetition of specific syntactic structures, development by addition and accumulation, etc. In contrast, a 'visual' mode of writing is available in Arabic, but is seen as distant and non-interactive. Its salient features include linearization, elaboration of sentences and paragraphs, complicated thematic structure, and a clearly delimited ending. Although the characterizations for an 'aural' style is similar to Ostler's analyses, Sa'Adeddin makes the important point that Arabic writers have the option to write in a 'visual' style, much as English writers do, but that it is culturally dispreferred (see also Zellermeyer 1988 for a similar comparison between Hebrew and English).

Hatim (1991) reinforces the point that Arabic writers have historically had the option to develop arguments in writing in terms of balanced counter-arguments, presenting the opponent's view, but then countering it. In modern Arabic, however, this option is not preferred; instead, a preference is given to argumentation which either makes no reference to an opposing view or presents a lop-sided argument with an explicit concessive (e.g. *although*). For both Hatim and Sa'Adeddin, the issues of audience and an interactive stance with the reader appear to play prominent roles in discussing linguistically observable differences between Arabic and English rhetorical preferences. It is worth noting, in passing, that a common critique of Ostler's study, that it only examined ESL writing, is not the issue with Sa'Adeddin or Hatim. Both of their studies support distinctions noted in Ostler. The primary difference of opinion is with the interpretations as to what these differences represent.

7.7.10 Spanish

Perhaps the most common contrastive rhetoric comparison is that between Spanish and English. In the early 1970s, a number of dissertations examined aspects of Spanish-English rhetorical contrasts. In the 1980s, additional studies have examined both linguistic and rhetorical differences. Four studies, in particular, lead to the notion that Spanish writers prefer a more 'elaborated' style of writing; that is, Spanish writers, whether writing in Spanish or in English, will typically make greater use of both coordination and subordination in clause structuring.

1. Reid (1988) first pointed out that Spanish ESL writers wrote longer sentences, used more coordinate clauses, and used as many subordinate clauses as English L1 writers. At the time, she suggested that these results might indicate a pattern of 'loose coordination' as discussed in Ostler (1987).
2. Montaño-Harmon (1988, 1991) compared secondary school Spanish writers in Mexico and English L1 writers in the USA, and observed that Spanish writers wrote longer sentences, used fewer simple sentences, and used more coordinating clauses. In this case, the comparison was made across two groups of students writing in their own first languages.
3. A third study by Lux (1991; Lux and Grabe 1991) compared university level Ecuadorean Spanish writers and University English L1 students in the USA. Once again, the results revealed that Spanish writers wrote longer sentences. They also made greater use of subordinate clauses, but there was no difference in the use of coordinate clauses.
4. Reppen and Grabe (1993) compared the writing of Spanish-speaking elementary ESL students with low socio-economic English L1 students. Once again, Spanish writers wrote longer

sentences (T-units), used more coordinate clauses and used more subordinate clauses. While one might argue that the coordination is a reflection of low proficiency in English, such an argument does not match the results of either Montaño-Harmon or Lux.

Taken together, the results of the four studies consistently argue for a more elaborated style preference for Spanish writers. This consistent pattern applies across ESL student writing and Spanish writing, across a range of distinct cultural contexts, and across adults, adolescents, and children.

7.7.11 Research using multiple textual parameters

Another important area of investigation in contrastive rhetoric involves the use of multiple textual parameters derived from linguistic feature analysis. Carlson (1988), working with samples from the Test of Written English (TWE), found that predictors of holistic scoring varied by language group. This was in part due to different overall language abilities in English, but she also suggested that language background itself may be a cause of the differences in the predictors that explained holistic scoring.

Looking specifically at a comparison between Brazilian–Portuguese and American–English editorial writing, Dantas-Whitney and Grabe (1989) examined the texts for linguistic features that would reflect functional dimensions of text structure (cf. Biber 1988, Grabe 1987). For example, texts which make extensive use of linguistic features such as first and second person pronouns, subordinators, infinitives, and general hedges appear to be more *interactionally* oriented than texts which make low use of these features but high use of repetition in prose. In this study, Dantas-Whitney and Grabe found that there were significant differences between the two samples in terms of *abstract/formal* versus *situational/informal* presentation of information. This dimension was represented by high use of nominalizations, prepositions, and words per sentence for abstract/formal style versus low use of these features and high use of third person pronouns and locative adverbs for situational/informal style. There was also a tendency for Portuguese editorials to appear more *interactional* than the English editorials, which were more *informationally* oriented, though results were not statistically significant.

In a second analysis examining multiple functional dimensions, Lux (1991, Lux and Grabe 1991), studying the writing of tertiary level students in Ecuador and the USA, argued that Spanish-language writers, whether as L1 or as L2 students, wrote more 'elaborated' prose than did English-language writers. On the basis of a multivariate analysis of 22 linguistic features, Lux proposed four factors which were useful in interpreting the comparisons among writing groups. Most important for the purposes of this discussion was the 'elaborated style' factor noted above.

A third multidimensional approach to contrastive rhetoric, though somewhat different from the above methods, follows from the work of Purves and his colleagues in the International Educational Assessment (IEA) study of written composition (Gorman *et al.* 1988, Purves and Takala 1982, Vahapassi 1988). In this study, students in 14 countries and at three age levels wrote on eight different writing prompts (Purves and Hawisher 1990, Purves and Purves 1986). As a result, the project was able to compare writing across different age levels, across countries, and across task and text type. Purves and Hawisher (1990) describe one study in which 100 essays from each country were rated on a number of functional dimensions:

(1) personal–impersonal
(2) ornamented–plain
(3) abstract–concrete
(4) single–multiple
(5) propositional–appositional.

These dimensions involved, respectively, references to the writer's thoughts; to the use of metaphors, imagery, and figures of speech; to the amount of specific information; to the perceived narrowness and unity of topic; and to the types and numbers of connectives used. Results of their study suggested that writers from different countries could be placed in a multidimensional profile. For example, the Italian writers were rated 'high' in all five categories; that is, the writing was judged as highly personal, ornamented, abstract, single-focused, and propositional. In contrast, the Finnish writers were rated low on all five dimensions. In this way, students from 14 different countries were rated. While this approach is intriguing, it remains to be seen what specific consequences of this research will be forthcoming, and what implications will be suggested for writing instruction.

These multidimensional studies are only suggestive of the potential research options that are available. In the future, research on contrastive rhetoric will require studies of a wide variety which relate linguistic and discourse-structure counts to functional/textual dimensions of text. In this way, the many individual findings can be corroborated and explained in terms of the functional structure of discourse. Unfortunately, such research, done on a large scale, requires considerable time and resources.

To summarize the review of the research on contrastive rhetoric, there is considerable evidence that different cultures have different rhetorical preferences for the organization of written text. While contrastive rhetoric research is a complex undertaking, there is now sufficient reliable evidence that contrastive rhetoric preferences not only shape written text in distinct languages and cultures, but tend to manifest themselves consistently, if subtly, in the writing of students learning a second language. When combined with the evidence on discourse variation from other disciplines and the logical arguments for contrastive rhetoric, the issue should centre on ways to understand differences revealed by contrastive rhetoric, rather than ask whether contrastive rhetoric is a fruitful avenue for research (Connor 1995, Leki 1991).

7.8   The uses of contrastive rhetoric

One difficulty in early contrastive rhetoric research lay in the fact that it concentrated on the final product without giving adequate attention to the ways in which text was produced. It has become clear in recent years that the basic questions repeatedly raised with respect to contrastive rhetoric cannot be answered by looking exclusively at final products. A *second problem* in early contrastive rhetoric research lay in the failure to compare similar text genres, and therefore led to repeated attempts to compare student writing with the writing of professional writers or, at least, the writing of skilled writers. Those researchers working in this area have learned to control experiments so that genres actually are comparable.

A *third difficulty* that marked earlier contrastive rhetoric research was the failure to determine whether the writer being studied was able to produce effective prose in his or her native language. It is likely that an individual with constrained ability in his or her native language will not exceed those constraints in a second language. A *fourth difficulty* in early contrastive rhetoric research lay in the fact that deductions were made by examining deviation from the norms of English only, rather than examining the discourse of the L1. This last difficulty has been substantially overcome through the research cited above referring to particular languages; much more is known now about the rhetorical structures of at least some other languages, and research in this area is continuing. But *the most serious problem* lies in the fact that there is no universal theoretical model for contrast; it is regrettably the case that the findings of various scholars cannot easily be compared because results were often derived from different research paradigms and from different empirical bases. (This is not just a problem for contrastive rhetoric, but for all of discourse analysis as a field of research; see, e.g., Kaplan 1991; cf. Biber 1995.)

These problems constrained the usefulness of contrastive rhetoric both as a research base and as a base from which to make pedagogical decisions. What is clear is that there are rhetorical differences in the written discourses of various languages, and that those differences need to be brought to consciousness before a writer can begin to understand what he or she must do in order to write in a more native-like manner (or in a manner that is more acceptable to native speakers of the target language). Precisely because written language has relative durability (it can be held in place and examined) and permanence (it can be stored and brought forth at some other time and place), readers expect a precision and a clarity in written language that they are willing to forgo in oral language; that is, they will easily tolerate breakdowns in pronunciation, syntax, lexicon, and top-level structure in oral language that they will not tolerate in written language (cf. Sa'Adeddin 1989). In oral language, communicability counts, but in written text accuracy becomes more important.

It is not only in the area of mechanics that contrastive rhetoric can be of assistance in the pedagogical setting. Students need to be made aware of the fact that the ability to compose in one language does not assure a comparable ability to compose in another. It is very difficult for students to break out of a 'simplistic' frame of organization (such as the five-paragraph essay) in a second language if they do not have access to the 'simplistic' framework to begin with. While the teaching of organizational models is not currently a popular pedagogical strategy (cf. Smagorinsky 1992, Stolarek 1994), it is a well-recognized approach in other areas of instruction involving creativity. In art and music, students are taught basic forms so that they then have frameworks to manipulate and to deviate from in original ways. (It should be noted that this argument is not an argument for a current-traditional approach to writing instruction; it only points out the need for L2 students to understand organizational aspects of written text.)

Similarly, it is necessary to have practice in particular genres to becomes skilled in those genres (Bereiter and Scardamalia 1987, Martin 1989). There may be no absolute constraints on the organization of larger blocks of text structure, but there are, in many genres, preferred expectations about the way information should be organized (Atkinson 1991, Swales 1991). These preferential expectations can be examined in English prose; non-native students can be made aware of the preferences and they can work with these patterns of preferential organization pedagogically through a number of activities (e.g. metacognitive skills training, summarizing, paraphrasing, putting in paragraph boundaries, unscrambling blocks of text, placing details and examples into a summary, examining and writing organizing sentences for texts, and looking for markers of superstructure; Evenson 1990, Harris 1990; Pressley *et al.* 1989).

7.9   Contrastive rhetoric and the development of a theory of writing

It is always hazardous to move from a discussion of a theoretical notion to its implications for teaching. It is more commonly the case that theory does not lead directly to instructional implications; rather, the theoretical insights suggest a need to have students understand a notion or set of notions, but not a particular method which necessarily represents the pedagogical answer. This relation holds true with the notion of contrastive rhetoric. It is evident that contrastive rhetoric offers some implications for what students need to know; it does not clearly provide answers for exactly how to facilitate this understanding for a student. Leaving aside the question of how to teach 'towards an important notion', it is important to consider, in a general sense, the implications for instruction raised by contrastive rhetoric.

It is reasonable to suggest that contrastive rhetoric focuses attention on seven types of knowledge important in the teaching of writing.

1. Knowledge of rhetorical patterns of arrangement and the relative frequency of various patterns (e.g. exposition/argument: classification, definition, etc.).
2. Knowledge of composing conventions and strategies needed to generate text (e.g. pre-writing, data-collection, revision, etc.).
3. Knowledge of the morphosyntax of the target language, particularly as it applies at the intersentential level.
4. Knowledge of the coherence-creating mechanisms of the target language.
5. Knowledge of the writing conventions of the target language in the sense of both frequency and distribution of types and text appearance (e.g. letter, essay, report).
6. Knowledge of the audience characteristics and expectations in the target culture.
7. Knowledge of the subject to be discussed, including both 'what everyone knows' in the target culture and specialist knowledge.

Clearly, this list is primarily, though not entirely, concerned with product; however, it is worth reiterating that it in no way endorses a 'current-traditional' approach to writing instruction (Berlin 1987; cf. Silva 1990). While the emphasis is on the text rather than on the mental processes through which the composition is generated, these latter processes have not been, and cannot be, ignored. Extended discussion of these practical implications of contrastive rhetoric for writing instruction is addressed in Grabe and Kaplan (1989). Many of the specific recommendations for instruction in Chapters 10 through 12 also suggest ways that insights from contrastive rhetoric support instructional practices.

It should be clear from the discussion in this chapter that insights from contrastive rhetoric are applicable to research on composing, and that there are a number of pedagogical implications that can be drawn for writing instruction in L2 contexts. How contrastive rhetoric is combined with other theoretical notions to build a theory of composition is the goal of the next chapter.

Notes

1. Kaplan prefers the term 'notion' over that of 'theory'. Contrastive rhetoric does not yet comprise a fully articulated set of principals and methods that define this area of research.
2. Labov (1971) makes a strong argument for the power of converging evidence.
3. While the distinction between parallel patterns versus linear patterns was an oversimplification, it has served to galvanize a useful discussion.

8

Towards a theory of writing

> If we think of a theory as a machine to think with, a
> device for organizing and interpreting events with the
> aim of bringing other questions and other forms of
> evidence into conjunction, then it is not at all un-
> reasonable to aspire to a theory of how writing
> contributes not only to our understanding of the world
> but also of ourselves.
>
> (Olson 1994: xvii)

8.1   Introduction

In the first seven chapters, major trends in writing research and differing contexts for writing and writing instruction have been discussed. Together, these seven chapters provide the background for a reconsideration of the nature of writing, covering issues in textual structure, cognitive processing, and social contexts. In this chapter, we would like to step back and consider once again the basic question, 'What is writing?' This will be explored first through an ethnography of writing; then the various issues raised by the ethnography will be reconsidered through a taxonomy of writing skills and contexts; finally, a descriptive model of communicative language processing will be suggested as a means for integrating the cognitive, social and textual domains of a theory of writing.

One often finds discussions similar to the model proposed in this chapter in instructional contexts. For example, 'the rhetorical triangle', treats writing as a combination of writer, reader, subject matter, and text. It is interesting to note, in contrast, how so much of writing research is not contextualized within such a larger framework. For example, Cooper and Matsuhashi (1983) emphasized textual issues, de Beaugrande (1984) and Bereiter and Scardamalia (1987) emphasized processing issues, and, more recently, Flower (1994) has emphasized the combination of cognitive and social contexts.

Witte (1992), in a general theoretical discussion, is one of the few researchers who has argued that a theory of writing needs to synthesize the cognitive, social, and textual (linguistic) factors. We, in our turn, would like to suggest a synthesis which incorporates these three major domains commonly discussed in writing research, but seldom integrated. As these domains are integrated, the goal is to arrive at a balanced interpretation of what it means to be able to write.

8.2   Towards an ethnography of writing

Perhaps the best initial way to consider the overall set of concerns involved in writing is to apply an ethnographic approach to our current understanding of writing. This approach, applied to the study of spoken language, has led to the sociolinguistic field of ethnography of speaking and conversation analysis (Poole 1991, Schiffrin 1991). An equivalent effort has not been applied to writing, in part because many linguists, including many sociolinguists, remain convinced that written language is derived from spoken language (e.g. Basso 1974, Biber 1988, Olson 1994). However, as we have argued in Chapter 1, there are sufficient reasons to reconsider the relationship between spoken and written language, and to attend as carefully to written language as we have to spoken language.

One of the best ways to attempt a first ethnography of writing is to ask the basic question (e.g. Cooper 1979):

Who writes what to whom, for what purpose, why, when, where, and how?

Providing a taxonomic answer to this question will lead to an initial approximation for an ethnography of writing.

8.2.1   *Who*

A first requirement of the ethnography is a taxonomy of writers. Is the individual a beginning writer or a mature experienced writer? Is the individual experienced in a wide variety of writing or only in a narrow range of writing? Is the writer a student who expects to be evaluated academically or a journalist who earns his keep by writing? These and many other related questions form a complex matrix that must be analysed if any classificatory system is to result.

Knowing who the writer is (the characteristics of the writer rather than, perhaps, his or her persona) can have an important bearing on the nature of the writing that is studied. For example, the young adult who does not have extensive experience in writing, but must write a report in a second language, will write quite differently than the skilled adult writer who has experience in the writing task and is writing in the L1. This difference in the characteristics of the writer will be quite independent of other influences (e.g. audience) which impact the writing situation – and it is not simply a general proficiency issue.

8.2.2   Writes

The term 'writes' might normally suggest an action or process. The issue of process, however, is discussed below (see 'how', subsection 8.2.8) and the notion of 'writes' is used here to examine the linguistic nature of texts, the writing.

The study of the writing situation requires a theory of the text itself, a theory of text construction. What are the linguistic parts and how do the parts work together? What are the linguistic resources? To what extent do linguistic features reflect some functional purpose in the writing? How do sentences link together to form a larger text (if indeed sentences are involved)? How are we to understand the notion of coherence? And what part of this notion resides in the text?

These and many other issues were explored in some depth in Chapters 2 and 3. The text itself is an important independent component of the overall writing situation. Only through analysis of the text can researchers examine the uses of particular linguistic structures, transition devices, and lexical choices, as well as the functional roles these uses might play in the context of the entire text. Study of the text reveals the (in)appropriate use of formal conventions such as opening statements, external reference, stages in the sequencing of information (Atkinson 1991), and the rhetorical arrangement of information (Bruthiaux 1993). Study of the text also reveals patterns of information structuring in terms of 'given–new' information ordering, 'topic–comment' arrangement, and 'theme–rheme' structuring. A theory of text construction contributes independently to the writing situation in that it provides a framework for the various linguistic tools available to the writer as well as combinatorial choices which create the flow of information and the notion of coherence. The linguistic elements in text construction also aid interpretation of other factors in the writing situation such as audience considerations, writer's purpose, the writing context, and the genre required by the task.

8.2.3   *What*

The most basic definition of *what is written* is some message and some type of content. For our purposes, the *what* of writing will be discussed in terms of content, genre, and register. These concepts suggest a number of questions for writing: What are the types of writing the writer typically engages in creating? What sorts of general background information does the writer need? To what extent is knowledge of specialized registers necessary for writing? How can we define a theory of genre? To address these and related questions, a theory of writing must take into account the phenomenological world (a theory of world knowledge), a theory of genre, and some specification of register.

Typically, we can think of the *content* as background knowledge, for example, as schema theory. In addition to general background knowledge, schema theory suggests that specific sets of knowledge stored as integrated units are accessible for retrieval (or reconstructing) and are used in understanding and producing content knowledge. Schemas also provide frames for our knowledge of appropriate register in different contexts and our knowledge of genres as ways to organize discourse for specific purposes (Swales 1990). The basic influence of schema theory (or similar theories of the mental organization of knowledge) on writing is apparent in research which shows that students write more when they are writing about information with which they are familiar (e.g. Freidlander 1990 for L2). Background knowledge provides content and genre-structure resources for writing.

It should also be noted that background knowledge is, at least to some extent, culturally derived. Our culturally shaped background knowledge can lead to misunderstandings because this knowledge is not typically recognized as varying by culture. As a result, we are often unaware of the assumptions and presuppositions that guide our logic and our conclusions; rather, we think of our own ways of knowing as common sense. However, when two cultures come into contact, what is common sense, what 'goes without saying', is by definition not the same. Even within a given culture, differences may exist across generations, across social groupings, across genders (Atkinson 1993, Lemke 1995). Thus, some framework which explicitly represents background knowledge is critical for text construction research.

Genres might simply be described as discourse types that have identifiable formal properties, identifiable purposes, and a complete structure (i.e. a beginning, a middle, and an end). Genre is a concept which applies to both oral and written language, though the primary issue, for our purposes, is the occurrence of genre in written discourse. While it may be possible to discuss genres in broad macro-generic terms such as expository prose, persuasion, and narration, genres are more typically defined by narrower contexts and more specific formal features. The following provides a few examples of discourse types which can be considered written genres (e.g. Martin 1985, Rothery 1989, Swales 1990):

fiction novels	grant applications	progress reports
ransom notes	course syllabi	survey articles[1]

Until recently the notion of genre has been relegated to a secondary status in writing theory, though it is used widely in writing instruction and in text-linguistic and psychological research. In the past decade, however, the notion of genre has been receiving increasing recognition as an integral factor in the writing situation, one which makes an independent contribution (e.g. Berkenkotter and Huckin 1993, 1995, Bhatia 1993, Freedman and Medway 1994, Lemke 1995). For example, the text of a fictional narrative will be consistent in certain ways with other fictional narrative texts and will differ from texts that are not fictional narratives in ways which cannot be predicted specifically and completely from information about the writer, the audience, the writing process, the topic, the writing context, or the purpose of the writer. Thus, a reader might expect a descriptive setting in a fictional narrative (even if not at the very beginning) but will not expect a similar setting sequence in a letter or a newspaper editorial.

Register, as independent from genre considerations, is defined by the topic of the writing, the medium (always writing in this case), and interpersonal tenor (Halliday 1978, Halliday and Hasan 1989, Martin 1992). Seen in this way, register also appears to have an important influence on writing. Writing about vacations and travel will be different from writing about economics, anthropology, physics, medicine, or law, and will lead writers to use different linguistic resources. While certain topics will predispose a writer to select particular genres, it is also true that research articles, popular articles, and introductory textbooks dealing with music and photography will be different from the same genres dealing with physics and biology (Grabe 1987). Register aspects related to interpersonal relations are treated in detail below in the discussion of audience. Taken together, content knowledge, genres and registers comprise social, topical, and cultural resources which strongly influence writing.

8.2.4 *To whom*

Another major issue for a framework of writing is the development of a theory of audience. Audience is essential to the creation of text and the generation of meaning. In terms of audience, the following and many other related questions can be raised.

Who is the intended reader of the writing? Is the reader an abstraction? Is the reader invoked equivalent to the reader addressed (intended)? Is the reader a known individual? If the audience is known, how close or distant is the reader? How much shared background knowledge exists between the reader and the writer? How much shared specific knowledge of a particular topic exists between the reader and the writer?[2]

Some definition of the person(s) *expected* to read the writing has a major influence over the discourse of the written text. Within the general concept of the reader, or audience, are a number of factors which constrain the decisions of the writer (Kirsch and Roen 1990). It is perhaps even preferable to consider 'parameters of audience influence' rather than specific features in order to provide a more thorough account; at least five such parameters would appear to play important roles in textual variation.

1. One parameter of reader influence on the writing is the number of persons who are expected to read the text. A text intended for oneself, a single person, a small group of people, a large group of people, or a general audience will influence the text structure. A related issue is the extent to which the audience is an invoked audience for a rhetorical purpose rather than a 'real' audience definable by the writer (cf. Long 1990, Willey 1990); that is to say, the writer provides cues which indicate the persona (invoked)

which the reader should take on during the reading. Another related issue is the extent to which the specific audience for a text is the intended audience. A diary may be intended for the use of the writer, but ever since Samuel Pepys's diary was published, some diary writers write not for themselves but for posterity.

2. A second parameter of audience variation is the extent to which readers are known or unknown. Writing to a known person, a less familiar colleague, or a stranger is likely to alter the text. This is well documented for oral language interaction in Wolfson's (1989) 'theory of the bulge'; that is, those who are recognized to be in the wide middle ground between stranger and close colleague typically require more elaborate responses, and usually require more hedged language expressions. Thus, degree of closeness to the reader is likely to determine the extent of interactional and involvement features which appear in the writing (Biber 1988, Tannen 1987, 1989).

3. Along a third parameter, that of status, the writing will vary according to whether the reader has a higher status, an equal status, or a lower status than the writer. In oral language contexts, Wolfson (1989) has demonstrated that status also creates discourse variation, with higher and lower status listeners receiving much less interactional negotiating. In a somewhat different context relating to status, the knowledge that a particular person (e.g. a well-known scholar) will be a reader may influence the writing, though there is no research yet which specifically addresses this issue.

4. As a fourth parameter, the extent of shared background knowledge will influence the writing to a considerable degree; that is, readers with a high degree of shared background knowledge are likely to influence the writing in particular ways. Writing for readers who are familiar with current events in certain cultural contexts will allow the writer to anticipate general knowledge on the part of the reader, and to allude to types of knowledge which separate those who know from those who do not (e.g. newspaper editorials, professional journal articles).

5. As a final parameter, the extent of specific topical knowledge shared by the reader and the writer will influence the writing. The extent and choice of detail, the need for defining ideas and assumptions, the use of common versus specialist terms, etc., will all affect the writing (Lemke 1995). Difficulties created by this parameter are evident in the writing of grant proposals in which

only one or two (20 or 30 per cent) of the reviewing committee may have equivalent specialist knowledge.

8.2.5 *For what purpose*

This analysis will consider purpose as a functional categorization. Purpose raises important questions for writing, such as:

- To what extent is it possible to define purpose in a writing task?
- Are there multiple purposes in every writing task?
- How does purpose interact with genre and audience?

and many others.

The purpose for writing may, in a general sense, be said to represent an attempt to communicate with the reader. Most discussions relating rhetoric to writing instruction assume this relation.[3] Apart from personal notes, most recognizable forms of writing are intended for an audience other than the writer; indeed, even such 'personal' items as diaries and research notes may be intended for other audiences. In considering his or her functional purpose(s), the writer recognizes that he or she has specific intentions as well as informational content to convey. Because the reader assumes these purposes on the writer's part, both the reader and the writer will understand and interpret writing purposes from certain accepted linguistic, psychological, and sociolinguistic principles:

1. Gricean maxims – the need to be informative, factually correct, relevant, and clear; and their systematically interpretable violations.
2. Speech acts – specific features in the writing which signal speech acts by the writer, and the degree to which they are negotiable.
3. Conventions for conveying status, power, situation, intent, and attitude. (These indicators are not necessarily the same as features which mark genres.)
4. Predictability of cognitive structures which anticipate and implicate larger patterns of organization: schemata, scripts, frames, citation patterns, goals, ethos and pathos in rhetorical persuasion, aims of discourse, etc.

All of the above are implicated in the writer's purpose and the ability of the reader to discern the purpose of the writing.

The application of Gricean maxims to writing provides the means for making inferences as to the writer's purpose in much the same way as a listener can infer a speaker's purpose. It is worth noting that the writer's awareness and application of Gricean maxims in writing allows him or her to convey purpose beyond that signalled by a genre form. Thus, writers of letters of recommendation who violate maxims of quantity or relevance send a message quite apart from the message conveyed by the genre itself. That is, writing a letter of recommendation implies a recommendation; however, the specific inferences which may be derived from the amount, accuracy, relevance, and clarity of the letter convey much additional information.

Much the same argument can be made for each of the other three principles above. For example, specific speech act verbs may indicate purpose independently of genre. Markers of writer or reader status, choice of salutation, number of directives used, etc., all indicate writer's purpose apart from genre choice. The choice of rhetorical patterns of organization, types of persuasive appeals, and types of references cited all indicate an author's purpose in ways independent of genre. So, too, will presuppositions and cultural stereotypes (Schröder 1991).

It would seem, then, that the purpose for writing must be addressed on at least two levels. On a general level, the overt purpose is related to the concept of genre; the 'purpose' influences the text structure itself, selecting appropriate genre options. However, the parameter of 'purpose', as used here, also addresses functional issues which are independent of recognized written genres. For example, people write in order to apologize, invite, inform, praise, threaten, complain, order, explain, reject, etc. – speech acts for which there are no specific genres which may be consistently invoked. This parameter of 'purpose' is an independent dimension of writing, potentially separable from genre and audience, since a person could write two texts to the same audience and in the same genre but have each text serve different functional purposes (e.g. apology, reprimand, invitation) and convey different messages according to applications of Gricean maxims. It would seem that this functional category accounts for speech act theory in written discourse as well as for applications of Gricean maxims to writing contexts.

It is also important to consider the problem of *lacunae* in cross-cultural writing environments; that is, certain genre/purposes may simply not exist in one cultural environment as compared with another.[4] Lacunae occur at the discourse level, omitting certain genres, audiences, purposes, etc.

8.2.6 Why

The concept of why people write refers to the *underlying intentions or motives* that may or may not be revealed by functional purpose. Under what conditions does a writer not want to communicate fully? Are there attitudes and notions which are difficult to convey in writing? In what situations will some group of readers not be able to see the purpose of the writing?

It might be best to see writer's intentions as indicated along a cline of transparency. *Genres* (subsection 8.2.3) represent the most overt indication of intention and serve to facilitate schema instantiation. As such, intention constitutes a level which is, in one way, strongly constrained by audience and topic. The *purpose for writing* parameter (subsection 8.2.5) is independent of genre (or the question *what?*) in the sense that there may be many purposes not existing in a one-to-one relationship with a given genre – independent of genres that are signalled in writing. These purposes are assumed to be related to communicative intention and, therefore, to be relatively transparent. Even when a person violates Gricean maxims, as in the letter of recommendation, it is done in a way that is understood by the knowledgeable reader. The reader can readily infer the writer's purpose. A third level of writer intention, *underlying intentions or motives* (the focus of this section), may be represented by the extent to which the writer wishes to manipulate the reader to attend to the content, and the writer may not necessarily value transparency for the reader above other considerations. It is also possible that the writer is struggling with the content to the extent that transparency for the reader is not attainable.

The extent to which our present parameter (*why*) influences text depends on two constraints. One is the extent to which a writer wants the reader to recognize a hidden message – the more hidden the underlying message, the more likely it is that the reader will only recognize the functional purpose of the text (e.g. Lemke's (1995) discussion of technocratic discourse). The second situation is one in which a complex or exacting content takes precedence over reader friendliness (e.g. legal documents, technical specification, gang graffiti). Situations may also arise when a writer does not want to present a set of arguments too simply and thereby insult informed colleagues who may be the primary audience (Swales 1990: 64). In this way, the discourse community of the specialist group acts to make the writing less accessible to other readers.

One conceptualization of this notion is Steiner's (1978) four levels of difficulty. This system of variable difficulty derives from the author, the text, and the environment as they influence the ability of the reader to comprehend. The first type is *contingent* difficulty, which arises from arcane and technical reference, but which can be corroborated at some time and in some way. The second type is *modal* difficulty, which arises from inaccessible or alien interpretations of the human condition. The third is *tactical* difficulty, which arises from the relative desire of an author to be understood only up to a point. The last is *ontological* difficulty, which arises from the constraints imposed by the language itself (see Figure 8.1 on page 215).

8.2.7 When and where

It is not clear to what extent the notions of when and where a person writes are critical to the general taxonomy for an ethnography of writing. In fact, the relative non-importance of these issue for writing points out a major distinction between an ethnography of writing and an ethnography of speaking. The immediate situation of language use in speaking is of critical importance in determining the purpose of speaking and interpreting specific language use. The context of 'here and now' appears to be much less important to a theory of writing. This is not to say that the influence deriving from 'when' and 'where' a person writes is negligible or non-existent; rather, these parameters play a much smaller and less consistent role as factors which contribute independently to written discourse. This is so because a writer may work late into the night, under the influence of some substance, or in difficult circumstances (e.g. E.A. Poe, S.T. Coleridge), or, by contrast, a writer may work in a comfortable office with state-of-the-art equipment, but the reader is not likely to know. Such information becomes available usually only long after the fact, in biographical studies, and then only if the writer has achieved a modicum of fame.

Knowing the approximate date of a handwritten message (e.g. a grocery list) may well be important for the person reading it. Similarly, it is important to know when a letter was written to interpret any deictic references contained in the letter appropriately. It is also important to know when a certain research article was written in order to interpret the importance of the claims being made; but this is more a concern for making an informed reader's interpretation rather than a matter which influences the writing of the producer. The same issue may influence letters of many sorts as well as the writing of graffiti. Typically, the dating of a piece of writing is often all that is needed (or available) to allow appropriate reader interpretation, neither the process of writing nor the form of the writing being otherwise influenced.

8.2.8   *How*

As the final parameter in an ethnography of writing, understanding *how* written discourse is produced centres around a theory of on-line writing production, or, in simpler terms, a theory of the writing process. It is noteworthy that channel (physical means of communicating) may be less significant in written text than in oral text. Whether a writer generates text with a pen, a typewriter, or a word processor seems to have limited implications for the structure of text, though this perception may be derived from the fact that little research exists. Some tentative studies suggest that the editing capabilities of a word processor do influence both length and rewriting at least in teaching situations (Bangert-Drowns 1993, Cochran-Smith 1991).

The cognitive mechanism for production rests at the core of a theory of writing. It provides methods of empirical research which complement research on the written text, and also provides the means for exploring notions such as audience, content, and writer intention from a processing perspective. Among the important questions which arise are:

- To what extent can research inform us about important issues in the writing process?
- How useful are models of the writing process?
- Does the writing process vary from culture to culture?
- Is there more than one writing process, and if there are many processing models, what implications does this variability hold for writing theory?

214 Theory and Practice of Writing

Two groups have dominated research on the writing process(es) over the last 15 years, and have shaped current conceptual understandings of how writing is produced. The work of Flower and Hayes (Chapters 4 and 5) has opened up research on the writing process and has presented theories which, though sometimes criticized as too vague, have greatly influenced the way writing research is conducted. Bereiter and Scardamalia, in a series of research studies (see Chapter 5), have argued that there must be more than one writing process, that the writing process used for skilled academic writing is a development out of a more general writing process and is not mastered well by all writers, including university students.

What emerges from the current research on writing processes is that many basic findings are now widely accepted and influence instruction (e.g. Johnson and Roen 1989, Krapels 1990, Raimes 1987, 1991, Silva 1990, Zamel 1987 for L2 influences). At the same time, there are still shortcomings in the writing process research which will need to be addressed in the future. For example, although some researchers (e.g. Perfetti and McCutchen 1987) view linguistic skills as a primary concern, they do not extend such linguistic concerns to the influence of the formal features of genres or to the requirements imposed by certain rhetorical intentions of the writer. More generally, cognitive processing research privileges the reader/writer contract over influences on writing deriving from the topic, the genre, or the writer's intentions. As Swales (1990: 63) points out:

> While Flower (1979) and her co-workers may be generally right in their theory that the immature writer produces 'writer-based prose' and the mature writer 'reader-based próse,' it would seem equally clear that in certain genres mature writers also produce 'writer-based prose' [appropriately].

8.2.9 Summarizing the ethnography of writing

This attempt to develop an ethnography is tentative. Regardless of how the final form of such an ethnography evolves, it should be clear that the purpose is to provide at least a descriptive account for the question posed at the outset of this chapter, 'What is writing?' The ethnography also provides a foundation for a more comprehensive theory of writing: the availability of such a theory would then be useful for situating results from any one parameter of writing within a larger interpretive framework.

Sociolinguists studying oral interaction would not interpret their results outside of some ethnography of speaking framework, yet research on written discourse seldom seems to be similarly compelled to frame research in larger contexts (cf. Kress 1991, Lemke 1995, van Dijk 1988, Wodak 1989, 1990). This is, in part, due to the extensive research on written discourse by cognitive psychologists, many of whom do not see the need to situate writing socially as part of their explanations, and often do not even see a need to recognize different types of writing. While the ethnography sketched out here may not be an equally suitable interpretation of the 'writing event' for all researchers, some framing context for writing is needed – one which goes well beyond the simple communication schemes which relate communicative function to writing only in a general way.

One way to organize the various parameters of this ethnography of writing is to retain the general sequence of the communicative orientation to writing, but to incorporate into the structure a wider range of influencing considerations. One framework attempting to do that (Kaplan 1991) is reproduced in Figure 8.1.

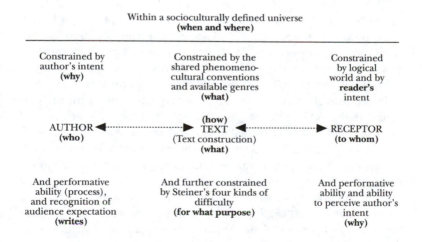

Figure 8.1   Model of parameters involved in writing

In this model, the phenomenological world may be said to include the constraints imposed by various discourse communities and the degree to which those constraints are understood by the participants in the instantiation, including such variables as the function and distribution of different genres.

8.3   A taxonomy of writing skills, knowledge bases, and processes

A second way of organizing the full range of information involved in the above ethnography and the simple model of parameters is through a detailed taxonomy of writing skills and contexts. The development of a taxonomy of writing should not be seen as an alternative to an ethnographic description but rather a way to build upon it. The taxonomy organizes the full range of information in a form that is readily accessible and useful for finding gaps and establishing new areas of inquiry.

8.3.1   *Background assumptions to the taxonomy*

The taxonomy offered here tends to reflect two theoretical bases. One is the general approach towards communicative competence in language first developed by Canale and Swain (1980, Canale 1983, Harley *et al.* 1990; cf. Bachman 1990, Celce-Murcia *et al.* 1994, Chapelle *et al.* 1993); the other is the ethnography of writing framework outlined earlier in this chapter. The development of the taxonomy began by asking about the sorts of writing situations that exist for writers (and particularly students) in terms of settings, tasks, texts, and topics. These situational parameters are then reflected in some way by the writer's goals, combined with the particular writer's intentions, attributions to the task from past successes and failure at similar tasks, and emotional states. In addition, writing obviously requires control over specific linguistic skills as well as over discourse and sociolinguistic skills. Earlier chapters have made the argument for considering linguistic knowledge as a critical component of writing ability and the foundation for text construction. Incorporating a socio-cognitive perspective, one must also consider sociolinguistic skills which play a role in writing (e.g. audience considerations). The writing process also suggests many component skills and strategies essential to writing instruction.

The taxonomy presented below reflects this effort to structure the writing situation and the skills, knowledge, and processes used by the writer. The taxonomy is not in any way intended to be a definitive representation of all aspect of the writing situation – the current state of knowledge would not permit the development of an inclusive taxonomy, and any taxonomic effort necessarily reflects the biases of its compilers. Indeed, it can be anticipated that significant alterations would be a necessary part of using such a taxonomy since knowledge of writing is continually changing and improving. To the extent that gaps become evident, this awareness, in itself, validates the purposes for generating a taxonomy.

8.3.2   A taxonomy of academic writing skills, knowledge bases, and processes

I. *Educational settings for writing*
  A. Classroom
  B. Office
  C. Home
  D. Library
  E. Writing centre/laboratory/corner
  F. Computer centre
  G. Dormitory lounge

II. *Educational writing tasks*
  A. Notes and memoranda
  B Lecture notes
  C. Letters
    1. Personal
    2. Invitation
    3. Acceptance
    4. Refusal
    5. Complaint
      (a) strong
      (b) mild
    6. Recommendation
      (a) positive
      (b) neutral
      (c) negative
    7. Business
    8. Apology
    9. Request
    10. Confirmation

D. Journals/diaries
E. Free writing
F. Recounts (forecounts)
G. Narratives
   1. Fictional (novels/short stories)
   2. Non-fictional
H. Recipes
I. Reports/(expository) essays
   1. Description
   2. Definition
   3. Exemplification
   4. Classification
   5. Comparison/contrast
   6. Cause/effect
   7. Problem/solution
   8. Analysis/synthesis
J. Poster boards/diaramas
K. Interviews/surveys/questionnaires
L. Argumentative essays
   1. Logical stances
   2. Ethical appeal
   3. Emotional appeal
   4. Empirical stance
   5. Appeal to authority
   6. Counter-arguments
M. Timed essay tests
   1. In-class
   2. Take-home
   3. Part of standardized test (commercial or academic)
N. Newspaper reporting/columns
   1. Headlines/world and national news
   2. Local news
   3. Sports news
   4. Book/movie review
   5. Social/political/cultural columns
   6. Editorials
   7. Advertisements
   8. Comics/cartoons
O. Poems
P. Plays
Q. Laboratory reports
R. Charts/tables/graphs/maps/figures
S. Abstracts

T. Research papers
U. Grant proposals/applications
V. Theses/dissertations

III. *Educational texts used and produced (most items in section II also apply here)*
    A. Textbooks
    B. Novels
    C. Short stories
    D. Poems
    E. Plays
    F. Journals/diaries
    G. Newspapers
    H. Magazines/trade journals
    I. Essays (narrative, expository, argumentative)
    J. Charts/graphs/tables/figures/maps
    K. Workbooks
    L. Dictionaries/encyclopaedias/grammar and usage books
    M. Research journal articles
    N. Professional texts/books/chapters

IV. *Topics for academic writing*
    A. Personal expressive
    B. Imaginary narratives
    C. Personal recounts
    D. Biographies
    E. Bibliographic works
    F. Topics from family, community, regional, national life
    G. Topics from social, cultural, economic, political issues
    H. Topics from academic humanities fields
    I. Topics from academic social sciences fields
    J. Topics from academic natural sciences fields
    K. Topics from professional disciplines

V. *The writer's intentions, goals, attributions, and attitudes*
    A. Writer's reinterpretation of the task
    B. Awareness of complexity of task
    C. Willingness to be understood (perhaps only up to a point)
    D. Awareness of previous success with task type and topic
    E. Attitude toward task type and topic
    F. Willingness to elaborate and experiment with task and topic
    G. Motivation to perform to capacity
        1. Grades
        2. Higher proficiency
        3. Learn new information
        4. Future job/promotion
        5. Impress teacher/other students

H. Degree of creativity intended
I. Attitude towards teacher, other students, institution
J. Willingness to learn
K. Awareness of metacognitive strategies
L. Awareness of differences across languages and cultures
M. Awareness of writer's own intentional, attributive, and attitudinal differences in different languages

VI. *Linguistic knowledge*

  A. Knowledge of the written code
    1. Orthography
    2. Spelling
    3. Punctuation
    4. Formatting conventions (margins, paragraphing, spacing, etc.)
  B. Knowledge of phonology and morphology
    1. Sound/letter correspondences
    2. Syllables
      (a) onset
      (b) rhyme/rhythm
      (c) coda
    3. Morpheme structure (word-part knowledge)
  C. Vocabulary
    1. Interpersonal words and phrases
    2. Academic and pedagogical words and phrases
    3. Formal and technical words and phrases
    4. Topic-specific words and phrases
    5. Non-literal and metaphoric language
  D. Syntactic/structural knowledge
    1. Basic syntactic patterns
    2. Preferred formal writing structures (appropriate style)
    3. Tropes and figures of expression
    4. Metaphors/similes
  E. Awareness of differences across languages
  F. Awareness of relative proficiency in different languages and registers

VII. *Discourse knowledge*

  A. Knowledge of intrasentential and intersentential marking devices (cohesion, syntactic parallelism)
  B. Knowledge on informational structuring (topic/comment, given/new, theme/rheme, adjacency pairs)
  C. Knowledge of semantic relations across clauses
  D. Knowledge to recognize main topics
  E. Knowledge of genre structure and genre constraints

F. Knowledge of organizing schemes (top-level discourse structure)

G. Knowledge of inferencing (bridging, elaborating)

H. Awareness of differences in features of discourse structuring across languages and cultures

I. Awareness of different proficiency levels of discourse skills in different languages

VIII. *Sociolinguistic knowledge*

A. Functional uses of written language

1. Apologize
2. Deny
3. Complain
4. Threaten
5. Invite
6. Agree
7. Congratulate
8. Request
9. Direct
10. Compliment

B. Application and interpretable violation of Gricean maxims

C. Register and situational parameters

1. Age of writer
2. Language used by writer (L1, L2, ...)
3. Proficiency in language used
4. Audience considerations
5. Relative status of interactants (power/politeness)
6. Degree of formality (deference/solidarity)
7. Degree of distance (detachment/involvement)
8. Topic of interaction
9. Means of writing (pen/pencil, computer, dictation, shorthand)
10. Means of transmission (single page/book/read aloud/printed)

D. Awareness of sociolinguistic differences across languages and cultures

E. Self-awareness of roles of register and situational parameters

IX. *Further audience considerations*

A. Reality of audience (perceived real or invoked audience)

B. Number in audience

C. Degree of familiarity with audience (specifically known or not)

D. Status of audience with respect to writer (peer/employer)

E. Extent of cultural, social, and world knowledge of audience

F. Extent of specialist/subject-matter knowledge of audience

X. *Knowledge of the world*
  A. Declarative (semantic, topical)
  B. Episodic (events, personal experiences, interactional)
  C. Procedural (processes, routines, conventions)

XI. *Writing process skills (on-line processing skills; not linear)*
  A. Goal planning routines
  B. Lexical and structural activation (generating content)
  C. Propositional integration
  D. Text-model production
  E. Mental model interpretation
    1. Inferencing
    2. Match to processing goals
    3. Match to writer's intentions (reinterpreted task)
  F. Rapid production routines
  G. Revising routines

XII. *Writing process strategies (executive control or metacognitive strategies)*
  A. Monitoring text production
  B. Generating additional content
  C. Considering task problems
    1. Audience considerations
    2. Purpose considerations
    3. Rhetorical considerations (discourse knowledge)
    4. Problems created by additional content
    5. Language of preference for problem consideration
    6. Compensating strategies for weaknesses in linguistic, discourse, sociolinguistic knowledge
  D. Using invention strategies, 'topics', brainstorming, free writes
  E. Considering alternative solutions
  F. Re-reading already produced texts
  G. Using reading resources (texts, dictionaries, data, etc.)
  H. Rejecting content/rhetorical information/alternatives
  I. Holding in storage content/rhetorical information
  J. Summarizing/paraphrasing/reordering information
  K. Predicting future outcomes to match goals
  L. Using notes/outlines/drawings/other self-created materials
  M. Getting assistance
  N Reassessing/changing goals
  O. Recognizing mismatch with processing goals, author's intentions
  P. Editing texts
  Q. Reassessing content/rhetorical strategies
  R. Reassessing content/rhetorical revisions
  S. Getting feedback from others
  T. Considering individual style concerns (voice)

The above taxonomy is one attempt to account for the many variables that may need to be considered when describing the nature of academic/professional writing, conducting research, interpreting from theory to practice, and planning a writing curriculum. Too often, research is conducted without adequate attention to many other variables which may impact the outcome of the study. Researchers also are sometimes willing to overstate the results of research, without giving full consideration to a number of factors which might mitigate their claims. A taxonomy can serve as a useful reminder in these cases. The taxonomy also allows researchers to plan alternative studies which incorporate additional issues. Further, The taxonomy allows researchers to reconsider research questions and to adjust research hypotheses. Finally, and perhaps most importantly, the taxonomy, by its nature, forces some type of order on the many variables that impact our understanding of writing.

On a more practical level, the taxonomy provides a framework for curriculum considerations. Certainly any serious effort to plan a writing curriculum will lead to some type of taxonomy of writing skills, even if outlined only informally. The purpose for the above taxonomy is not to examine every possible feature for a writing curriculum but rather to decide what to emphasize and how to order goals in the light of the many other concerns and constraints operating on an educational curriculum.

8.4   Towards a model of writing

In both of the two previous sections (ethnography and taxonomy), the goal was to use generative mechanisms to establish the range of issues important in a theory of writing. In each case, the mechanism provided a means for ordering the range of information within the domain of writing. What neither approach does is to suggest how the various factors might work together in an integrated fashion to generate whatever writing would be appropriate. In this section, we shall sketch a model of writing abilities which primarily views writing as a communicative activity, and attempts to account for the skills, knowledge bases, and processes as they are used in the course of writing. The model is not based on any specific set of supporting data; in fact, from our perspective, it is unlikely that any relatively comprehensive model will be established on any specific subset of data. Rather, the goal is to account for the results of research in various domains of writing and to integrate this information within a framework that could also, in its turn, generate further hypotheses about the nature of writing.

8.4.1   A communicative approach to writing

In Chapters 1 and 2, it was argued that the primary purpose for writing in almost all contexts is to communicate. Most writing is usually undertaken to communicate with one or more readers for a variety of informational purposes. Even when writing for oneself, there is a likelihood that the writing will, at a later point, be used to communicate with others. When there is no other anticipated reader, and the writing is truly personal and private, one could argue that the writer serves as a reader, and thus the writing remains as a communicative act.

Starting from the position that writing is a communicative act, theories of communicative language use, or communicative competence, provide an important resource for developing a model of writing. Recently, a number of alternative communicative conceptualizations have been proposed for developing models of written language. Flower (1994) has developed a socio-cognitive model which incorporates contextual influences into the cognitive processing of the writer, but the limitation of the Flower model is seen in the minimal integration of textual factors. Martin (1992), from a Hallidayan functional perspective, proposes a model of discourse which is adaptable to writing in particular. Martin's model accounts for textual and social issues, but ignores cognitive-processing factors. Witte (1992) has recently proposed a social semiotic perspective, which discusses the needs for integrating social, cognitive, and textual components.

From an applied linguistics perspective, the models developed by Bachman (1990), Canale and Swain (1980), and Hymes (1972) provide a foundation for the model of writing described here. Drawing on Hymes's initial discussion, Canale (1983) proposed that communicative competence could be discussed in terms of grammatical (linguistic), sociolinguistic, discourse, and strategic competence. These four components of communication would account for a person's linguistic skills in the following ways: (1) phonological/orthographical, morphological, syntactic, and semantic knowledge; (2) sociolinguistic awareness and rules of appropriate language use; (3) knowledge of the ways that discourse is sequenced and abilities to structure discourse effectively; and (4) knowledge of skills and strategies that either enhance communication or repair miscommunication. This perspective on communicative language use has been central to applied linguistic discussions for the past decade (see, e.g., Bachman 1990, Celce-Murcia *et al.* 1994, Harley *et al.* 1990). Recently, Chapelle *et al.* (1993, Grabe and Chapelle 1995) have proposed a model of communicative language use for academic purposes which converges with the synthesis presented in this chapter. We summarize a revised version of this model briefly and then discuss its application to writing situations.

8.4.2   A model of communicative competence applied to writing

Chapelle *et al.* (1993) developed a model of communicative language use which is intended to account for academic language performance in all four skill areas (listening, speaking, reading, and writing). That model is adapted here specifically to writing performance and is modified somewhat to take into account the discussion in the earlier sections of this chapter. Overall, the model specifies communicative language use as comprising a *context* for language use and a representation of the language user's *verbal working memory* (see Figure 8.2). Included in the 'context' are components that integrate *situation* and language *performance* output. The 'situation' itself comprises *participants, setting, task, text,* and *topic.* The 'performance' accounts for the actual *textual output* produced as a result of the processing in 'verbal working memory'. The 'textual output' provides an additional influence on components in verbal working memory as it becomes available for inspection in the 'context'. All of the context variables together comprise the external social context of the writing situation.

The 'text' component in the 'situation' accounts for expected register constraints, genre constraints, communication purposes (speech acts), norms and conventions of language use, and constraints of the communication channel, thus incorporating textual resources as part of the situation. The other subcomponents of the situation (participants, setting, task, topic), along with 'text', are specified in detail in the earlier taxonomy (headings I, II, III,

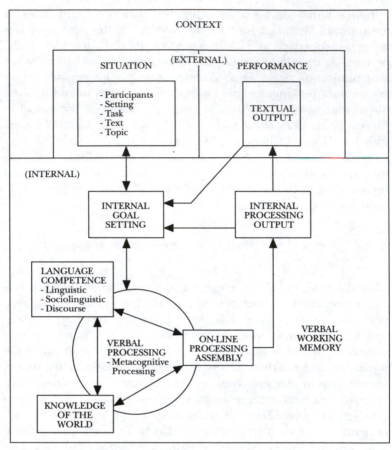

Figure 8.2 Model of writing as communicative language use

IV, VIII, IX). More detailed interpretations of these components may be drawn from the taxonomy of writing and the ethnography of written communication presented earlier.

The second major component to the model is the processing activities of the language user in *verbal working memory* (as opposed to visual memory, for example) while carrying out a language task.[5] Generally speaking, all verbal operations are assumed to take place in a person's working memory (see, e.g., Barsalou 1992, Just and Carpenter 1992). The 'verbal working memory' component has three subparts: *internal goal setting, verbal processing,* and *internal processing output.*

'Internal goal setting' allows the language user to set goals and purposes for writing based on the contextual situation (participants, setting, task, text, topic), internal motivations, performance attributions (beliefs about how well similar past efforts were evaluated), interest, etc. Internal goal setting also provides an initial task representation consistent with the goals created. This task representation (e.g. a one-page summary, a filled-out form) will activate a cycle of operations in 'verbal processing'. The arrow line between internal goal setting and verbal processing indicates that 'context' influences on verbal working memory will always be mediated by the internal goal setting. Metacognitive awareness and monitoring is an important aspect of this subcomponent. It is likely that metacognitive awareness and control abilities are possible throughout all of working memory space except the on-line processing. It should also be noted that 'internal goal setting' is the primary locus for the various affective factors which colour and alter an individual's perception of the external context, and especially the writing task to be carried out. Thus, 'internal goal setting' generates lenses through which the writer attempts to match the external 'context' with internal resources.

'Verbal processing' itself is composed of three parts: *language competence, knowledge of the world,* and *on-line processing assembly.* 'Language competence' and 'knowledge of the world' are parts of both long-term memory and verbal working memory – that part of long-term memory activated for processing.[6] This interpretation follows current views of working memory and its relation to long-term memory (Barsalou 1992, Just and Carpenter 1992). For purposes of the model, however, Figure 8.2 only represents these components as activated in working memory.

In the figure, each of the subcomponents of verbal processing are depicted as partly within, and partly outside, the 'verbal processing' circle. This arrangement is intended to indicate that each subcomponent 'activates' a set of information and resources in relation to the 'context' and the 'internal goal setting'; however, only those aspects of each subcomponent which are used for a given processing cycle are within the circle. Other resources in each subcomponent may still be activated, but they are not used for the immediate processing task.

The 'language competence' component is made up of three competencies discussed in earlier models of communicative competence: linguistic (grammatical), discourse, and sociolinguistic.[7]

These are given detailed specification in the taxonomy presented earlier (VI–IX; see also Bachman 1990, Celce-Murcia *et al.* 1994). These three parts in the language competence activate relevant linguistic resources based on internal goal setting and the cues from the contextual situation. In a number of respects, therefore, information specified in the 'context' will also activate parallel language resources in 'verbal working memory' – particularly in the discourse and sociolinguistic subcomponents of competence. For example, the 'text' (e.g. narrative genre) and 'participant' (e.g. equal status, distant reader) components in the context will activate, in turn, similar information from the discourse and sociolinguistic units of the language competence.

The second major component of verbal processing is 'knowledge of the world'. Whether this component is specified in terms of schemas, frames (e.g. Barsalou 1993), dual-coding theory (Paivio 1986), or some other representation of knowledge resources, the important issue is that the knowledge of the world is also initially activated by the topic in the context and by the internal goal setting, and it interacts strongly with the language competence component (perhaps sharing the lexicon). The 'language competence' and 'knowledge of the world' components generate further information interactively, engaging in iterative problem solving (knowledge-transforming potential). The two components, together with the internal goal setting, activate, at the same time, the 'on-line processing assembly'.

The on-line processing assembly is the component that integrates the informational resources generated by 'language competence' and 'knowledge of the world'. On-line processing refers to the various processing skills that are relatively automatized and procedural in nature. These skills might include lexical access, initial parsing structures, non-problematic propositional integration into a text model, predictable bridging inferences, writing production factors, etc. The results of on-line assembly will be available internally as the 'internal processing output' and provide a mentally 'observable' unit of textual representation.

One of the major functions of the verbal processing unit as a whole is to carry out 'metacognitive processing' which will support the on-line assembly processing and, when that doesn't work efficiently, to alert the 'internal goal setting' and 'internal output' components. All three components, then, can engage interactively in repair strategies. The term 'metacognitive processing' clearly represents a simplification for all the processing activity that requires directed attentional resources, but it serves here to distinguish itself from on-line processing and account for the problem-solving nature of many writing tasks.

It should be noted that metacognitive processing in the verbal processing unit is the locus (along with goal setting) for activating the type of processing which Bereiter and Scardamalia call 'knowledge transforming'. For example, as verbal processing employs the resources from the language competence and world knowledge components, goal setting may need to be adjusted, and new plans created, in order to coordinate the array of language and world knowledge information. In some cases, goals might be simplified so as not to overwhelm an inadequate initial goal setting with too much information.

The final component of the internal operations is *internal processing output*. As processing is carried out, the output is compared to the internal goal setting component in order to match goal setting and processing output. This matching, then, will lead to further processing, to an acceptable match and an end to the processing cycle, or to an unacceptably poor match and a discontinuation of the processing cycle. The 'internal processing output' unit and the 'internal goal setting' unit are strongly influenced by metacognitive strategies.

The details of how such a model might be specified would take us well beyond the scope of this chapter, though various models from cognitive psychology research suggest directions for specification. The purpose of this sketch is to argue that such a model, or some similar model, provides a way to integrate the three major concerns for a theory of writing: a writer's cognitive processing, the linguistic and textual resources that instantiate the writing task, and the contextual factors which strongly shape the nature of the writing. As a processing sequence it is not very different from either the Flower and Hayes model or the Bereiter and Scardamalia approach. What distinguishes it from these other models is the incorporation of textual influences, the explicit specification of the context, and the built-in comparison mechanism between the goal-setting component and the three sources of processing/processing outcomes (verbal processing, internal processing output, textual output). In the next section, the model is summarized and a writing situation is outlined to illustrate how such a model might account for a given writing activity and its context.

8.4.3   *Applying the model*

The model outlined above was originally intended to encompass all language performance (listening, speaking, reading, and writing) in academic settings. In the case of writing, the processing sequence would begin with an initiating activity/motivation coming either from the internal motivations of the individual writer in 'internal goal setting' or from the 'context,' though these two sources of initiation are not so easily separable. Instances of writer-initiated motivation might be a diary entry, a letter, or a summary of an important academic text. Instances of situation-initiated activity might be an essay assignment, a memo, or a revision of an essay.

Whether initiated from the writer or from the 'situation', the first processing step would be to activate goal setting for writing. This goal setting would involve an assessment of the context, an initial representation of the writing outcome, an assessment of the potential difficulties in carrying out the task, an initial activation of features of the genre and conventional forms to be part of the task, and an organizational plan. These initial processes in the goal setting component will, in turn, activate the three components in the verbal processing unit. The language competence component will generate the language information needed to respond to the task-setting requirements, including considerations for audience, topic, setting, register, organization, etc. The world knowledge component will activate relevant information which, in turn, will generate more language resources.

The verbal processing unit is, at this time, using metacognitive processing as needed, and assembling the set of world and language knowledge for on-line processing assembly. This on-line assembly, then, sends textual representations to internal processing output. The internal processing output, in its turn, is continually matching verbal output to goal settings. When problems are recognized, metacognitive processing may need to reassess goals, task interpretations, organizational plans, types of world knowledge used, types of language knowledge used, and/or the interactions among these resources and plans. Reassessing the goal setting, at a certain point in the process, would also be dependent on the developing text, now available in the context (as textual output in performance); that is, from the moment that text is produced, the many textual variables in the 'textual output' will begin to interact with contextual factors and cognitive processing factors. Of course, the text already written also requires that reading processes interact with writing processes. One benefit of the model discussed here is that it is also possible to account for reading contexts, goals, processes, and outcomes, and such processing must also be an essential part of any model of writing.

When the writer is satisfied that the processing output is sufficiently close to the internal goal setting, and also to the task requirements established by the context, the internal verbal working memory operations will discontinue generating information to satisfy the task requirements. The text at that point is both a representation (of some type) in the verbal working memory and also fully part of the performance in the context.

An extended example with a specific writing task will illustrate how the model would account for many of the considerations raised by the earlier ethnography of writing and the taxonomy of writing skills. In this example, the writing task, set by the teacher, is to produce a one-page summary of a twelve-page reading. The *participants* are the students as writers and the teacher as a real, evaluating audience. The status of the audience will be superior and the degree of solidarity expressed through the writing will be minimal. The *setting* for the writing may be at home, in the school library, or in the classroom. The *task* is to produce a one-page summary – genre and organizational conventions should restrict the writing to a few central ideas and their main supports. The *text* constraints will include the following: the writing will not be a critique of the reading text; details, examples, lists, and processes will be collapsed to single superordinate descriptors; the language used will be formal and academic. The text may also be typed. The *topic* is rain-forest ecology.

The student will engage the *internal goal setting* and set a physical goal of one page of writing. The summary genre and format will be assumed as familiar to the writer, so success is expected. Moreover, the reading is interesting, so the writer is motivated by the topic. The writer also wants to receive a good grade, so he or she will spend more time on this task. The functional goal is to summarize the text – find the main points and report them. The organization of the summary will probably follow the organization of the text. There should be little need to generate additional world knowledge resources because the writer is familiar with the information in the reading text. The topic (re-inforced by the reading of the text) as well as the internal goal setting will generate world knowledge and language resources that are appropriate to describing main points. The student may begin production by brainstorming or noting main ideas in order to generate a stronger organization plan. This pre-writing stage will then lead to a more developed planning/drafting sequence. For both the pre-writing and the drafting, the generated informational and language resources will be integrated by the on-line processing assembly. As processing output begins, the writer begins to produce text on paper (or computer screen).

The summary writing that appears, as *textual output* in *performance*, can be evaluated against internal goal setting, against expectations for text construction (e.g. text coherence, language proficiency), and against summaries typically produced by other students for such tasks. The performance, as text, is open to evaluation by the writer (and by others in collaborative settings), and the many considerations of coherence and text construction are open for assessment. The ongoing production may also create a change in the internal goal setting processes and may lead to new requirements for language resources and world knowledge from the *verbal processing unit.* The repeated sequences of text production, as well as the verbal processing and reassessment of goal setting in verbal working memory, will eventually come to an end when the text product achieves a reasonable fit with the goal setting and matches the constraints and expectations of the context.

From this example, one set of dynamics for the model is highlighted. As the various parameters of the context, and the resources in verbal working memory, change, so also will the dynamics of the model and the text output. Since there are virtually limitless options for different writing scenarios, a model of writing will need to be sufficiently flexible to respond to these differing scenarios. We believe that this model, though tentative and incomplete, has the potential to account for almost any writing activity that typically occurs.

8.4.4 *Uses and limitations of a theory of writing*

This model of writing, adapted from the more general model proposed by Chapelle *et al.* (1993), will need to be elaborated further, as would any model, if it is to account for a number of ongoing issues in writing research and instruction. For example, it will need to incorporate something like the Hayes *et al.* (1987) discussion of revision processes (Chapter 5). It will need to explore in some detail how the various subcomponents of language competence interact among themselves and with world knowledge and processing mechanisms. It will need to specify the full range of factors that should be attributed to the internal goal-setting component; this specification will help research to move beyond listing types of goals and plans, and to consider a number of additional factors which influence goals and plans (e.g. motivation, interest, prior experiences, emotional attitude, etc.). The model will need to account for the notion of writing as a social construction (rather than a social interaction) and describe how notions such as 'shaping at the point of utterance' are to be handled. Further, it will also need to explain how different levels of a writer's language proficiency (and in different subcomponents of language competence) will interact with other components and explain different types of writing output. The model will also need to be suitable for hypothesis generating, and it will need to generate relevant implications for writing instruction in many different contexts (and cultures) as well as suggest possibilities for writing curricula.

Aside from the many issues for which the model would eventually need to account, it also must respond to less tractable questions in interesting ways. Foremost among these is the general issue of how the model of writing changes when the various components of the model have different values and salient features. For example, how does collaborative writing or writing under time pressure alter the dynamics of the model? How does a low level of proficiency in the language or low motivation influence the model dynamics? How do different levels of topical knowledge affect the dynamics? These questions, and many more, become interesting issues as research on writing attempts to situate itself in a model of writing of the type presented here.

The limitations of this model are similar to the limitations noted for many other models: the exact specifications are somewhat vague; the full set of interactions and outcomes are not clear; and the direct implications for instruction are not obvious. At the same time, this model does attempt to address three issues which are not commonly considered in other models of writing.

First, the model incorporates issues related to the social context, to cognitive processing, and to the textual product. This three-way integration is distinct from most other models of writing. Second, because the model builds upon a notion of communicative competence, it is able to incorporate a stronger language component than is normally considered in other models of writing. This greater emphasis on the language component allows more options for capturing the patterns of variation exhibited by many different groups of writers. Third, the model is able to incorporate the information described in the earlier ethnography of writing and taxonomy of writing skills – particularly the specification of the 'situation'; this flexibility suggests that the model is well adapted to the much wider range of concerns discussed by applied linguists as compared to composition researchers. For example, there are probably more L2 students in the world learning to write in English than there are L1 students; yet, aside from applied linguistics discussions, relatively little consideration given to the many different groups of students who would fall within L2 writing contexts, or how a theory of writing would account for these students.

The goal of producing a descriptive model is to understand better the nature of writing, account for important research and writing practice, and rethink what is involved in writing under many different circumstances. However, it is unlikely that any one model will tell us most of what we need to know. One goal of proposing a model is to generate critiques which, in turn, allow our knowledge of writing to progress: the model described in this chapter is proposed in this light rather than as a definitive statement on writing. The model is both a culminating synthesis of research to this point and also a starting point to examine writing anew. It allows for a consideration of useful insights from research and also of shortcomings that need to be addressed.

8.5 Moving from theory to practice

In this chapter, we have presented three variations on a theme. The theme is the question asked at the beginning: 'What is writing?' As a first approximation, the initial ethnography of writing provided the means to situate the parameters that any theory of writing should explain and refer to when considering implications for instruction.

The taxonomy of writing skills, knowledge bases, and processes provided a means for organizing and ordering the many factors which both influence and contribute to writing variation. This reordering as a taxonomy permits an easier reassessment of the many issues involved in writing, the ways that these issues should be specified, and the alternatives that need to be included or substituted. The model, in its turn, suggests ways in which the accumulated information on writing could be integrated so that writing can be understood as a combination of the cognitive, textual, and social factors that are commonly discussed in various research approaches. If we have not answered the basic question as directly as one might wish, we leave it for others to do so and improve on our attempts at synthesizing the relevant writing research.

A second major question which needs to be posed centres on the pedagogical implications that follow from a theory of writing: 'How does one develop writing instruction from a theory of writing?' The most realistic answer is that the movement from theory to practice is not necessarily direct, nor is it necessarily straightforward. One does not simply 'apply' a theory and thereby produce a means of instruction. At the same time, the discussion of theory in this chapter makes a number of strong suggestions for designing writing curricula. These implications will be explored in the next chapter as the discussion moves from theory to application.

Notes

1. Other possible genres include talltales, research articles, editorials, society columns, local news reports, jokes, festschrifts, letters of reference, business letters, fables, research reports, memos, personal letters, condolence letters, biographies, proverbs, travel narratives, business reports, legal briefs, legends, service manuals, short stories, poems, textbooks, research monographs, recipes, diaries, advice books, shopping lists, legal summonses, college handbooks, almanacs, reprint requests, conference handouts, myths, abstracts, research 'letters', classified ads, product ads, sermons, religious tracts, short-answer responses, graffiti, job application forms, etc.
2. Widdowson notes that writers sometimes assume sophisticated knowledge of an immediate audience for the sake of not insulting those in the audience who do possess such sophistication (in Swales 1990: 63–4).

3. Well-known examples include the 'communication triangle', Burke's 'pentad', Jakobson's 'functions of communication', Moffett's 'universe of discourse', Kinneavy's 'aims of discourse' (cf. Lindemann 1987).

4. This problem of lacunae is most easily demonstrated at the syntactic level; e.g. languages such as French, German, and Spanish contain, in their pronominal systems, the possibility of distinguishing between formal and informal second-person modes of address (*tu/vous* in French, *sie/du* in German), but English *lacks* this distinction. This particular feature does not generally pose serious problems; other aspects of modes of address may create more serious difficulties. For example, the use of first names, last names, titles, etc., have significantly different implications in different cultures, as do eye-contact and other paralinguistic features.

5. 'Verbal' processing is the common cognitive psychology term for linguistic processing. It is intended to apply to all linguistic processing in any of the four traditional skills.

6. It is not possible at this time to argue whether or not the 'on-line processing assembly' is also directly part of long-term memory. It would seem reasonable to think that processing routines of many types are part of long-term memory and only the subset needed for a given processing task would become activated in verbal working memory. The question of distributed processing versus stable representations is particularly problematic for this component and takes us well beyond the scope of this discussion, and beyond the purposes of the model proposed.

7. The earlier notion of strategic competence is not parallel to the other language competencies and it is not directly represented in this model. Instead, it is accounted for primarily by the metacognitive processing throughout 'verbal working memory'.

9

From theory to practice

9.1 Introduction

The previous chapters surveyed research on writing which encompassed issues of learning to write in both a first or second language. While no one book can hope to provide a comprehensive overview of research activity in all areas involving the development of writing abilities, the previous chapters do permit us to emphasize those aspects of research which should influence planning for instruction. The purpose of the present chapter is to explore those design criteria which guide and constrain instructional practices. Chapters 10, 11 and 12 will then address practical techniques for writing instruction in various contexts.

The transition from theory to practice will be based upon major research findings on writing as well as a thorough analysis of the social contexts of writing instruction. The research results influence the ways in which a writing curriculum should be designed and suggest effective instructional practices. The social context analysis ensures an appropriate and systematic transition from theory to practice, which must take into account at least the following issues:

- Insights from writing theory and writing research
- The student writer
- The writing teacher
- The educational institution
- The role of instructional materials
- Instructional approaches.

9.2   Insights from writing theory and writing research

This overview highlights those research findings which should be incorporated into planning for a writing curriculum. The section will, for the most part, highlight L2 research findings that allow for direct comparisons with L1 writing research. It appears that a number of L2 research findings differ from those of L1 writing research, and require a consideration of the L2 student writer in a somewhat different light. A recurring theme running throughout this review is that L2 writers, however they might be defined, do not appear to be identical with L1 'basic writers', though there are unquestionably a number of similarities.

9.2.1   *The text product*

The first set of insights from research argues that the written product, and formal aspects of writing, cannot be disregarded in instruction (Leki 1992, Raimes 1991). For L2 writers, greater language proficiency (however defined) will lead, at some point, to better writing quality. Recent research from a socio-cognitive perspective points out the need for models of writing and the raising of student awareness with respect to the ways in which words, structures, and genre forms all contribute to purposeful communication (Berkenkotter and Huckin 1995, Cazden and Gray 1992). In this regard, even the five-paragraph essay and paragraph writing may be useful for students in certain contexts, though not necessarily in the ways in which these notions have been discussed as part of 'traditional instruction' (Smagorinsky 1992). In addition, Fathman and Whalley (1990) have argued that focusing on written form during feedback is no less effective than focusing on content for L2 students (cf., however, Robb *et al.* 1986, Zamel 1985), though focusing solely on form or solely on content appears not to contribute to great improvement in revisions. Similarly, the use of sentence combining has been shown to improve students' abilities to write more complex and varied sentences. However, sentence combining, in order to have a salutary effect, must not be dealt with mechanistically.

Considerations of how discourse is structured have also led to numerous findings which emphasize the importance of discourse features of writing. Vande Kopple (1986, 1990) and Witte (1983b) have shown that the general principle of 'given' before 'new' is adhered to more consistently in better writing and that main ideas are typically marked by topical chaining. Work on cohesive harmony has also shown that higher quality writing has a higher index of cohesive harmony. Recent work on 'involvement' by Tannen (1989) points out features of text which tend to draw in the reader and build coherence. On a somewhat larger scale, research on genre structure has indicated that its role in conveying purpose and assisting the reader's interpretation is critical in effective writing.

Work on contrastive rhetoric has demonstrated that students from different L1 backgrounds, and with a history of culture-specific educational training and socialization, will prefer certain forms of textual organization over other forms in particular writing contexts. As a number of L2 researchers have argued (Leki 1992, Raimes 1991), making students aware of these different preferences can have an important impact on L2 students' composing processes.

Silva (1992, 1993), comparing research on L1 and L2 student writing, has argued that many text-based studies point to distinct issues which should be addressed in L2 writing instruction. Among the differences he noted for L2 students (as compared to L1 students) are:

- different organizational preferences;
- different approaches to argument structuring;
- different approaches to incorporating material from text into writing (e.g. paraphrasing, quoting, style);
- different perspectives on reader orientation, on attention-getting devices, and on estimates of reader knowledge;
- different uses of cohesion markers, in particular markers which areless facilitative and create weaker lexical ties;
- differences in the ways overt linguistic features of the text are used (such as less subordination, more conjunction, less passivization, fewer free modifiers, less noun modification, less specific words, less lexical variety, predictable variation in the purposes of syntactic structures, and a simpler style).

Thus, it cannot be assumed that L1 research findings apply automatically to L2 contexts (Leki 1992, Silva 1992, 1993).

9.2.2   *The writing process*

The notion that writing is not strictly linear in its planning or production is central for instruction, as is the idea that writing is a goal-driven activity. Research on writing processes indicates that good writers:

- plan longer
- have more elaborate plans
- review and reassess plans on a regular basis
- consider more kinds of solutions to rhetorical problems in writing
- consider the reader's point of view in planning and writing
- incorporate multiple perspectives into the drafting
- revise in line with global goals rather than merely editing local segments
- have a wide range of writing and revising strategies to call upon.

Research comparing composing processes of ESL and Native English Speaking (NES) students has often argued that composing processes are similar across L1 and L2 contexts for writing (Jones 1985, Krapels 1990, Richards 1990, Zamel 1982, 1983). More recently, however, research has suggested a number of differences between ESL and NES students (for overview, see Leki 1992). Raimes (1985, 1987, 1991) found that L2 students often spent much more time rehearsing what they wanted to write, were not as bound to local contexts or a concern for making errors in their writing, and were not inhibited by efforts of teachers to correct or edit their work. She suggests that L2 students should not be viewed as L1 writers, nor should they be seen as 'basic writers'. Campbell (1990) found that in using a reading text as a basis for writing, L2 students were more bound to the text in generating their writing. Silva (1992) noted that ESL students could not make use of intuitive editing the way L1 writers can by re-reading texts to see if they 'sound' right.

L2 writers' performance does not always reflect language proficiency; L2 students often reveal more sophisticated composing abilities which have previously been developed in the L1. L1 students, in contrast, have high linguistic proficiency but may not have adequate composing skills. Thus, both language proficiency and composing abilities must be considered in evaluating L2 writing performance.

Other writing process research has accepted the distinction between proficiency and composing skill, and has established that a student's L1 often appears to have a positive influence on L2 composing, as opposed to the generally accepted view that the L1 is only a source of interference (see Krapels 1990). The L1 represents a resource, reflecting what the learner already knows about writing (Edelsky 1982); it assists in the development of content, organization, and details (Friedlander 1990, Lay 1982); it allows the writer to access appropriate lexical items and phrases and to consolidate ideational relations across languages (Cumming 1990a); it permits more sophisticated thinking on the writing topic (Cumming 1989, Leki 1992), and it does not constrain writing time or writing quality (Friedlander 1990). Reviewing this evidence suggests that many composing processes tend to transfer positively, though they do not necessarily represent the same processing used in L1 writing (if for no other reason than L2 writers combine resources from two languages).

Research on the writing process provides many important insights into the ways skilled writers perform, and the ways in which learning to write can be improved.

9.2.3   The social context

The third general insight is that the social context – that of the classroom, the other students, the interactions among the teacher and the students, and the larger world outside the classroom – has a profound impact on the development of writing ability (Heath 1993, Johns 1990, Raimes 1991).

It also appears from recent research that differences between skilled and less-skilled writers are strongly affected by the socio-cognitive aspects of writing. For example, Collins and Williamson (1984) have shown that better writers vary their writing more in line with specific audience and genre constraints. They also have shown that weaker writers are less able to provide explicit structural information for reader interpretation; that is, less-skilled writers are less considerate of the audience – perhaps because they are less aware of the audience (Hillocks 1986). Some researchers have argued that students should not be overburdened with information about audience until they are able to handle the added planning complexity resulting from the availability of such information. Other researchers have pointed out that even weak writers can handle audience concerns if other aspects of the task are made manageable (Bonk 1990, Collins and Williamson 1984).

The related emphasis on writing purpose and task variation has led to a reconsideration of the concept of genre in writing development. While writing instruction in many traditional approaches was guided by model texts which demonstrated specific generic patterns of organization, the current reassessment of genre relates to its formal role in writing purpose and task. It is now recognized that genre form has evolved out of a consistent and conventionalized means of addressing specific purposes and tasks in writing. Thus, genres are conventionalized ways to achieve meaning – to solve rhetorical problems – and students vary their writing according to genre structures which match their purposes for writing. Research along this line argues that the various genres and tasks which are useful for academic contexts need to be practised extensively, not as arbitrary models, but as means for achieving academic goals and purposes (Atkinson 1991, Christie 1992, Crowhurst 1990, Swales 1990).

The influence of genre on writing has been examined from a number of perspectives. Empirical research has indicated that genre is a critical factor in shaping the written text. Students, assigned to write on different tasks and for different purposes, systematically vary their grammatical, lexical, and organizational choices to conform to expected genre constraints. Moreover, skilled writers appear to be much more sensitive in this regard than less-skilled writers (Bereiter and Scardamalia 1987, Crowhurst 1987, 1990). Australian approaches to writing development, influenced by Halliday's functional theory of language use, have similarly investigated the role of genre in content-centred instruction and concluded that attention to genre structure is a critical component of which students need to be made aware, and with which they need to practise (Christie 1992, Gray 1990, Martin 1989).

Another socio-cognitive approach to writing development has evolved out of Vygotsky's theories of language and literacy development. From this point of view, the student learns to write by working with a more knowledgeable person on the skills and knowledge needed to perform specific purposeful actions through a kind of apprenticeship. Seen in this light, writing development involves an apprenticeship which requires considerable practice, under expert guidance. Moreover, students gradually learn by appropriating the teacher's goals and purposes for writing, as well as the appropriate language forms, in the process of the writing activity and through feedback on the writing. Such an appropriation occurs in what Vygotsky terms the 'zone of proximal development' (ZPD) – that level of knowledge between normal student performance and what a student is capable of attaining with expert assistance. Empirical research by Bereiter and Scardamalia points out that students often are capable of writing performance well beyond their normal writing output.

The commonly assumed notion among composition researchers of generalized transfer of learned writing skills across tasks, purposes, genres, and topics is not an inference to be drawn from a Vygotskean approach to writing. Rather, children learn to internalize and self-regulate those writing purposes and tasks in which they have had extensive practice and guidance. This approach:

- accommodates the interactive roles of experts and peers;
- stresses purposeful writing tasks;
- stresses the interaction of language skills in the accomplishment of specific tasks; and
- highlights the importance of practising those writing tasks and goals which students need to learn rather than assuming general transfer of writing skills across purposes, tasks, topics, and genres (Newman *et al.* 1989, Rogoff 1990, Tharp and Gallimore 1988).

9.2.4 Research on instructional techniques

The fourth general insight into writing from research derives from studies testing the effectiveness of various instructional techniques. These techniques include direct instruction – especially metacognitive strategy training, types of group interactions among teacher and students, techniques for guiding the drafting and revising stages of writing, and techniques for providing effective feedback on writing. The research which has important implications for instruction includes the specific training experiments of Bereiter and Scardamalia, and those of Flower and Hayes. In earlier work, Flower and Hayes have pointed out the importance of multiple drafting, time for planning, the role of recursion among planning, drafting and revising, and the essential problem-solving nature of writing. In more recent work, they have extended research into revision processes, pointing out the importance of, and difficulty with, global revision of writing. Very recent work by Flower examines the interactive influences of the writer's cognitive processes and the social contexts of the writing situation.

In Flower's recent work (Flower 1994, Flower *et al.* 1990), she demonstrates:

- that skilled writers consider more perspectives in relation to the rhetorical problem at hand and are good at representing the problem;
- that task representation has a major impact on writing;
- that students need to develop a strategic awareness for meeting writing goals appropriately; and
- that students have difficulty transferring their writing knowledge from one context to another.

In addition, Bereiter and Scardamalia (1987) have shown:

- that greater topic familiarity does not always lead to better writing (cf. Richards 1990);
- that greater essay length tends to correspond with indicators of writing quality and maturity (cf. L2 reverse findings, Leki 1992);
- that general knowledge about how to perform a writing activity will not ensure that students will be able to carry out the task;
- that many writing assignments produce poor results not because student are overloaded by the process but because they are bored by the process;
- that teacher modelling and support for revising strategically can improve students' revising abilities;
- that the goal of writing instruction is to have students see writing as a problem-solving activity involving self-regulation, evaluation, diagnosis, and reflection (see also Cumming 1990a for a similar L2 perspective).

A key proposal for developing critical skills is to have the teacher modelling and thinking aloud while composing (Bryson and Scardamalia 1991). Such strategies for writing development have also been suggested for L2 contexts (Raimes 1985, Cohen 1990).

Bereiter and Scardamalia also provide a number of suggestions in order to help students develop a knowledge-transforming ability in writing:

- instruction should induce a simplified version of the complex strategies needed by students and then that these strategies may be gradually appropriated by students;
- writing tasks should be developed which will gradually help students to transfer advanced skills to new domains;
- students need to have teacher-modelling of problem-solving composing processes;
- students need to be aware of the goals of writing and need to be given challenging tasks; and
- students should be shown how to provide support and assistance to others.

In related research on expertise and the problem of ill-defined task representation, the skilled writer is again shown to be able to work through writing tasks as problem-solving activities. What typically leads to expertise in writing is not well understood, since writing is complex, locally dependent, and relatively ill-defined: it can be made more or less complex depending on the writer, the perceived reader, the complexity of the topic and the depth of explanation intended, and the demands of the text (e.g. genre constraints, length, purpose). Scardamalia and Bereiter (1991) define writing expertise as a gradually building dialectic process between domain knowledge of the writer and the specific tasks. For many beginning writers, a challenging writing task leads to the discovery of additional knowledge of the domain, which, in turn, leads to a more effective execution of the writing task. As Scardamalia and Bereiter note, 'Experts acquire their vast knowledge resources not by doing what falls comfortably within their competence but by working on real problems that force them to extend their knowledge and competence' (1991: 174).

This line of research suggests that instruction should promote extensive practice within a set of related contexts, using challenging tasks which build on the solutions of earlier tasks (M. Carter 1990, Spiro *et al.* 1987). Bereiter and Scardamalia argue that expository assignments offer the best context for developing problem-solving tasks in writing and opportunities for students to work with their own knowledge. Expository tasks force students to clarify meanings, discover implications, establish connections, formulate problems for intended goals, and evaluate decisions. An approach which relies predominantly on expressive writing and on narrative recounting does not typically make as great a set of demands or provide as many opportunities for knowledge transforming.

Research on writing tasks in classroom environments has shown that certain pre-writing activities are particularly useful for students. Also the more traditional heuristics for writing 'invention' appear to be useful for better writing (e.g. Hughey *et al.* (1983), Richards 1990, Young *et al.* 1970; cf. Bereiter and Scardamalia's (1987) concern that pre-writing activities sometimes make writing tasks too simplistic). Such devices for planning and goal-directed idea generation are similar to Bereiter and Scardamalia's instructional interventions referred to as 'procedural facilitation,' but students make use of the cues in procedural facilitation *while* they are writing rather than *before* they write (Bryson and Scardamalia 1991).

Other insights from classroom contexts involve research on feedback and revision instruction. While there are a number of questions about the effectiveness of various revision and feedback procedures, Leki (1992) points out that students need to learn how to revise more effectively, whether the learners are international students, or immigrant or L2 minority student in tertiary institutions.

9.2.5   Research and curriculum design

The research reviewed in this section points out the range of issues and concerns which must be considered in developing curriculum design. No theoretical perspective nor set of research findings should be reinterpreted as having a one-to-one relationship with curriculum design. Rather, the goal is to recognize that research occurs in contexts not typically equivalent to the language classroom; it also creates constraints and/or opportunities/ resources which are not typical of the language classroom. The goal in making the transition from theory to practice is to recognize the relevance of research insights and their potential for informing curriculum and instruction.

9.3   The student writer

One of the first tasks of curriculum design is to establish who the instruction will be for, what the learner needs, wants, and is capable of, what factors will cause individual learner variation within a given group, and how other curriculum constraints interact with this particular set of issues. The potential diversity of learners in writing instruction is enormous.

In addressing this diversity, an applied linguistics perspective is assumed, and thus various L2 contexts as well as L1 contexts need to be considered; no attempt to privilege a particular subset of students or writing contexts for the discussion of writing has been taken (except that learning-disabled students are not considered in any context). In some respects such an approach is obviously problematic, as this section will highlight. At the same time, any strict delimiting of the perceived student in this discussion of writing would remove from consideration important research findings and instructional issues, as well as interesting writing practices. The purpose of this section, then, will be to highlight the different types of constraints that accompany different groups of students, to the extent that differences can be systematically recognized. Variations in student background due to language, culture and preferred learning style, educational training, age, and individual differences all must be considered in relating theory to practice.

9.3.1 L1 versus L2 student writers

Within the domain of L1 literacy development lies variation created by the ages of the learners, the social and cultural group identities of the learners, the extent of access to educationally valued literacy practices, the extent to which the learners' dialects/idiolects depart from the educationally valued dialect, and the range of individual differences in terms of learning styles and strategies (see Chapter 1).

The range of L2 learners is even more complex,[1] as these learners may come from literally thousands of different L1 backgrounds. They will not only fit into all the ranges of divisions for L1 learners but will also vary considerably in terms of the contexts of L2 use and the purposes for needing/learning a second language.

The picture which emerges from attempting to describe student variables in planning writing instruction is one of great complexity. In ESL contexts, consideration needs to be given to:

- the extent of L1 literacy;
- social practices and expectation in L1 literacy;

- the L1 educational background;
- the extent of previous and current contact with English speakers;
- the social and cultural distance of the student from the dominant and educationally valued English-speaking group;
- the intended length of stay in an English-speaking environment (any such environment, not necessarily the one in which instruction occurs).

EFL contexts may be even more complex. Consideration must be given to:

- country of origin;
- length of prior English study;
- extent of access to English;
- linguistic typological distance of L1 from English;
- social and political attitudes towards English and English speakers generally;
- training and expertise of the English teacher;
- extent of L1 literacy training;
- social practices and expectations in L1 literacy;
- major field of study or educational track in school;
- potential for economic opportunities; and
- cultural expectations for learning.

While the total picture is rather overwhelming, the fact is that most teachers, institutions, and materials developers do not have to deal with the full array of student variables. The purpose in sorting through the range of variation is to sensitize the reader towards the concerns of writing teachers in many different contexts. An example should illustrate the importance of this context sensitivity and also point out important differences between L1 and L2 writing students – in this case, the differences between international ESL students and English-speaking students in a tertiary-level writing course context.

9.3.2   *The international student*

The international ESL student studying in the tertiary-level writing course in an English-speaking country works within a very different set of constraints than do other students working at the same level. Leki (1992) carefully reviews the many differences between international students and English-speaking basic writers, two populations often placed in the same courses in US tertiary-level institutions and often assumed to be similar in backgrounds and needs.

According to Leki (1992), international students have linguistic, cultural/attitudinal and academic experiences which distinguish them from the English-speaking basic writer. International students are often seen as having *composing* problems by the teacher when, in fact, they are dealing with *linguistic* problems. International students are typically trained in more formal registers of English ('book language') which is an advantage in academic contexts; however, teacher efforts to simplify language by using informal registers often makes comprehension more difficult for these students. International students:

- are likely to misunderstand class interactions, teacher talk, and orally given assignments;
- have difficulty participating orally in class;
- often misread non-verbal cues which cause numerous attitudinal conflicts;
- are not able to rely on native speaker intuitions when using language, so reading papers aloud may not be a suitable teaching technique;
- expect to return home after finishing their studies, and may not see English as critical for their future careers.

Attitudinal and cultural differences create major distinctions between international and native English-speaking students. In most basic writing courses, international students recognize hostility among some native English-speaking students who resent being placed in the same class as international students (whose linguistic limitations may be wrongly interpreted as signs of stupidity). The implication in such a situation is that the native L1 speakers do not know their own language. Since international students do not have a cultural identity with the forms of English they use, they can more easily abandon their uses for more academically 'correct' language. Many international students also stand apart because they come from economically privileged backgrounds (foreign education is intrinsically expensive) and have very sophisticated world outlooks (their wealth/position in their home communities has exposed them to high-quality education, etc.).

Academically, these students also present quite different

profiles from other students, and are often surprised by the behaviour of their hosts in the classroom and by the level of informality exhibited by both teacher and students.

International students also experience many disadvantages that are not always recognized by teachers (particularly in the USA).

- They do not have a full range of host country cultural experiences (e.g. TV, sports, holidays, political system, economic system (i.e. a credit economy), etc.).
- They may come from countries with ambiguous political relations with the host country, marked by simplistic stereotypes of host country people and situations.
- They are perhaps often painfully reminded that host country people know, or want to know, very little about their cultures.
- They experience some degree of culture shock – disorientation – and something as simple as shopping for shoes or buying food can become overwhelming.
- They may experience unique academic problems (especially in the USA), and are often surprised by course requirements in host country tertiary-level institutions – such as regular attendance, homework, and periodic tests.
- They are unaccustomed to the idea that any theory is relative, open to criticism by the teacher and to comparison with conflicting views.
- They are often unfamiliar with the rigidity of assignment deadlines, and the legalistic concerns of plagiarism.
- They often find it difficult to express an honest opinion that conflicts with the view by the teacher.
- They may find such techniques as conferencing to be problematic as they may out of politeness feel compelled to agree with, but not comply with, all teacher suggestions.
- They may experience frustrations when they recognize their inability to express complex academic ideas which they know they can express adequately in their own language.

When one recognizes that many detailed group differences can be similarly drawn between Native American and Black students and their white middle-class peers in US secondary schools, between Spanish-speaking minority students and English-speaking Anglo students in elementary classes, between EFL students learning English in tertiary institutions in their own countries and international students learning English in the USA, etc., it becomes clear that student considerations must enter into any planning for a writing curriculum.

9.3.3   The role of the student

The obverse side of understanding the experiences of the students and their range of variation is to recognize those skills and attitudes which are important for the good learner. Hughey *et al.* (1983) describe good learners as students who take an active role in their learning; these students set goals and take responsibility for their learning. To explain what is needed to become an active learner, Hughey *et al.* (1983: 50–4) and Leki (1992) address a number of areas which help define the good learner.

They note that, first, learners need to have *a positive approach.* Learners must have some empathy for the language that they will use and try to write whenever appropriate to do so. They will need to:

- believe that they will be successful in their writing development;
- have an open attitude to their academic environment and to the sorts of writing tasks they will be asked to perform;
- willingly pursue issues and not think they already have all the knowledge they might need; and
- be willing to practise and revise their writing, recognizing that writing development is a gradual process which requires much hard work.

Second, learners need *appropriate skills* in order to carry out writing assignments. They need a reasonable degree of control over the language and some ability to manipulate the language in response to varying needs. They need to have an appropriate level of control over vocabulary and the rhetorical structures of the language. Students need adequate reading skills as well in order to read what they write and read other sources for information, for contrasting views, and for alternative ways to view writing.

Third, learners need some *set of workable learning strategies* which are applicable to the writing context. They need strategies for planning and setting appropriate goals, for working with words and language structures, for developing information and arguments, for attending to the rhetorical constraints of the task, for re-reading texts and revising effectively, and for evaluating their writing and comparing it to other writing.

Fourth, learners need to be *motivated* to invest the time and effort, whether the motivation comes from perceived economic opportunities, from better grades, or from a desire to develop better communication skills. While a certain amount of extrinsic motivation is typically used to motivate students such as well-designed assignments, relevant topics, and interesting materials, intrinsic motivation must be developed as well if the student is to become an active learner.

The role of the learner represents one aspect of the matrix of issues which contribute to curriculum design. Another major component in the planning process involves the nature of teaching: Who is the teacher and what role does the effective teacher play in writing instruction?

9.4   The writing teacher

9.4.1   Teacher training

A writing curriculum must give consideration to the strengths and training which the teachers bring to instruction. Once again, a number of basic distinctions tend to group teachers in important ways. Among the basic considerations are whether or not teachers are themselves native (or near-native) speakers of English. Another consideration is whether or not they have had explicit training and/or experience in teaching writing. A third issue is how skilled and well-trained teachers are as teachers. While any programme would like to assume that all teachers are excellent, well trained in writing instruction (and native speakers of English), such is not often the case, and curricula should be planned in light of realistic estimates of teacher strengths and weaknesses.

The situation with respect to the non-native English speaker as writing teacher is particularly complex. In certain countries in which English is a foreign language without special emphasis in the educational system, the extent of writing ability and practise needed to become a writing teacher may actually be minimal, and often teachers' own skills in writing are rather weak. In these situations, teachers quite naturally are not interested in certain approaches to writing instruction (e.g. the process approach to writing, an approach which might reveal the English language limitations of the teacher). Non-native English teachers in ESL situations in which English is a major language in the educational system (e.g. the Philippines) may also have distinct instructional preferences. Such teachers may not like to cede control of the classroom to students since doing so might be interpreted as a weakness in English language knowledge or writing skills; similarly, allowing students to choose topics for writing – or not correcting errors diligently – may be seen as signs of linguistic weakness. The essential point is that local contexts of instruction often determine the effectiveness of instructional approaches. Sometimes an approach which is appropriate in the context of an English-speaking country may be less effective in other contexts if for no other reasons than those deriving from misperceptions by students.

Another set of issues pertains to the knowledge of language and writing that teachers possess. Among these issues are the extent of creativity and innovation with language and writing, degree of skill in writing itself, knowledge of the pragmatics of the language being taught, interest in examining/studying writing, writing habits and practices, and motivation to write. Teachers also need experiences with specific genres and registers that are important for the writing curriculum.

It is true that the above issues are not all-or-nothing propositions; teachers, both native and non-native, will be represented fully along each continuum: English language skills, teaching skills, writing skills. In some respects, while in-service training may serve to improve teaching skills and, in particular, the skills implicit in teaching writing, it is somewhat more difficult to assess or to address the training needs of the non-native English writing teacher.

A large number of particular teacher attributes should also be considered in planning writing instruction. These attributes may have an important, though not always obvious, impact on the success of a writing curriculum. The following list points out individual variables which occur among any group of teachers. Individual teacher characteristics will vary at least by:

- age
- general educational and social background
- cultural expectations
- time since completion of teacher training
- professional affiliations
- years of teaching experience
- academic subject knowledge/interests

- philosophical views on teaching and learning
- willingness to cede formal control in the classroom
- preferences for class structuring
- extent of adherence to materials/curriculum
- gender (and gender stereotypes)
- linguistic competence in L1 and L2.

Differing perspectives on many of the issues noted above will influence how any teacher will approach writing instruction.

9.4.2 *The role of the writing teacher*

Aside from examining the variation which typically occurs among groups of teachers and within these groups, it is also important to recognize the types of tasks the teacher must carry out in the course of writing instruction, and the strengths that many teachers bring to the classroom. In planning a writing curriculum, the teacher must at various times be a motivator, an interpreter of the task, a designer of meaningful tasks, an organizer, a resource, a support person, an evaluator, and a reader for information. Somewhat more specifically, teachers need to show a positive attitude, believing that students are capable of doing the work in the curriculum; and when students are found to be struggling with specific assignments, teachers need flexibility to adapt these assignments to ensure reasonable opportunities for success. Teachers need to provide students with a wide range of opportunities for writing, opportunities which are interesting for students and which serve important developmental goals. Teachers need, also, to develop among students a sense of community and sharing so that writing can become a collaborative and cooperative endeavour.

A final requirement for good teachers is that they have productive insights about writing and the writing process. They need to be aware of all of the following issues in writing and convey these insights to students:

1. Writing takes time to develop, and instruction should be planned accordingly.
2. Students need to be made aware of the role of language form as the medium of meaningful communication, as well as the types of language constraints which are reflected in different genres and purposes for writing.
3. Writing development requires extensive practice.

4. Writing can sometimes be difficult and frustrating, and students need positive feedback and enough success to maintain a willingness to work.
5. Students will occasionally vary in their performance and should be made aware that this variation will occur.
6. Students should be encouraged, at times, to take risks, to innovate, and to rethink assignments in more complex ways.

The role of the teacher is very complex; the teacher must balance various pedagogical insights which will have to be rethought somewhat differently for each student in the class.

9.5   The educational institution

To this point, the emphasis for instruction has been squarely on the teacher. But responsibility for what happens in the classroom must be shared with the institution within which the teacher functions and with the system in which that institution is embedded. While the purpose of this section is not to suggest that any given teacher must be prepared for all potential instructional contexts, it does point out that planning a writing curriculum occurs in many different places with many diverse institutional goals.

Institutions typically decide the goals for learning:

- They plan and operationalize the curriculum, usually in accord with the institutional norms for a country, a region, or a set of related bodies.
- They react to the requirements of an inspectorate.
- They decide how much time in the curriculum to allocate to writing instruction and support systems.
- They decide how much money to allocate for writing instruction and support equipment.
- They decide the teacher-training courses, and how much training teachers need in order to teach writing courses.
- They decide how much to pay teachers, how many students should be taught in any class, and how many classes should be taught by any given teacher during a given term.
- They decide how much writing instruction different students need and for what purposes.
- They decide whether or not to support teachers for further training.

- They decide the relative importance of writing in relation to other components of the curriculum.
- They decide how to integrate writing with other components of the curriculum (ESP courses, etc.).

The institution's decisions play a major role in shaping a writing curriculum. As one example of this impact, many elementary schools in the USA are restructuring language arts curricula to integrate writing with other language activities and are simultaneously moving towards the consideration of writing in content areas; thus, content-centred approaches and integrated-skills approaches are bringing writing together with subject-matter instruction rather than maintaining writing as a separate skill with its own discrete and isolated block of time in the curriculum.

9.6   The role of instructional materials

Writing instruction makes use of a wide variety of information and resources. Some of these resources are straightforward in terms of a writing context; others are less obvious but equally effective. Resources for writing can be classified into texts, libraries/media, realia, student-generated resources, activities, and discussions. The latter four types of resources are discussed in detail in Chapters 10, 11 and 12.

Texts for working with writing instruction would include rhetorics/writing texts (for academic contexts); language arts texts (for lower grades); anthologies of readings for writing; workbooks and usage/grammar handbooks; dictionaries; encyclopaedias/biographical sources/atlases; novels and short stories; articles from magazines and journals; newspapers; non-fiction books; and textbooks from subject-area fields. Some of these resources are designed explicitly for writing instruction and tend to reflect specific approaches to instruction; other materials provide resources for reflection, information, and argumentation.

Writing textbooks, of course, are not objective, scientific works; on the contrary, they exemplify the biases of the writer, of the publisher, and of the market. It is a regrettable reality that publishers are required by their Boards of Directors to earn money – they are, presumably, profit-centred organizations. Thus, they are inclined to make decisions in marketing terms, not in instructional terms. In sum, textbooks that are likely to sell are likely to get published, and for this reason, teachers should not accept a textbook at face value but should examine it carefully to determine whether it coincides with the methodology adopted for instruction, whether it is appropriate to the intended instructional audience, and whether it is reasonable in terms of the cultural parameters in which the instruction is being offered.

Another obvious resource for materials is the library, either in school or in the community. Library visits allow students to browse through book topics and examine a range of topical possibilities which might be completely new to the individual or the group.

The issue of materials and resources is another important area. Often, one hears that classes cannot afford the materials and resources they would like to enhance the curriculum. Resources will obviously vary enormously in different instructional situations, but any class can generate its own range of materials and activities to stimulate topics and tasks for writing if the most up-to-date resources are not available. In some respects, the creative use of student-generated materials provides the best avenue for initiating exploration of issues and topics, both personal and academic.

9.7   Instructional approaches

There are three potentially separable domains into which one can sort a discussion of instructional approaches: the general 'schooling' domain, the tertiary-level domain, and EFL/ESP domain. The first context involves approaches at the general 'schooling' level but most particularly at elementary grade level; discussions typically centre on whole-language versus more traditional language arts approaches (but also on content-based approaches and genre-centred approaches). The second general set of themes converge from discussions of tertiary-level and pre-tertiary-level settings (e.g. intensive EAP programmes), whether the students concerned are English L1 students or ESL students in English-speaking academic contexts. The third domain might best be represented as an EFL/ESP or L1 work-based grouping which typically does not enter into the frays which excite the first two groups. In fact, most discussions in this third group are decidedly atheoretical – writing instruction is seen as following the dictates of the general EFL language curriculum (usually with little writing emphasis), or the dictates of specialized student/institutional needs such as writing for airline mechanics, medical technicians, missile battery operators, etc. There are, of course, other potential groups, though they are seldom addressed in the general writing literature and the professional journals (e.g. adult education writing, deaf students, 'learning-disabled' students, etc.).

9.7.1   Elementary contexts

In elementary contexts, there are three potentially discernible positions with respect to writing approaches:

1. Traditional language arts approaches (with some process writing included)
2. Whole-language approaches
3. Genre-centred approaches.

In fact, there is considerable potential overlap among these approaches, and sometimes the debate centres on philosophical issues rather than focusing on radically different curricula and techniques for teaching/learning writing.

9.7.1.1   Traditional language arts

Traditional language arts curricula are typically textbook-based and often – though not necessarily – combine language arts texts with basal readers. Such approaches often use simple assignments from the text which involve student-centred expressive writing, narratives, and occasional reports/descriptions. This approach includes options for teaching grammar, spelling, and vocabulary. Most texts of this type now stress a process writing approach, though it is not clear to what extent teachers follow through with such text recommendations (Applebee 1986, Ley *et al.* 1994).

9.7.1.2   Whole-language approaches

Most whole-language variations represent strong reactions to the frustration with traditional language arts approaches to writing

(Edelsky *et al.* 1991). The movement also represents, in general, an effort to place the teacher and the students at the centre of the curriculum rather than having instruction mandated by a school or district plan.

There are many important principles and instructional practices which have been advocated by whole-language practitioners. These principles and practices are currently having a major impact on writing instruction in the USA and Canada, and some influence in New Zealand, Australia, and the UK. Since whole-language practitioners make strong claims for their approach, it is important also to examine some of the limitations of this approach. First, the theoretical framework for whole language is somewhat protean in nature. It includes references to M.A.K. Halliday and Vygotsky; but, in contrast:

- Halliday stresses the crucial role of language structure as mediator of social interaction and purposeful communication (Halliday 1993b);
- Vygotsky stresses the distinctions between oral and written language in the sense that the latter requires socio-cultural mediation and support – moreover, a Vygotskean approach stresses attention to the skills to be learned through a social apprenticeship and a gradual appropriation of others' goals and language use through direct instruction.

The protean nature of whole language also prevents comparisons between itself and other approaches since evaluative measures and empirical orientations arise out of the other approaches and are seen as inappropriate means for evaluating whole language.

There are practical criticisms that whole-language classes, being learner-centred, do not provide support for many students who need a more structured learning environment. Such students may need teacher modelling and assistance, and they may not, by nature, be creative and inquisitive on the kinds of tasks/cycles which focus the whole-language classroom. The notion that the curriculum should come from the interests and choices of the students is perceived by some as an abdication of the role of the teacher as a more knowledgeable other, an evaluator, and a teacher. All of these teacher roles, in the right contexts, are necessary for effective student learning (Genesee 1994). Teaching the writing process, for example, does not mean a teacher should avoid actively guiding students' writing processes. The assumptions of universal learning processes and skills also de-sensitize teachers, preventing them from seeing that students conceivably come from very different social, linguistic, and cultural backgrounds, with different expectations about language use in class contexts.

A somewhat less ideological perspective on elementary language development and whole-language activities is seen in Enright and McCloskey (1988). They present a view of language development among elementary-grade students which incorporates many whole-language methods, integrates language skills, emphasizes purposeful language use, and combines language learning with content area learning. In this more flexible approach, the content plays a stronger role and creates the opportunity to relate language activities to content within existing curricular frameworks.

9.7.1.3 Genre-centred approaches

The genre-centred approach is currently being practised in Australia (Christie 1992, Christie *et al.* 1991, Cope and Kalantzis 1993, Hasan and Martin 1989, Martin 1989, 1993). This approach, based on Halliday's functional systemic views of language and his social semiotic theory of language development (see Chapter 5, section 5.3), stresses the social nature of language learning but also stresses the mediating role that language form plays in purposeful communication (Halliday 1993b). In essence, this approach brings in the role of language form in learning language and combines it with notions of writing process, integration of language skills, meaningful communication, peer collaboration, and, in many instances, content-based instruction (Collerson 1990, Derewianka 1990). An important theme in this approach is that students develop a sense of the shaping role of genres in writing, and how language structure and genre form constrain the ways in which language communicates information.

9.7.2   *The influence of instructional approaches*

The role of different instructional approaches in the teaching of writing has been quite influential. Often, teachers are exposed to a general philosophy of writing based on one approach or another and are assured that there is strong evidence for the various insights claimed for the approach. In many cases, rationales given for instructional approaches are themselves taken as evidence and cited in later descriptions as research support for the approach. It is important to sort the discussions of supporting empirical and observational evidence from those sources which describe an approach and provide logical/intuitive rationales for the approach as well as appeals to similar earlier articles and appeals to authority. In this way, it should then be possible to consider the insights from instructional approaches in light of research findings. From this relationship, it should also be possible to find generalizable instructional ideas which can underlie the principles of a writing curriculum.

9.8 A generalized approach to writing curricula

The preceding discussion has attempted to determine the range of evidence which is available from research and to consider how that research can be categorized and related to other knowledge (see also Chapter 8). The influence and roles of the student, of the teacher, and of instructional material have all been considered. The influences of various instructional approaches to writing have also been discussed. It has been necessary to look at instructional approaches independently because many views proposed in instructional approaches are presented as though they are supported by evidence, without making the evidence explicit; other views depend on appeals to teaching experiences or logical/theoretical arguments from rhetoric, psychology, education, linguistics, or language learning. It is important, then, to compare these approaches and to determine to what extent their underlying philosophies overlap, their instructional methods match, and their theoretical bases receive support from research. The final aim of this chapter is to distill useful generalized notions of what should be involved in good writing instruction on the basis of these several sources.

9.8.1 An idealized writing curriculum

An idealized writing curriculum would combine emphases from the writing product, the process, the social context, and the subject-matter content (Raimes 1991).

1. The course would be content-driven and present topical issues and writing tasks which motivate and engage students, while at the same time being challenging and providing opportunities for learning. Students would work within a coherent content-based conceptual framework and would explore the complexity of thematic issues, leading to more challenging writing tasks, the learning of new content, and knowledge specialization as opposed to writing what the teacher already knows (Bartholomae and Petrosky 1986).

2. The course would see writing as an apprenticeship training in which teachers:

   (i)   act as knowledgeable experts who can model effective writing practices;
   (ii) raise student awareness of relevant strategies;
   (iii) engage students in problem-solving planning;
   (iv) help students sort through formal linguistic choices;
   (v)   guide the development of the strategies and skills which will let students perform similarly without teacher support;
   (vi) develop activities which allow the gradual transfer of these skills to other (related) contexts.

   Such a view of instructional guidance draws heavily on meta-cognitive strategy research, research on the development of expertise, and Vygotskean views on literacy learning.

3. The course would engage students in the writing process, recognizing that writing is a recursive process in which writers continually plan, write, revise, and refine; thus, the course would use multiple drafting, student selection of tasks, many opportunities for feedback, and reaction writing and free writing for the exploration of ideas and issues related to the writing tasks. Students would learn how to generate plans and call up content information, how to organize plans through invention and 'topics', how to write fluently, how to draft without expecting a final text, how to revise – develop the inner reader, and how to elaborate and refine.

4. The course would incorporate cooperative learning activities for peer feedback, for exploration of ideas, for interaction which will enhance writing strategies and skills, and for opportunities to improve learning as the student recognizes alternative interpretations of information and of the writing

tasks themselves. Students learn from each other in many ways, including access to prior successful performance (improved attribution), positive attitudes (motivation), a wider range of accessible content, and alternative sets of underlying assumptions brought to the tasks. Group work would usually be partly directive so that specific tasks would be guided with work sheets or oral directions up to the point at which students can provide effective feedback and be good audiences (R. Stahl 1994).

5. The course would require the integration of language skills. Students would read extensively; would spend much time writing about their readings and relating the reading to the writing tasks; would discuss the readings and their writing; would write more based on their discussions and those discussions would lead to additional readings, which would, in turn, lead to more writing, etc. Such a perspective combines Freirean and Vygotskean views with research on the interactive benefits of reading and writing together – research which suggests that this interaction leads to better learning and promotes greater interest/involvement.

6. The course would attend to formal constraints of the language which serve to signal writing purpose, the role of genre for reader expectation, and the flow of discourse information. This aspect of the course would provide a focus for group analysis of texts, for teacher modelling of writing, for verbalized goal planning and problem solving, and for explanations of formal language constraints as they arise naturally – giving students the appropriate metalanguage to discuss these issues directly and explicitly. Such an emphasis would allow students to address more complex discourse and organizational issues with a specific vocabulary – giving students true control over the language through the metalanguage. Revisions of texts, whether by teacher or by peers, would include analyses of formal aspects of text, and not only in the final stages of drafting. Lower-level writers would be given writing tasks such as composition modelling, guided composition, sentence combining and other activities, which is particularly important for L2 contexts, allowing students to attend to formal aspects without being initially overwhelmed. It should be noted that these activities should not be done *in place of* other writing activities or as a preliminary requirement to other writing activities.

7. The course would provide careful consideration of the audience, as well as the influence of the social context, on the writing task. Students would be made aware, through the teacher composing aloud and through misunderstandings by other readers, how audience considerations must be given careful attention, whether they be seen in terms of Gricean maxims, power and politeness relations, or register parameters and expectations. The course would look to incorporate a range of audience sources, whether in the form of letters to others; competitions for writing; presentations of projects, posters, diaramas, or reports sent to other readers; or publications of writing production.

8. The course would provide ways to introduce early writing activities and encourage experimentation without harsh evaluation, promoting a sense of language play. Varieties of English would be respected, though standard forms would also be developed and used as the means for becoming bidialectal and gaining access to the school-valued educational genres. Writing development would move from the personal to the academic, from those tasks in which students have access to information to those tasks which require a search for information and the complex development of information presentation.

9. Writers would practise a range of writing tasks and learn to work with a variety of genres and rhetorical issues. Students would also write extensively, carrying out the idea that writing proficiency requires constant practice, even if writing quantity, by itself, is not sufficient for writing improvement. Students and teachers would negotiate some subset of the total set of assignments in the class; most commonly, students would choose specific topics of interest within broader curricular themes.

10. The course would offer a variety of options for feedback, some of which would be evaluative; other feedback would be non-evaluative. Assessment of writing development would be carried out in a variety of ways, through in-class writing, out-of-class writing, journals, conferences, free writing and reflective writing, portfolios, evaluation of final drafts of essays and projects. Students would take an active role in assessment by participating in feedback, in developing content resources, and in interaction and discussion.

9.8.2 The realities of curriculum planning

The ideal curriculum described above is, perhaps, not one which is fully applicable to any single real context. As the other sections of this chapter have pointed out, each context for writing instruction will consist of a unique set of constraints: different students, teachers, institutions; different resources, time allocations, and access to information; and different individual abilities, expectations, social/cultural backgrounds, and linguistic backgrounds. At the same time, the above idealization does synthesize research and practices which appear to improve writing. In this respect, these feature should be incorporated into a writing curriculum to the extent that it is feasible to do so. At the very least, they represent guiding notions for the planning, implementation, and/or evaluation of a writing curriculum (see also Hilgers and Marsella 1992).

Given this set of guiding principles, it seems reasonable to turn to the set of issues for which many practising teachers have a primary concern:

- What specific techniques can be used in the teaching of writing?
- How can they be adapted to different contexts?
- How might they fit within a rationale such as that noted above?

Chapters 10, 11 and 12 explore specific instructional techniques for beginning, pre-academic, and academic writing instruction. While these chapters will, in effect, present 'pieces', it must be noted that writing techniques must be considered within a given curriculum design and a given theoretical motivation. Only those techniques which are motivated by the goals and assumptions of a given curriculum should be adopted. The techniques which follow, then, are not a set of activities to be tried out 'next week', but rather a set of options which should be considered for use only to the extent that they serve the general goals of the curriculum adopted and the preferred instructional approach of the institution.

Note

1. For ease of discussion, the following treatment of second language students will assume that English is the second language. The following categorization could be replicated with other second languages in non-English speaking countries.

10

Teaching writing at beginning levels

> What is learning to read and write? Fundamentally, it is an extension of the functional potential of language. Those children who don't learn to read and write, by and large, are children to whom it doesn't make sense, to whom the functional extension that these media provide has not been made clear or does not match up with their own expectations of what language is for.... Fundamentally, as in the history of the human race, reading and writing are an extension of the functions of language.... This is what they must be for the child equally.
>
> (Halliday 1978: 57)

10.1   Introduction

As we have stressed throughout this volume, we believe writing to be first and foremost a communicative activity. Second, writing is commonly an internally motivated activity; that is, outside the school world, people often write because they believe they have something to say. The teaching of writing in schools, by definition, violates these two constraints. That is, teachers *assign* writing tasks; the tasks are not internally motivated. Moreover, some tasks that teachers must necessarily assign are not essentially communicative. While we do not condone these artificialities in the various teaching methodologies intended to instruct writing, we recognize that instructional needs may outweigh other considerations. At the same time, we believe that teachers can do much to improve the communicative orientation of even the most mundane writing tasks.

In this and the following two chapters, we shall outline 75 instructional **themes** (see pp. 427–9) which are relevant to writing and which suggest teaching **techniques** and ideas. The themes and techniques draw on the theoretical positions outlined in Chapters

8 and 9. Thus, an emphasis on certain aspects of the writing process is assumed, particularly the notions of brainstorming, multiple drafting, peer support, multiple audiences, and attention to form at the later stages. The notion that students should write for meaningful purposes as much as possible is also assumed, though the concept of meaningful writing should not be taken to an extreme. There are a number of enjoyable and interesting writing activities which do not have a purpose outside of the class but which are useful for the development of writing skills.

In this chapter, the various instructional themes present many sample activities for writing practice. It is part of the nature of beginning writing that students will need many different opportunities for writing, some of which will be, for one reason or another, less carefully sequenced with larger curriculum objectives. Nevertheless, the many specific activities suggest an array of options for getting students involved in writing. Because of the large number of specific activities, certain themes and techniques presented in this chapter could be viewed as isolated practices and techniques. We would prefer to see the various ideas for writing instruction as resources which can be used to support content-based instruction or some larger project in which the whole class or student subgroups are engaged.

The themes and techniques in this chapter emphasize writing activities which are appropriate for beginning students; we also recognize that such a label is a convenient fiction. There is no one group of students that can be labelled as beginning writers. However, there are a number of groups of students who do fit the characteristics of beginners learning to write in English.

Certainly children in English-speaking elementary school classrooms fit the characterization of beginning writers; this is true whether the students are learning English writing skills in their first language, in their second language, or in an additional language. For purposes of general classification, beginning elementary students learning to write would include children in early education. Most secondary school students do not fit within the classification of beginning writers, though English L2 immigrant students who enter secondary schools will be beginners in English, regardless of their literacy skills in their L1. There is certainly a difference, however, between students who have learned how to write in their L1 and those who have not. Finally, there are adult immigrants from non-English-speaking countries. They, again, can be divided between those who have writing fluency in their L1 and those who do not. Adult courses will also sometimes involve or include L1 illiterate adults.

The extent to which these distinctions are important will be addressed in our discussions of various themes and techniques. It is important to note that the 'theme' and 'technique' designations are not intended as a strict hierarchical division, nor are there any strong claims attached to the designation of some topic as being a theme rather than a technique. In general, themes characterize larger issues and/or guidelines for instruction rather than specific tasks or assignments.

10.2   Themes for beginning writers

The themes for beginning writing discussed in this chapter involve various issues which can make writing a more productive experience. While some fluent adult writers think of writing as a difficult process, children initially do not have the same attitude, and the teacher should try to ensure that writing is not seen as a frustrating and unrewarding skill. Rather, students should be encouraged to feel that writing is an important and effective means of self-expression, communication, and information-gathering. Themes discussed here (though certainly not all-inclusive) are grouped to highlight major concerns in beginning writing instruction.

The 25 themes are organized into five overarching principles:

1. Preparing students for writing
2. Assisting and guiding writing
3. Working with writing
4. Writing for different purposes (Genres)
5. Extending the writing curriculum.

These five principles – and corresponding themes – provide a way to explore various aspects of writing instruction.

In beginning to write, students need confidence to feel that they can do what is being asked of them. The section on *preparing students for writing* offers five themes which promote this goal. Second, students need guidance as they carry out a given writing task. The section on *assisting and guiding writing* highlights ways to support the development of student writing. Third, students need to engage in writing activities which cover a wide variety of topics and tasks. The themes of *working with writing* present a range of ideas which can be applied to writing instruction; all of these themes can be integrated easily into content-based or project-oriented instruction. Fourth, students need to work with *different types of writing*, even at early levels. The themes that address writing for different purposes provide options for working with a variety of text types and genres. Finally, students need to *expand their uses of writing*, to be given more independent opportunities to write and to pursue topics of personal interest.

Many of the activities and techniques discussed in this and the next two chapters are described in a number of resources on writing. In quite a few cases, good ideas appear in multiple sources. Rather than cite sources for each technique or approach, it is simpler to refer to a number of basic resources which we found particularly useful, and which the interested reader should also find relevant. Among the most practical and insightful resources for writing instruction referred to in Chapters 10 to 12 are the following: Frank (1979), Hedge (1988), NCTE (1983), Newkirk (1993), Peregoy and Boyle (1993), Raimes (1983c, 1992), Reid (1993), Tompkins (1990), and White and Arndt (1991).

10.3 Preparing students for writing (themes 1–5)

Five themes centre around preparing students for writing and making students aware that writing is a means of communication. Integrating these themes into classroom instruction can help students develop writing skills as well as positive attitudes to writing. These themes include: (1) using print in the classroom, (2) writing daily, (3) promoting discussion prior to writing, (4) tapping student interest, and (5) providing reasons for writing. These themes are designed to raise student awareness, generate interest, create topics for writing, and get students started.

10.3.1 *Using print in the classroom (1)*

The teacher and students should find as many uses for print in the class environment as possible. For classes composed of the same students all day – common in elementary grades – there are many options for print display in the classroom. Classroom wall space can be used for organizing weekly and monthly activities; for generating lists of ideas and topics; for posting the class roster; for displaying stories, in-class notes, out-of-class letters, and reports, etc.

Many of these uses of print in the classroom can evolve gradually as units are taught through the school year. Others can be recycled; for example, captions, labels, stories, letters, and reports can be changed on a monthly basis. Students can work individually or in groups to create print for display or to assist others. The possibilities for displaying print in the classroom are endless.

The principle behind these practices is critical. Students need to see that print is used in a wide variety of contexts, and they need to explore the ways that print informs, entertains, displays intentions, and enhances learning.

10.3.2   Writing daily (2)

If writing is to be seen as a basic means of learning information, exploring the world, and interacting with others, it must be a common practice. Writing should be practised in the classroom every day. Following from theme 1, above, it is possible to use writing for a variety of purposes beyond essay and narrative writing. Some writing tasks can be brief; others may be a springboard for more complex writing purposes.

Recent research has shown that students should begin writing from their first year at school. Early writing, including drawings and creative spelling, appear to have a positive influence on later writing development. Early writing activities establish the importance of writing for communication and raises students' awareness to the uses of writing. Early writing also appears to have an important positive influence on reading development (Adams 1989, Zamel 1992) and is most readily accommodated through Language Experience Approaches (LEA) (see subsections 10.4.1 and 10.5.1).

10.3.3   Promoting discussion prior to writing (3)

Students should be encouraged to recognize the resources that they each bring to writing, the information that they have but do not know how to access. By means of class discussion, students discover and create additional knowledge for writing. The time for discussion also provides teachers with opportunities to shape and extend student ideas, giving students additional resources to use in their writing. Students also have the opportunity to learn how to work in discussion groups to support one another. Often a discussion begun as a class activity can lead to a simple group task to generate additional ideas that are reported back to the class. In this way, class discussion before writing can lead to the beginnings of cooperative group learning.

The generation of various types of lists and labels for objects from class discussions provides an important resource for beginning students. The generation of lists also builds vocabulary resources for each student. Further, the recording/drawing-up of lists, tables, maps, outlines and object labels on the board permits both teacher and students to explore various ways in which information can be reorganized.

10.3.4   *Tapping student interest (4)*

In addition to discussion which generates lists and other sets of information, discussion can focus on tasks and topics that interest students and about which they would like to write. Students need the opportunity to contribute to the selection of tasks and topics as a motivation for writing. This does not mean abdication of topic choice to students, as some might suggest, but a judicious balancing of teacher and curriculum needs with student initiative and involvement.

Students often do not know the range of writing activities and topics open to them. Nor do they know about the various ways in which a specific topic or task can be adapted as a source for a wide range of different activities. Brainstorming with the whole class and in groups allows students to recognize the options that are open to them, and also to explore the types of information that they will need for a range of specific writing activities.

10.3.5   *Providing reasons for writing (5)*

Students should be encouraged to carry out writing tasks which serve a purpose. Not all tasks and activities serve purposes or audiences outside of the classroom; in fact, many useful activities involve self-discovery and reinforce important information from content-areas such as social studies. While these activities do not invoke audiences and uses for writing beyond the classroom itself, they represent real uses of writing which are a basic part of ongoing learning in school. As such, they need to be regarded as real and authentic writing activities.

Many writing tasks can also be created to extend beyond the usual writing assignment. For example, writing can involve other classes at the same grade level or at a different grade level. These activities can include letters to other students, school personnel, parents, city officials, etc. Projects and reports can be displayed for other classes or in a project fair. Essays, stories, and reports can be displayed on a thematic bulletin board. Writing can be used for plays, debates, presentations, poetry reading, etc. There are many extended uses of writing which can be incorporated into the writing curriculum. In the various themes that follow, a number focus on audiences other than the teacher and beyond the immediate classroom.

10.4   Assisting and guiding writing (themes 6–10)

A second set of themes centres around supporting students as they carry out writing tasks in the classroom. In addition to preparing students for writing, it is important to provide support for students while they are writing, to assist them with ideas for organizing their writing and adding information, and to respond as a reader as well as the teacher. These themes focus on (1) using sheltered instruction, (2) literacy scaffolding, (3) attending to vocabulary development, (4) responding and feedback, and (5) helping those who cannot get started. In these themes, the teacher provides the support and assistance that will give students confidence and motivate them to take risks.

10.4.1   *The use of sheltered instruction (6)*

With beginning students, it is important to provide continual support, to shelter students as they learn to develop some basic competence in writing. The teacher:

- should offer students both verbal and non-verbal cues to help them recall information, organize their ideas, and use strategies for planning;

- should remind students of the brainstorming and discussion activities that took place before writing, show pictures and drawings, demonstrate some concept or notion, and provide redundant explanations;
- should review and reinforce the purposes for writing as well as the potential uses of the writing when possible;
- should monitor comprehension and help students make writing more appealing and accessible for potential peer readers;
- should also take advantage of the opportunities that arise to suggest new vocabulary or other ways of presenting information without insisting on students changing the text.

Motivation and encouragement are also important aspects of sheltered instruction. The teacher needs to keep students motivated and on task. Ways to increase motivation can include short writing periods, 'competitions' for the best beginning, sharing a paper, writing with students, pointing out good starts and good organization, and presenting rewards for the best final papers. Sheltered instruction also provides opportunities for group work of various types. Students can be asked to help each other find a good example, remember some information from a class-generated list, comment on illustrations, or write a joint story or report. The key concept is that the teacher needs to assist students actively as they write, without taking responsibility away from them. The teacher should, at the same time, exercise good sense in responding to student writing. Not everything needs to be graded. The teacher should also avoid imposing interpretations on student efforts; if a text is ambiguous, a perfectly valid strategy lies in asking the student what the text is trying to say.

A particularly effective way to provide sheltered instruction is through Learning Experience Approach (LEA) activities. These activities build primarily on stories dictated by students to the teacher (or to class volunteers or students from higher grades); or, the students' written stories are read back to them by the teacher. In this way, they experience success with reading and writing beyond their normal abilities. This approach increases interest and allows for systematic follow-up of the language in the stories. Students can underline words that are most meaningful to them, write them on word cards, and form a word bank. Students can cut stories into strips and rearrange them. In some ways, LEA is like Freire's approach to generative themes and words since the themes and words come from the students who can then reflect on any information they find important. Teachers can also ask students to re-read stories, illustrate stories, read stories to others, revise stories, underline difficult words, circle words that they know, and take dictation from their stories (Dixon and Nessel 1983, Peregoy and Boyle 1993).

10.4.2   Literacy scaffolding (7)

In assisting students in their writing, it is important to use language that is repetitive and easily understandable. Teachers should recycle important vocabulary and elaborate on words with additional information and examples. Discourse routines that support student writing should be repeated so that students become familiar with the expectations of both teacher and task.

Teachers should also provide students with basic metalinguistic vocabulary and routines so that they can talk about their writing. Even at early ages, students can talk about difficulties in finding the right words, about a problem with organization, about a less-than-clear example, etc. Students cannot be expected to do this without learning how to do so from the teacher. The teacher needs to present many models and guided examples of how to look at writing, assess the strong and weak points, look for better alternatives, and recognize the language structures and vocabulary that go with specific genres and tasks. These insights and routines should be incorporated gradually into ongoing student interactions while they are writing, and thus become part of their own active writing over time.

10.4.3   Attention to vocabulary development (8)

Much as writing leads to improved reading abilities and a more elaborated knowledge of certain important vocabulary, the development of writing itself calls for an ever-increasing vocabulary. In the various activities involved in writing preparation (e.g. pre-writing discussion or brainstorming), or in providing support for an ongoing writing task, it is important to take advantage of useful vocabulary which arise naturally out of the situation. As students generate lists and ideas for writing, certain words will be new and can be a source of discussion, or even of a writing activity. For example, the introduction of new words can lead to a number of the following writing activities.

Lists of *important, useful, interesting,* or *personal* vocabulary can be created from student writing. Students can, for example, keep a personal word bank – a list of meaningful words in the back of a notebook – and can share certain words when new activities call for their use. Attending to vocabulary is a basic part of expanding students' repertoire of resources for writing. It also provides reasons for cooperative group-work; students can ask each other to explain certain words in their writing, or to use certain words as part of a group writing activity. Vocabulary development not only supports reading and writing, it also promotes syntactic flexibility and creates a foundation for further learning. Further ideas for vocabulary development and use are presented in a number of themes (see, e.g., subsections 10.5.1, 10.5.2, 10.5.3, 10.5.5).

10.4.4   Responding and feedback (9)

At beginning levels of writing development, the purpose for responding and feedback is to support student efforts; teachers need to encourage students to continue, to feel good about their writing, and to carry the activity through to completion. In this regard, Frank (1979) provides a useful set of guidelines for teachers working with beginning writers:

1. Build a helpful spirit and give directions for appropriate criticism (e.g. find the funniest sentence; find two good words; find something good about the opening; find any sentence that is not clear; think of something that might be added).
2. Start with anonymous pieces from outside the classroom for class criticism and ease into the process of critiquing slowly.
3. Focus on the positive.
4. Separate revising from editing.
5. Do drafting together.
6. Work often with short pieces.
7. Give specific responses: point out sentences that do not make sense, strong or weak openings, the need for more descriptive words, the over-repetition of vocabulary.
8. Decide what techniques need to be refined.
9. Recycle editing experiences into the next writing activity.
10 Avoid false praise.
11. Do not persist in an activity if students are resistant.

10.4.5   Helping those who cannot get started (10)

Even at the beginning, some students will have difficulty getting started. Sometimes the task creates the problem; sometimes a student is not having a good day, and sometimes a student is just overwhelmed by situations that extend beyond the writing task. Frank (1979) also has useful advice in this situation:

1. Spend more time collecting/generating ideas.
2. Give some time off from the writing activity.
3. Do not announce writing ahead of time.
4. Encourage other forms of expression (e.g. art).
5. Go back to words and word lists.
6. Return to the oral – talk a rough draft.
7. Accentuate the short as good.
8. Choose other high-interest writing topics for a while.
9. Let students write under a pseudonym.
10. Stop re-writing for awhile.
11. Write in class with a lot of assistance.
12. Combine writers into pairs.
13. Be aware of rigid constraints imposed by specific tasks.
14. Provide more direction.
15. Try transcribing ideas/copying information.

These suggestions should help a teacher to step back and consider how to make writing less threatening and more interesting. The teacher's role is to assess the situation in which students are struggling, find the best way to make writing tasks useful to the students, and give them a sense of accomplishment so that they will be better motivated for the next writing activity.

10.5   Working with writing (themes 11–16)

A third set of themes proposes basic activities for working with beginning writers. These activities provide ways to get students to generate text. They also represent sets of activities which are easy to accomplish, giving students a sense of satisfaction and motivation to continue. Activities should capitalize on students' early positive attitudes towards writing and should support those students whose prior encounters with writing have been insufficient or unmotivating. Six themes that present these basic writing activities include: (1) using big books and Language Experience Activities (LEA), (2) generating word lists, (3) working with phrases and sentences, (4) copying and dictation, (5) working with poems, and (6) working with pictures.

10.5.1 Using big books and Language Experience Activities (11)

An important early goal of a writing programme is to familiarize students with books and to connect books with their own writing practices. Students will then accept books as a resource and support for writing. The use of big books represents one effective way to introduce beginning writing. The teacher provides big books for the class or the class makes big books. Smaller groups can also make their own with teacher assistance. Using big books, the teacher reads to groups and to the class. These books can be re-read and the teacher can point out difficult vocabulary, assist with letter-sound correspondences, check for meaning, and select words and phrases that interest students. These books have predictable patterns and assist students with many word-listing and sentence-making activities. A further activity employing a shared book is a mapping of the story line. This activity teaches text organization as well as comprehension and vocabulary. Students can respond to big books in a variety of ways. They can fill in response sheets in groups, make dioramas of a scene, develop a timeline, expand on a character, or make a collage that fits the story.

A variation on big books is the use of picture books without words. Picture books have sequences of pictures which students can present orally as stories, either individually or in groups. These stories can then be written down and combined with copies of the pictures. This can be done by having students select their own picture sequences. Later, working in pairs, students share their own stories with one another. These picture books can thus be the starting point for writing, or for a Language Experience Approach (LEA) activity.

Another activity involves the creation of concept books. Students begin by choosing a simple concept such as big, small, good, happy, green, ABCs, etc. Students can then collect pictures and make illustrations which centre around the concept. They can add words, captions, and simple explanatory sentences. A more advanced variation, for example, could involve a no-number book-let describing what the world would be like without numbers. Start with a list of ideas: no bus-line numbers, no mathematics, no zero, no checks, no money, no addresses, no telephone numbers, no computers, no calendars, no birthdays, etc. Students collect illus-trations and pictures which involve the use of numbers or which depict life without numbers. These are combined into a book along with supporting descriptions. The writing can be limited to phrases and sentences, or it can be expanded into descriptive and explanatory paragraphs. (This idea can be used to teach systems using various number bases; e.g. 24 hours, 60 minutes, 7 days, 52 weeks, etc.)

Students can also make a class handbook which describes, for example, the rules of the class. After discussing class rules and deciding on a final set for the class, students put together the rules in a class handbook. A group of students, appointed as an editorial team, could be in charge of changing rules and adding student-generated rules. This makes a good LEA activity. Subsequently, students can look at and discuss historically import-ant sets of rules (e.g. in the USA, the Bill of Rights).

10.5.2   Generating word lists (12)

Many beginning writers need to have a way to begin to generate ideas and bits of language. One way to do this is by creating word lists which become resources for writing. Students are not intimi-dated by the activity, and they can be led to realize that they have many personal ideas from which to draw. This activity also rein-forces important vocabulary and allows students to explore relationships between new and known words. Finally, the genera-tion of word groups and word lists, when practised consistently, provides students with an independent strategy for starting to write.

Working with words and lists, in their most basic forms, involves the teacher and students in collecting words from the class environment. Students can be asked to collect different types of words which can then be sources for stories, 'poems,' essays, and a variety of LEA activities. Students can collect busy words, happy words, convincing words, etc. Among the simple activities which involve word collecting are:

1. *Word tasting.* Students select a word – milk, for example – generate words that tell how it feels, tastes, smells, looks, sounds. They can add a word that describes how it feels in the mouth, how it feels when it is swallowed, and an aftertaste word. These words can be organized into sets of phrases and sentences, or can be arranged in a poem-like pattern. As a follow-up activity, students can add words for the types of people who like milk.

2. *Prepositions for silly stories.* After students select a preposition that they like (e.g. out, down, in, on, up, with, for, to), they look for it in a simple reading book. They can then tell a silly story using as many occurrences of this preposition as possible.

3. *Five key words.* Students are asked to select a reading passage from a text. They then choose the five (or *x*) most important words that must be preserved from the text if all others are taken away. Students explain orally, or write, why they would keep these words by sharing them with others in a group, and can then generate sets of phrases and sentences with the chosen words. They can tell a story with these words, or make a 'poem' with someone else's words. The most interesting words can also be placed in a personal word bank.

4. *Feather words.* After a discussion of birds or an experiment with falling objects, students can put together a list of words that are light or 'like a feather' (e.g. floating, soft, light, airy, slender, twirling, free). Each student can make a 'poem' or a paragraph from the words, or students can compare word lists and compose a group text.

5. *Colour association.* Students may pick a colour and assemble a list of words and phrases to associate with the colour. These words can then be used to make a set of interesting phrases and sentences, which can also be written in different colours. Students can try to tell a story with these words or compare their words with those of other students. They can then consider whether their statements and words about any colour can be generalized.

6. *Thinking like an animal.* Students can pick an animal and make a list of words that fit the animal. For example, if a student picks a lion, he or she can list words that interpret the animal; e.g. words describing how a lion eats or sleeps, or walks, etc. The student can search for some 'lion-like' words, then tell a lion story or explain how a lion lives.

7. *Come to your senses.* Students are asked to think of an emotion;
e.g. happiness, anger, sadness, excitement. Students then
describe (orally or in writing) these words by using the five
senses: how it tastes, feels, smells, looks, sounds. Students then
meet in groups with other students who have chosen similar
emotions. They may combine their words and make a word
chart. These charts can constitute part of a unit on the five
senses, on emotions, or on metaphorical meanings.
8. *Pick a food.* Students write ten words that describe a food they
like or do not like. Students compare these lists and determine
which foods everyone likes and which foods are not popular.
The two groups of foods can then be described through the
combined word lists generated by students.

A variation on student-generated word lists is to have students
look for relevant words in the print environment around them.
Instead of writing words themselves, students cut out words from
magazines and newspapers. These words can be pasted together
to tell a story or to describe/explain a concept. The words can
also be combined to make a bigger story or report as a group
activity. Students can then add pictures to illustrate the work. The
final products can be displayed on a 'found' writing bulletin
board. The teacher can keep a pile of such words and phrases in a
box, alongside a box full of interesting pictures, as a possible
ongoing writing option in the writing corner.

More organized and advanced activities which reinforce vocabulary development and ideas from writing include semantic feature
analysis and word clustering. Semantic feature analysis can be carried out in a number of ways. For example, based on a current
topic in class, students can select words from their word banks and
from elsewhere that may fit the topic. The teacher can set up a
grid of words so that the words themselves run down the side.
Students then select characteristics that fit some subset of the
words and fill in the grid to match words to their characteristics.
They can also write sentences which explain word groupings. This
activity builds word meanings, but also builds up a concept matrix
for important ideas.

In clustering activities, students may also nominate words on a
topic for writing. After many words are nominated, student groups
can cluster words together, then clusters from different groups
can be compared and, where appropriate, connected. The

students decide which clusters are most important for the writing that they will do, and why, and use these clusters to write sentences or a paragraph on the topic.

10.5.3   *Working with phrases and sentences (13)*

Another effective set of activities for beginning students involves the creation of interesting phrases and sentences, which then serve as a springboard for other activities. One of the simplest ways to get students to write more complex sentences or work with a new sentence pattern is through patterned sentences. After choosing a simple concept or pattern, students experiment with the patterned organization. Patterning examples include the following (doubled here to show the pattern):

> I used to …, but now I …
> I used to …, but now I …
>
> I used to be …, but now I am …
> I used to be …, but now I am …
>
> I can see …, I can see …, I can see …
>
> I seem to be …, but I really am …
> I seem to be …, but I really am …
>
> I'm good at …; I'm not so good at …
> I'm good at …; I'm not so good at …
>
> I like …, it looks like…, it feels like…, it tastes like …
>
> I am the one who likes …,
> I am the one who takes …,
> I am the one who has …,
> I am the one who plays …
>
> If…, if…, if…, then *subject* and *verb*
>
> When…, when…, when…, then *subject* and *verb*

These patterns, which students repeat five or six times, can be used to create simple poem-type arrangements. The patterns, which act as a scaffolding, allow students to exchange ideas and vocabulary as well as experiment with descriptions, concepts, and specific structures.

Students can work with new sentence structures in other ways, particularly as part of making sentences to organize ideas and information. For example, students can think of warnings, problems, events, or changes. They can make a sentence list starting each line with *If*. They can also make a list of daily habits that people have or activities that they do. They then write a sentence list with one sentence for each idea. Other options include making a list of events that do not normally happen, or of events that regularly occur during the year, and begin each sentence with *When*.

A second type of sentence-generating activity is to present good news/bad news. Students may select a person or situation and think of five (or *x*) good things and an equal number of bad things; they may then write a good/bad sequence; e.g. fortunately A, unfortunately B, fortunately C, unfortunately D. Students can recall a personal experience on a good news/bad news day. They can also make a good news/bad news sequence for a famous person.

As a third activity, students can write a set of sentences that begin with the same sound (or letter). After writing five (or *x*) sentences, they can decide if one could be the source for a story. Students with the same sound (or letter) can compare sentences and students in groups can also combine the sentence sets in interesting ways. Similarly, students can select five (or *x*) foods and write a sentence for each, describing each food in such a way that it sounds awful/wonderful.

As a fourth activity, students in groups may select a sentence from a text or one that a student has written. Each student in a group adds a word to the sentence. This may also be done in groups with some sentences from each student's latest essay. In this way, students focus on the types of words that can improve the descriptive or explanatory power of sentences. Students can also record particularly interesting words in their personal word bank.

Another useful approach to working with phrases and sentences is with information gap activities. All information gap activities involve a pair or group of students; one group or individual has information that the other needs, and vice versa. Many activities can be set up as information gap tasks. For example, students can introduce pictures, ads, or posters and split these visuals in pairs so that each member in student pairs has a set of pictures, etc. Individuals (or groups) can then describe the pictures to the other partner(s). Partner(s), in turn, give written description back. Both work together to create a final version of a written description. Students can examine how the description was misleading and determine what is needed to make a description accurate. These activity can work well when students are learning to describe settings or backgrounds in larger writing projects.

A further set of activities which focus on sentences involves the use of sentence strips. In these activities, the teacher selects a paragraph that is relevant to a larger theme-unit or project and cuts it into strips, or into words and phrases. The students are then expected to reconstruct the original text. The teacher can also discuss with students how they made their decisions for the reconstruction. The same approach for a more complex set of sentences can use an illustration to help the students. In addition, the teacher can scramble words or phrases in a student story and ask the students to reconstruct the story. The reconstructed versions can then be compared with the original. Students can also add sentences to the reconstruction and compare the expanded text with the original text.

Finally, activities with phrases and sentences can centre around the creation of lists for various purposes. The general guideline is to generate a list of interest to students and follow-up with a more focused writing task. A number of examples of list activities include the following:

1. *Ten (or x) friendly things to do.* Students make a list of ten (or *x*) friendly things to do and discuss why they make their choices. Students alone or in groups may rank the list items in order of importance. (How many of these things have they done lately?) Student groups compare their lists with other groups and compile a top-ten list for the class. Students can then make a poster of 'best things to do' and discuss how many of these activities they have done lately.
2. *Your worst day.* Students can list ten (or *x*) things that happened on their worst day. From this activity, they can tell a story about their worst day. The class can also discuss what someone should say to a person having a bad day and make a short list of things to say. Students can also list ten (or *x*) things that might happen on a very good day.
3. *Yes.* Students make a list of ten (or *x*) things to which they would say 'yes'. Students can start by thinking of good words in groups. The class can then organize these things into various categories and students can then think of headings for each group. Students can discuss the values and ideas in the headings and

write a short explanation or description for one of the groups of ideas.

4. *Ten (or x) things to do.* Students begin by thinking of ten (or *x*) things to do last, to tell their mother, to learn about, to do quickly, to do first, to do slowly, to do in their town, to forget about, to remember, etc.

5. *Excuses.* Students can make a list of ten (or *x*) excuses for not taking out the garbage, for not doing their homework, for sleeping late, etc.

6. *Five (or x) reasons.* Students can make a list of five (or *x*) reasons for growing tomatoes, getting good grades, going to school, watching TV, having a pet, having friends, eating, seeing a movie, writing (or not writing), etc.

10.5.4   Copying and dictation (14)

For students who have difficulty getting started, or for students who need to gain fluency with the mechanics of writing, copying words, sentences, and texts form an excellent beginning. While some students have no inhibitions with free writing and creative spelling, other students, particularly older ones, may want more security in their early attempts at writing; both copying and dictation provide a higher level of support for accurate and appropriate writing.

At the simplest level, students can copy words from the board; copy a daily sentence; copy information of immediate importance (such as announcements, class information, semantic maps on the board); copy part of a class magazine; copy new words into word banks, etc. Copying can also be a lead-in activity for word-generating activities and work with phrases and sentences.

Dictations provide students with additional practice in writing mechanics, word recognition, and sound-letter correspondences. They also improve fluency as well as related skills such as memorizing and note taking. With true beginners, the teacher can use cloze dictations so that they only need to fill in selected words as they listen.

10.5.5   Working with poems (15)

There are many ways to introduce students to 'poem' writing. Students often enjoy finding words that rhyme and sentence groups that exhibit a metrical rhythm. While it is important to distinguish simple poem-like writing activities from good poetry, students can produce interesting and enjoyable arrangements of words and sentences. The extent to which the teacher extends poem writing to encompass more complex aspects of poetry writing is an individual choice. These activities provide an ideal way to engage in word play and structure variation. Many poem activities can be an extension of other writing activities (e.g. word lists and sentence patterns). Some options for including poetry in beginning writing are as follows:

1. *Texts to poems.* Students can start with a simple news article, advertisement, picture caption, or story, and physically rearrange the sentences or move phrases around to form new sentences. They can also choose interesting words and arrange them into a poem. The words can be organized into groups with similar meanings, similar shapes, or similar sounds; they can be moved into lines; they can be arranged into rhyming sets; or can be subtracted from lines.

2. *Mathematics poem.* Students can generate a list of ten (or *x*) mathematics words. They can write a poem using these words and any other math words that can be added. Students can then form groups and compare and revise their poems.

3. *Alphabet poem.* Students can pick a letter of the alphabet and generate a list of interesting words beginning with that letter. (They can be encouraged to use a dictionary or an encyclopaedia for this activity.) They can then arrange words into a poem that shows their one letter of the alphabet, e.g.:

    K is king of the Kentucky kneepads,
    K has kennels, keys, kerosene, kites,
    K knocks, kneads, knows, keeps, kicks, kids,
    K is always on kettles, kilts, kinfolk,
    K is a kindly kinetic keeper with a kit of ketchup.

4. *Garbage.* Students often like to explore 'messy' topics. One example is the word *garbage*. For each letter of the word GARBAGE, students can write words and phrases that describe trash. They can then arrange these words into a poem. The most interesting descriptions can be displayed on the class wall, pasted on a cut-out poster of a garbage can.

5. *Junk.* Students can generate lists of words that name kinds of junk. Using these words, students can write sentences that

include one or more pieces of junk. These sentences can then be rearranged to form poems.

6. *Cans.* Students can generate a list of things that come in cans, and can then make phrases and sentences from these words to make a poem about items that come in cans. A second focus can be on pleasant or unpleasant things that come in cans.

7. *Diamond poem.* Students can combine words with visual displays. In this activity, students place words in a visual display that moves from one extreme to the other and produces a poem in a diamond shape:

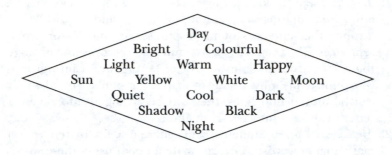

10.5.6   *Working with pictures (16)*

Virtually every book on writing instruction includes activities involving pictures, and there are almost no limits to the possibilities for using pictures to generate writing activities. One good first step before using many picture-based activities is to collect a large number of interesting pictures from magazines and keep them in boxes for student use. Students should also be encouraged to collect and bring pictures for their own writing files to be kept in the writing corner. Below are some of the options that can be tried as writing activities. Teachers can also keep in mind that any theme-based curriculum unit or project may include many pictures as a focus for writing activities.

1. *Make a photo essay.* The teacher and students can collect some photos and pictures and arrange them to tell a story. Students can create drawings to fill in missing parts of a story line. After sequencing the photos and drawings, students can write the story in prose under the pictures and create a booklet. These booklets can be posted around the room for other students to

read. Picture sets can focus on hobbies, cars, sports, family, neighbourhood, etc.

2. *Working with picture sets.* Students can tell a story based on a set of pictures distributed by the teacher (see also subsection 10.5.1). Each student can then write the story and recount it to their group. Alternatively, groups receive the picture set, tell the story, and write up the story together. In simpler versions, beginning students can describe individual pictures in a set, then make a group story together. Groups of students can rearrange picture sets to tell a different story. Picture sets can also be used in information gap activities. With picture sets, half of each student group gets the first two or three pictures; the other half of the group receives the remaining two or three pictures. Each subgroup tells a story from the pictures; then the subgroups meet and tell a complete story from the pictures. After this activity, individual students can generate their own stories from a similar set of pictures.

3. *Select an animal.* After selecting an animal from a picture set or a book, students can look up information on the animal in the class library and in books on animals collected by the teacher. Each can then write a small report of one or two paragraphs, and all students in the group can combine the set of reports into a class book on animals of interest.

4. *Food pictures.* Students can locate a picture of some food that they find interesting. They can then write ten (or *x*) descriptive words about the picture. Using these words, they can describe a person who would eat the food.

5. *Picture fortunes.* Students can first make a list of words and phrases that can be used to tell a fortune. They can then select a picture of an unusual man or woman and can tell, or write out, this person's fortune.

6. *Visualizing what happens.* Students can choose a picture that is unusual or interesting. They can write about what happened before the picture was taken; about what happened after the picture was taken; and about what is outside the frame of the picture that might be important. If it is a picture of a room, students can describe the contents of the next room, or the characteristics of the entire house or building. Students can use pictures, advertisements, cartoons, comics, etc., as a starting point. They can also discuss what might have caused the situation in the picture.

7. *Room descriptions.* The teacher can provide pairs of students with pictures of two different rooms for description. Each student pair writes a description of one of the rooms; then they trade the descriptions. Pairs compare and discuss organization and perspective; they can consider different ways to describe a room, the number and kind of details to be included, and the pattern of description to be followed.

8. *Animals and people.* The teacher and students can find pictures of animals and people of proportional size on the printed page. Students can cut the animals and people in half and recombine the people with the animals. They can then describe these new creatures: What are they like? What do they do? Where do they live? Students can follow this activity with one in which they tell a story about their new creatures.

9. *Pictures and poems.* Students can collect pictures and poems on a topic of interest: feelings, seasons, holidays, sports, sounds, movie stars, music, nature. Students can paste or copy these pictures into a notebook and can add poems or write their own poems for the pictures in the book. Students can then compare books and solicit the help of other students to find more pictures/poems. They can complete the book by writing a concluding essay that explains the book.

10. *Captioned!* The teacher and students can collect comics and cartoon strips. The students can cut off (or white-out) the writing and add their own scripts. Students can trade cartoons or keep them. The teacher can also develop a large set of cartoons in the writing corner. Students can trade their completed cartoons and strips with other students and give advice or add a second version.

11. *Advertisements.* Students can bring in advertisements that they like or think are effective. The teacher can also keep a set of advertisements in a box in the writing corner. The class can discuss why some advertisements are effective and others are less so. Students can then write an advertisement for x. In the advertisement, they can try to convince people of the value of x. In addition, they can design a larger brochure for the advertised subject. They can include an endorsement by a famous person and write out the lines that the famous person has to say.

10.6   Writing for different purposes (themes 17–20)

The fourth set of themes focuses on four well-recognized text types. With beginning students, it is reasonable to expect that they learn how to tell stories, write simple letters, provide a description or a procedural sequence of events, keep records, and write a simple report. When they begin to write, most students already know the basics of telling a story or relating an event so this genre is a good text type to use for building fluency and mechanics (in addition to using free writes, word generating, copying, dictation, and journals). There are also many opportunities for students to engage in letter writing, descriptions, procedures, and reports in early grades, particularly in a content-based and project-oriented curriculum. Four themes address these basic text types: (1) telling stories, (2) writing letters, (3) providing descriptions, directions and procedures, and (4) keeping records and writing reports.

10.6.1   Telling stories (17)

There are many ways to encourage students to generate simple stories. In fact, many of the word-generating and sentence-generating ideas described previously can be concluded with a brief story-writing activity. When students are engaged in story-writing tasks, the teacher can take advantage of the opportunity to point out the important aspects of writing good stories: a strong descriptive opening, a vivid setting, interesting character sketches, a point of conflict, an exciting opening episode, a sequence of events to entertain, a climactic event, and a suitable ending. These stories also allow the teacher to highlight the specific types of language features which contribute to a strong story: action verbs, descriptive adjectives with strong images, the specific words which detail a character's personality, the time-oriented transition words that keep the sequence of events in order, adverbs which convey the emotions and attitudes of the characters, etc. In short, there are many ways to help students work with the structuring of a good story. While many stories can be designed to follow reading activities and specific content-based activities, the following are a few additional ideas which can lead to story writing.

1. *Cliff hangers.* The teacher can hang paper from a coat hanger and spread the paper across students' desks. Students begin to

write a short story on the paper. When students are at an exciting part they stop. Students then move to another hanger and
finish the story. The teacher hangs the stories up for others to
read. In another variation, the teacher or students hang a picture or a photo from a hanger. On pieces of paper, students
add words and phrases that describe the picture and put them
on threads to hang from the hangers. Students then look at the
hangers and write sentences from other students' words.
Groups then get together and write stories from the hangers.
2. *Telegrams.* The teacher should first show students a few actual
telegrams to provide an opportunity to talk about the conditions under which telegrams are sent and received. Students
generate 15 (or *x*) words that can be used in a telegram and
use these words to write an urgent message. In the telegrams,
students refer to something important that has happened (or
in a story they have just read). Students can then switch telegrams and tell a story of what happened after they received an
urgent message.
3. *Story telling.* After a brainstorming session on a topic, the
teacher can begin a story and stop it at a certain point.
Students can then continue the story individually. Alternatively,
students can begin a story from descriptive words that have
been generated by the brainstorming activity (e.g. dangerous,
quiet, raining, explosion, noisy, fire).

10.6.2   *Writing letters (18)*

Writing letters is an easy and natural writing activity which can be
expanded in a number of interesting ways. Students can write to
many different people and organizations for a variety of purposes.
These possibilities provide genuine alternative audiences for students and allow for discussion of audience expectations that
change as students write different types of letters. The differences
in audience and writing purpose can also provide opportunities to
point out the features of language that vary consistently along
with readership and writer's purpose. In this way, letter writing
allows the teacher to discuss conventions of writing: down-toning
words to qualify assertions, adding strong descriptive adverbs and
adjectives, highlighting points or reasons in making an argument
or taking a position, and using modality appropriately to convey
the right attitude and emotion. Below are a few of the many

possible uses of letter writing in a writing class. Many letter-writing opportunities will also follow from content-based instruction and curriculum projects.

1. *Writing to others* – Letters can be written to a variety of people. Students can write letters to students in other classes or in other schools; or to the principal suggesting a change that should be made in the school; or to the local authority describing the biggest problem facing the city and what the city should do about it. Students can write letters that congratulate, invite, apologize, or direct, and can also set up a class mailbox for which the teacher can arrange 'pen pals' (or 'pen pals' can be contacted through electronic mail; see subsection 10.7.5).

2. *Protest.* Students can write a letter of protest to some company about its product. The teacher and students can first talk about words and phrases that are important for a letter of protest. They can then decide on a company to whom they can write. Students can also write a protest letter about some school rule, or they can write a protest letter to the city about some issue that is affecting their school.

3. *Greetings.* The teacher and students can collect birthday announcements for famous people from calendars, newspapers, television, and radio. Each student can select a famous living person who was born on or near his or her birthday. Each student can then make a birthday card and send it to the selected person. On the back, students can explain why they are sending their cards.

10.6.3 *Providing descriptions, directions, and procedures (19)*

In beginning writing, it is important to expose students to a variety of writing purposes and tasks. In addition to stories, letters, and expressive writing, students need to practise types of writing which engage them with content-centred informational materials and tasks; these types of writing should be practised regularly for a number of reasons, even though they may be perceived by teachers as more difficult.

First, if they are indeed more difficult, students would benefit from more practice rather than less. Second, informational genres of writing are natural extensions of content-based and project-oriented curricula and are important means for integrating and learning content-area information, even in the early grades. Third, these types of writing are natural extensions of stories and expressive writing activities. Often, students can develop descriptions or procedures as part of a story telling, and certain projects involving expressive writing can be followed by descriptive and procedural assignments that oblige students to explore additional resources. Fourth, some students do not have much exposure to informational types of writing at home. These students need early exposure in school to informational genres if they are not to fall behind more advantaged students in their writing development. Fifth, students are naturally curious about the world. Information genres provide another means for exploring the world, and they let students organize this information for other purposes. While many activities in this chapter begin with generating information from personal resources, students should be encouraged to explore topics which will lead to writing about the world around them rather than consistently writing about themselves.

The teacher needs to focus attention on the language features and organizing principles which tend to be consistently part of descriptions, directions, and procedures. Students also need to be aware of the words and phrases that clearly signal the intended organization of the writing.

Early activities involving word lists, phrase and sentence writing, and writing poems can easily be expanded into description, direction giving, and procedural writing. The following are just a few of the many additional possibilities.

1. *Favourite food.* The class identifies favourite foods and makes a list of class favourites. The recipes can be collected for a class recipe book.
2. *A special place.* The teacher can describe a special place and explain why it is special. Students can then think of their own special place, visualize it, and describe it in a few sentences.
3. *Shoe personality.* Students can begin this activity by collecting pictures of shoes. They can then describe the shoes and the personalities of the people who wear them.
4. *Giving directions.* Students should think of situations in which people often give advice and specific directions. The class can brainstorm a list of situations – as well as words and phrases – used in giving directions, and can then give directions for a

selected situation. For example, they can tell someone how to do something: eat with chopsticks, make papier mâché, brush their teeth, cook a turkey, make a hamburger, make a sandwich, water a plant, feed a pet, write a recipe, etc.

5. *Favourite sport.* Students can form groups and nominate their favourite sports. They can then describe this sport and its rules to someone from another planet.

10.6.4   Keeping records and writing reports (20)

Students need to become familiar with report writing. They should practise collecting and recording information on a topic, sorting the information, and generalizing from it. They should also practice writing about the information in a clearly organized and logical presentation. This may seem to be a daunting task, but activities can be developed which systematically lead students into such writing and which follow naturally from other classroom activities. Particularly in project-oriented and content-area instruction, students need to practise working with sets of information that can genuinely inform others, whether they be classmates, students in other classes, parents, or others.

The teacher can also point out formal features of report writing. This will represent natural opportunities to focus on the language used in reports and the organizational frameworks that will be effective. For example, students can focus on the need to generalize away from specific examples, to classify information into larger groupings, and to use qualifying terms rather than absolute statements. Students can also become more aware of ways to signal the organization of their texts through transition devices.

There are many possibilities for report writing with beginning students. Students can begin by brainstorming ideas; generating words and phrases; focusing on specific topics of interest; making observations of objects or events; writing up simple recounts, descriptions, directions, and journal entries; and trying to find more information from the teacher and the class library. This sequence of activities, over time, should lead naturally to simple report writing. Below are a few examples of the types of activities which lead to report writing.

1. *Touch and tell scrapbook.* Students collect items that are interesting to touch (e.g. foil, plastic, paper, cardboard, sandpaper,

cheesecloth, corduroy, glue, burlap, foam, leather, satin, nylon, leaves, sawdust, velour, wood chips, cement pieces, etc.). They put samples on each page of a scrapbook and write down some words for each piece (appearance, feeling, source, use). The items can be organized into groups, appropriately labelled, and the resulting scrapbooks can form the basis for a simple report on types of materials in our world, what they look and feel like, where they are found, and what they are used for.

2. *Pet feeding and cleaning.* In this project, students write out a schedule for the care/feeding of a pet. The pet can be either at home or at school. A record is kept of eating habits, times for eating, preferred foods, etc. This notebook can then be the source for a simple report on the feeding routines and eating habits of the pet.

3. *Data sheets.* Students can keep a daily record of an ongoing experiment. Such an experiment can include plant germination, ant farms, fish behaviour, humidity recording, etc. After a set period of time, students can write a final summary of their observations and determine whether or not such observations can be generalized.

4. *Making a questionnaire.* The students can plan a class or group project to examine student interests in some topic. Students can nominate a topic of interest from a set listed on the board and create a simple set of questions to gather information from classmates. Students can also survey family members or students from another class, and can write up the results of the survey as a group project. Students will need to determine the generalizations, if any, that can be made from the information gathered.

5. *Taking notes.* Students can practise note-taking through many simple tasks and activities in order to develop a sense of the key words and phrases that are important. One such activity involves taking notes on a short reading, a simple lecture, a video presentation, or the comments of a guest speaker. Students can compare notes in a group, then compare their notes with the notes of the teacher. They can use the various sets of notes to fill in useful words and phrases and to improve the accuracy of their own notes. Students can then briefly write a summary, or a response, or fill in a chart. This type of activity should be simple and should be repeated often: it should also be done with information that students need for another purpose.

10.7   Extending the writing curriculum (themes 21–25)

A final set of themes suggests ways to enhance the writing environment and assist students in carrying out writing tasks. These themes indicate extensions that are natural and necessary for writing development, lead to positive attitudes towards writing, and introduce a wide range of opportunities to practise writing. Five themes appropriate for these purposes include: (1) using a dialogue journal, (2) publishing completed work, (3) establishing a writing corner, (4) including extensive reading, and (5) providing early access to word processing.

10.7.1   Using a dialogue journal (21)

A good way to have students extend their writing opportunities and also use writing to communicate is through dialogue journals. In highly structured approaches, the dialogue journal requires writing every day: at a given time, students regularly open their dialogue journals and write an entry for that day. The journals are collected periodically by the teacher who responds to student entries. The responses are not meant to be evaluations of writing or suggestions for writing; rather, the dialogue journal is an opportunity for the teacher and the student to communicate informally in the written medium. The teacher responds to a student's ideas and engages students in a dialogue on whatever topic they have chosen. Of course, the teacher is free to nominate other topics of interest, much as any conversational partner would do (Peyton 1990).

The dialogue journal does not have to be a daily routine, but it should be a consistent one if it is to be seen as a genuine means of expression and communication. The writing should occur often enough to be seen as a regular part of classroom activities. Enough time should also be given to journal writing to ensure that it is not a hurried session squeezed in between other activities or before the end of the class day.

There are a number of benefits in using journals. They provide students with additional reasons for writing and further practice, and they allow students and teachers to nominate topics of interest which can become sources of other writing activities and projects. The journals also become an outlet through which students can express their feelings and their attitudes towards school and other assigned activities. Journals can occasionally be shared with other students to let them see what their peers are writing about. Similarly, journals can be a source of discussion in class and a resource for brainstorming (Staton *et al.* 1988).

10.7.2   *Publishing completed work (22)*

A second useful extension of writing for beginning students is publishing certain writings. This process can be relatively informal, using a space on the bulletin board for the publication of the week. It can involve the production of a cover and some artwork, which are then combined with the writing and stapled together as a book for other students in the class to read in a reading corner or class library. It can also involve a more elaborate publishing of the writing. Many classes use a word processor to finish a writing task for publication. The writing itself goes through an editing process and then is published.

The use of publishing is a strong motivator for students. They feel a sense of pride in their accomplishment because the published work often looks very good. Nevertheless, the use of publishing requires a sense of moderation and proportion. Publishing should not be used for every writing task; rather, it should be saved for special projects, longer and more involved assignments, and group projects that are of some special value. A class book of favourite poems or stories, for example, is a project which might deserve publication. Publication should also be reserved for good work. Students and teacher both recognize writing tasks that reflect special efforts; and these are good candidates for publishing. Because publishing is special, it should only be used for special writing otherwise it loses its value and students will not see books as major productions that require considerable effort (and provide great satisfaction).

The creation of a small newspaper is also an important authentic outlet for student writing. A monthly two-page newspaper can be taken home to parents and can include class announcements, student writing, and plans for upcoming projects.

10.7.3   *Establishing a writing corner (23)*

Writing activities can be extended into a writing corner, an area of the classroom designed to promote writing, whether as part of a writing assignment or as a resource for individual activities. In many cases the writing corner can be the place where students and student groups go to explore options for interesting writing tasks. In classes that use student portfolios (see Chapter 11, sub-section 11.7.2; and Chapter 13), the writing corner is where they are kept, and students can then review their previous writing and decide whether to complete it or revise it. Various editing and references materials can be stored in the writing corner, such as student dictionaries, resource books, encyclopaedias, and editing guidelines, etc., for checking writing before it is published.

The writing corner can also be a place where many resource collections are kept to motivate students to write. The writing corner can include cans and bags which have story starters: these can be titles, first lines, or first paragraphs for a story. Students can select one from a bag and finish the story. Another bag might include papers with sets of words on them from which students must make a poem or short story. Another bag can contain newspaper headlines for which students have to write the accompanying news story. A box can contain pictures which students can describe or use as a starting point for a story or poem. A bag can include addresses of people to whom students can write letters (e.g. addresses of schools, city and governmental offices, corporations, informational assistance addresses, etc.). A large metal can, containing group-writing activities, can be used to get groups started on a writing task or project. These and other writing starters can all be components of a writing corner, one which should motivate students to explore writing on different tasks and topics, and for different purposes.

10.7.4 Including extensive reading (24)

One important extension for writing is the incorporation of extensive reading in class. Reading and writing are reciprocal activities; the outcome of a reading activity can serve as input for writing, and writing can lead a student to further reading resources. A good way to incorporate extensive reading into the classroom is through Sustained Silent Reading (SSR). In SSR, the teacher and students stop other activities in order to read silently. The teacher must also read to model extensive reading. This should be done on a regular basis (3 to 5 times per week) and can last 10–15 minutes per session. The time can later be expanded as students become more comfortable with sustained reading. Students can introduce their own reading material or select material from a good class library.

Another way to promote extensive reading which can lead to many writing activities is by using high-interest class sets of readers. Reading time is set aside on a regular basis and everyone quietly reads the same book. After 15–20 minutes, students stop and record their progress. They might also write a line or two on their response to the day's reading. Class readers provide opportunities for group projects, dramatizations and acting out scenes from the book, additional creative writing about a character in the book, pre-reading activities to set the scene before the book begins, or continuing the story to tell what happens after the book ends. These and many other options become available with the use of a class reader.

10.7.5   *Providing early access to word processing (25)*

Increasing numbers of students are gaining access to computers. As a consequence, educational norms expect students to be familiar with writing in this way. Many schools have a computer lab or a few computers in the class. These resources should be used to develop students' facility with the technology and, more importantly, to give students writing practice with powerful resources. The computer gives the students opportunities to write longer pieces, to revise easily, to work with different formatting, and to keep files of past work. Computers provide a new dimension for group work because students can work on a given assignment either together or at different times, and the text remains clean. Finally, graphics options and clean print-outs tend to motivate students to write for longer periods of time.

A further advantage of computers is that writing tasks can be transferred to other sites. Students can trade diskette files with other classes, either to complete a project or as a mail delivery. Further, students can write to other classes through e-mail; not only can they set up 'pen-pal' exchanges but also engage in informative projects which exchange information on cultures, holidays, important people, and classroom practices, among other activities. Computers provide important options for writing which increasingly cannot be overlooked. Much like writing itself, computers need to be seen by students as a medium for communication and a powerful resource for their own development.

10.8   Adapting themes for the adult beginning writer

Much of the above discussion is primarily designed for the young student beginning to write, and it assumes students in the elementary grades. Many of the issues raised, however, apply equally to the adult beginning writer. Adult beginning writers need extensive encouragement and support; they need to be given many opportunities to succeed; they also need to feel that the progress they make is not trivial or useless. In this regard, many themes outlined above can be adapted easily to the adult context. Adult students need to be able to discuss what they will write about, and they need to brainstorm information on a topic.

- They need to build a productive writing vocabulary for expressing their more complex ideas.
- They need to write on a daily basis and for a variety of purposes; the essay is not the preferred goal for beginning adults, it is rather frequent short writings for different real purposes.
- They need to focus consciously on the wide variety of print in the environment and on its many formats and purposes.

Too often, adults focus only on the difficult forms of writing that they feel unable to produce.

In terms of writing support and guidance, adults also need to be supported by sheltered instruction and literacy scaffolding. They need much modelling, tasks that they can accomplish, and stimulating and meaningful activities. In addition, they need to learn a metalanguage for talking about writing so that they can discuss their own writing and the writing of others, and can engage in giving and accepting feedback in a productive way, which is a particularly difficult skill to develop as adult beginners are generally vulnerable to criticism from others.

The need to extend writing practice in a variety of ways is perhaps even more important for adult beginners. Since adults have less time to develop the necessary skills than young children who will be in school for many years, adults need to practise many different types of relevant tasks and gain control over many genres in a relatively short period of time. Dialogue journals are a particularly useful way to engage adult writers in serious exchanges of written information in writing without critiquing their writing form: they allow adults to feel as though they are communicating about ideas and issues from their real world as they exchange dia-

logue journals with teachers. Teachers need, however, to emphasize that they are *not correcting writing errors* in the dialogue
journals; otherwise, students may assume that anything a teacher
reads and does not mark is correct.

A class which includes a writing corner may also motivate adults
to engage in interesting activities either individually or in groups.
The same is true in terms of opportunities to publish, most likely
in the form of well-written letters or newsletters to a variety of
people and groups. Similarly, access to computers can motivate
students if word processing is well supported and modelled. The
need to integrate writing with reading is also a more important
issue for adults than for young learners. Adults need to see various
types of printed texts and learn larger sets of informational and
topical vocabulary. They also have a greater need to feel a sense of
success and accomplishment with reading and writing than do
young children because they have little time and few opportunities to recover from the influence of unfortunate past
experiences.

One added challenge involves those adults who arrive in class as
true illiterates. In these cases, student activities and teacher roles
become quite different. The teacher is faced not simply with
students who cannot write, but also with students who do not
understand the relationships between sound and print, who have
no knowledge of alphabetic units and little sense of how writing
forms are shaped by writing purposes. Also, they cannot read as a
way to gain access to forms of writing, at least not initially. In these
cases, a basic literacy programme which stresses the alphabetic
principle, the need to build a simple sight vocabulary of basic
words, and control over the mechanics of writing become the primary goal. In such a context, students can begin to write by
copying, starting with word lists which they self-generate and
which include vocabulary important to their needs. Only after
adults can control the mechanics of writing and have successful
experiences in short assisted writing tasks with teachers (e.g. LEA
activities) should they be given a wider range of opportunities for
self-expression. Adults, more than children, are aware that they
are not writing appropriately, and false encouragement and frustrating writing activities should not be allowed to damage a
sensitive adult ego. The transition to a beginning writing stage in
which some familiarity with writing is assumed is a decision that
should be negotiated between the student and the teacher.

10.9 Conclusion

The themes for writing introduced in this chapter are meant to raise awareness of the many options available for writing with beginning students. The compendium of themes, however, is not meant to be seen simply as ideas for 'something to do' the next day. Rather, the many specific techniques discussed throughout the themes are intended as activities that can be used within larger projects and content-units in a class. The themes provide some simple guidelines to assist their integration into the development of larger curricular units.

It should also be evident that there are certain instructional notions that run through many themes. First, it is important to set up an assignment at the students' level. Even for beginning writers, this is possible if the task is simple at first (and simple does not mean simple-minded). Often the starting point is the generation of words and phrases and their association with some props. In other cases, the use of lists, pictures, and sentences all provide the sorts of sheltering that students sometimes need and that can be the beginning of a larger, more complex activity. Second, students need to work in groups on a regular basis to see how other students are conducting the activity and to compare their own work with others in a non-threatening environment. The teacher, however, should also use groups to provide feedback that is timely and that does not always single out students individually. Third, students should be encouraged to explore ideas and information in a variety of ways. And while there is a greater emphasis on expressive and narrative ideas in this chapter, there are also many activities which can be used to explore the students' world. Fourth, students should also explore many aspects of language form and language use through these activities. These types of activities provide teachers with opportunities to focus on language aspects as they arise out of the assignment. Such opportunities represent important ways to raise student awareness about language, point out the effective uses of language, and give students opportunities to explore a variety of writing situations and their attendant linguistic constraints.

In the two chapters to follow, additional principles, with accompanying themes and activities, will be presented with more advanced students in mind. Many of those activities build on the simpler activities presented in this chapter. It is also important to keep in mind that the themes and activities in this chapter are not only applicable to beginning writers; many ideas can be adapted to become more complex tasks, appropriate for intermediate and even advanced writers.

11

Teaching writing at intermediate levels

11.1 Introduction

As students have more experience with writing in English, and as they move into educational contexts with more demanding learning tasks, writing instruction takes on new dimensions. Students need to be able to organize more complex sets of information and develop fluency with a wider range of genres and formal structures of written discourse. While basic fluencies and abilities, as discussed in the previous chapter, remain important components of writing instruction, there are many additional abilities which must be developed and many resources for writing which must be invoked.

The intermediate student is one who is able to write on a basic level[1] and now must use writing to learn a wide range of other academic information; someone who uses writing to learn about history, science, literature, social studies, mathematics, art, and foreign languages. Students at this level must learn how to read from multiple sources and write from these sources. Often these students will be engaged in longer projects which require specific types of analyses, syntheses, and critical evaluation. At the same time, intermediate students are continually gaining control over additional vocabulary and more complex sentence structure while also gaining a greater degree of stylistic maturity, a reflection of a growing sense of purpose and audience in their writing. All of these changes in writing expectations reflect a greater emphasis on informational writing and its various genres and constraints.

There are two major groups of intermediate writers who need to improve their writing for academic purposes. For the student in the public school context, the intermediate writer is seen as the secondary school student, roughly grades 6–11 (ages 12–17). These students presumably have mastered the basic skills for composing simple messages and the mechanics of writing. They have also typically gained a fair amount of experience in writing narrative and expressive tasks. A smaller subset of secondary students have already gained a range of experiences writing various expository and argumentative tasks: these latter students have developed strategies for organizing information in logical frames which are appropriate for their purposes. Many of these students have also worked with thematic projects and content-area information integrated with an emphasis on literacy and writing.

Unfortunately, research has revealed that, for the majority of students, emphases on expository and argumentative writing have not been a consistent part of the educational curriculum. For the majority of students, then, it is imperative that they gain access to the more powerful forms of writing during their secondary school experiences. It is well known that expository and argumentative forms of writing require much practice in a variety of contexts; thus, students need many opportunities to work with these types of tasks. A writer cannot move to an advanced level of writing without such extensive practice, even if these students do find themselves in a tertiary environment and believe themselves to be ready for tertiary-level work. This group includes both English L1 and English L2 students. While it is important, on general principles, to differentiate the needs of L1 and L2 students, for the purposes of this chapter, their similar backgrounds in secondary school settings provide strong rationales for treating them alike. (For other purposes, they certainly would have to be distinguished; Leki 1992, Silva 1993.)

A second well-defined group of intermediate students is the international ESL student who seeks to enter an English-speaking tertiary-level academic institution but has only an intermediate level of English language skills. These students have typically mastered the mechanics of writing in English, and have developed some basic fluency in writing through practice. They commonly take English academic preparation courses either in their home countries or on arrival in the English-speaking country before they are ready for tertiary-level work.

A third possible group, adult literacy students, often do not move beyond basic literacy abilities in their classwork. For this reason, they do not represent a major group of students requiring intermediate-level writing instruction. While it can be argued that adult literacy students should be explicitly represented in a discussion of intermediate writing development, the political reality is that they do not, in fact, form a large group of students in comparison with the two above groups.

11.2 Themes for intermediate writing instruction

This chapter will focus on a set of 25 themes which are important for developing writing abilities beyond a basic level. It builds upon the themes and activities addressed in the previous chapter, extending and incorporating basic writing activities into the context of intermediate instruction. Again, it must be pointed out that the themes in this chapter are not intended to represent isolated sets of issues or stand-alone techniques which do not fit into a larger writing curriculum. Rather, these themes are intended to highlight critical issues for curriculum design and options for assignments, and they should be integrated within an overall instructional framework, preferably a content-based instructional framework.

The themes for writing instruction in this chapter are again organized into five general principles:

1. Preparing students for writing
2. Assisting and guiding writing
3. Working with writing
4. Writing for different purposes (genres)
5. Extending the writing curriculum.

The first set of themes addresses pre-writing concerns, presenting general issues which support subsequent writing activities. A second set of themes focuses on issues which are important during the time of writing, particularly in the case of larger writing projects over a period of time. These themes deal with ways to improve writing as it moves through the writing process of multiple drafts and extension activities. A third set focuses specifically on various types of writing activities. A fourth set addresses the need to introduce and practice additional genres. The final five themes address issues which often exist outside the framework of specific writing tasks. These 'extension' themes consider additional types of knowledge or abilities (e.g. sentence combining)

which can be integrated into a curriculum as they are most useful
and appropriate.

11.3   Preparing for writing (themes 1–5)

The five themes in this section highlight major approaches to
building a writing curriculum and ways to prepare students for
writing. These themes include: (1) cooperative learning and
group work, (2) content-based instruction as a framework for writing development, (3) an awareness of audience, (4) free writing
and brainstorming, and (5) semantic mapping and graphic organizers. Together, the five themes offer students ways to prepare for
writing and opportunities for generating many relevant ideas.

11.3.1   *Cooperative learning and group work (1)*

Group work is commonly discussed as an important component of
writing instruction. However, there are few consistent research
results which support the general notion of group work as an
effective approach to writing instruction (cf. Spear 1988). Rather,
there are certain types of group work which appear to be effective
for many types of learning, including the development of writing.
Foremost among these more effective approaches is the general
notion of cooperative learning and its several variations, almost all
of which are supported by a strong set of research studies
(Fathman and Kessler 1993, Slavin 1990; see also Chapter 13).

Cooperative learning is a type of group work (though certainly
not all group work is cooperative learning). The goal of cooperative learning is to engage students cooperatively in inquiry and
interaction for the purpose of working towards some joint goal.[2] It
is a carefully structured approach in which all learners are
responsible for the group outcome. Students in each group are
assigned distinct roles: to direct the group, to promote interaction, to record progress, and to report to the outside world.
Students are engaged in solving problems together and supporting each other. The goal of the teacher is to model strategic
behaviour, facilitate group interaction, monitor progress, and clarify the problems and the means to solve them.

Cooperative learning approaches have a number of points in
common. First, they allow varying options for grouping students;

second, they teach social and interactive skills explicitly; third, they foster a sense of cohesiveness among group members; fourth, they promote shared leadership within groups; fifth, they emphasize the perspectives of various members of the group; and sixth, they use structured tasks to promote cooperation and learning. Many approaches also stress group and individual responsibility for accomplishing the task.[3]

Five main types of cooperative learning are commonly cited: the Group Investigative Method, the Learning Together Method, Jigsaw, the Structural Approach, and Student Team Learning. Each of these approaches is readily adaptable to writing instruction, particularly in a content-based, or thematic, writing curriculum (Fathman and Kessler 1993, R. Stahl 1994). The Group Investigative Method (Sharan and Sharan 1992) proposes a large project in which each subgroup investigates one part of the larger theme. Each subgroup is responsible for planning, carrying out the study, and reporting back to the class. The Learning Together Method (Johnson and Johnson 1991) emphasizes the importance of working together on a project through team-building activities, discussions, and teacher support. Jigsaw (Aronson 1978) promotes group cooperation and cross-group interaction. Each member of a group receives a different set of information and students must leave their group to work with other students who received similar information. Groups then reassemble and combine their information to accomplish a larger task. The Structural Approach (Kagan 1992) teaches students a variety of means for organizing and presenting information to others. These structures are the building blocks for larger activities, encouraging different types of cooperation. Finally, Student Team Learning (Slavin 1990) is an approach specifically designed for content-area learning. This approach emphasizes individual accountability, team rewards, and multiple opportunities for success.

The various approaches to cooperative learning all fit well with more complex writing tasks and projects and are especially effective when writing is also used to learn and work with specific sets of information. Students using cooperative learning approaches have demonstrated significant gains in reading and writing abilities as well as superior content-material learning (Fathman and Kessler 1993). While there is a general preference for 'group work' among writing teachers, few methods can match the research results and demonstrated improvements that have been shown by true cooperative learning. For this reason, writing teachers need to be aware of cooperative learning methods and to consider whether they can be applied to their various writing instruction contexts.

11.3.2   Content-based instruction (2)

The use of content-based instruction is no longer a new idea, but it is one that is extremely effective for both content and language learning, and, in particular, for writing development (Batholomae and Petrosky 1986, Crandall 1993, Enright and McCloskey 1988, Mohan 1986, Readance *et al.* 1989, Santa and Alvermann 1991, Tchudi and Huerta 1983). The basic goal is to keep content at the centre of instruction and to build various language learning activities and projects around major themes. Themes and projects should be interpreted broadly so that a variety of topics and tasks can be sequenced to meet learning objectives. Writing activities should develop directly out of the themes and allow for natural discussion of ways that different genres of writing serve different purposes; they should also highlight the ways that appropriate language use supports specific genres and purposes for writing. These notions are applicable to writing instruction from elementary grades through tertiary-level courses (Bartholomae and Petrosky 1986, Enright and McCloskey 1988, Manning *et al.* 1994, Meinbach *et al.* 1995, Tchudi and Huerta 1983, Walmsley 1994).

Content-based instruction is effective because students are motivated to learn both content and language. The various uses of language are not artificially developed but arise as part of the more general process of inquiry. This approach also allows for more realistic complexity of the information with which students are asked to work. Students will each develop somewhat unique sets of knowledge from the resources they refer to and read. When they work together in groups, they then have genuinely distinct sets of knowledge and insights to contribute (cf. many information-gap writing activities in ESL texts). Further, writing assignments themselves can be sequenced so that simpler tasks build into more complex tasks, all of which build naturally to the completion of a major project.

A good way for a teacher to develop content-based instruction is by collecting information and nominating useful themes for the class to explore. These could include explorers, dinosaurs, monsters and myths, trees, the 1950s, volcanoes, underwater exploration, heroes, space, etc. Each of these themes, in turn, can be the source for a number of more specific topics; for example, the explorer theme can focus on geographical explorers (on earth or in space), but it can also include scientific discoveries, the use of robots for research, the first airplanes, or exploration of the human mind. Topics might include the geography of exploration, the record keeping required in exploration, financial aspects of exploration, the sociology of exploration, the politics of exploration, etc. Topics should be organized in such a way as to build up from easier tasks to more complex and difficult ones. Further, content themes and topics should be organized in a coherent manner so that an entire curriculum can work from an ever-increasing set of knowledge as a resource for various writing activities. (See subsection 11.5.2 for additional discussion.)

Content-based instruction also provides a natural framework for cooperative learning, strategy instruction, the use of graphic organizers (visual representations of text structure and discourse organization), and a range of Language Experience Activities (LEA). Many of the specific ways to develop tasks and activities for cooperative learning, as discussed above, are especially well suited to content-area instruction. Students can keep learning journals and progress logs for sequenced tasks. Well-designed information-gap activities are also appropriate since students who deal with an extensive amount of content information remember and synthesize the information differently; thus, they generate natural information gaps through discussions and writing activities. Students, in addition, will be able to ask, and respond to, informational questions without needing artificially constructed tasks. Content-based instruction also lends itself well to discussions about writing assignments and generates extensive information on specific topics.

11.3.3   Audience awareness (3)

Intermediate students need to focus greater attention on a consideration of audience. While it is possible to raise such concerns with beginning writers, they do not often give serious consideration to who the reader is, how the reader may influence the writer, and how the writer may influence the reader. Writers need to

310 Theory and Practice of Writing

recognize that readers also have expectations, attitudes, interests, and objectives. Readers assume that texts will be organized in certain ways and that sufficient signals of the writer's intentions will be available in the writing. Readers also have specific attitudes towards the content of a text – whether the content is useful or not, entertaining or not, sympathetic or not, etc. In addition, readers have their own interests, and texts need to be shaped to consider reader interests. Finally, readers have objectives in the sense that they want a text to provide a thorough explanation, a complete story, an interesting point of view, an honest interpretation, or a challenging assessment.

Audience factors may also include consideration of a number of variables; whether or not:

- the reader is known;
- the reader is an individual or a group;
- the reader will evaluate the writing;
- the reader has approximately the same level of general knowledge;
- the reader knows a lot about the specific topic of writing;
- the reader will be empathetic;
- the reader has a different power status.

An attempt by a student to present an argument, and provide reasons for the position taken, should be shaped to some extent by the various audience factors noted here.

Activities to raise awareness of audience may include rewriting an argument text from the perspective of the opposing viewpoint, telling the same story from the perspective of a different character, rewriting a text for a younger audience, rewriting a text in the form of a letter to the local newspaper, rewriting a letter of complaint or protest as a letter to a friend explaining your complaint or concern, or reworking an informational text into a poster for public display. In each of these cases, it is possible to include exploration of how a different audience will influence the way that a student will write (see also Schriver 1992).

11.3.4 Free writing and brainstorming (4)

Both free writing and brainstorming provide additional resources for student writing. Free writing, allowing students to write for a short period of time on any chosen topic, is a useful way to get students to 'find' topics of interest, to recognize ideas of which they were not aware, and to nominate possible topics for writing activities. A more directed form of free writing occurs when a teacher suggests a general idea and students write on anything relevant to that general idea. Similarly, students can free write after a class discussion to explore ideas of interest or worthy of a response of some sort. The most controlled type of free writing occurs in response to a specific question raised by the teacher. Often, specific aspects of a student's free writing can be nominated as a new source for more specific free writing. This looping activity is a commonly suggested option in textbooks and among writing teachers.

Free writing has a number of benefits for student writing:

1. It is not evaluated and students can feel free to say what they want about a topic or an idea.
2. It allows students to overcome writer's block and develop greater fluency in writing.
3. It is a good source for ideas that can be used for later writing assignments or future class activities.
4. It gives students a chance to explore, or become aware of their individual voice – how they write (how they sound) without conforming to some set of external constraints.

In other brainstorming activities, students can reflect on some event, concept, or controversy and discuss this as a whole class. They can write individual reactions to some issue and then use these responses to discuss the topic. Another possible way to gather and organize ideas occurs through note-taking during a discussion and subsequently through reorganizing content by working with groups. Generating lists, making word associations, and creating semantic maps (see also subsection 11.3.5) provide further brainstorming activities. Responding to a short reading or to a visual display such as a picture, chart, table, or graph can also introduce ideas for writing.

11.3.5 Semantic mapping and graphic organizers (5)

Working out the relationships among sets of information and recognizing the levels of discourse and information structuring is an important type of brainstorming, but such an activity goes beyond brainstorming to matters of overall text structure and the organization of information. Through semantic mapping and graphic organizers, students and teachers explore ways to examine the organizational framework of a text and structure information.

Semantic mapping (or webbing) is now a well-known technique for generating information, connecting ideas, finding ways to organize the information, and using the information to develop an effective written text. Typically, semantic mapping begins with students generating words that they associate with a topic or central idea. These words are written on the board and then organized into groups of words that appear to go together. This reorganizing of the words can be done individually, in groups, or as a whole-class activity. Once groups of words are agreed upon, students can nominate topic headings for each subgroup of items. Class discussion can then determine which groups of ideas are more or less important. The class can also decide whether or not each group of ideas contributes important information to the central idea; whether or not the writing tasks should focus on the central idea in the map or on one or two of the sub-ideas as a more focused activity; and whether or not there are other ways to organize/add information. The results of these activities then serve as a major resource for vocabulary acquisition, reading comprehension, information learning, and writing assignments. Semantic maps can also be 'translated' into more linear informal outlines to assist writing activities. Overall, semantic mapping is recognized as an effective technique which improves both content learning and language development (Heimlich and Pittelman 1986, Nagy 1988).

Graphic organizers are primarily intended to represent conceptual relations between sets of ideas. The term refers to visual structures which organize information and guide reading comprehension and planning for writing. There are many types of graphic organizers and many ways to use them. Information can be organized into flow charts, hierarchical tree structures, classification arrays, charts, tables, figures, histograms, diagrams, matrices, maps, or outlines (Armbruster 1991, Mohan 1986, 1990, Tierney *et al.* 1990). These displays can be created by the students and teachers; they can be given to students as a guide; they can be partially completed, leaving gaps to be filled in by students; or they can be presented as empty frames to be filled in by students. Working with graphic organizers can be done individually or in groups, and they present good tasks for cooperative learning activities. Graphic organizers can be used as pre-writing and as post-writing activities. Ideally, the use of graphic organizers on a consistent basis should lead students to use them independently to examine conceptual relations and organize information. Many studies show that this approach is effective for both content and language instruction (Armbruster *et al.* 1991, Mohan 1990, Pearson and Fielding 1991, Pressley *et al.* 1989, Tang 1992).

11.4   Assisting and guiding writing (themes 6–10)

The five themes addressed under this principle reflect the more challenging demands placed on intermediate writers as well as the more complex set of factors influencing writing activities and writing development. These themes include: (1) strategy instruction, (2) peer response groups, (3) the writing process, (4) movement from controlled to free writing, and (5) awareness of language and genre structure. These themes extend the notion that effective writing requires attention to both the process of working with text and the output which conveys the intentions and ideas of the writer. Together, these themes make students more aware of the options they have while writing.

11.4.1   *Strategy instruction (6)*

In preparation for writing, and at various times during the writing process, a focus on writing strategies (e.g. summarizing mentally, revising plans, providing examples) is an effective way to prepare students for independent strategy use. Strategy instruction can be presented to the whole class or as part of small-group activities. In either case, the most effective means for presenting writing strategies is through explicit modelling and follow-up discussions. The teacher can model a writing assignment by talking aloud while composing at the blackboard or on an overhead projector. Students note important or interesting choices made, and during the discussion after the composing activity, students ask the teacher about various aspects of composing. At the same time, the teacher is able to point out a number of conscious planning and composing strategies that he or she has used (e.g. audience awareness, added information). In this way, a number of important composing strategies are brought to a conscious level and consistent attention to these strategies becomes an important component of writing strategy instruction.

An additional goal of strategy instruction is to have students consciously attempt important strategies on their own. One method for developing independent strategy use is through reciprocal teaching and a community of learners approach (Brown 1994, Brown and Campione 1994, Brown and Palincsar 1989, Palincsar and Klenk 1991). In this approach, the teacher works with a group of students, taking turns composing aloud. As students compose aloud, they can explain the sorts of strategies they are using. Students can also focus on planning strategies, revising strategies, elaborating strategies, or evaluating strategies. Feedback from the teacher and other members of the group will highlight additional strategies used or not used. Consistent practice, with students taking the role of the teacher, will eventually lead to independent control over a range of writing strategies. This approach allows the teacher to point to specific aspects of discourse structure which support the goals for writing such as attention to cohesive relations, information structuring, text organization, and rhetorical goals.

A second method for developing writing strategies is through procedural facilitation (Bereiter and Scardamalia 1987, Pressley *et al.* 1992, 1994). In a series of studies, Bereiter and Scardamalia trained students to use cue cards while writing. The cards each had a strategy written on the reverse side to cue strategic writing behaviour when the student was not sure what to do next. Cuing was designed both for narrative topics and expository topics, and cues were developed for planning (think of a new idea, improve plan, recall major goal, etc.), for evaluating, and for diagnosing problems. Evaluating cues, for example, would include statements such as the following:

1. People won't see why this is important.
2. People may not understand what I mean here.
3. This is a useful sentence.
4. I'm getting away from the main point.
5. I'd better give an example.
6. I'd better leave this part out.

(Bereiter and Scardamalia 1987: 270–1)

As students gradually became comfortable with these cues, they consulted them more freely. Results of research on this seemingly mechanistic approach revealed significant improvements in writing and in appropriate strategy use when used over time.

11.4.2 Peer response groups (7)

The use of peer response groups is widespread in writing instruction, and it is promoted at all levels of instruction, from beginning to advanced. Theoretically, peer revision is well supported in that it is consistent with Vygotskean perspectives on learning; it can draw on research and instructional insights from the cooperative learning literature; it is supported by social-construction theory as an important way to establish dialogue about writing, nominate appropriate information, and get assistance from real readers; and it is consistent with strategy-instruction approaches such as reciprocal teaching (Nystrand 1986, Nystrand and Brandt 1989, Spear 1988, Zhu 1994).

Peer response groups, however, do not implicate a single method or technique; rather, the approach can be carried out in many different ways. The choices depend on the views of the teacher, the types of students and teaching situations, and the time and resources available for instruction. For example, intermediate-level students in grade 8 may have difficulty in understanding how to comment on peer writing effectively. These students cannot simply be left to their own resources but need to be guided if they are to give helpful critiques. Zhu (1994) classifies five parameters of peer response approaches: small group vs. large group, student-selected vs teacher-assigned groupings, teacher-directed vs student-directed groups, role-specific vs non-role-specific groups, and oral response vs written response groups. Many of these distinctions centre around the degree of teacher intervention.

To work effectively, peer response groups need to be modelled for students. Teachers need to guide students through several sessions so that students become effective readers and responders. Moreover, students and teachers need to work together to establish positive interactive environments in which all students work together to help each other. Spear (1988) argues that effective peer response groups are task oriented – that is, they stay on task; they focus on more global aspects of student writing; they give accurate and specific feedback; they interact as peers rather than as surrogate teachers and students; and they promote student trust and support for their writing efforts.

There are many ways to help students become more effective, sensitive, and insightful readers for their peers' writings. Spear

(1988) discusses feedback in terms of three types: supporting feedback, challenging feedback, and editing feedback. The first builds trust and support; the second provides ways to rethink the ideas and the structure of the text; the third attends to the formal aspects of writing that typically are expected by readers. This taxonomy highlights different types of feedback that can be useful to students; it does not suggest that these types of feedback are necessarily exclusive of one another. Spear also suggests that, through the use of reader free writing, reader note taking, and close structural analysis of reading, effective guidelines for responding can be developed. At the same time, she argues against the use of highly constrained task-oriented revision checklists which reflect categories of a writing handbook (e.g. diction, paragraph structure, sentence structure, mechanics). These latter guides are typically stated negatively and encourage group members to slip into surrogate teacher–student roles rather than negotiating the text under discussion: such checklists block real discussion of the text. Useful guidelines for effective peer responses are also suggested by Elbow (1981) and Reid (1993) (see also Chapter 13).

11.4.3   *The writing process (8)*

The writing process has become a widespread instructional approach over the last 15 years. It is seen as a major improvement over traditional methods of writing instruction. Many case studies and observational accounts support a writing process approach (Calkins 1986, Graves 1984); however, there is relatively little empirical evidence that the writing process itself leads to significantly better writing or that it is being carried out effectively even in classes labelled as writing process oriented (cf. Applebee *et al.* 1994). This is not a counter-argument to process instruction as much as it is a caution that a method for organizing writing processes cannot be expected, by itself, to overcome many of the difficulties encountered in teaching writing; the approach cannot be seen as a mechanical sequencing of techniques that automatically produces good writers.

The writing process, in general, is described as a five-stage process: pre-writing, drafting, revising, editing, and publishing. The first three steps will typically be recycled as many times as needed. Activities which are usually associated with the writing process include brainstorming, semantic mapping, free writing, journal writing, reading, class and group discussion, peer response, teacher conferences, mini-lessons on aspects of language, revision and editing based on the student papers, and teacher feedback for revising and editing. The teacher facilitates topic selection and helps students to focus their writing activities; the teacher also helps students find further information and encourages them to develop their ideas before being concerned with formal editing.

For younger students, Frank (1979) suggests, in addition, that students write on a daily basis, that the process be varied for different assignments depending on student interest and energy level, and that not all phases of the process need be involved in every activity. For example, she notes that students sometimes do not have the concentration to take a difficult task through all the stages. Frank also suggests that teachers make the writing process fun, make it easy, take small steps, avoid over-evaluating, save unfinished pieces, make a non-writer into a class observer who takes notes, and not worry about the progress of every student on each assignment. With younger students, such a relaxed atmosphere may often be more motivating in the long run than one which is consistently demanding.

11.4.4   Controlled, guided, parallel, and free writing (9)

Students who are making the transition from beginning to intermediate writers need to gain access to the means for more effective writing for differing purposes, and they need to be shown explicitly how to do this. They need not only the words and ways to talk about writing, but they also need specific models which point out how language and text form are tied to specific purposes for writing. They need to see how certain discourse conventions are used in clear and simple examples (Smagorinsky 1992). This use of examples does not mean that students are taught to write in simple ways that they will not use later; rather, the goal is to give students an initial framework for building more complex routines and organizational patterns as they encounter more complex information and more demanding writing tasks (Stolarek 1994).

Controlled writing can be as simple as changing a paragraph from first person to third person, filling in certain cloze gaps, adding a final sentence, combining simple sentences, or filling out an outline from a matching text. These and many other activities can be done not only with commercial materials (e.g. Kaplan and Shaw 1983) but also with texts generated by students or by the teacher from previous joint or group writing. Thus, there is no need to treat controlled writing activities as unrelated to larger curriculum topics and projects. Even the simplest activities involving changes in writing, or requiring analysis of the structure of writing, can come from materials generated by students or for other purposes by the teacher. These activities then provide a way to examine the form of purposeful writing and to explore relations between language form and textual function. These controlled activities also allow students to gain fluency in writing, to see appropriate writing models, and to know that the changes they make are not merely guesses but are likely to be appropriate because the task has not overwhelmed the student.

The gradual movement from controlled to free writing is meant to provide support for student writing, not to require error-free writing. As students practise various activities in controlled writing, they can also engage in *guided-writing* assignments in which they produce one of the paragraphs of an essay from information given, fill in an outline, or develop an essay from sentence combining. In *parallel writing*, students can read a simple model paragraph or two, fill in an outline that allows students to write on a parallel topic, then produce the one or two paragraphs. *Free writing* follows from reading some model texts and writing either a similar text or a response of some kind. In this final step, students are not directly guided or supported through the text materials themselves. It is worth reiterating, in describing this sequence, that students are as free to be creative, or to proceed without being completely accurate, as the teacher will allow. In many ways, the movement from controlled- to free-writing activities can be seen as an extension of Language Experience Approaches to writing into an intermediate writing context (e.g. Allen 1976, Cantoni 1987, Tierney *et al.* 1990). Students' writing development is limited or assisted not by the technique itself but by the teacher's choices in using the technique.

11.4.5 Awareness of language and genre structure (10)

An important component in writing instruction is the integration of formal aspects of writing with the writing process. To say that formal aspects of the language be considered resources for writing does not imply an emphasis on grammar instruction in the traditional sense. Hillocks (1986), in a careful review of research on formal grammar instruction, has argued convincingly that formal grammar instruction provides few positive results when taught as a school subject. However, many researchers and practitioners recognize the need for students to attend to formal aspects of their writing when they work on revising and editing. Moreover, many writing activities lend themselves naturally to examining formal aspects of language structure as they apply to writing. These opportunities may be used to stress how language works as a resource for better writing.

One of the major shortcomings of the relation between the structure of language in written genres and the teaching of writing has been the training that most writing teachers receive in modern grammar (if they receive any). There is little that North American generative grammar can contribute to writing instruction; rather, the completely theoretical emphasis of modern grammar, as it is commonly taught in the USA, for example, offers no explanation for the use of language structure as a resource for making meaning in various registers and genres of writing. In contrast, various researchers in systemic linguistics, most prominently in Australia, have pointed out the strong relation between variations in language form and the specific demands on language resources made by particular genres of writing (Christie 1992, Cope and Kalantzis 1993, Martin 1989).

This functional-theoretical perspective on language emphasizes the relations among a theory of language structure, a social theory of language use, and their implications for literacy development. For example, systemic research points out ways that informational writing makes greater use of complex noun groups and nominalizes many verbs and adjectives. It also demonstrates ways that argumentative writers rely on a modality system to provide the rhetorical power of persuasion. These and many other aspects of written texts can be explored directly with students as they become aware of the different language resources which can serve various purposes (Christie 1990, Christie *et al.* 1989, Collerson 1990, Derewianka 1990, Hasan and Martin 1989). Of course, teachers also need to be made aware of the patterns of language variation that serve writers' purposes if they are to help students in this way. In brief, the issue is not whether language forms and structures are useful, but whether students can recognize the relations between language structures and the roles they play in conveying appropriate meaning. Such awareness of language-as-a-resource gives students access to what Martin (1989) calls the discourses of power – ways of writing by which people organize and influence the world around them.

Teachers can use students' writings to develop tasks that will raise their awareness of structure, organization of information, and informational flow. A simple activity involves the use of sentence strips which have to be reconstructed into paragraphs that are coherent. The same basic activity can be done with paragraphs from a reading or a longer essay. A second activity is to provide an incomplete paragraph and have students complete the paragraph appropriately. Students can also examine cohesive ties by identifying them, filling them in, or considering how different cohesive ties would change the text and perhaps make the text less effective.

Another type of awareness activity is to examine sentence arrangements and information ordering. Students can examine given–new relations in student-written texts and see how information is presented. In prepared paragraphs, students can be asked to fill in the best continuing sentence at given points and discuss what make a sentence most appropriate. Students can also focus on first and last sentences of a paragraph; they can either fill in a first or last sentence, or add additional sentences. In these cases, students can focus on the best sentences to provide a transition to a new paragraph or to a new topic. They can also propose the best transition sentences for the beginning of a new paragraph.

Students can focus on organizational sentences that highlight the topic and signal text organization; students can discuss what types of sentences provide useful organizational information and why. Students can also examine word choices and explore how word changes influence writing. In particular, students can examine the effect of changing verb groups to nominalized words and phrases, and the influence of compressing clause information into prepositional phrases, participial phrases, relative clauses, and adjectives and adverbs (and also show how adjectives and adverbs themselves can be nominalized). Students can compare paragraphs that are heavily nominalized with paragraphs that retain the verbal processes as actions and states. Students need to be made aware of the differences that such changes make in a text and the conditions under which each type of writing style is more appropriate.

11.5   Working with writing (themes 11–15)

As students work on various writing tasks and projects, there are a number of supporting activities and skills that students can use and practise for their writing. In this section, five themes and supporting activities are presented for these purposes: (1) gathering information, (2) working with content-based material, (3) summary and response writing, (4) awareness of language uses, and (5) editing texts effectively. All of these themes provide information and resources that allow students to develop more complex but more controlled writing.

11.5.1   Gathering supporting information for writing (11)

The most obvious way to gather information for writing is from discussions and books: books from home, from the class library, from the school library, from a teacher's special collection for a project. There are also a number of other ways to collect information. A popular option is for the students to develop a survey or simple questionnaire and then hand the instrument out to other students, to another class, to five (or *x*) friends, or to parents and relatives. The surveys and interviews can also be used with people who work in the school.

Short field trips, in particular, provide useful ways to use questionnaires and surveys developed by students; the technique places some responsibility on students for collecting useful information (e.g. subsection 11.6.2 below). A simpler variant is to invite a specialist into the classroom. The invited person can explain a process or a job, or the person may demonstrate a skill or a process to students. In this case, there is an additional emphasis on note taking since the information would not be constrained by a survey or questionnaire format.

Writing letters and collecting brochures is another easy way to assemble a range of information on a topic. An investigation of diseases and public health might include a letter to the local health authority, or, in the USA, to an organization such as the Center for Disease Control. It might also include a letter to the principal asking for an explanation of school health policies. Students may also enquire if their parents work in places that have specific health and safety policies, what those are, and what purposes they serve. Brochure collecting is another useful way to amass information. Brochures may be collected for future planning for schools, employment, vacations, or for a study of available local tourism information. Students might also explore who uses brochures and flyers to disseminate information, what information is included, who the anticipated target audiences are, and how effectively the information is presented. Such a project may be combined with letter writing as well as with interviews and surveys.

Observation is another important tool for information collection, though it is often overlooked. Students can observe a group of people who meet regularly, or observe a person in a public context (e.g. school secretary, postman) and note what these people do in as much detail as possible. Students can select a person or a group to observe and consider whether they are doing a good job. If the student were the boss, would he or she be pleased with the work done?

11.5.2   Developing content-based instruction (12)

There are virtually unlimited options for creating content-based units and topics which will engage students and provide for a range of relevant writing activities. In most cases, teachers can designate a number of general content-units within which a range of topics and projects can be nominated by the teacher and the students for further investigation. Such content-units and topics can explore personal values, activities and pastimes, world and national affairs, scientific discoveries and technologies, famous and important people, people and communities, foods, medicine, etc. Teachers can begin planning by selecting a set of major content-based units and gathering resources for a class library. These resources can be supplemented by student resources and library materials. Teachers and students can explore possible topics and projects by considering curriculum requirements, student interests, values clarification exercises, and informational resources available to the class (interesting video tapes, a person with unusual expertise, a major current event, etc.).

Content-based units can cover a wide range of issues and topics, and they can be the source of a set of projects and writing tasks. In most cases, these content units can be used to bring in information from other classes and to incorporate that information into the writing and information-gathering activities. Moreover, these content units can be extended across a number of classes beyond the language/language arts school periods if other teachers are willing to cooperate (e.g. the social studies teacher).

A good example of a content-based unit generating multiple topics and activities is given in Enright and McCloskey (1988). In their unit on 'heroes', they develop 12 activities and projects which were selected after brainstorming the content-theme with the class. Similarly, Tchudi and Huerta (1983) use a content-based unit on 'the elderly' and list 20 possible topics in a number of different academic areas which could extend the theme. They suggest topics on the elderly in the areas of science, mathematics, art and music, social science, history, civics, vocational education, and athletics, and they list 33 specific activities and projects related to the theme of 'the elderly'. (See also Meinbach *et al.* 1995, Walmsley 1994.)

11.5.3   Summaries and responses (13)

Unlike the previous two themes which concentrate on generating information, this theme suggests a means for organizing and controlling the information for later use. Writing summaries and responses to information are relatively well-accepted practices in secondary schools and constitute an important strategy for academic learning at higher levels. Summary writing can begin as a controlled or guided activity. One good beginning exercise is for students to complete summaries that only need one or two more sentences. Alternatively, they can write summaries that involve sentence combining of given structures. They can also write a summary that is parallel to an example summary, or write a summary with the first and last sentences already given. In groups, students can trade summaries and note the differences. As students gain some sense of the choices made in summary writing, they can then write short summaries from outlines of readings they have finished. They can also begin to write summaries from longer texts that they have read.

Summary writing does not have to be the difficult and challenging activity that students often consider it to be. If summary writing is an early goal of a writing curriculum, it can be incorporated regularly in a non-threatening fashion. In early months, students can be asked to write out the main idea of a reading in one sentence; then students can compare these one-sentence synopses and decide what makes a good summarizing statement. In the following few weeks, students can summarize in one sentence and then write a second sentence to add some explanatory information or a second main point to the summary. In two or three months, students can write out three-sentence summaries. By the fifth month, students can write four or six sentence summaries which nominate only the major points, arranged coherently.

Another basic way to present summaries is for the teacher to use a reading and line through the least important information, find the topic sentences, and condense/remove lists and examples. In this way, students learn a few simple rules of summary writing: (1) remove examples, (2) remove dates, (3) remove descriptive details and explanations, (4) remove concluding comments, (5) combine sets of points into a single general statement, and (6) find the topic sentence or create one if none exists. If practised over a period of time, these rules become relatively easy for students to control.

As a variant on the basic summarizing activity, students should expand a teacher's summary of an existing text by adding examples, descriptive details, and explanations. Students can then compare their expanded texts with the original from which the teacher developed the summary. The basic principle is that the underlying text should be recoverable to some extent from a successful summary. Such an activity would also raise awareness of the various principles used in summary formation.

In addition to summary writing, students should also be able to respond to ideas generated by other activities. Any activity which requires students to take a position on a topic will involve not only summarizing abilities but also an ability to respond to the information and present a point of view. Responses can begin with the simple task of students writing what they thought, or felt, with respect to some discussion or information source. As students become more comfortable with summary writing, they can add an evaluative paragraph of three or four sentences following a summary which may represent a critique of the summary information, a supporting commentary on the summary, or argue a position noted in the summary. Response writing provides a way into more complex persuasive and argumentative writing; it does not demand any complex arrangements of arguments and counterarguments because the response is primarily a continuation of the summary.

Both summary writing and response writing need to be practised in meaningful contexts so that they are seen as purposeful
writing activities and skills. As students become involved in more
complex writing tasks and as content information increases with
higher grade levels, students will need to use summary writing and
responses to keep track of important information and to assess
their views on more complex issues. These writing activities should
be incorporated into writing curricula as a natural extension of
working with academic information and writing critical commentary.

11.5.4   Awareness of language uses (14)

Students, as they progress through grade levels, need to recognize
the uses of print that are relevant to academic purposes. A study of
print in the classroom context and in the home context is a useful
activity for raising student awareness. There are, in fact, many uses
and purposes for print and these should be brought to students'
attention. Uses (and purposes) for academic print include the following: journals, biographies, stories, letters, résumés, histories,
editorials, commentaries, newspapers, case studies, posters, etc.
(cf. Tchudi and Huerta 1983, Frank 1979).

Students also need to be made aware of the role of language in
various less-standard environments. In the process, students can
engage in activities which make use of their expertise and provide
training through cognitive apprenticeship. In a recent set of studies, Heath (1993, Heath and Mangiola 1991) explores ways to
make students aware of language and reflective towards its uses by
making them experts in language teaching and language-based
projects. Heath (1993) reports on the use of drama and play writing in community centres as a strong source of oral and written
language development. Students write their own plays and perform them for real audiences. In the process, they devote
considerable amounts of time to literate activities and demonstrate skills which are not reflected in their performance with
school-based literacy activities.

These activities lead students to reflect on oral and literate uses
of language (including conventional editing), and, in the process,
lead students to work much more intensively with written language than they would as students in their own class. Heath
and Mangiola (1991) report on three other projects which

transformed students into literacy experts: (1) cross-grade tutoring with note taking and reporting on the younger students' progress; (2) students writing a book to the parents of the younger students involved in cross-grade tutoring – these books discuss the literacy needs of the younger students; and (3) analysing observations of spoken and written language in their community and family, and using their data to develop ethnographic analyses of language use (see also Kutz *et al.* 1993). Drama, play writing, cross-age tutoring, and ethnographies of spoken and written language all provide ways to raise student awareness of appropriate language use.

11.5.5 *Editing (15)*

At some point in writing instruction, and in the writing process, some emphasis needs to be given to editing, ensuring that the writing fits conventions and formats appropriately. Editing, unlike revision feedback, should occur in the final stages of writing; it represents an effort to make the writing acceptable to a critical audience. Editing involves checking a wide variety of surface aspects of the text: punctuation, capitalization, hyphenation, page formatting, titles and subtitles, spelling, appropriate word choice, grammatical sentence structure, and a coherent sequence of information.

Editing should not be an activity that is suddenly sprung on students long after they have become comfortable with only minimal concern for editing. At a fairly early stage in the educational curriculum, teachers need gradually to show students basic conventions of writing. Students, after all, are well aware that there are conventions in writing to which edited texts all conform. Parents, also, often remind students of the importance of certain conventions such as spelling, punctuation, and handwriting skills. A good way to begin attending to writing conventions is to examine aspects of well-edited texts which are being used for a content-based unit. Students can be given an altered version of a paragraph from a text they are using, which has editing errors throughout. They then play the game of 'can you find 20 (or *x*) differences' between the original text and the 'changed' version. This can be done on a regular basis with scores recorded through the year. Over time, students will begin to perceive the acceptable conventions of edited writing.

Editing can also be demonstrated regularly through teacher think-aloud protocols on texts that the class produces. Unlike previous teacher think-aloud demonstrations, the teacher is making overt various editing strategies. Thus, the teacher can verbalize the editing skills he or she would normally apply in silence. Another regular practice is to place two sentences on the board every day. In each sentence, there is one editing (but not necessarily grammatical) error; students must identify and correct the sentences. This takes little time; the practice sentences can be from student papers or related to a content unit currently being taught, and students gradually come to recognize the critical patterns.

Other activities can also promote editing skills. Spelling contests are one good way to focus attention on correct spelling. Group contests to find the editing errors in a paragraph are another means to build editing skills. Editing with peer group assistance is also helpful. Many handbooks have extensive exercises for editing texts and attending to grammar and vocabulary problems. For the most part, the ideas are right but the context is wrong. It is important to have students work with texts that are meaningful to them. For example, writing essays that will be read by other classes, writing books for younger students, publishing books, writing a newspaper, writing letters to outside audiences, etc., all place responsibility on students to produce conventionally appropriate texts, and these texts should drive home the need for editing skills.

11.6 Working with different types of writing (themes 16–20)

In Chapter 10, four types of texts were considered as part of writing instruction (telling stories; writing letters; descriptions, directions and procedures; recording and reporting information). In this section, five text types are considered: (1) autobiographies and biographies, (2) surveys and questionnaires, (3) newspaper writing, (4) informational reporting, and (5) personal writing. In each case, these extend the types of writing often done by intermediate students, and support the various other themes presented in this chapter.

11.6.1   *Autobiographies and biographies (16)*

One effective way to develop fluency in student writing is to have students explore issues related to themselves and their histories, and then extend these explorations to other people.

One simple activity is to have students describe and discuss important events in their lives. The events can be displayed as a group project, as important moments in their lives, and each event description can be accompanied by a brief autobiography of three sentences. They can write autobiographies describing who they are, where they are from, what they are currently doing (e.g. student in 8th grade), and what their interests and hobbies are. Other activities which will result in an autobiography include writing about an important accomplishment in their lives.

The autobiographical activities can also lead into a long autobiography project. Students can 'collect' events and people in their lives: accomplishments, difficult times, vacations, schooling, relations with family members and friends, etc. Students can ask parents for pictures, or students can illustrate events. The most relevant information can then be assembled in a time-line chart on a poster board. Students then write a number of different paragraphs (or more) on paper which are subsequently fastened to the board, aligning them with the appropriate place on the time line. These time lines can be displayed for other students to read.

As an alternative to the project above, students can write biographies based on the study of biographies of one or two other persons. Students can choose someone from a content-based unit and write a brief sketch of that person. This activity can centre on an important person, a person the student admires, a famous person (e.g. a TV actor), or someone in history whom the student would have liked to have met. In groups, students can decide ways to organize a person's biography; for example, discuss what information is needed, and why those persons' lives are important or relevant to the students. Students can then use biographies to consider what events, information, and organizational goals would be necessary to write an autobiography in a similar way.

11.6.2   *Surveys and questionnaires (17)*

Surveys and questionnaires provide important ways to gather information and serve as useful resources for many other writing activities. They can be used to collect information about people and their opinions about events, rules, politics, society, schools, etc. These sets of information allow students to make comparisons and draw conclusions. They can also be used to gather information on specific individuals, events, and situations for more careful analyses; thus, students can use this information for writing job descriptions, biographies, and procedures and techniques.

Surveys and questionnaires, however, require careful planning and writing if they are to be used successfully. Planning needs to begin with class discussion of specific goals for information collection. The students and the teacher then have to design questions that will be clearly understood and easy to answer. Attention has to be paid to the number of survey items or questions so that the questionnaire is manageable. The surveys and questionnaires also have to be formatted in such a way that students using them do not become lost or find themselves without sufficient space for recording additional information.

Results of surveys and questionnaires also have to be organized efficiently and examined carefully if the collected information is to be useful. The teacher may want to introduce tally sheets or sheets divided into columns to sort the information. If there is to be a summarizing of numbers from specific items, sheets should also be designed to make adding and averaging easy. The results of the surveys and questionnaires also need to be analysed through class and group discussion. Students need to consider the goals of the survey/questionnaire, which of the collected information complements the goals, how the information can be presented, what conclusions can be drawn, and how the survey or questionnaire could have been done differently. Students should then summarize the conclusions and write a report describing the information collected and the possible importance of the information for some other project purpose.

11.6.3 *Newspapers and media (18)*

Writing for student-generated media represents another source of writing practice. The most common option is writing regularly for a class newspaper or newsletter. A school or a community newspaper also provide viable options. Writing for newspapers, for plays, for TV episodes and commercials, and for class anthologies all extend writing into different text types.

The newspaper genre actually comprises a number of text types. Students can write a sports column following their favourite school or professional teams. They can also write profiles of famous sports stars for a monthly newspaper. Other students can be in charge of an editorial and letters-to-the-editor page. These writing tasks require students to summarize and critique events of importance to the class and school. Students can focus on curricular units, school events, school rules and regulations, food in the cafeteria, safety problems in the school, how the school money is budgeted, etc.

Other students may want to focus on column and feature writing. Students can write a series of reports on teaching methods, on the status of the library or the computer lab, on the planning for school lunches, on choices for textbooks, on school clubs, etc. Columns can focus on specific individuals in the school, including behind-the-scenes people; students can conduct interviews with maintenance people, cafeteria workers, secretaries in the principal's office, and even the principal. Students can also interview different teachers each month to write up profiles of teacher backgrounds and interests. They can also interview recently arrived students. Finally, students can be assigned to be front-page reporters. They can investigate the most current stories about the class, specific students, the school, teachers, community decisions about the school, etc. The newspaper and its various text types can also be tied to specific content-based units, particularly for writing editorials, features, and columns.

Other media genres can also provide many useful writing activities for students. Students can use information from a content unit to write a play, involving events and people being studied in other parts of the school curriculum. The play can add a creative option to exploring characters, personalities, and other information. The powers of persuasion can also be tapped through writing newspaper, magazine, and TV advertisements (using camcorders). Newspaper advertisements can be published monthly and TV advertisements can be scripted and videotaped. After a number of TV advertisements have been videotaped, the class can have a TV advertisement festival and show all the advertisements to other classes. Students can also plan a TV news show in which all news, weather, sports, and commentary are scripted and delivered to the video camera for later 'broadcast'.

In all cases of media writing, it is important to let students create the scripts and critique each other. These text formats offer students responsibility and demand acceptable performances in front of their peer audiences. These text types combine the need to demonstrate creativity and the need to report accurately. Since most of the audience will be aware of the news and features being reported, there will be a natural constraint on writers and scriptwriters to 'get it right'. All of these media options can also be incorporated into curricular units and projects. Features can focus on major student projects; editorials can critique the projects; features and columns can explain the goals of projects, the methods used for finding information, and present interviews of real or fictional personalities; TV shows and advertisements can focus on outcomes of projects and announce coming events; and front-page news can report on the latest progress or unexpected discovery during project work.

11.6.4 *Informational reports (19)*

Students in secondary schools who need to write for academic purposes require extensive practice with informational writing. This type of writing requires students to present information according to acceptable formats. These would include, for example, (1) comparing and contrasting different events, issues, results, outcomes, or processes; (2) writing about posed or real problems uncovered during information collection and explaining them in terms of a problem–solution organization; or (3) writing about a process, object, or concept that is complex and requires definitions, descriptions, and examples. The essence of informational reporting is organizing information into patterns of arrangement that are expected and understood by the reader. Students need to be made aware of the options and possibilities available to them as they report and synthesize information. Basic patterns of arrangement include: definition, classification, cause and effect, comparison and contrast, problem–solution, and analysis.

Definitional writing focuses on the means for delimiting some object, process, or concept. It provides the information needed both to relate a concept, for example, to other concepts and, at the same time, to distinguish it from these other concepts. Definitions typically include a topic sentence frame such as: 'An __x__ is a __y__ that does __z__.' This format is then followed by a variety of strategies: relating and distinguishing, giving examples, providing behavioural and physical attributes, describing functions and uses, etc. Classification arrangements extend the definitional notion to include sets of objects, concepts or issues; the primary goal of this pattern is to highlight relationships and differences among groups. Classification patterns do not fully specify the number of branches needed to describe the information: as a new type is created in the classification, a new branch is added. Definition and classification are reciprocal processes, the former placing an individual into a class and the latter dividing a class to distinguish an individual.

Cause/effect and comparison/contrast patterns of organization represent two types of logical organization that can, at times, overlap, though they are logically distinct. Cause and effect patterns delimit causes and consequences. The pattern defines a causal relation that makes a strong claim. Comparison and contrast patterns define relations without necessarily asserting any causation. This pattern also represents a powerful resource for setting up argumentative, problem–solution, and synthesis texts.

Analytic patterns of organization provide yet another powerful means for persuasion, critiquing, and problem–solution. The force of this arrangement pattern comes from the assumption that the analysis accounts for all of, and only, the important variables. An analysis of how a watch works neither leaves out important parts of the watch nor discusses parts that do not fit in the watch. An analytic arrangement assumes that all of the critical components are included; the parts that are presented explain the larger concept being studied. An analysis of a political debate, like those which appear on an editorial page, assumes the authority to claim knowledge of all the critical issues, and an ability to recognize the essence of a political event. Put in these terms, it is easy to see why students would have difficulty with a pattern of arrangement that presumes so much authority and expertise. Nevertheless, such a powerful pattern is important for students if they are to move beyond a passive participation in their education.

The key to using patterns of arrangement for information reporting is not to introduce them in isolation or as decontextualized activities; rather, students working with information through content-based units and projects will already have a wide range of information, and one of their major difficulties will involve ways to present the information accurately and effectively. In this context, teachers need to show students how this can be done. The teacher can model thought processes for arranging information as well as the decision-making processes involved. The teacher can point out to students how appropriate patterns of arrangement are used in some texts with which the students have worked, and the teacher can guide students in groups to practice using patterns of arrangement that fit the information they have collected. Patterns of arrangement need to be seen as resources rather than as goals for writing; and students need extensive practice in seeing these patterns in the informational texts they work with, and in realizing that such patterns represent methods of effective communication.

11.6.5 *Personal writing (20)*

Personal writing is not constrained by expectations of information reporting but involves the views, emotions, and creative resources of the individual student. It may involve fictional accounts and narratives; it may involve writing TV advertisements or plays; or it may simply involve explaining a personal point of view. What makes personal writing unique is the authority taken by the writer to be seen as an expert. The expertise lies in the personal interpretation that must be recognized in this type of writing. Recognizing expertise, of course, does not mean that any writing produced is good, only that the idea or concept behind the writing should not be challenged as inappropriate; after all, it is the purpose of personal writing to recognize the creative power of the students.

The most direct form of personal writing which students can practise are diaries, journals, and learning logs. In the case of journals and logs, the writing is more responded to than evaluated. Diaries may remain the confidential property of the students if that is the class policy. These forms of personal writing may be very useful for generating ideas and topics for other types of personal writing as well as for finding sources of interest for thematic units and larger projects. Other forms of personal writing are highlighted in a number of other themes in this chapter. Plays, autobiographies, personal information gathering, and free writing all provide potential avenues for personal writing. Students involved in a content-based unit or a project can also use personal writing to decide what is most interesting, most important, or most disturbing about the information being used to develop the unit. In writing responses to reading assignments or group work, students can examine and reflect on the information that was most striking.

There are several additional ways to focus on personal writing. Students can work individually from writing tasks in a writing corner, or can work on class or group assignments with the following activities:

1. Students can see themselves as time travellers: Where would they go and why? Whom would they see? What would they do? When would they return? What would they bring back with them?
2. Students can decide what they would do with ten million dollars if they were given the money the next day.
3. Students can choose a person whom they admire and describe the appealing qualities or characteristics of that person.
4. Students can relate an embarrassing moment: What happened? Why was it so embarrassing? What did the student learn from the experience?
5. Students can discuss a strong feeling, emotion, or attitude they have towards some object, event, person, concept, etc.
6. Students can be asked to give spontaneous speeches with one minute's preparation. For one minute they can write down ideas and phrases that will help them.
7. Students can use an opening sentence from some book, story, article, or text and continue in their own words in any way they wish. Sets of starting sentences could be stored in the writing corner.
8. Students can tell a modern tale. They may take some fairy tale, fable, myth, or proverb that is well known and tell a story that is a modern-day version of the tale, etc. They can also change the outcome to fit a modern perspective.

11.7   Extending writing (themes 21–25)

In this section, five themes are discussed which represent useful extensions for writing practice. Each theme could also be used to support content-based units and task-based curricula. The five themes include: (1) sentence combining, (2) portfolios, (3) values clarification activities, (4) double-entry notebooks, and (5) student presentations. The themes provide ways to expand student resources and to explore the form and the content of their writing.

11.7.1   Sentence combining (21)

Students need to become aware of the possibilities for varying structure, combining ideas, and highlighting and backgrounding different sets of information. It is no simple matter to have students recognize these options in writing, and sentence combining is one of the few recognized ways to accomplish such goals. In addition, sentence combining activities build writing fluency, improve tacit knowledge of structure, promote flexibility, and allow for more complex writing. Sentence combining should not be treated as a grammatical matter, but should instead be seen in a discourse context, recognizing the function of the output combination within the larger text structure. While sentence combining, by itself, does not guarantee improved writing quality over a short period of time, despite strong claims by adherents, it does add an important component to writing skills and instruction. Sentence-combining textbooks are commonly available for use in writing classes; however, sentence combining, like all other aspects of the writing curriculum, is best generated out of the writing of the students as well as the supporting material used for content units and curriculum projects. Using this approach within a meaningful context is more likely to motivate students and lead to greater fluency and complexity in student writing.

There are a number of ways to use sentence combining in a writing programme. The most basic approaches to sentence combining involve lists of heavily redundant sentences which require the combining of groups of three or four sentences as a single more complex sentence. The list of sentences, when combined in this way, should form a reasonably complex paragraph. Another fairly standard version of sentence combining is to include connector cue words at the end of each sentence which indicate how one sentence should be combined with the next. Introducing students to sentence combining can begin with simple exercises which ask them to combine two and three sentences into one sentence (Linden and Whimbey 1990).

Incorporating sentence combining into the class context is possible by using material from relevant texts and from paragraphs written by students themselves. Students can look for the underlying simple sentences in a brief text segment from textbooks read by all the students. In a five-sentence edited text, for example, students look for all the possible simple sentences they can find and try to recombine the simple sentences in different ways. Students can also look at their own writing in the same way. They can also add additional simple sentences to their own texts, making the final recombination more complex than the original paragraph.

11.7.2   *Portfolios (22)*

Portfolios have become a major topic of discussion in writing research and practice (see Chapter 13). It is important to recognize that much more research needs to be done to assess the exact benefits and limitations of using portfolios in different ways and in different contexts. At the moment, many strong claims are being made for the benefits of portfolios. Recognizing that some of these claims will need to be tempered in the future, the potential of *portfolios for writing instruction* is still quite exciting. Portfolios can be seen as a place to store all writing activities that include creative input from the student. These portfolios can be visited regularly by students who are free to work on any piece of writing already in the portfolio. One student can also share some pieces of writing with another student and ask for a response. Between peer feedback and their own later reassessment of pieces in the portfolio, students learn to become more critical of their own writing and begin to discriminate between more and less interesting writing.

Portfolio assessment involves the presentation of final work to the teacher for evaluation. In this case, students recognize the need to present their best work and to make final revisions. This type of writing evaluation gives language minority and at-risk students a better opportunity to present their best work without the time pressure of exam writing or of a grade based on a single writing.

11.7.3   *Values clarification (23)*

As students begin to deal with more complex issues and topics, many of these topics will include difficult problems and dilemmas which need to be examined thoughtfully as part of the writing experience. Initially, such problems can be proposed by the teacher through specific exercises. The goal, however, is to have students recognize and raise problematic issues and dilemmas independently as they work with more complex information. On a basic level, several types of activities can be used to generate problem posing and possible resolutions. Straightforward topics for this purpose could include: reasons for banning some object, chemical, activity, or habitual practice in a given setting; examining jobs done in the home and redistributing work expectations; finding ways to conserve resources such as water used in the home or school; working through a dilemma that is posed; and/or trying to see a situation from the perspective of another person.

One approach to such activities is to set up a problem which requires some difficult decisions and ask the students to explain their decisions in writing. For example, some specific scenarios could involve the following: (1) with a simple description of ten (or x) people, students decide which of them to save if they are ill and there are vaccinations for only four (or y) people; (2) starting with ten job descriptions, students decide who should keep their jobs if three jobs have to be cut to save money; (3) starting with descriptions of six local communities and businesses which need a regular water supply, students decide which two groups should receive a 10 per cent cut in water supplies and why; (4) starting with five locations for building a modern government-funded hospital, students choose the one site that will best serve a wide range of patients and communities. (To enable students to answer item (4), they will need a general geographic description of the region, a simple explanation of the resources and obstacles existing at each site, and a brief economic impact statement. Students can then make a reasoned decision based on the data.)

A second general approach to values clarification is to begin with students' listings of their most important activities, most valued friends, most interesting TV shows, most frequent work or chore, favourite food, least favourite activity, etc. From these lists, students can consider questions such as: What interests do they seem to have in common with peers? What do these common interests indicate about underlying values? Where do such values come from? Are any of the general interests or values potential sources of problems? Are any worthy of change? Are any worthy of encouragement and further development?

As a third approach, students can examine other people's values and develop surveys and interviews which investigate other people's interests, preferences, goals, pastimes, disinterests, etc. Students can use the results to explore general attitudes and values and compare group results to their own views.

11.7.4   Double-entry notebooks (24)

When students use journals in classes, one option is to have students write only on the right-hand side of the notebook. The left-hand side is then free for other students (or the teacher) to write comments after reading the entries. This double-entry approach can be used for learning logs, note taking, interactive journals with the teacher, and journals that are shown to other students. The extra space allows sufficient room for the responder to write out a full commentary directly opposite the initiating section of the original entry.

The double-entry concept can easily be extended to other writing formats. Rough drafts can be written only on one side of the page. Responders can then add comments and suggestions in a way that is immediately accessible. Students can also return to their own writing and have sufficient space to respond with additional information, revisions, or critical commentary. In this way, students learn to return to their own work and develop the habit of revising their ideas. In a sense, the students can, over time, engage in a running dialogue with themselves (Berthoff 1981, Raimes 1992).

11.7.5   Presenting the text (25)

When students have completed their writing tasks and need to use the texts for additional purposes and different audiences, a good general approach is to present the writing to others. Presenting texts can vary: reading a text out loud to a group or to the class, performing a script, making a video, recording an advertisement, trying to make a sale, publishing a book and reading from it, putting on a debate, or providing a public poster session in which each student has to explain his or her poster to others.

A critical component of making student writing meaningful is to create realistic applications for the writing. A number of these options have been examined in some detail in previous themes. In the case of media presentation, the opportunity to present writing is an important experience. For example, publishing a book should not be the final step for students; they should also read from it, either to their own class or to another class (perhaps to a lower grade). They can also explain to students from lower grades what they had to do to publish a book, going through the writing and editing processes.

Reading their own texts aloud to other students in a group or to the whole class is an important way to present their ideas. Once students get into the habit of reading aloud, they will edit their own texts quite differently, given appropriate support. One or two readings with frequent phrase misreadings, hesitations because of wrong words, and lost clauses in convoluted sentences will motivate students to improve their revising and editing skills. The regular practice of reading texts aloud to the class also provides an opportunity for feedback from classmates. Students in the audience recognize the added pressure of public performance and usually try to assist the performing student; this assistance leads students to comment constructively on the text being read. When this approach becomes a regular feature of writing activities, students take seriously the task of providing useful feedback since they all know that they will also be in the position to ask for assistance.

11.8 Conclusion

In this chapter, five overarching principles and 25 corresponding themes for writing instruction have been considered with the intermediate audience in mind. Of course, many of these themes can also be adapted to beginning or advanced writers. In many ways, the themes on preparing for writing represent a natural extension of themes that encouraged beginning students to build fluency and confidence. Similarly, the themes that involve writing assistance and writing practices are meant to extend the discussion in Chapter 10.

Of course, this chapter also discusses the increased writing demands imposed on students as they move towards greater writing proficiency. Reflecting this transition is the greater emphasis on types of writing and the concurrent increased attention to the formal and organizational aspects of writing. In short, while this chapter builds and extends the discussion begun in Chapter 10, it also adds new dimensions to writing instruction. This is only fitting as students move towards more complex academic uses of writing. The trend towards greater academic demands and more complex uses of writing is continued in the next chapter, exploring writing instruction for advanced students.

NOTES

1. It is possible to set an arbitrary level for intermediate writing ability, such as an FSI level or an ACTFL level, but the discussion of writing, and the range of student writers we consider, is too broad for us to provide a specific definition characterizing the difference between beginning and intermediate writers.
2. There is ample evidence that much scientific and technical writing (including proposals, research reports, etc.) is actually a collaborative effort. Students need at least to get a sense sof this real-world activity; thus, the motivation here is twofold – to take advantage of the benefits of cooperative learning as an educational strategy and to prepare students for the cooperative writing environment in the real world beyond the classroom.
3. This discussion assumes a 'Western' orientation. In educational systems heavily dependent on rote learning approaches, such an approach may in fact be counter-productive.

12

Teaching writing at advanced levels

12.1 Introduction

Students in advanced academic contexts have needs for writing which go beyond the basic goals for communication and for learning new information. For students who are finishing secondary schools, in post-secondary institutions, and in post-graduate programmes, the uses of writing evolve to take on new dimensions. Writing is no longer seen as primarily for personal expression or presenting school-based information, though they remain important issues. Rather, the advanced writer is also often concerned with analysing and interpreting information critically, synthesizing disparate sets of information, creating information, arguing alternative perspectives, and presenting and promoting research. While these uses of writing call on many of the skills that have been discussed in Chapters 10 and 11, some more specialized academic skills are also required in advanced writing.

The themes in this chapter both expand and contract the focus of writing instruction. The expansion of themes is seen in terms of the additional genres discussed and the in-depth exploration of textual patterns of arrangement with more specialized writing tasks. The narrowing focus is seen in the discussions of more specialized contexts for writing. As writers take on more complex writing tasks, these tasks – which reflect the increasing specialization of purpose and audience, and the processes involved – necessarily address narrower audiences and require more specific writing formats and conventions. In this way, discussions of advanced writing cannot simply be seen as an ever-expanding set of more complex generalized processes. Instead, advanced writing must begin to separate into specific streams and channels. Genres become more specialized and academic communities impose distinct expectations.

For the purposes of this chapter, the term 'advanced student' includes tertiary-level undergraduate students and those academically proficient students in English-speaking countries who are in their final years of secondary school and have expectations of continuing for additional academic preparation. These students require more complex writing skills if they are to be successful in their studies. At post-graduate levels, the need for advanced writing skills is even more critical as this becomes the most important linguistic mode for meaning making and information presentation. The themes in this chapter address the changing needs of these writers as they move from the secondary school to the more demanding expectations of professionalism.

12.2   Themes for advanced writing instruction

The themes in this chapter follow a similar format to that of the previous two chapters, though the principles themselves are somewhat different, reflecting the changing goals and requirements involved in advanced writing. The five organizing principles include:

1. Planning for writing
2. Organizing information and attending to conventions
3. Assisting and guiding writing
4. Working with different genres
5. Extending the writing curriculum.

A first set of themes considers issues which assist planning for writing and provide information for writing. In particular, there needs to be an emphasis, at advanced levels, on critical reading and the ways information and arguments are presented. The second set of themes expands upon the concern for organizing information while working with more complex writing tasks. It also addresses supporting activities which can maintain and improve writing skills, making the complexity of the task more manageable. The third set of themes highlights classroom activities and writing tasks which assist and guide writing, and thus also respond to the greater complexity required in advanced writing tasks. The fourth set of themes considers additional writing genres which expand the range presented in earlier chapters and represent types of writing that are more important for advanced academic students. The final set of themes considers issues which extend the uses of writing, address specific contexts for writing, and highlight the importance of convention, genre constraints, and writing style.

12.3   Planning for writing (themes 1–5)

The five themes in this section help students plan for writing; these themes include: (1) building a climate for writing, (2) working with multiple resources, (3) reading critically, (4) guiding discussion, and (5) exploratory writing and writing exercises. At the most basic level, advanced writing requires an appropriate classroom atmosphere as well as access to more complex sets of information. This information is gathered from many sources, especially through guided discussions and critical reading. It is also important not to overlook exercises and activities which allow students to speculate occasionally in less constrained ways.

12.3.1   Building a climate for writing (1)

The need to establish a positive atmosphere for writing is as true of advanced classes as it is for beginning classes. Teachers need to show enthusiasm and interest in the writing curriculum and in students' efforts. In addition, teachers need to provide students with the time to write, the encouragement to write often, and opportunities to explore a number of ideas without a constant concern for evaluation and grading. At times, it is important for the teacher to encourage innovative ideas and risk-taking. In all of these respects, the teacher must assume the role of expert, guide, resource, and facilitator. The role of teacher as evaluator is a necessary aspect of the writing class, as it is of every academic context.

The teacher needs to participate in writing activities in the class by *modelling* expert performance in terms of both the process and the product. This does not mean that the teacher should also do the tasks assigned to the students. Instead, the teacher should find opportunities to brainstorm and compose, not only *with* the class, but *for* the class. Teachers should take a lead role in composing aloud (thinking aloud) for a class assignment, developing an outline or some other visual display for a writing task. In addition, the teacher should think aloud while carrying out the activity in front of the students. This allows students to see the planning and decision making that occurs in mature composing. Students can ask the teacher questions about the strategies and choices made while writing for the class and the teacher can point out specific choices made and concepts developed through effective details and examples.

At other times, the teacher can begin by composing aloud while writing, using an overhead projector, and then ask students to contribute. As the activities develop, students take on greater responsibilities as composers, and the teacher can mention alternative choices that can be made. The class composing and the possible alternatives can then be discussed in terms of reader expectations, writing organization, information highlighting, and variations in writer's perspective. The critical notion through these teaching–writing activities is that the students observe, then comment, and assume some of the responsibility for composing.

From a broader perspective, the teacher must not only maintain a positive climate by giving thought to how the curriculum will fulfil course expectations and established criteria, but must also find time to encourage the free exchange of ideas, and to promote a willingness by students to assist each other.

12.3.2 *Working with multiple resources (2)*

Writing from resources involves an important transition from writing with personal and easily accessible information to writing from complex sets of information which are collected from multiple sources. This is a major transition that students need to make if they are to be successful in advanced academic contexts. Unlike beginning and intermediate writing activities, which can often call on personal experiences and impressions as a primary source of information, advanced academic contexts seldom place great store in personal knowledge and impressionistic interpretations. Instead, advanced academic contexts require information from other sources, and a main goal of advanced complex writing activities is the analysis, synthesis, and interpretation of information from a variety of sources.

Readings are the most common and the most productive resources available for advanced writing situations. Since so much of academic writing in different disciplines involves working with readings, it is important that students receive as much practice as possible in working with, and writing from, readings. The writing course – with direct supervision, guidance, and support – is usually the students' main chance to master these complex skills.

A second critical resource for advanced student writing is the use of the library. Students need to be given an orientation to library resources and then be *expected* to use these resources in their writing. This process can be developed gradually through a brief sequence of writing activities which require: (1) finding and using a particular resource in the library, (2) including a source of their own choosing in their writing, and (3) referring to two different sources in the same writing assignment. Students need to recognize the possibilities that library resources offer when they write for academic purposes.

Besides extensive reading and the use of library resources, students can carry out their own research and data collection to support a writing activity. This can be done through a case study method with extended periods of observation and note taking. Students can decide to interview a relevant group or an individual expert on their chosen topic. Students can also develop a survey which can then be distributed to a larger group of people; the tabulation of the survey can provide useful independent evidence for a position or an argument being made. Students can also telephone a variety of offices and request information on a topic they are investigating. In the USA, for example, various government agencies are often able to provide a range of resource information; such options can extend from census bureau information on different population groups, to forest service information on hiking trails, walking maps, and policies on tree cutting in national forest lands.

12.3.3 Reading critically (3)

Students are often asked to read (or find) a text which appears to be relevant to their needs. However, for a variety of reasons, many students do not seem to be able to exploit the textual resource to its full potential. In many cases, they are unable to perceive underlying assumptions guiding the text, or follow the intertextual relations revealed in the text. A major goal for academic writing, then, is to make texts truly accessible in terms of the logic of a complex argument or of the different subtexts running through a text. This level of text interpretation is not a matter of basic reading comprehension, but is an expectation of successful academic performance. Moreover, a major goal of insightful academic writing is the use of texts in sophisticated and non-obvious ways, in some ways a peeling back of layers of a text; this is particularly true in cases of a text viewed as central to an academic course or used as the basis for interpretive writing.

Students should not be expected to know how to read critically; rather, they need to be taught *explicitly* how to do so. They also need considerable practice in this activity, since it is a complex skill which draws on many interpretative resources. One way to help students with critical reading is for the teacher to read a text with students, or to students, and, through a think-aloud process, reveal to students what the text invokes through teacher interpretation. A teacher can read an important but difficult text and stop every few lines to discuss the various ideas that come to mind: for example, the authority the writer has, who the writer draws on for theoretical authority, the strengths or weaknesses of the arguments, the standard alternative views, a text that interlinks with this text in support or in opposition, etc. This process of inquiry is useful for students to witness since students seldom 'see' a text directly questioned by an expert reader.

Teachers can also begin to answer the questions that might arise with respect to a given text; that is, the teacher can name and describe alternative texts which provide counter-arguments and the relative degree of authority of the counter-sources. The teacher can identify the oddity or centrality of the argument to the expectations of a given discipline or field of study. The teacher can also point out the sub-arguments being made and their relationship to an overall theoretical position taken by the author.

Such interpretation takes considerable expertise and students are seldom even aware that others read in this way, but practice in doing so and writing with this knowledge gives students an authority and voice which can significantly change their writing practices. After students have seen a teacher 'demonstrate' the critical reading process a number of times, they can be encouraged to engage in some critical commentary of their own. They will be in a better position to do this if they have already been exposed to a number of texts on a similar topic, if they have discussed the various motivations and theories guiding different authors, and if they have practised commenting on the strengths of arguments, sources of background evidence, and linkages between a given text and various other important texts.

12.3.4 Guiding discussion (4)

Another important resource that can change the way students plan their writing, and read and comment on their own texts, is through carefully guided discussions. Discussions can easily be sidetracked or be only exploratory in nature, and careful analyses of reading and writing require them to be specifically focused. Even a persistent questioning by the teacher of the ways that students are interpreting various texts can lead students to a different perspective on the textual information as well as on the writing activity itself.

In discussions of readings, a major goal for the teacher is to lead students to reassess sources of evidence, examine more carefully the logic of certain polemic arguments, reconsider the consistency of a theoretical position, and question the interpretative conclusions drawn from a complex set of data/evidence. Students can also be asked to outline a complex argument (either orally or in writing), permitting them to examine points where the argument is weak or requires a great degree of inference. Students can also be given a short list of analytical questions which they can learn to use themselves as they listen to a classroom discussion of a reading or to some other source of information (e.g. a video, a guest speaker, a radio talk-show).

The guidance needed for critical analysis of discussions, again, is not easy, and the process requires continual practice. Students have to learn how to challenge each other but to do so in a way that is not personally threatening. Students have to be willing to be persuaded that another position is, at least for the moment, better supported; they have to recognize that most positions can be strengthened or weakened by referring to further resources or bringing in additional perspectives. They also need to recognize polemic arguments and opinions masquerading as evidence. The goal of the writing course, and of the teacher, is to place these skills and their development in the context of writing activities and content-topics that are central to the writing curriculum. Guided discussions as well as critical reading should not be divorced from the central content and topics proposed for the course; rather, guided discussions, as well as critical reading, need to be seen as central to the inquiry that constitutes successful academic writing.

One important set of resources for supporting these critical skills is through a regular sequence of writing responses to assigned readings and classroom discussions. These responses can be in the form of fairly standard prose assignments which call for a summary and reaction to the materials. Alternatively, students can work through schematic representations of the information. For example, teachers can provide students with an outline frame only partially filled in, and students can complete the outline. The students can also represent information graphically by means of flow charts, tables, figures, time-lines, etc. These resources are a good check on comprehension of the information; they lead students to interpret the information in ways that the teacher sees as useful; they become resources which students can share and discuss; they provide a means for students to synthesize and evaluate the information; and they create a framework for using the information for other writing tasks.

12.3.5   *Exploratory writing and writing exercises (5)*

The converse of carefully guided analyses of writing resources lies in providing opportunities to explore ideas speculatively. Rather than always demanding a controlled assessment of writing resources, students, at some points, need to be allowed to consider less clearly supported alternative positions, to explore their own views in writing, or to take an opposing point of view and see ideas from a new perspective.

Just as beginning writers employ various activities to initiate writing, advanced writers sometimes need to return to basic exercises to break free of comfortable positions. Since advanced writers often feel affinities towards given views – the result of many years of schooling – the ability to explore other views is not a simple matter. One way to see other possibilities is for students to generate lists of words on a topic, or to argue for a position opposite to their own, or to examine ideas that some students have rejected.

Students can also write speculative comments on ideas that are important to them but have not been discussed or have been of little interest to the class previously. Some students may wish to write about a problem that has concerned them in the treatment of a given topic, even if they have difficulty explaining why the problem deserves more attention, or why it has been overlooked. The major goal of these writing exercises is to train students to speculate and adopt alternative points of view; the aim is to encourage students to explore additional ideas, make room for speculative thinking, and recognize that there may be a number of alternative positions or perspectives, even if they have not all been given equal attention in the main activities of the class.

12.4   Organizing information and attending to conventions (themes 6–10)

The themes in this section point out the importance of organizing information and attending to reader expectations in academic writing. The five themes include: (1) outlining and structured overviews, (2) using heuristics for organizing writing, (3) using patterns of essay organization, (4) paragraphing and text formatting, and (5) starting writing and ending writing. The advanced writer needs to be aware of the many ways to organize writing and the constraints on writing imposed by expected forms of organization.

12.4.1   *Outlining and structured overviews (6)*

Writing at advanced levels requires greater attention to the organization of the writing, the logic of the arguments, and the sequencing of information. All of these concerns suggest that mechanisms such as outlining and structured overviews are useful supports for writing. It is important to note, however, that the use of outlining in writing does not necessarily refer back to traditional outlining practices in which a writing topic had to be fully dissected in an elaborate formal outline before writing began. Instead, the goal of outlining is to work out the most appropriate logic for assembling information and arguments. For some writers, this may mean writing out a fairly unstructured set of notes which are then reassembled more carefully as a useful working outline. For other students, a careful outline is an important preliminary step in writing; if the formal process works for these students, it should not be discouraged because it is too strict for others. Still other students gain most from outlining when they develop a careful outline after writing the first draft. This practice allows students to see weaknesses in the structuring of the information and problems in the logic of the writing.

Outlining – to whatever degree of formality is effective for a given set of students – is a skill that cannot simply be explained once or twice and then assumed. If it is to be an effective *support,* some type of outlining activity should be included in any larger writing task. One of the easiest ways to incorporate outlining is to work from semantic maps and other forms of organized brainstorming. Often semantic mapping will provide a central theme, much terminology and a hierarchy of information one or two levels deep.

Outlining is also a useful activity for peer revisions. Asking the other members of a group to construct an outline that reflects a given piece of writing can be very revealing not only for the students writing the essay but also for the other cooperating students in the group. It also allows peer students to offer suggestions for revision which should become readily apparent to the student whose paper is being reviewed/outlined.

Other options for displaying the structure of a text are possible. Rather than working from the same outlining format every time, students may want to experiment with other visual displays (graphs, charts, other types of figures, etc.) which reflect the logical organization of the text. A tree-branching display for a classification paper may be an effective way to fill in gaps or to consolidate information. A time-line may be a useful display for historical cause and effect analyses. A flow chart with several branching options at different points may capture the complexities of interacting concepts or processes better than an outline format because it better depicts the dynamics of options at different points. These alternative formats can be as complex as the detailed formal outline in displaying the order of information and the logic of the writing.

12.4.2   Using heuristics for organizing writing (7)

In writing informative and argumentative texts, there are several stages at which guidelines of various types can assist the writer. These guidelines, often in the form of sets of questions, can reveal for the writer options that should be explored and extensions that should be considered. In the more formal terminology of rhetoric, these guidelines are termed 'topics'; in less formal terminology, they can be seen as schemes for organizing writing and considering options at various stages in the process.

Raimes (1992) provides a useful set of these topics for writing. She provides schemes for question forming, schemes for generating ideas, topic development schemes, purpose schemes, schemes for supporting a thesis, 'openings' schemes, drafting schemes, and editing schemes. For example, in her scheme for generating ideas and information on a topic, Raimes refers to the standard journalistic format: *What?, When?, Where?, Who?, Why?, How?* She then follows up with an extensive sequence of exploratory questions which can be applied to any type of writing. For persuasive writing, she sets up the following scheme:

What do you know about ....?
What do others need to know about ....?
Who believes .... now?
Who is affected by ....?
How is everyday life affected by ....?
How will things change if people change their minds about ....?
How can people's opinions about .... be changed?
When did people first begin to think the way they do about ....?
When did/do views about .... change?
Who feels strongly about ....?
Where is support for .... found?
Where is opposition to .... found?
Why is it important to convince people about ....?

(Raimes 1992: 41–2)

In another set of schemes, Raimes provides guidelines for reviewing a first draft and supporting the thesis statement. These are presented as ways that writers support a thesis:

Provide facts or statistics
Provide examples or illustrations (tell stories)
Provide sensory details
Use chronological or spatial sequences to describe events or scenes
Compare or contrast two persons, things, or ideas

Analyze or classify people, objects, or ideas
Examine causes and effects or problems and solutions
Give definitions
Examine what others have said.

(Raimes 1992: 65)

It is no accident that these guidelines for thesis development reflect basic logical patterns for organizing informational texts in general, and highlight the need to develop a thesis along the lines of a framework that structures the writing as a whole.

There are a number of other important schemes for organizing ideas for writing. Perhaps the best known among these is the set developed for writing by Young *et al.* (1970), based on a tagmemic framework for linguistic theory and a set of Aristotelian concepts.

12.4.3   *Using patterns of essay organization (8)*

One of the most basic topics for writing instruction centres on the set of patterns of organization which underlie much of expository and argument writing. As discussed in Chapter 11, these patterns are important for the logical development of informational writing. Recognizing these patterns in writing, however, is not enough for advanced writers; they must develop facility with the many possible variations on these patterns that will lead to effective writing and assist the reader of the text.

These patterns of organization, as described in many writing texts, are intended to provide the writer with an efficient yet constrained way to address different types of issues and concepts. If the goal is to describe a situation, setting, or process, the patterns for organizing texts will define, describe, classify, and develop a setting/procedure. It would make less sense to present a description in terms of a comparison/contrast or a cause/effect relation unless the writer intends to signal more than a description through the text. In this way, writers' arrangements are signalled and reader expectations are activated based on patterns that conventionally structure information. The patterns are typically classified as follows: definition (by taxonomy, by function, by example, by analogy), description (spatial, temporal, process), classification, comparison and contrast, problem and solution, cause and effect, analysis, and synthesis.

These patterns of arrangement do not represent major genres

of writing; rather they are means for organizing information within a number of genres and text types (e.g. narrative, argument, report writing, letters, sermons, lectures). Patterns of organization need to be made explicit through critical readings, outlines, visual displays, model texts, and group analysis of student texts. Rather than employ decontextualized lessons and exercises, teachers should look for ways to exploit reading material, make use of semantic mapping and information generation, and focus on analyses of student texts as ways to raise student awareness. Peer feedback and teacher responses to writing can also enquire about the organizational logic of students' writing.

12.4.4 *Paragraphing and text formatting (9)*

At a certain point in advanced academic writing, the adherence to conventions and the appropriate use of specific writing formats become an important part of the presentation of the text for the reader.

One particularly important convention is that of the paragraph. While historically the paragraph has been perceived as a visual entity intended to improve the physical symmetry of the text and make reading easier, the notion of the paragraph has taken on a new purpose in the latter half of the twentieth century. It is now expected that paragraphing, aside from matters of display and reading ease, reflects the psychological units of textual information. The paragraph, as currently used in informational writing, is intended to signal a coherent set of ideas, typically with a main theme and supporting information. Whether or not an explicit topic sentence is provided, readers expect the paragraph, as a unit, to convey a sense of information which can be summarized in a single sentence, and which contributes to the organization of the total text. This modern view of the paragraph fits psychological models of language comprehension as developed by Kintsch and van Dijk (1978, van Dijk and Kintsch 1983) and Singer (1990).

The development of organized and logical paragraphs cannot be assumed, even for advanced writers. The point of instruction is not to engage in an endless series of paragraph writing exercises, but to raise awareness of the role of paragraphing in writing, to discuss its relation to careful outlining and other visual displays of information organization, and to examine the effective use of paragraphing in model texts being explored for writing assignments and projects. Of course, if students do have difficulties with appropriate paragraphing, it is important to address those problems directly rather than hope that the advanced writer will resolve the difficulties naturally. Also, it cannot be assumed that advanced writers are fully aware of the power and purpose of the paragraph, since this aspect of writing is often ignored or treated in a simplistic way at lower levels of writing instruction.

12.4.5   Starting writing and ending writing (10)

A major problem for many writers, including advanced writers, centres on appropriate ways to begin and end writing. As students learn to work with new genres and new types of academic tasks, the simpler notions of openings and closings often are no longer adequate. It is not sufficient for students to recognize that openings state a thesis and indicate an organizational plan; students must also recognize that openings for different academic purposes will provide specific types of information and references to theoretical positions or concepts that ground a particular piece of writing.

A good way to raise student awareness of openings and closings is to collect sets of openings from various sources, particularly from readings used for the writing class and from student writing, showing effective and less-effective openings. The openings from edited texts can be examined for the consistent features common to many openings; they can also be examined for features that vary from topic to topic, from purpose to purpose, from genre to genre, and from audience to audience. These patterns of consistent and varying features can, in turn, be used to construct guidelines for looking at student openings in writing for various purposes.

The ending of a writing assignment is as important as its opening. In many cases, a useful essay strategy in timed writing exams is to stop near the end of time, no matter how seemingly incoherent the break might be, and compose a clear two-sentence conclusion that can then be fitted to the text as well as possible. A clear ending will make up for many inconsistencies along the way. And since the conclusion is indeed the last information read by the reader, the text is likely to give the reader a better impression. However, even outside of examination contexts, the ending pro-

vides a useful check for the reader and re-establishes the major
issues and goals of the text.

12.5   Assisting and guiding writing (themes 11–15)

In working with more complex writing tasks and assignments, students need to consider more than information sources and the
general organization of the text; they also need to consider how
arguments and positions are presented and how they can be made
more effective. There are two important issues in this regard: (1)
using persuasive information and arguments with factual support
(rather than unsubstantiated opinion), insightful examples, and
illustrative details; (2) providing students with feedback from
expert sources that will make them more effective writers. The five
themes in this section consider both of these concerns as they
address: (1) distinguishing fact from opinion, (2) developing
appropriate detail, (3) responding to student writing, (4) presenting texts for class revision, and (5) teacher–student conferencing.

12.5.1   *Distinguishing fact from opinion (11)*

Effective academic writing typically marshals a variety of evidence
to support the main points of a text and the veracity of the writer's
arguments. A major change in advanced academic writing is the
recognition of weak or spurious arguments, or of information and
arguments that are supported by opinions rather than by factual
information. While inappropriate reporting of information is a
serious concern for academic argumentation, the problem of separating fact from opinion is a broader and more basic concern.

All students, whether L1 or L2, need to develop a clear sense of
the difference between fact and opinion. Arguments and information supported by a belief system, a set of personal experiences, or
the assertions of other students do not provide evidence that
would be considered factual. Rather, students need to recognize
and use factual information as illustrated in the following: (1)
carefully controlled case study information; (2) survey and questionnaire data which includes some information on the
methodology of data collection; (3) quantitative data reported
from reliable sources (e.g. government documents, census information, major reference publications); (4) empirical experimental

results which include some explanation of the methodology employed; (5) visual display resources such as maps, charts, diagram, figures, tables, etc., derived from recognized reference sources; (6) carefully presented ethnographies and participant–observer discussion; and (7) theoretical arguments which combine informational resources with support from multiple sources of evidence.

Having suggested useful resources for factual information, it is important to acknowledge that all information and all facts can be seen as 'constructed' in some sense. However, there are clearly different degrees of control over the 'constructing' of fact, as was discussed in Chapter 6 (referring to Bazerman's (1983, 1988) discussion of 'passive constraints' on theorizing and actual information). It is also true that all academic writing retains a degree of rhetorical framing (even in the most seemingly informational of texts, such as professional science articles or annual business reports to stockholders). Nevertheless, it is important to see the use of factual information and the rhetorical framing of the information, or a set of arguments, as two distinct issues, and students need to be made aware of this difference.

There are also situations in which L2 students will have profound difficulties with the distinction between opinion and fact. In particular, students from certain cultures have difficulty understanding this distinction since polemic presentation may be, in their cultures, a valued method for organizing an argument and providing information. For such students, teachers need to address explicitly the issue of fact versus opinion, analyse differences between fact and opinion in various readings, and explore student composing processes in the development of argumentative or persuasive writing.

Teachers are aware of a number of well-known techniques which can raise awareness of the uses of factual information, and which can help students work more effectively with facts. For example, teachers and students can make lists of causes, evidence, examples, data, and theories which relate to a specific issue. These resources can then be organized in terms of their factual emphasis, and this listing may become a resource as students develop a visual display or outline of their draft and begin to write.

As a second example, teachers and students can explore a number of texts that they have read for a thematic unit or a project and examine the sorts of evidence used. These sets of evidence can then be classified as empirical fact, theory, inference, or opinion. Discussion of the choices should help to raise students' levels of awareness.

12.5.2   Developing appropriate detail (12)

In addition to a concern for using factual information appropriately in writing, there is a need for writers to provide vivid detail – the striking analogy and the effective illustration. Used in conjunction with a variety of factual resources, these details build a relation between the writer and the reader, a sense of involvement, as Tannen (1989) would argue.

The use of figures of speech includes similes and metaphors – ways of making less familiar information more understandable through example and illustration – and vivid detail can also be drawn directly from the data resources being reported. Typically, when there is extensive data display and discussion, the detail that might make the information more manageable is missing. Good writers, in contrast, know when to focus on a small segment of the data and when to make its appropriateness and importance clear for the reader. Thus, the detail can serve as the most persuasive aspect of a complex and demanding written presentation.

There are a number of ways to develop a student's sense of effective detail in academic writing. For a writing project, students can begin by making lists of details, examples, and illustrations that they can remember from various sources and these lists can then be combined into a master list. Within a few weeks, this list should be reviewed two or three times to allow new items to be added. The teacher can also remind students to look for details in their readings and point them out to the class. The teacher and students can also explore ways in which details, examples, etc., vary from one academic genre to another. As another general activity, students can review readings used in class for the variety of details in these texts. These can then contribute the basis for a taxonomy of effective details to be used in writing.

12.5.3   Responding to student writing (13)

Teachers need to provide helpful and informative feedback to students at a variety of points during the writing process; these feedback mechanisms will also need to vary with the teacher's purpose and the individual student's progress. Students need both informal and formal feedback from teachers, whether the feedback be assistance with brainstorming, informal feedback during class discussions, or more specific and formal feedback on written drafts.

From the beginning of a writing task, the teacher can provide assistance with brainstorming and organizing, reviewing heuristics, and exploring the extent of content information available. Teachers can provide feedback during class discussions, in reaction to free-response writing on a topic that students might pursue, in response to initial outlines prepared in groups, and in reaction to class lists of student-raised topics and informational resources. Teachers can remind students of the various ways they should consider organizing information, and the various places they can look for more information. Much of this initial feedback will be informal and will not involve specific evaluation mechanisms; however, the teacher can create activities which assess early efforts to develop drafts and give formal evaluative feedback. Given the typically evaluative nature of most academic writing, the pressures of formal evaluations might best be postponed until later in the process unless students need extrinsic motivation.

The feedback process commonly involves reading the first drafts for content and organization (e.g. factual information, logic of presentation). In many classes, student peer-revision occurs in conjunction with the first draft; however, the first draft provides a better opportunity for the teacher, as expert writer, to help students consider fundamental issues in the organization and content of the writing without becoming too committed to the original writing plan. During feedback on the first draft, and during subsequent class discussions, the teacher can provide supporting comments so that students may attend to important features of their writing (e.g. information structure, and details of grammar, logic, and fact). Students can then form groups, following class discussions and individual feedback on rough drafts, and identify three or four concerns which should be given priority while working on the second draft.

The teacher needs to decide how feedback can be provided most effectively for the final draft (or the draft that will go into a portfolio). The teacher has the option to give both instructional and evaluative feedback on final drafts. The instructional feedback might point out important issues that were discussed but that were not addressed adequately in a given final draft. The teacher can also ask students to write a reflection page on their experiences writing the paper, on the feedback from the teacher on the final draft, and on changes that the student might make in a later revision or for another paper. A variety of feedback options are examined in detail in Chapter 13.

12.5.4   Presenting texts for class revision (14)

A common, and very effective, technique for teacher feedback is a whole-class critique of one or two texts written by students in the class (or from another class). The technique also provides opportunities for quick reviews of previous issues and allows the teacher to think-aloud through ideas for revision in front of the class.

The most important concern when using student papers for whole-class revision sessions is to design the activity in a positive way. Students need to be convinced that feedback from the class offers additional benefits to feedback from a peer group. The teacher needs to keep the authorship confidential, preferably presenting a retyped version for the class. In addition, the students need to be assured that they will all have some piece of their work reviewed in this way, so all students will have the same experience and no student will be singled out inequitably. In cases in which emphasis is to be given to some particular aspect of writing, such as opening paragraphs, the teacher can choose to present three or four introductory paragraphs for class work. In this way, all members of the class know that three or four students have a part in the exercise, and no one student is receiving all the revision responses.

Teacher-fronted class revision activities can focus on a wide variety of topics and issues. First, the teacher can focus on ways to develop a rough draft and on concerns for overall organization. The teacher can read through a student's text, then put the text aside and outline how he or she would do it differently using the same information. This think-aloud process allows students to see alternative approaches and to ask questions about choices made by the teacher. The teacher, in turn, can comment on choices made and explain motivations guided by audience, purpose, content, and task. Students can take notes while the teacher is thinking aloud and then meet in groups to decide on the two or three most important changes or considerations proposed by the teacher. The class discussion to follow will allow the teacher to emphasize important points for drafting and revising. This feedback should help students not only in writing but also in developing their own feedback abilities during peer revision sessions.

The teacher can also guide a class discussion of a student's paper (cf. Beach 1989). Students may begin by reading the paper silently, noting places in the text at which a comment may be made, and selecting two points to make. The teacher can read the paper aloud so that all students hear the rhythm of the text and recognize problem spots that they might have overlooked. The teacher can also offer guidelines for the critiques so that the comments are taken constructively. For example, the teacher can ask all reviewers to begin with some positive comment or some interesting idea that is suggested even if it does not actually appear in the text. Students can then describe something that they think would improve the text. The goal is to focus more on larger issues such as organization, audience, content, purpose, coherence, detail, illustration, etc. If a student would like to comment on structure, then the student should propose an alternative structure. A final five minutes should be provided to enable students to write out their critiques on their copies of the text which the teacher collects and later gives, as an entire class set of ideas for revision, to the student whose paper was critiqued.

These class revision techniques provide opportunities for students to work with meaningful texts and to engage in constructive commentary in peer writing (see also Chapter 13).

12.5.5   Teacher–student conferencing (15)

Teacher–student conferences are an effective, if time-consuming, alternative to class feedback and written feedback on individual papers (Beach 1989, Freedman 1987). Such conferences can be used as a regular feature of the writing curriculum, with a number of regular conference times scheduled, or they can be conducted two to three times during a semester.

Conferencing, when it is possible and feasible in a given instructional context, should provide students with unique learning opportunities. Recent research on cooperative learning suggests that intensive interaction with teachers will improve learning

(Fathman and Kessler 1993, Slavin 1990). Similarly, a Vygotskean interpretation of conferencing would argue that conferences will lead an apprentice writer to perform at a level not possible without expert assistance (Newman *et al.* 1989, Rogoff 1990). Collaborative learning research in composition also suggests that the writing conference is a productive way for students to learn (Flynn and King 1993, Golub 1988). Finally, research on tutoring in educational contexts suggests that intensive interaction is a powerful means for learning complex higher-order skills (Wasik and Slavin 1993).

Conferencing, however, is no panacea for writing success. There are a number of issues which have to be attended to if conferencing is to be effective. First, the teacher needs to know how to share the power relation in the conferences and not be overly directive. Second, the teacher must listen and give the student time to consider answers. Third, the teacher needs to know when particular information and assistance will be most useful. Fourth, the teacher must structure the conference so that the ground rules are clear for the students. Fifth, the teacher has to make students feel at ease and confident, and also have students recognize that the conference is a time for work. To have a conference work well, the teacher should discuss conference methods with students, describe expectations and goals for conferencing, explain why it will improve students' writing, and provide a set of written guidelines for what should happen in conferences.

In conferences held on a regular basis, students should recognize the shared responsibility for this interaction. Students should bring in-class and homework papers, questions from assignments, papers from other classes, and, more generally, be willing to discuss their progress in the writing class. For conferences held once or twice during a writing course, the dynamics of the conference will also include discussion of progress in the class, feelings and attitudes towards the class and the writing tasks, and expectations for learning to write from the class.

Despite the greater complexity and time requirements of conferences, there are a number of advantages that make them serious options for writing instruction. Students receive, and give themselves, detailed feedback in situations in which they feel free to ask more questions and in which the teacher can probe in more detail. Teachers can also provide a range of important feedback for students:

1. Carefully evaluate writing progress
2. Examine past writing assignments
3. Provide help with brainstorming, topics, details, etc.
4. Examine and discuss portfolio progress
5. Introduce more detailed heuristic schemes with carefully guided practice
6. Practise those skills that students should be using in class peer-revision sessions.

12.6   Working with different types of writing (themes 16–20)

At advanced levels, it is important that students expand their range of writing abilities into additional genres and also develop specific skills useful for more demanding academic contexts. This section examines five genres which are important for the development of advanced writing abilities: (1) critical reviews, (2) argument writing, (3) case study writing, (4) interpretive essays, and (5) the research paper.

The research paper represents, in some respects, the final stage of advanced student writing. While the research paper is sometimes viewed as an abstract and time-consuming exercise in writing classes, it is, in fact, the best opportunity that students have to grapple with the full complexity of academic writing and academic expectations. Genres which are even more complex or specialized than the ones discussed in this section typically only emerge in a graduate student–faculty or apprentice–mentor relationship that represents initiation as an active member of an academic discourse community. The more complex genres typically indicate sufficient expertise in writing that the term 'writing student' is no longer appropriate and mastering these advanced genres does not typically include the need to develop general writing skills further.

12.6.1   *Critical review writing (16)*

The ability to analyse a text and provide a critical review is a major academic task in most fields of study. In advanced learning contexts, it is not assumed that course lectures provide all the information that students are expected to learn. The most common source of additional information is through reading other text material. The additional content gained through reading is not expected to be inert, but to be used and integrated with other academic content. The most efficient way to assess the reading material is through a critical review. It provides a summary of the information, and forces the reader to approach the material with a sceptical and enquiring manner. Many courses, particularly at the graduate level, make regular use of this genre, and it is an important one for students to have practised.

Students are also expected to evaluate longer readings and books through the critical review essay. In simple form, the review essay first summarizes the author's work as neutrally as possible. This is followed by the author's position and intentions, both overt and covert. The review then typically describes the text's strengths and weaknesses, which usually indicates acceptance or rejection of the text. The review often ends with a reviewer's interpretation of the value of the text and its appropriateness for other readers.

Before students can develop skills with this genre, they must read books and longer articles which raise important issues and discuss these issues with some degree of complexity. One good way to introduce students to critical reviews is to have them read a book and find a set of reviews of that book. The teacher can also provide a commentary on a published review that is handed out to the class: the teacher can include an outline of the organization of the review, a discussion of the highlighted issues that motivate the review, a critique of the review's summary as well as the shaping of the summary to meet the author's intentions, and an evaluation of the reviewer's rhetorical strategies.

Students can also find a review of a book they have read and outline the organization of the review. Students can point out places in which the reviewer indicates a positive or negative evaluation, issues which guide the review, the summary of the book, and the analysis of the book in terms of the issues highlighted. Students can then work in groups or as a class to write a review of a book read by the entire class. In a brainstorming discussion, students can outline a plan for the review, list important topics in the book, offer genuine criticisms of the book, and nominate issues which students could use to focus the review.

12.6.2   *Argument writing – taking a position (17)*

A standard genre that students are expected to master is the argument paper, in which they take a position on an issue. Argument papers typically propose a thesis and then support the thesis through a set of evidence (facts, logic, examples, etc.). Writing assignments in which students are to take a position require them to learn how to consider both sides of an argument, describe the alternative positions effectively, note the strengths and weakness of both positions, and provide a persuasive explanation for choosing one position over another.

The first requirement for having students write argumentation essays is the availability of a set of information which genuinely establishes alternative positions or points of view. This is easiest to do in the context of a content-based unit, a project, or a set of readings on a topic, as these formats raise a number of issues which should allow different perspectives. These alternatives should be explored in group discussion with students taking notes and the teacher summarizing the main points of the discussion on the board. Students should then seek additional information which can support the positions for which they would like to argue.

Information collected should be reformatted as a set of supporting arguments. This set should be discussed in class, and the teacher should provide optional frameworks for presenting the arguments. Teachers also need to point out that a strong argument is one which includes discussion of weaknesses with the preferred position, but which responds to these weaknesses with reasonable counter-arguments.

Argument papers can be the source for, or the consequence of, a class debate on a particular topic. In either case, the work done collecting information for the essay becomes an important resource for the debate. Argument papers can also be combined into a more elaborate report which can be sent to an appropriate outside institution, for example, a local authority.

12.6.3   *Case study reports and simulations (18)*

Students are often asked to explore an issue or a situation for which there is no simple solution (see also Chapter 11, subsection 11.7.3). These situations typically are presented as a set of problems or decisions to be made on the basis of information available. This is a common teaching approach in a number of academic disciplines and it can be a powerful means for introducing students to the goals and methods of a discipline.

Case studies and simulations can involve a range of possible scenarios: the building of a hospital or a freeway; the use of pesticides or fertilizers; water rights or dam construction; government funding decisions; the costs and benefits of business relocation into the local community. These and many other scenarios can be designed to explore issues associated with the content of an academic course, including a content-based writing course.

Such case study reports and simulations force students to take a position in writing based on specific sets of data, specific methodologies for analysis, and specific alternative options, all of which typically have advantages and disadvantages. The writing of simulation and case study reports constrains the options available to students and teaches students to work with methods of analysis which are preferred by some academic disciplines (i.e. some discourse communities).

12.6.4   *Creative and interpretive writing (19)*

A further important type of writing, or perhaps a number of types of writing, could be classified here under the label of creative and interpretive writing. Students at advanced levels might engage in at least four types of writing which might be considered creative or interpretive: (1) creative fiction and poetry, (2) creative non-fiction, (3) the interpretive critical essay, and (4) the interpretive theoretical synthesis.

Creative fiction and poetry is, of course, of interest to students who wish to pursue writing creatively. While students seeking degrees in English come immediately to mind, there are, in fact, many other students who would like to develop some abilities to write short stories, poetry, screen plays, etc. These students are interested in learning to write in new genres. Moreover, the work of Heath (1993, Heath and Mangiola 1991), studying performance-arts writing of disadvantaged youth, shows that creative writing can be an important resource for developing writers, particularly for students who are considered to be at-risk.

Creative non-fiction provides another option for writing. As a growing field of professional writing, creative non-fiction typically refers to travel writing, to reflections on personal experiences, or to interviews with persons who are not explicitly named for a variety of reasons. Both forms of writing typically include a narration but are not fictional. Students may also be encouraged to write creative non-fiction as part of certain academic courses (e.g. anthropology, sociology) as well as in a writing course. In some sense, creative non-fiction is the mature version of expressive writing done at earlier stages of writing instruction.

The interpretive essay is a genre which is common in humanities disciplines. In many courses, students are expected to read literature or philosophy and provide an insightful interpretation of what the reading means to them. This is typically a difficult genre to master since it often presumes a wide range of background knowledge, a finely honed sense of intertextuality, an ability to read on multiple levels and to recognize symbolic structure in a text, and a knowledge of ways that critical theory is used in interpretation. While it can be seen as a genre that extends beyond the writing student, in fact students are often asked to work in this genre whenever there is an emphasis on literary, cultural, religious, or philosophical texts. Unfortunately, it is very difficult to teach students this genre without an intensive apprenticeship and attendant practise.

The interpretative theoretical synthesis is a different type of writing, one which synthesizes information and arguments from a number of sources and infers a larger theoretical foundation for the sources. Often this type of writing summarizes a number of research studies and interprets them in a way that attempts to unify the various results. This type of writing is fundamental to academic activities which look to find patterns and generalizations in sets of information, perhaps the most fundamental purpose underlying any academic enterprise. It is not uncommon for students in writing classes to look for patterns and generalizations across sets of readings and, in effect, build a theory. Such an approach to writing is the foundation also for Bartholomae and Petrosky's (1986) writing curriculum, *Facts, artefacts, and counterfacts*. It is also a basic goal for writing curricula which seek to problematize commonly held cultural assumptions, and, as such, are seen as Freirean approaches to writing instruction.

12.6.5   *The research paper (20)*

The research paper is a well-known option for advanced writing, and one which has moved in and out of favour at different times in writing pedagogy. For advanced writing, students need to learn how to work with sets of information, how to synthesis knowledge from multiple sources, how to use and cite resources appropriately, and how to explain a complex issue in a manageable format. The research paper (or research project) can provide a reasonable way to promote these goals, and promote exploration and enquiry on some topic of interest to students.

The research paper provides a manageable type of writing which can incorporate other genres presented in this section. At the same time, the research paper is sufficiently general that students can carry it out without the task becoming overly difficult. Students can be expected to explore some topic of interest related to the course curriculum and teachers should provide guidelines and assistance for focusing the topic, for information collection, and for using an appropriate format for the paper itself.

In most cases, the research paper involves an extended investigation and collection of outside resources on a topic. Teachers should offer guidelines throughout the process of writing the research paper, and can discuss various possible topics and variations on a theme. They should schedule library activities which teach students how to make use of library resources and should also provide a time-table of assignments which will keep students on task. Many of the brainstorming, drafting, and writing activities that are useful for shorter writing activities are also important for writing the research paper.

The research paper can assume various formats and conventions; nevertheless, it is a widely recognized genre in academic courses and in advanced writing classes. It is also an important way to introduce students to synthesizing and information reporting, basic activities in all academic classes.

12.7   Extending writing (themes 21–25)

This section raises a number of issues which reflect differing demands of writing in different disciplines. How these various concerns can be incorporated into a writing curriculum, or the extent to which they can be incorporated, is the focus of the final five themes; these include: (1) content-based writing and writing across the curriculum, (2) discourse communities, (3) working with visual displays, (4) working with media, and (5) style and the individual writer.

12.7.1   Content-based writing courses and writing across the curriculum (21)

Throughout the previous three chapters, as well as in a number of the other chapters, a basic orientation to writing has been in terms of content-centred instruction. Such an approach does not guarantee successful instruction, nor does it make the issues and problems in writing instruction any less complex. It does, however, offer genuine academic learning experiences in the writing classroom and give writing instruction a realistic content: while writing itself could be seen as content, and it often is in writing textbooks, most students are not persuaded by such rationalizations. For advanced writing instruction to be effective, writing itself must be used in much the same way that it would be used in any academic context. This realistic context is what content-centred courses can bring to writing instruction.

There are many ways to carry out content-based writing instruction. One common option at advanced writing levels is to use a major theme with which students can connect. The thematic curriculum by Bartholomae and Petrosky (1986) presents a detailed discussion and rationale. Their curriculum, centred on adolescence, allowed students to bring expertise and authority to the issues; at the same time, the curriculum emphasizes dialogue and discussion, extensive reading, many writing activities, a thematic progression from self to other's views of adolescence, and a progression in writing from personal to academic theory building. A number of other topics can be used in similar ways, giving students some amount of expertise, while also sequencing writing towards more complex academic tasks. Such themes might include education, technology, the future, culture, academic culture, etc. (See also Kutz *et al.* 1993.)

A second curricular format is to develop subtopics around loosely related sets of content material. In this format, the curriculum is centred around three to five topics, some of which may be connected. The connections need not be made across all topics, and topics can, in part, be the choice of the students, assuming that the teacher has collected information on a number of options for units. Aside from the need to develop a motivating sequence of writing and reading activities for each topic, the teacher should also find ways to strengthen relations across topics. This can be done by links across main topics at times, but it is also possible to connect topics in other ways. For example, a set of subtopics (apart from the main topic) may focus on a famous person, an important set of consequences from an event, an issue that cannot be easily resolved, or some abstract concept such as responsibility, technology, etc. The recurrence of sub-issues across topics can be exploited to build coherence into the curriculum, and a set of connections can bind the content of the various topics. This option should not, however, be seen as a rationale for a composition 'reader'. Such composition texts do not allow for the open development of a topic, nor do they lead to student input or motivation. Many 'readers' tend to be frozen in concept and literary-classical in orientation: the spontaneity and creativity needed for interesting content/topic development is generally missing from these texts.

A further option for thematic writing curricula is the often discussed notion of Writing Across the Curriculum (WAC). The goal in this case is to bring the writing instruction to the content class rather than the reverse. While there are a number of good rationales for WAC, there is no clear evidence that it promotes writing/learning in ways beyond writing-class instruction (Ackerman 1993). Of course, the more opportunities that students have to write, the better they should become as writers in a discipline. While WAC, in theory, is a good idea, it is not guaranteed to improve writing instruction. In WAC contexts, introducing sets of writing techniques, exercises, and activities which are not integral to the content curriculum will not lead to any significant improvement in academic writing. In fact, content-area teachers often resent the intrusions that many writing techniques represent when they are not well-integrated into a curriculum, and when suggested by the well-meaning writing specialist without careful consideration of the goals of the content-area courses (Kaufer and Young 1993, Spack 1988).

In spite of these real concerns by content-area teachers, the ideal of students engaging more intensively in writing across a range of courses is a goal that should be a priority of academic programmes everywhere. Many content teachers are well aware of the genre-specific writing demands of their disciplines. The attention to writing, while also focusing on the real content of a discipline, provides opportunities for meaningful writing activities which should motivate students. An effective WAC programme could have a profound effect on writing development, but it is difficult to implement and requires considerable negotiation and coordination (McLeod and Soven 1992).

12.7.2   *Discourse communities (22)*

The significance of the concept of discourse communities for writing development has been discussed in Chapter 5. Nevertheless, it is important to point out the practical implications of this concept for writing instruction. Academic discourse communities are typically discipline-specific groups of academics who share sets of theoretical, methodological, and conventional notions about their discipline. One important issue is whether or not such communities see initiating students into their discourses as a goal when teaching advanced students. In a recent book examining writing in various undergraduate disciplines, Walvoord and McCarthy (1991), in fact, found this to be a primary consideration of many faculties. Many faculties are motivated to have students undertake writing tasks which model real writing activities carried out by professionals in the outside world. Thus, the notion of the discourse community is an important one for advanced writing instruction.

Discourse communities provide a resource for real and realistic writing activities. Specific discourse communities make extensive use of different genres and conventions which will be important for students to master. Some of these genres and conventions will be specialized, but others will generalize across a number of disciplines. For example, the ability to form a coherent and well-supported set of arguments from multiple, and sometimes conflicting, resources is a skill that is valued in a number of disciplines. Similarly, the ability to write a critical review of a major text is widely valued. A number of disciplines also value the ability to construct a set of valid recommendations from case study scenarios and simulations of problems. In these respects, the study of writing uses in different discourse communities can have a strong impact on the design of writing courses and the integration of WAC with various academic discourse communities.

Writing specialists must recognize the genres and conventions of writing in different disciplines and look for ways to support writing activities which both improve writing and prepare students to carry out activities valued by a discipline.

12.7.3   *Working with visual displays (23)*

A skill in advanced writing that is valued in many academic contexts is the ability to write with visual displays (e.g. incorporating a table of data into the prose discussion). From earlier sections, the notion of a visual display can mean a visual representation of the text organization used to generate an essay. In this section, the concept of visual display is extended to mean also: (1) an alternative (e.g. visual) interpretation of the data discussed in a text, or (2) non-prose displays of information in the writing which add information and which may be partly explained in the accompanying writing. Both situations represent important writing issues for advanced students.

On one level, students in writing classes are often asked to write essays, informational reports, and arguments *based on* visual material: this sort of writing is sometimes done as a writing activity and sometimes as a test and evaluation of knowledge. Less formally, students write from displays when they write from semantic maps, time-lines, self-constructed charts and tables, and draft outlines to help organize their own information. There are no simple guidelines for these types of activities since various visual displays can invoke the full range of organizational options in writing. It is important to give students practice with assignments of these types, and such activities can be integrated into project work and summaries of content-based units. The writing from various visual displays can also be used to show the options available to students when converting outlines into connected prose.

On another level, students are sometimes expected to integrate visual material *into* their own prose writing. This type of integration between visual and linear prose is a different matter from using a display to provide information for writing. Visual displays accompanying writing can be used in a number of ways. The visual material can add further information not explained in the text. Alternatively, visual displays can be coordinated with the prose of texts and selected aspects of the display can be referred to explicitly. A third option occurs when the visual display summarizes the information in the text. In this case, the display completely overlaps with the text and functions primarily as an additional comprehension support for the reader. All three options may be required of academic students in certain disciplinary contexts.

Students may also be expected to create their own visual supports for their writing. This is another reason to incorporate visual displays in brainstorming, planning, and organizing writing. These planning and organizing formats then become potential visual displays to accompany texts. Again, there is no simple recipe for learning to use visual displays in writing, but consistent practice helps. In many cases, these writing activities can be incorporated when advanced students know that the skills are valued in their future academic disciplines. At the same time, it is important to recognize that the adept use of accompanying displays in writing often makes a notable impression on readers.

12.7.4   *Working with media (24)*

In the previous chapters on writing instruction, a number of writing techniques and activities have made use of media sources and used media activities primarily *as the impetus for writing* (Chapter 10, subsections 10.5.6, 10.7.1; Chapter 11, subsections 11.5.4, 11.6.3, 11.7.5). The uses of writing *for media purposes* may also be an important extension for advanced writing. As students develop writing skills and are asked to work with more specialized tasks, they may be asked to write text for a media project or write prose in conjunction with a media resource as a multimedia project.

At a fairly basic level of advanced writing, students can be asked to script a video production or an act from a play. Students can script and produce a debate or interviews with famous people from the past. Students can produce a TV talk show in which two 'correspondents' take a conservative view, and two other 'correspondents' take a more liberal view. A news feature report is another project which can follow an extended content-based unit and which can draw together different sets of information into a coherent documentary.

At more advanced levels, students can also produce a newspaper or a newsletter with information about the school, local events, class and group projects, and biographies of class members. The class can produce a book or an extended report which can be distributed to other classes and to other schools. For example, in Bartholomae and Petrosky's (1986) writing curriculum on adolescence, the class produces a set of student autobiographies which become the text data for discovering general patterns in adolescent experiences. Students can also write a report or a news feature which can be submitted to the school newspaper. It is important to recognize that, while students are at an advanced level, they still have much to gain by combining academic writing with other forms of media.

12.7.5   Style and the individual writer (25)

Advanced students will need to develop a strong sense of style in their writing. This individual style will include a recognition of how strongly a claim should be asserted, a knowledge of how and when to speak as an expert and to invoke authority, and a sense of appropriateness of form and convention in writing which matches the genre and situation of writing. The ability of students to find their own 'voice', and to develop a voice that is appropriately academic is a difficult task; it requires extended practise with expository and argument writing, and a long-range time commitment. The development of an appropriate academic voice is also likely to require some amount of discipline-specific apprenticeship. While many writing texts talk about students developing a voice in their writing, this usually means a personal expressive style that is similar to the way students relate ideas orally. This notion of voice will not typically translate into an individual academic style, demonstrating authority and confidence while writing for academic purposes.

The development of an individual academic style requires both a sense of stylistic options available to writers and a clear sense of valued academic and formal conventions of writing. One way to raise awareness of academic style would be to compare two writers on the same topic and explore ways in which the two texts differ stylistically. Two or three of these awareness exercises will allow students to see a few advanced options in writing such as the extensive use of appositive parenthetical clauses and absolutive clauses, variation in modality for modifying assertions, modification with final participial clauses, complex patterns of nominalization, the use of a variety of punctuation options (e.g. dash, colon, semicolon), and the use of passives and impersonal structures. Certain of these features can then be explored in the revision process with students' texts. Another option for raising student awareness lies in comparing an academic written version of a text to an oral version (see Christie 1992, Kutz *et al.* 1993, Martin 1993).

Students need to become aware that the formal conventions of writing are not only patterns which match academic constraints and the expectations of informed readers, they also signal a willingness to work within disciplinary expectations and to project an academic persona. While the need to edit texts carefully and produce 'clean' texts is important for evaluation purposes, this goal only indirectly reflects the real impetus for careful editing and appropriate formatting. Academic writers are careful about formats, conventions, and error-free texts because they know that other academics view such carefully produced text as a sign of respect and, for better or worse, a mark of careful scholarship.

The impressions given by the form of a text are not too important in lower levels of writing instruction, but they are critical in advanced writing. If, indeed, a student is an advanced writer, and is aware of the conventions and expectations of readers, then a poorly edited and stylistically weak text indicates some degree of contempt and disrespect for the reader. In the final analysis, there is no avoiding the need to combine insightful organization and stimulating content with a careful attention to the form of the text. It is the combination of these features of text which carries the ideas, intentions, and attitudes of the writer.

12.8   Relating writing instruction to writing theory

The themes addressed in this chapter, while focusing primarily on the advanced student writer, also, in many cases, are adaptable to students at lower writing levels. This and each of the previous two chapters present, as an organizing format, 25 themes for writing. However, many themes are applicable across all levels of writing instruction, for example:

- the writing process, in various forms
- writing for various purposes, for different audiences, and for different genres
- different ways to incorporate informal, personal, and creative writing
- the need to focus on conventions and formal aspects of writing.

Students at all levels need to generate and organize a large amount of information for writing, and they need to recognize appropriate patterns for organization. Students must also be able to combine reading and writing, and use many sources of information.

A number of general curricular guidelines, suggested in Chapter 9, provide the foundation for the discussion in this and the previous two chapters. Some of the guidelines are noted above; others, which can be observed across the various themes and instructional discussions, include an equal emphasis on product and process, the need for students to develop strategies for generating content and organizing information, the need for many types of feedback, an awareness of the uses of writing and the various purposes that writing serves, and a willingness by the teacher to provide many opportunities for writing – some of which will be non-evaluative (see Chapter 9).

In these three chapters on writing instruction, one can see an interdependence among activities, plans, intentions, and formats supporting overall guidelines for writing curricula. The critical notion underlying the many themes presented is that they are guided by theoretical concerns and research, though not in any direct or simplistic way. One cannot translate theory directly into a neat package of activities and exercises; the multiple worlds of student writers are much too disparate and complex for neat solutions. At the same time, it should be clear that the generalizations suggested in Chapters 8 and 9 are reflected here and in Chapters 10 and 11. The fit between general curricular guidelines and instructional practices suggests that theory and instruction can be integrated, though one should not expect a simple procedural blueprint for instruction. There are many interesting issues and problems associated with writing instruction, but there are no simple solutions.

12.9   Conclusion

This chapter, together with Chapters 10 and 11, has discussed a wide range of ideas for writing instruction. They could be read independently of the rest of the book, but that is not our intention. As the previous section suggested, many of the instructional concepts follow directly from theoretical perspectives on writing. Moreover, Chapter 9 represents an effort to bridge theory and instruction, allowing the ideas of these three instructional chapters to be incorporated into a principled philosophy of instruction and a well-reasoned curriculum plan.

This chapter, in particular, offers many suggestions for advanced writing instruction which should apply across many academic contexts, assuming instructional settings from the end of secondary schooling to the beginning of post-graduate education.

It is also true that advanced writing instruction begins to require specializations that are less amenable to general curricular plans; but this is an ongoing dilemma in many tertiary-level writing courses that are not embedded within a specific discipline. The tertiary-level writing course represents that point of partition into more specific disciplinary demands, and it produces pedagogical tensions in that the writing course cannot by itself meet all the needs of advanced students. The movement into writing instruction in specific disciplinary contexts and for specific purposes also, perhaps, represents the point at which a generalized notion of writing instruction comes to an end (see Swales 1990).

13

Responding to writing and writing assessment

13.1 Introduction

In this chapter we review research and practice in responding to writing and in writing assessment. In recent years, these areas have received much more attention than they had previously, both with respect to research and to practical implementation. At the same time, however, the issues surrounding responses to writing and writing assessment are still discussed more in terms of the questions raised and the concerns to be addressed than in terms of clear answers to difficult and important issues.

Responding to writing and writing assessment have important consequences for students as well as for teachers. *Responding to students' writing* can greatly influence student attitudes to writing and their motivation for future learning. Students can be easily confused by unclear, vague, or ambiguous responses and can become frustrated with their writing progress. Alternatively, students can be positively motivated to explore many areas of knowledge and personal creativity through supportive and constructive responses to their writing. Unfortunately, there is no clear set of universal guidelines that will guarantee such a supportive and positive experience for all students. In any given context for writing instruction, students will differ, teachers will differ, institutional expectations will differ, and tasks, topics, and resources will differ. Nevertheless, we do believe that certain results of research and practice provide important insights; these represent strong options and resources for teachers who are looking for ways to provide feedback on student writing.

The impact of *writing assessment* on students is apparent to any person involved in academic learning contexts. Writing assessment,

377

whether as in-class assessment of student progress or as standard-ized proficiency assessment, is a major determinant of students' future academic careers. Writing is commonly used to assess not only students' language skills but also their learning in many acad-emic content-areas. For this reason, among others, the ability to provide students, teachers, and administrators with fair and sup-portable assessment approaches is a serious issue. Not only do many decisions rest with writing assessments, but assessment processes have a great impact on student attitudes and their moti-vation for future work. All concerned in writing instruction need to have confidence in assessment approaches – approaches that are designed to permit students to perform to the best of their abilities and that are appropriately interpreted by decision makers and test-score users.

13.2   Response to student writing

Until the emergence of the process movement in writing instruc-tion, much feedback to students on their writing appeared in the form of a final grade on a paper, often accompanied by much red ink throughout the essay. This practice assumed that students would take to heart all the mistakes pointed out, infer the reasoning behind the grade, and be motivated to avoid the multiplicity of mis-takes on their next writing tasks. It is now apparent to most teachers and researchers that such an approach left many bewildered and confused students unable to work constructively on their writing skills. One of the major positive impacts of the writing process approach has been the thorough rethinking of responses to student writing. A direct outcome of multiple drafts and pre-writing activi-ties has been the exploration of ways in which teachers can assist students most effectively in their writing. Student revision and teacher response has become central at all stages of the writing process: pre-writing, first drafting, revising, and final-draft writing.

In addition to exploring the role of responses to writing at all stages of composing, research has examined many alternative methods for responding to students. These options run from teacher–student conferences and response journals to peer group responses of various types, to differing teacher responses on students writing, to analytic-guide questions and lists, to teacher–class discussions, and to using other audiences for feedback. These options all offer ways to promote effective responses to student writing, recognizing that different students may react differently to alternative types of responses.

13.2.1   Peer group responses

In the last ten years, the most popular means for providing student responses in English L1 contexts is through peer group interactions. As an example, students would enter class with their first or second draft completed. Students would then get together, or be assigned in groups of two, three, or four. The students would exchange or pass around the papers and receive comments from the other students in the group. This process would take 40 to 60 minutes. Students would subsequently use these comments and suggestions from their peers to write the next draft. Some peer sessions would involve the free exchanges of reactions to a given student's writing. Other peer sessions might require students to work with specific peer-review guidelines, and peer groups might be organized so that each student would be responsible for some specific task or set of tasks. Alternatively, students might be required to present a written response to each text read and to complete response sheets to be evaluated at some later point.

In fact, there are many variations on peer group responses, and much professional debate centres on deciding the forms that are most effective. These debates cover such issues as the amount and type of student training for such group work, the amount of peer group response (per session and per semester), the manner of peer group response, the number of students involved per group, the amount of teacher intervention, the goals set for peer group response, the types of follow-up procedures used, etc. The specific issues are numerous, and there is much research that remains to be done in understanding the effectiveness and dynamics of peer group interactions (see, e.g., Anson 1989, Carson and Nelson 1994, Connor and Asenavage 1994, DiPardo and Freedman 1988, Freedman 1987, Gere 1987, Golub 1988, Lawson *et al.* 1989, Nelson and Murphy 1993, Spear 1988, 1993, Zhu 1994).

The motivations for using peer response groups derive from a number of sources. From a practical perspective, writing process teachers and researchers recognize the need for audiences other than the teacher, and for alternative feedback on student writing. Responding to peer work will also involve students in each other's writing; in that process, students can learn the language of, and uses for, responding to texts. From this experience, students would then begin to see similar problems and weaknesses in their own writing as well as use innovative and creative ideas to which they are exposed. Students also would need to learn to accept reasonable reader responses and to use them constructively in their revisions. A number of arguments are offered to support the practice of peer group feedback.

Theoretical research in rhetoric, literacy criticism, and social-construction theory converge to argue that knowledge itself is constructed through the negotiations of a community. Knowledge does not reside outside of a community of scholars, and knowledge can change as the community reconstructs itself. This argument is used to promote peer groups in writing – students discover new ways of reading other texts and their own texts. This perspective is also compatible with recent reader-response and post-structuralist approaches to text analysis and interpretation: the coherence of texts is created and recreated by readers rather than being inherent in texts. The three fields, together, provide a strong rhetorical argument for effective ways for students to read texts and receive meaningful feedback (Bruffee 1986, Lawson *et al.* 1989).

A second theoretical argument for peer group responses derives from a combination of sociolinguistics and cognitive psychology. Socio-cognitive approaches to learning argue that knowledge is best acquired through negotiated interaction. The issue is not whether knowledge is created in this way (as claimed in social constructionist arguments), but that knowledge is best acquired and used through negotiated interaction (Flower 1994, Langer 1987, Nystrand 1990). According to this view, students will develop as writers more effectively as they engage in transactions over their own texts and the texts of others – negotiating real intentions to communication with real audience expectations.

A different line of support for peer group responses is one that is only now receiving attention among many teachers and composition researchers. This line of argument follows from research on cooperative learning as it is applied in K-12 educational contexts rather than in university writing courses (Fathman and Kessler 1993, Kagan 1992, Slavin 1990). In cooperative learning approaches to instruction, groups are used in various ways to collaborate on tasks and projects that promote learning and typically involve extended writing.

Peer group approaches are typically carried out in a number of distinct ways. In many cases, students are given little overt direction except to read each other's papers and comment. In other cases, teachers provide occasional training sessions with the whole class on how to take part in an effective peer group. In many peer group sessions, students can either bring their own papers and pass them around, or they can bring copies for each member of the group so that other students can read silently and write comments on the copies. In some cases, students read their own papers aloud while others listen; in other cases, a member of the group reads another student's paper aloud. Responding students can provide comments orally after the reading, or they can give written comments to the student who wrote the paper.

A more structured alternative is to provide each group member either with a worksheet for analytic feedback or with a guideline containing options for feedback. In the former case, the students work through the sheet and typically focus on mechanics, grammar, and word choice, as well as on the coherence of the main argument. Guidelines with options for feedback may include sets of questions that any member of the group can ask other members; these questions cover organization, planning, the frequency and distribution of main ideas, examples used, good points of the papers, perceived weak points of the paper, introductions, conclusions, etc. Specific sheets for recording student responses may be handed out by the teacher, or students can write out their own feedback based on questions and comments they offer during the group work. Students typically use these sheets in their revisions and attach the feedback from peer group members to the back of the next draft handed in to the teacher. The teacher then sees the work done by the student and the amount and quality of the feedback that other group members provided.

There are a number of composition teachers and researchers who object to the use of explicit guidelines in peer revision. They argue that students often use these guidelines as mechanical check-off sheets rather than as a way to provide meaningful support. It is certainly true that students may be tempted to use guidelines as simple checklists to minimize their roles as commentors. Guidelines also cannot act as a substitute for the teacher or for coaching on how to be an effective responder. At the same time, there is little evidence that peer groups without coaching and response guidelines perform better than groups with guidelines, or even as well as supported peer groups. Teachers and students need to recognize the uses and limitations of guidelines but, used effectively by the teacher, many guidelines offer students useful options for peer responses.

Guidelines for feedback with peer group responses can involve any of the following example formats from sources such as Copeland and Lomax (1988), Elbow (1981), Frank (1979), Leki (1992), Raimes (1992), Reid (1993), Spear (1988), and Tompkins (1990):

1. Writing group response

   Listener's Compliments
   I like the part where ...
   I'd like to know more about ...
   I think your main idea is ...
   You used some powerful words, like ...
   I like the way you described ...
   I like the way you explained ...
   Your writing made me feel ...

   Writer's Questions
   What did you learn from my writing?
   What do you want to know more about?
   What part doesn't make sense?
   Is there a part I should throw away?
   Can you tell what my main idea is?
   Did I use some words I need to change?
   What details can I add?

   Listeners Comments and Suggestions
   What is your favorite part?
   What part are you having trouble with?
   Do you need a closing?
   I got confused in the part about ...
   Could you leave this part out because ...
   Could you add more to this part because ...
   Is this paragraph on one topic?
   Could you combine some sentences?
   What do you plan to do next?

   (Excerpted from Tompkins 1990: 86)

2. Written peer criticism: getting the reader to respond

   Sayback: Ask readers: 'Say back to me in your own words what you hear me getting at in my writing.'

Movies of the Reader's Mind: Get readers to tell you frankly what happens inside their heads as they read your words.

Pointing: Ask readers: 'Which words or phrases stick in your mind? Which passages or features do you like best? Don't explain why.'

What's Almost Said or Implied: Ask readers: 'What's almost said, implied, hovering around the edges? What would you like to hear more about?'

Voice, Point of View, Attitude toward the Reader, Language, Diction, Syntax: Ask readers to describe each of these features or dimensions of your writing.

Center of Gravity: Ask readers: 'What do you sense as the source of energy, the focal point, the seedbed, the generative center for this piece [not necessarily the main point]?'

Believing and Doubting: 'Believe (or pretend to believe) everything I have written. Be my ally and tell me what you see. Give me more ideas and perceptions to help my case. Then doubt everything and tell me what you see. What arguments can be made against what I say?'

(Holt 1992: 385; excerpted from Elbow and Belanoff (1989) Peer Response Exercises)

3. Response questions

What is the main idea that the writer is trying to express in this draft?

Can you find any parts that do not relate to the main idea? Underline them.

Which part of the piece of writing do you like best?

Find two or three places where you would like more explanations, examples, or details. Write questions about them.

Did you at any point lose the flow of the writing or find places where the writer seemed to jump too suddenly from one idea to another? Were there any places that seemed unclear to you as a reader?

Did the beginning capture your attention and make you want to read on? Why or why not?

Can you summarize in one sentence the main idea of each paragraph? For each paragraph, complete the following statement:
Paragraph 1 says that ....
Paragraph 2 says that ....
Proceed in the same way for the remaining paragraphs.

(Raimes 1992: 64)

4. A process model for reading and revising

Read through the draft. Really read it. Understand what the author meant to say. Don't rely on one quick reading. Read it once to get a sense of the piece as a whole, again to look at details like what it says and how it is put together. Don't be too concerned with the exact words. Go underneath them to understand the ideas they represent.

Now take the draft apart. List what you think are the major ideas and state what seems to you to be the author's purpose. (This can be done either orally, going around the group, or in writing, during the class or prior to it.)

Under each major idea, note what the writer does to back it up.

Considering the purpose, the major ideas, and supporting information as you see them, what ideas affect you most strongly? What else might you need to know? What might you do differently? What would you like to hear more about?

Next, compare the outlines and comments prepared by each member of your group. See if the readers are consistent with each other in identifying the purpose, main points, and supporting information. See if their constructions are acceptable to the writer. What does the writer like *and* dislike about his or her draft? What does the writer regard as its strengths *and* weaknesses? If your group has differences of opinion, share them with the writer. Consider especially the additions and changes you were thinking about. Discuss what effects these changes might have and what the writer might do about them. (Remember, writers can't incorporate all suggestions: the idea is to use them to simulate thoughts on specific ways to revise the draft.)

(Spear 1988: 110–11)

5. Reader response worksheets

Worksheet: Reader–Writer Response

1. Writer: What one question would you like your reader to answer, or what one problem did you need a second opinion about?

2. Reader: Answer the question. Be specific. Then complete the following statements:
   a. The best part of this paper was ...
   b. When I finished the essay I thought/felt ...
   c. One place I disagreed was where you said ...
   d. One experience or idea I had that was similar to this was ...

e. When you said ...., I thought about ...

f. One suggestion I want to make to improve this paper is

...

Worksheet: Group Response

1. Reader: Ask the writer: 'How can we help you?'
2. Writer (who comes to class with notes that anticipate the question): Indicate specific areas in which you need help.
3. Reader: Listens and take notes, then offer verbal and written feedback and suggestions.
4. Writer: Listens and takes notes. (S/he retains full authority to evaluate the advice and make the final decisions.)

Worksheet: Descriptive Response

1. The subject/topic of this paper is ...
2. The intended audience for this paper is ...
3. The main ideas of this paper, in order, are ...
4. This essay has .... paragraphs (sentences).
5. This piece of writing is written from the point of view of a person who is .... (Describe the writer/narrator – this may be a persona, not the student herself.)

(Reid 1993: 211–12)

A final type of guideline resource for peer group feedback presents each group member with a long checklist of points to inspect in conjunction with the essay under consideration. This checklist, often improperly used as the only peer feedback mechanism, may play some role in an editing support group. The checklists would cover such topics as:

Topic and thesis
Composition as a whole
Reasoning and evidence
Sentence structure
Paragraph structure
Diction (word choice)
Mechanics and form

(From an example checklist in Spear 1988: 48–50)

Research on peer group approaches presents a complex set of findings. To summarize a few main points noted in previous chapters, Clifford (1981) and Nystrand (1986) provide empirical evidence which suggests that the employment of peer groups improves student writing. At the same time, Flower (1994), George (1984), Harris (1992), and Spear (1988) all point out a lack of improvement, or a variety of problems resulting from the use of peer group approaches.

Despite these mixed results for improved writing quality, various other benefits are claimed for the use of peer group approaches. There are, for example, results across a number of studies which show that peer groups promote collaboration, develop a better sense of audience, improve confidence, help develop a sense of community, lead students to consider alternative strategies, and expose students to a variety of writing styles (Gere 1987, Harris 1992, Nelson and Murphy 1992, Spear 1988). Many of these claims, however, rest on limited empirical support. In a particularly influential study, Freedman (1987) found that students were less satisfied with the results of peer group feedback than were teachers. Teachers, despite being associated with the US National Writing Project, were ambivalent over the benefits of peer group approaches.

The results to date suggest that the success of peer group approaches is heavily dependent on student variables, on the role of teachers, on the institutional goals, and on the classroom context. In research on ESL students, the diversity of student populations, differences in prior instructional socializations, and differing L2 command of English lead to different results for peer group approaches. For example, Carson (1992) notes that EFL students from China and Japan do not respond well to the educational assumptions underlying peer group work. In fact, sociolinguistic and educational expectations create problems for many L2 students (Allaei and Connor 1991, Fathman and Whalley 1990, Leki 1990, 1992, Nelson and Murphy 1992, Stanley 1992).

A somewhat different approach to peer group responses has been suggested recently in research by Flower (1994). In this alternative approach, students are asked to form groups for collaborative *planning*. Using audiotaped sessions, responders encourage the writer to discuss his or her plans, and to develop them so that they address many rhetorical concerns in writing. Student-writers then reflect on the planning session, listen to the taping of the session, and write up a plan for their assignment. The object of these collaborative planning sessions is to raise student awareness of the rhetorical issues that are involved in writing and to develop more appropriate planning strategies for writing. As Flower (1994: 142) states:

Writers are shown how to encourage each other to go beyond infor-
mation-driven plans 'to say' something in order to create rhetorical
plans 'to do' something in writing (1) by focusing on purposes, key
points, audience, and textual conventions, (2) by trying to consolidate these goals, and (3) by reflecting on their thinking. These three
moves reflect the long-term goal of collaborative planning: to help
... students develop strategies for constructive planning and to [help
students] gain more awareness of their own choices.

This approach seeks to move peer-group interaction beyond the
assumption that simple conversational interaction will be beneficial to students; rather, the goal is to promote negotiation of
rhetorical planning for writing. In this respect, Flower draws on
Vygotskean notions of activity in the 'zone of proximal development' and the concepts of task appropriation and the
intersubjective construction of goals (Collins *et al.* 1989, Newman
et al. 1989, Rogoff 1990). Apart from recognizing the importance
of task negotiation and conversational interaction, and the need
for direct guided support in training students, this approach
focuses on students goals and planning before they produce the
text rather than after they have written a first draft. To what extent
the initial results of Flower's (1994) work will be replicated in various contexts remain to be seen. It does, however, suggest an
interesting integration of peer group responses with rhetorical
strategy development and Vygotskean interpretations of learning.

Overall, the strongest conclusion which can be drawn from
current research is that peer group approaches vary in their effectiveness, depending on the extent to which:

- students are persuaded that such approaches will lead to writing
  improvement;
- students are trained to provide peer group feedback effectively;
- students have clear goals and guidelines for peer group work;
  and
- peer group members are held accountable for their feedback.

Peer groups appear to be most effective when students are motivated by the approach, when they are trained carefully to carry
out the group work, when they are given many suggestions and
guidelines for supportive feedback, when they are assisted in giving appropriate feedback, and when the feedback provided by
them is reviewed by the teacher (see, e.g., Elbow and Belanoff
1989, Golub 1988, Holt 1992, Leki 1992, Reid 1993, Spear 1988,

1993, Stanley 1992). The most reasonable position to take with respect to the use of peer groups is that they can be effective; however, they should not be seen as an answer to all of the students' needs (Whitworth 1988).

13.2.2   *Teacher–students responses*

While teacher–student feedback is often seen as a more traditional overall format for feedback, the range of possibilities for feedback are as broad as the variations with peer group feedback. Teacher–student feedback may involve:

- teacher whole-class discussion of major points for revision;
- teacher demonstrations of revisions with specific student essays;
- teacher mini-conferences in class;
- one-on-one conferences away from the class;
- written comments on essay drafts.

Each of these options includes many variations which can be adjusted to meet the needs of particular groups of students. Since they are often treated as distinct issues in responding to student writing, one-on-one conferences outside the class and written comments on drafts will be discussed in the next two section.

Teachers are often able to provide feedback to students not only on their essay drafts but also on their pre-writing and idea-generating activities. Teachers should demonstrate the types of skills that they want students to use, and should make strategies for brainstorming or invention real to students through think-aloud demonstrations. This is often done efficiently in a whole-class context with the teacher writing on an overhead projector and discussing the strategic choices made while brainstorming or composing. As students become more comfortable with the process, they can provide more of the information and text for such cooperative writing as they learn to appropriate the teacher's composing strategies.

The teacher can, in this way, provide feedback on a number of forms of writing that are used in the class. For example, students may be asked to do free writing from time to time. A teacher can demonstrate this by free writing aloud in front of the students. Students and teacher can then discuss some of the strategies used by the teacher and some of the ways that ideas were developed.

Teachers can also provide similar feedback on reaction-writing to readings or other assignments. If students are asked to read a text in front of the class, the teacher may begin the next class by asking students to write a brief (e.g. 15 minute) reaction to the reading or to some aspect of the reading. The teacher can then demonstrate appropriate strategies and techniques for such an activity by composing aloud while writing such a reaction assignment. Again, students and teacher can discuss what students thought they saw and what the teacher was doing. Teachers can also provide feedback on such tasks by reading and discussing the students' response writings, not in terms of their writing mechanics, but in terms of idea generation and missed opportunities for ideas to use.

Another type of teacher feedback can be provided by having students write evaluations of their essay drafts and then discussing these evaluations. This type of discussion can also lead the teacher into mini-lessons on such issues as controlling the topic, rethinking the organization of a paper, considering more carefully who the readers might be and what they expect as readers, etc. In this way, topics and issues in writing and rhetorical planning can be addressed within the context of the students' own interests and concerns rather than as decontextualized lessons.

Teacher feedback with the whole class can also involve the use of specific students' essays or essay excerpts (see also Chapter 12). The use of student writing, while requiring care and sensitivity to students' feelings, offers many options for teacher feedback. Examining students' writing can lead to discussions of certain problems that a number of students share in their writing. The teacher can bring in a number of similar excerpts that indicate a common problem and the class can discuss these problems together. For example, many students may not be using clear extended illustrations of complex ideas, and thus, their writing may require too much inferencing on the part of the reader. Students and the teacher can then work with a few excerpts from students' writing to develop strategies for generating clear and vivid examples.

A second major form of teacher feedback on students' writing occurs when the teacher works with one volunteer student's essay. This procedure has a number of benefits: the individual student receives feedback from the entire class; the teacher can give multiple readings and reader responses to the paper for the entire class to see and hear (e.g. a descriptive response, a personal response, an evaluative response), and the teacher can demonstrate a variety of feedback guidelines/issues and a set of appropriate strategies for revising. If this activity is done in a constructive way, other students may be willing to volunteer their papers for future sessions.

Teacher feedback can also be provided by engaging students in language awareness activities that are based on students' writings. These activities could include scrambling sentences in student essays to highlight cohesion devices, removing paragraph boundaries to determine useful logical breaks (and problems in trying to find them), looking for attitudinal and affective signals in student texts and discussing their effectiveness, highlighting opinion and argument markers and noting their relative effectiveness (see, e.g., White and Arndt 1991).

Finally, teachers often have opportunities for brief conferences with individual students in class while the rest of the students are involved in group work, generating ideas with pre-writing, writing first drafts, or carrying out other tasks or projects. These mini-conferences should last no more than 5–10 minutes and should involve feedback on a specific piece of writing by the student, or feedback on a writing journal or portfolio. The mini-conference should always balance critiques with positive commentary on some aspect of student writing. These brief conferences should conclude with the student stating what he or she will do next. Teachers should keep a record of mini-conferences and note the important points covered.

13.2.3 Conferencing outside of class

Conferencing with students either in a one-on-one situation or with a small group represents another major innovation in writing practice over the past 15 years. (This technique assumes that students and teachers are also meeting for regularly scheduled classes.) In typical conferences, a few students meet with the teacher for 15–30 minutes and discuss writing progress being made by those students. A conference can review previous writing in a portfolio, review the current draft of an essay assignment, or explore ways of improving specific aspects of class performance (practising peer responding, new strategies for planning, strategies for content generation and elaboration, or reviewing a self-assessment form for student progress in writing, etc.)

Research on the impact of conferencing on student writing is not extensive. While there are many accounts of case studies by teachers who discuss their use of conferences, there is as yet little empirical evidence which examines the role of conferences in student writing (cf. Calkins 1986, Graves 1983). Carefully controlled research on writing conferences focuses on two issues: the evaluations of teachers and students after conferences, and the nature of teacher–student interaction in sets of teacher–student conferences. Results of teacher and student evaluations support the notion that students receive more focused and comprehensible feedback during conferences than they do through written feedback (Carnicelli 1980, Sokmen 1988, Zamel 1985, Zhu 1994). Research on the nature of teacher–student interaction reveals that conferences can vary considerably in the extent to which they are helpful in improving student writing. Evidence suggests that conferences in which students participate actively *and* negotiate meaning (confirmation checks, clarification requests, revision confirmations, revision queries, etc.) are more effective than those in which students are passive recipients of teacher comments (Goldstein and Conrad 1990). The research on negotiation in writing conferences suggests that conferences must be well planned, and that both teacher and student must be prepared to negotiate aspects of the student's writing (Freedman and Sperling 1985, Walker and Elias 1987).

Conferences with students have certain obvious advantages and disadvantages. The teacher is able to work with students intensively, on a one-on-one basis or in small groups, and the teacher gets to know the students better on a personal level. Students have a more informal atmosphere in which to ask questions without embarrassment, and are able to receive more immediate and more elaborate feedback than they would through exclusively written comments. The teacher and students can work carefully and thoroughly through important strategies for improving student performance at all stages of the writing process and students are better motivated by the personal attention received. The teacher can help the students to establish clear and efficient goals for writing assignments and for overall writing improvement. The major disadvantages for the teacher are the much greater demands on time and the need to become skilled as an interactive negotiator. One way to lessen the disadvantages is to have students prepare a guideline which specifies certain objectives – changing for each round of meetings – for the conference ahead of time.

This format keeps the conference on task and may reduce the time needed for each meeting.

Conferences are typically described as following certain common sequences. Reid (1993), for example, describes the stages of a typical conference as follows:

Openings
Student-initiated comments
Teacher-initiated comments
Reading of the paper
Closings.

Reid also strongly recommends the use of conference planning worksheets which should vary according to the overriding goals of each particular conference. She provides specific examples of conference worksheets for initial planning, essay drafting, and revision planning; for example, the following is a revision planning guideline:

Revision Planning Conference

1. I thought the best part of my essay was ....

2. I thought the weakest part of my essay was ....

3. According to your [i.e. the instructor's] comments, the strengths and problems in the essay draft are as follows:

   STRENGTHS   PROBLEMS
   a. ....   a. ....
   b. ....   b. ....
   c. ....   c. ....

4. Based on the feedback, here is my plan for revising this essay (list specific steps you intend to take and specific paragraphs you intend to revise):
   a. ....
   b. ....
   c. ....

5. Three questions I want to ask you [i.e. the instructor] are:
   a. ....
   b. ....
   c. ....

(Reid 1993: 222–3)

In addition, Reid (1993: 222–3) offers a set of metacognitive questions/statements that students should draw on for any conference session. She also suggests that conferences should end with *students committing to 1 or 2 most important changes to make* so that they can form an immediate plan of action. Similar conference guidelines are provided by Taylor (1993), Tompkins (1990), and White and Arndt (1991).

Overall, the use of conferences is well supported by logical arguments, observations of teachers and researchers, and a small set of empirical studies. The conferencing approach can be applied flexibly to address pre-writing, drafting, revising, editing, and assessment issues in student writing (Tompkins 1990). From a research perspective, much additional work is needed to examine the impact of various formats and aspects of writing conferences. Until the results of such additional research becomes available, it would seem prudent to use writing conferences as one effective support for writing development, but not to expect it to be a panacea for improving student writing.

13.2.4 *Responding in writing*

A common format for responding to student writing is through written comments on drafts and final versions of student papers. Comments can be offered at any point in the writing process from planning, to initial drafting, to revisions, to final text. Teachers can also respond in writing to other shorter tasks such as free writings, journal entries, reaction assignments, and post-essay evaluations written by students. Not only does a teacher have access at many points to offer written response to student writing, but there are also a number of approaches and formats that a teacher can adopt while responding. The most common choices include descriptive written commentary (what the teacher thought while reading the essay), comments for revising major content and organization of the essay, and prose-editing responses on major editorial weaknesses.

While a number of researchers and practitioners feel that written commentary may be the least effective form of feedback for students, there is also persuasive counter-evidence to suggest that written commentary is a viable and effective approach when used appropriately (Fathman and Whalley 1990, Ferris 1995). Rather than make sweeping claims for or against written commentary, our goal is to understand the ways in which such feedback can be used effectively. One of the primary problems commonly noted with written feedback is that teacher comments are often vague, confusing, and provide little specific direction for students when they attempt revision. At the other extreme, teachers sometimes provide students with detailed editing comment on the surface form with minimal attention to major organizational and content issues. The idea is to find the middle road between these extremes.

Good responses to student writing work in much the same way as effective peer group feedback. The teacher should find some positive things to say about any essay, raise a number of specific questions which will allow students to carry out revisions, make suggestions for changing the organization or elaborating parts of the essay, and provide a small set of concrete suggestions for improving the structural and mechanical aspects of the text. Teacher feedback can be given on the student's draft, in a response note attached to the text, or on a tape cassette. Editorial comments should be presented clearly, whether as prose comments or as symbol notation (though there are drawbacks to the use of symbol notation). One effective preparation for teacher response is to have students mark and comment on sections of their texts before handing them in: this serves as a useful self-evaluation mechanism and alerts the teacher to problems and concerns experienced by the students.

Comments on a text should avoid exclusive attention to surface conventions (e.g. spelling, punctuation, paragraphing, hyphenation), and should also avoid vacuous commentary or notation (e.g. AWK). Comments should not overwhelm the students with a sense of failure (i.e. by noting absolutely every flaw), but should offer positive support (by praising what is genuinely good), ask what is meant at points where ambiguities occur (rather than putting words in their mouths), and address organizational issues by suggesting options rather than dictating solutions.

Specific guidelines and worksheets for teacher feedback on student writing should be used cautiously. Without careful use, they can be impersonal and intimidating. Training should accompany the use of such analytic guidelines so that students can take concrete steps for revision based upon such worksheets. Such guidelines are often used in final editing stages and for assessment feedback; however, such guides can also be used for informal teacher response without grading. Guidelines of this type are discussed in Hughey *et al.* (1983), Reid (1993), and Tompkins (1990).

13.2.5 *Other audiences*

Peer students and the teacher are not the only potential sources of feedback. Students should be encouraged to seek out other audiences and responders. Students can, for example, give papers to colleagues for feedback. The goal of this activity is to receive supportive feedback from additional audiences; and the additional readers should not engage in extensive editing and rewriting of the student's paper. An obvious concern is that other readers try to rewrite the essay, and the essay no longer represents the student's ability. Getting feedback from additional readers constitutes an appropriate part of the writing process for many advanced writers, and all students should be encouraged to view such opportunities similarly.

Students should also make use of writing centres and writing labs where those entities are available. Tutors in these centres can provide a distinct and honest reader interpretation, and they are able to provide useful assistance for revisions. Occasionally, tutors are available to individual students through class cooperation or learning-assistance centres; these teacher-in-training tutors are earning credit for teacher preparation programmes and often need tutoring experience. These tutors provide another audience resource for student writers which should be used whenever possible.

Outside readers can provide much the same type of responses as peers and teachers. Teachers should work with writing tutors and suggest ways for tutors to provide effective feedback. Teachers can provide tutors with various guidelines and options for feedback by showing them worksheets, response forms, suggestions for appropriate interactional negotiations, and various activities which focus on specific writing issues.

13.3   Writing assessment

Writing assessment involves both teacher responses and more formal mechanisms for student evaluation. The most common mechanisms involve grading of various types, though evaluation of writing does not necessarily require grading. Discussions of writing assessment typically occur in two contexts: the classroom context and the standardized testing context. The former context usually involves achievement assessment (both formative and summative) while the latter involves proficiency assessment. In the classroom context, any given assessment can be formative (emphasis on the process) or summative (emphasis on the product). Classroom assessment can also be used for diagnostic purposes and placement purposes, though this rarely happens. In contrast, standardized assessment is primarily used to make proficiency judgements (and, at times, placement decisions). It is often not a sufficiently fine-tuned tool for achievement testing in specific classroom contexts, nor is it typically useful for diagnosing student difficulties.

While it is possible to view responses to student writing and writing assessment along a continuum of formality, this chapter treats the two somewhat independently. Such an approach does not deny the similarities between responding to writing and more formal assessment, but it does recognize that certain issues in writing assessment are distinct from issues that are central to feedback on student writing. In this section, indirect, direct, and portfolio assessment will be discussed. To the extent that these categories include standardized assessment and in-class assessment contexts, both will be discussed under each main subheading.

13.3.1   Indirect writing assessment

Indirect writing assessment, typically multiple-choice measures that test students' grammar, vocabulary, and written expression knowledge, is largely limited to standardized writing assessment, i.e. any assessment situation which is not classroom centred and involves groups larger than the single classroom in a common assessment approach. Until 40 or 50 years ago, standardized assessment of writing was carried out by experts – the individual teachers and groups of teachers who subjectively assessed student writing on admission and placement writing samples. With increasing university enrolments, and a greater demand for accountability in terms of reliability, psychometricians argued for, and developed, indirect writing assessments (Camp 1993, Perkins 1983, White 1993).

The fundamental commonality across the large majority of indirect measures results from their attempts to assess writing ability by testing a subset of skills assumed to constitute components of writing ability. In most cases, this subset consists of vocabulary, sentence grammar, and points of writing usage. Most of these measures were developed during the 1950s and 1960s – the heyday of discrete-point testing and of psychometric priorities favouring reliability over other testing concerns. A number of these indirect measures continue in use today, though many of these are being retired in favour of direct measures of writing ability.

While now generally out of favour, these tests did establish two benchmarks for which all current assessment efforts must account: statistical reliability and some measure of validity. There is no question that indirect measures produced a strong reliability statistic when the tests were carefully developed. The effort to establish validity with indirect measures centred primarily around the concepts of predictive validity and concurrent validity. Indirect measures of writing, when designed carefully, did, to some extent, predict success in later academic work. Further, indirect measures exhibited high correlations with direct measures of writing and, therefore, were assumed to be accounting for much of what direct assessments measured (Breland *et al.* 1987, Camp 1993, Carlson *et al.* 1985, Perkins 1983, Stansfield 1986). The fundamental problem with these arguments is that writing assessment now gives much greater weight to content validity and construct validity, two issues which indirect measures cannot easily address.

Among the well-known instruments employing indirect measures were two early University of Michigan tests. Early versions of the Michigan English Language Assessment Battery (MELAB) for English L2 writers included a multiple-choice writing component. Similarly, the University of Michigan composition placement examination (for English L1 writers), in early versions, included multiple-choice questions. The Michigan Composition Board placement examination, required of all entering freshmen, consists now, and has for some time consisted, only of a direct writing sample holistically scored.

A second source of indirect writing assessment is the Test of Standard Written English (TSWE) for English L1 writers. Developed by the Educational Testing Service (ETS), it originated as a companion to the Scholastic Aptitude Test (SAT), the most basic and common pre-university assessment measure in the USA.

The TSWE is a 30-minute multiple-choice test consisting of 50 items. Two types of questions appear on the test: written usage questions, and questions on sentence grammar (Perkins 1983). Among native English-speaking populations, it has high reliability and some degree of predictive validity as well as concurrent validity with direct writing samples.

A third common indirect measure of writing ability is represented by section 2 of the Test of English as a Foreign Language (TOEFL). This section consists of 40 items to be completed in 25 minutes. The section comprises two types of questions: sentence grammar and written expression (usage). The section is highly reliable, and correlates well with holistic measures of writing samples (Carlson *et al.* 1985, DeMauro 1992). Despite high correlations, however, DeMauro (1992) expressly states that the TOEFL section 2 and the Test of Written English (TWE; see below), a direct measure of writing ability, are not parallel statistically.

There are a number of other indirect measures of writing ability that are noted from time to time. Best known among these are the Test of Ability to Subordinate (TAS) for English L1 writers, and the Michigan Test of English Language Proficiency (MTELP) for English L2 writers. The TAS is a 50-item sentence-combining test which appears to have some predictive and concurrent validity, but there is minimal documentation (Mullen 1987). The MTELP does not specifically include a measure of writing ability. It is, however, inappropriately used from time to time as a measure of concurrent validity. It should not be considered as either a valid or reliable indirect measure of writing ability.

Indirect measures of a different kind have been occasionally discussed as potential measures of writing ability. In particular, cloze tests, when properly designed and appropriately used, have demonstrated a high correlation with direct writing measures. For example, Fotos (1991) argued that cloze tests correlated strongly with essay writing for a population of English L2 university students in Japan. Similarly, Hanania and Shikhani (1986) argued that cloze tests and writing samples are both good measures of higher-order language abilities. In both cases, however, the authors refrained from proposing cloze tests as direct substitutes for essay texts; rather, they suggested that both essay tests and cloze tests are good integrative measures of overall language proficiency at advanced levels. It remains to be seen whether these relationships will be treated in greater depths in future research.

For the moment, the use of cloze testing is best viewed as a useful supplement to essay writing, providing a more effective overall measure of language ability (see also Jonz 1990, Oller 1983, Oller and Jonz 1994).

The use of standardized indirect measures of writing ability has decreased markedly in the past ten years, and indirect measures are not likely to regain popularity at any time in the near future (cf. White 1995). The increasing emphasis on construct and content validity – whether the test reflects what research understands writing to be, and what is normally covered by writing practices – will push future writing assessment further towards direct assessment approaches. Past concerns with the reliability of holistic scoring in direct writing assessment no longer represent a threat to direct assessment when such scoring is carried out appropriately. Since there is a strong general sense that good writing tests should involve students producing writing, indirect measures of writing ability are not likely to remain viable options in the foreseeable future.

13.3.2   Direct writing tests

Increasing concerns in testing theory with validity, particularly with content and construct validity, led many researchers to question the ability of indirect writing tests to assess students' writing abilities accurately. Beginning in the 1970s, many assessment measures of writing turned towards the production of controlled student writing samples. While this approach addressed the need for the assessment of a real instance of writing, it also raised a whole host of issues concerning the methods for collecting and evaluating a given writing sample as a true indicator of overall writing ability.

In the past ten years, standardized assessment with direct writing samples has focused research attention in a number of validity issues. In particular, research has focused on improving procedures for obtaining a valid writing sample, one which accounts for, or is at least reflective of, issues such as the impact of audience, task type, topic type, nature of the rater, rater training, assessment rubric for grade assignment, and the types of grading scales used. Many of these issues are also critical in discussions of holistic assessments in classroom contexts, but they take on greater importance in large-scale assessment situations since the consequences of the outcome scores are more serious for the students and for institutions.

In-class contexts for writing assessment, whether limited to a single class or as a school-wide activity, have moved even further from indirect measures than large-scale assessment. This reflects the less constrained environment of classroom-based assessment as well as the greater impact of instructional innovations on assessment approaches. Direct assessment issues will first be addressed in the context of large-scale assessment, followed by direct assessment in the classroom.

13.3.2.1   Standardized direct assessment

Most standardized direct measures of writing ability involve writing on a single topic for a relatively brief time. The essays are then scored holistically by a group of trained raters. In most reliable large-scale assessment environments, all essays are read by two raters and discrepancies are handled through a third reading by a 'head rater'. There is considerable debate concerning the validity and reliability of single-item essay writing samples and their holistic scoring procedures. This debate will be addressed briefly at the end of this section.

One of the largest direct measures of writing ability is the recently developed Test of Written English (TWE); TWE volume has exceeded a quarter of a million candidates per year for the last five years (ETS 1992, Test of Written English Guide 1992). The test is a single-topic essay prompt on which test takers write for 30 minutes. The test has perhaps undergone the most extensive set of validity and reliability studies of any essay-writing measure, and many of the results of these studies have directly contributed to improvements in prompt development, task and topic comparison, time for writing, essay rater training, and essay scoring (Carlson *et al.* 1985, Golub-Smith *et al.* 1993, Hale 1992, Henning 1992, Stansfield 1986, Stansfield and Ross 1988).

A commonly used British examination with a holistically scored writing sample is the International English Language Testing System (IELTS) examination, a joint product of The British Council and the University of Cambridge Local Examination Syndicate (UCLES). This test is representative of direct writing assessment on a number of British examinations for English L2 subjects (e.g. University of Cambridge Local Examination Syndicate examinations, Royal Society of Arts examinations, University of Oxford

Delegacy of Local Examinations; see reviews in Alderson *et al.* 1987). In the IELTS test, students write on essay prompts which reflect either 'academic writing' or 'general training writing' (as described in 1995 IELTS Handbook). In the earlier (ELTS) version, test takers wrote a single essay; in the revised International English Language Testing System (IELTS), test takers write two essays. In earlier tests, test takers were given subject-area options; most recent versions have dropped the subject-area options in favour of a choice between academic or general writing (cf. Alderson 1993b).

In almost all cases of British tests that include a component for L2 writer proficiency, there is a greater emphasis on communicative language use and expert judgement in test development and less emphasis on psychometric concerns for quantitative reliability and validity specifications (Alderson 1987, Alderson and Buck 1993). For test users with an orientation towards statistical reliability, this difference is unfortunate, since many of the tests developed in the UK include innovative test-taking options and interesting prompts. If future efforts are made to address issues of validity and reliability (e.g. further development of the IELTS), these tests would likely receive even wider acceptance as options for large-scale writing assessment.

Large-scale writing assessment also takes place in many other countries, providing measures of writing abilities for both English L1 and English L2 students (see also Blok and De Glopper 1992). For example, The Australian Second Language Proficiency Ratings (ASLPR) is a major exam in Australia for English language proficiency which includes an essay examination (Ingram 1990, Ingram and Wylie 1984). A major examination in Hong Kong is the Hong Kong Certificate of Education Examination (HKCEE). Annually, in Hong Kong, 150,000 16–18-year-old students take this examination as a qualification for tertiary-level admissions and for many employment opportunities (Milanovic 1987).

In Australia, the responsibility for language curricula and assessment rests with the individual states, and different states have experimented with different solutions to the assessment issue. At the same time, research is being carried on through the National Languages and Literacy Institute of Australia (NLLIA), headquartered in Canberra but supporting specialist centres in various parts of the country. Important work in various contexts of language assessment is being undertaken at the Centre for

Applied Linguistics and Languages at Griffith University in Brisbane, at Macquarie University in Sydney, at the University of Melbourne, and at Monash University.

In New Zealand, the process is centralized; the Ministry of Education is in the process of developing a revised National Curriculum in which English and other language instruction is central. At the same time, the New Zealand Qualifications Authority, separate from the Ministry but working cooperatively with it, is developing appropriate assessment instruments. In both instances, developments are of such recent date that very little information is readily available in published form.

In the USA, major English L1 testing efforts that have devoted considerable attention to reliability and validity include certain US universities and university systems. Two exemplary programmes are the Michigan Composition Board and the California State University Composition Board. The University of Michigan Composition Board, begun in 1979, assesses the writing abilities of all incoming undergraduates to the university (approximately 6000 per year). Students write a 50-minute essay and, based on the results, are placed in one of three levels of the writing programme. More recent versions of this test have employed multiple-trait scoring procedures, and these changes have been seen as successful (Hamp-Lyons and Condon 1993).

The California State University English Composition Board administers a 2-hour writing test that consists of two objective measures and a writing sample. The writing sample consists of a single essay prompt, and students are allowed 40 minutes to write a response. The writing samples are sent from the 20 campuses of the California State College and University System to a central scoring location, and beginners are placed in the English writing programmes on each of the various campuses based on these results. Prompt designs and scoring procedures are carefully controlled, and the test achieves high reliability measures (Greenberg 1988).

A different type of large-scale assessment approach is carried out in the USA by the National Assessment of Educational Progress (NAEP) programme for writing assessment (Applebee *et al.* 1986, 1990a, 1990b). This US-based programme (housed at ETS in Princeton) is funded by the federal government to monitor changes in educational progress across the range of student groups in elementary and secondary education contexts. Since its inception in 1969, the NAEP has carried out five national assessments (1969–70, 1973–74, 1978–79, 1983–84, and 1987–88). Over these five assessments, randomly sampled groups of students write on one to four writing prompts (out of 12 options) ranging across informative, persuasive, and personal/narrative tasks. Students participating in the NAEP receive a booklet and are given one hour to complete a set of background questions and a set of brief reading and writing tasks. The most recent NAEP assessment, in 1992, has expanded the time allotted; students are now given more time to respond to writing prompts (25- and 50-minute periods) (Gentile 1992). Overall, more than 1,300,000 elementary and secondary students have participated in the programme over the past 25 years. Based on the results, the NAEP provides reports which extrapolate from the sample to statements about the progress that US students make in writing development.

These writing samples are scored though a primary trait rating procedure, scoring each writing on the extent to which it carries out the task. Prompts are reviewed for bias and validity criteria, and the reliability measures are high (most in the 0.87 to 0.95 range). While there are serious criticisms of this programme in terms of testing design and procedures used, it does produce a large volume of data for assessing writing, for developing scoring procedures, and for interpreting the results. Moreover, many of the criticisms of the NAEP programme are no different from recent criticisms addressed to most large-scale direct assessment single-item approaches. (Other large-scale assessment programmes at Educational Testing Service (USA) which involve writing samples include the Advanced Placement (AP) testing programme for high school students and the General Education Development (GED) programme which awards equivalency for high school graduation.)

A final major international effort to understand writing development across a range of countries has used direct writing samples; carried out by the International Association for the Evaluation of Educational Achievement (IEA), the project is known as the IEA Study of Written Composition (carried out primarily in 1982–83). The testing design for the project required students at three different grade levels in 14 different countries to write on eight different writing prompts, ranging across pragmatic tasks (bicycle description, letter of advice) and essay-type tasks (persuasive essay, narrative essay). The prompts were extensively reviewed and piloted by an international review board, and the study developed strong criteria for validity and reliability of scoring. Results of this research have appeared in various places, though most are not easily accessible (Degenhart 1987, Gorman *et al.* 1988, Purves 1984, 1988, Purves *et al.* 1984, Vahapassi 1988).

13.3.2.2   Scoring approaches

There are a number of approaches to grading writing samples in large-scale assessment. The most commonly used type of scoring is a holistic score representing the overall quality of the writing. Other types of scoring include primary-trait scores and combined multiple-trait scores. Writing assessment in classroom contexts might alternatively include analytic scales and non-quantitative assessment. These latter two options will be discussed in a later section.

Holistic rating is the most common form of scoring for large-scale writing assessment, though in-class writing assessment can also use this approach. Its popularity is a direct reaction to the use of multiple-choice writing measures (Perkins 1983, White 1993). Holistic scoring is achieved by reading a text and deciding on a general, and subjective, score based on a numerical scale ranging anywhere from 1–4 to 1–9. The numbers on the scale are often described briefly as specifications on a scoring rubric (see, e.g., Test of Written English Guide 1992). When holistic scores are used, efforts should be made to socialize a rater to the ways other raters assign grades and their rationales for doing so. This 'anchoring' constitutes an important support for generating consistently reliable scoring (White 1994, 1995).

Primary-trait scoring is a grading scheme that is not so commonly used in either in-class or large-scale writing assessments (except in experimental studies). The use of primary-trait scoring is not a very economical approach since primary-trait guidelines should be rewritten for every writing task (White 1993). Because the goal is to match the salient characteristics of the task requirement to the primary trait that is evaluated, it is necessary to assess beforehand the potential of the task to highlight fairly that trait in the students' writing. Questionable validity is a further problem with primary-trait scoring. As Hamp-Lyons (1991c) argues, it is seldom the case that raters of essays rely on the visibility of single traits in an essay to arrive at the score. In observed studies of essay rating, it is apparent that raters rely on multiple traits as they are high-lighted at various points in the students' essays (see also Perkins 1983, White 1993). For this reason, primary-trait scoring is not a preferred option for student writing assessment.

The one well-known consistent use of primary-trait scoring with large-scale assessment is its use in the US NAEP testing. Writing assignments are designed to reflect specific tasks that students must carry out. Students are rated as successfully completing a persuasive task, a story-telling task, or a letter-writing task. Scoring is designed specifically to reflect success in carrying out the task (Applebee *et al.* 1990a, 1990b).

The use of *multiple-trait scores* is seen as a preferred option for writing assessment that requires more refined profiles of student writers, and it is particularly useful for diagnostic purposes if the scoring instrument is designed and used appropriately (Hamp-Lyons 1991c). In multiple-trait scoring, a rubric is designed which allows the rater to consider a number of aspects of the essay; some rubrics may be more general in nature and some may be designed more specifically (e.g. a general rubric might require a holistic score for accuracy, one for overall coherence, one for content, etc.).

The potential danger with multiple-trait scoring lies in the fact that it is difficult to design and use rubrics appropriately. In cases in which multiple trait scoring has been used without careful scor-ing rubrics, there are serious questions about the validity and reliability of results (e.g. Canale *et al.* 1988, Cumming 1990a, Hamp-Lyons and Henning 1991). Raters have difficulty in scoring student essays along independent dimensions in a reliable man-ner if they do not have clearly defined rubrics to support their rating. While this issue is more a matter of concern for research and for large-scale assessment, it nevertheless suggests caution when providing weakly detailed and specified multiple holistic scores on in-class student essays (such as for accuracy, style, and content).

13.3.2.3 Performance assessment

Performance assessment is often referred to as a type of testing procedure which stresses authentic and direct measures of abili-ties. It is also typically associated with complex problems, higher

order skills, context sensitive strategies, and student choice (see
Baker *et al.* 1993, Messick 1994 for current overviews). In many
contexts, such as science learning, engineering, or architecture
certification, performance assessment may be carried out in a
number of different ways.

For writing, this type of assessment has been discussed in two
contexts: in classroom and institutional assessments (including
portfolios; e.g. Dunbar *et al.* 1991, Faigley *et al.* 1985), and in
national assessment by the National Assessment of Educational
Progress programme. In both of these contexts, performance
assessment employs a variation on primary- and multiple-trait
scoring approaches in that it is designed to assess a specific type of
writing ability for a specific purpose or set of purposes rather than
to assess general writing proficiency (Faigley *et al.* 1985). The distinct specification arises from a carefully designed prompt which
determines the type of writing to be evaluated. It is like a primary-
trait assessment in that one specific facet is being assessed; the
difference is that the specific facet is not a measurement criterion
(e.g. coherence) but the type of writing that is to be assessed. For
example, a performance assessment would have students write a
classification paper, and assessment might focus specifically on the
extent to which the paper meets the demands of the rhetorical situation, establishes appropriate categories for classification, and
classifies items in these categories. (A primary-trait score, on the
other hand, would only measure the extent to which the overall
task was carried out.)

Performance assessment is most likely to be carried out using a
carefully constructed multiple-trait scoring rubric, one which
addresses specific aspects of the writing and which should be
appropriate for placement and diagnosis. Such a scoring
approach may not be very useful in most large-scale assessment
programmes, but it is likely to have potential in institutional-level
testing such as in a university placement programme for subsequent writing instruction. Efforts to develop performance
assessment for different purposes are discussed in Allaei and
Connor (1991), Baker *et al.* (1993), Faigley *et al.* (1985).

13.3.2.4   Classroom-based direct assessment

Students' in-class writing abilities are determined almost entirely
on assessments of student writing samples. However, classroom

contexts for direct assessment is primarily concerned with providing the student with evaluative feedback of some kind which should lead to improved performance. If class assessment is not used in this way, its primary function as a learning tool is being missed. There are a number of specific ways that in-class writing assessment can be carried out, and a number of options for assessment exist which can be matched to student, teacher, and institutional goals.

In-class assessment, for example, can be based on a single writing task, a series of related writing tasks, a long-term writing project, or a writing portfolio. Assessment can be ongoing or final; it can be based on in-class writing or out-of-class writing; it can be focused on formal, rhetorical, or content aspects of the writing; and it can be focused on writing as an independent language skill or integrated with other language tasks (primarily reading). Assessment can be carried out via a conference, a negotiated contract, a specific written sample, or an ongoing record of teacher observations. Assessment can be based on teacher evaluation, student self-evaluations, or a negotiation between the two. Finally, assessment in class can be oriented towards mastery of certain skills and strategies (process and criterion-referenced) or towards student performance compared with other student performances (norm-referenced). Grading can be based on a holistic score or on a set of analytic scales which reflect course emphases. Accordingly, teachers and institutions have numerous options for carrying out appropriate assessment of student writing.

The most traditional formats for writing assessment (typically summative) often involve a single essay based on a relatively simple prompt and administered over a relatively limited time. Such measures of student writing for in-class contexts are now considered, by themselves, to be of questionable validity. A second, more acceptable, option resulting in a single essay involves a longer period of time preparing students to develop a given topic, and then giving students more time, and multiple-writing sessions, for the essay itself. For example, a common format uses the last week of a semester to introduce students to a topic, to discuss a set of readings, and to develop a topic through pre-writing activities, discussions, and information drawn from the reading material. After a week's study of the topic, students are given a prompt and allowed one to two hours to write a rough draft. The next day, students return to revise for an hour. While this format still preserves the single essay evaluation format, it does allow the students to engage in the writing process while preparing for the final essay, and it gives students adequate time and resources to write to the best of their capabilities under time constraints.

The latter option, an extended period of class time for writing evaluation purposes, is more consistent with current instructional practices. Teachers spend much time convincing students that good writing involves pre-writing, brainstorming, planning, and revising. It is important that summative writing evaluation be consistent with the ongoing instruction. Having students work through the various writing processes as part of the evaluation preparation is one reasonable option for maintaining similar goals across instruction and assessment.

Ongoing (formative) assessment of essays written out of class – as the result of multiple drafting, feedback, and revision – represents a different, though still traditional, context for evaluation, one which is more compatible with the practices of a writing class than is an in-class time-constrained evaluation. In this case, both ongoing and final evaluations of student writing are based on assessments of the final versions of a set of essay assignments written throughout the course. A variation on this collective assessment option lies in including other types of writing in the evaluation: summaries of readings, critical reviews, reaction papers, etc., as additional evidence of writing development and improvement.

A third writing assessment option lies in having students write a series of shorter assignments during the final week of a course and then deriving an assessment over the combined performance on all of the writing tasks. These tasks might include a reading and writing summary, a position paper, a written self-assessment, and a synthesis of a first reading with a second reading. The advantage of such an approach is that the assessment is not dependent on a single writing sample or a single genre/task type. The disadvantages include the development of appropriate multiple prompts, the possibility of student (and teacher) fatigue, and a more complex weighting of grades for the various writing samples.

In all of these cases, assessment procedures must consider the development of appropriate and engaging prompts for writing, specific tasks which allow students to perform to the best of their abilities, evaluation schemes which are fair and readily interpretable, and constructive feedback based on the evaluation.

Recent research would suggest that the matter of appropriate prompts, tasks, and evaluation schemes is not simple. Hamp-Lyons (1991b) and Horowitz (1991), for example, argue that different writing prompts are likely to produce different results, as are different writing tasks. For this reason, Horowitz suggests that prompts and tasks for evaluation be situated in topics that are familiar to students and also be appropriate to the students' specific fields of study (see also Kroll and Reid 1994, Reid and Kroll 1995).

13.3.2.5 Assessment options in classroom contexts

Classroom contexts for writing assessment open up a number of scoring options which are not used in large-scale assessments. In addition to a relatively easier adaptation of performance assessment and portfolio assessment (see below), classroom contexts also permit the effective use of analytic rating scales, non-quantitative assessment, and alternative assessment.

Analytic scale rating has been, and remains, a popular way to assign a grade to students' writing and to provide feedback on specific aspects of the writing. The best of these analytic rubrics is that developed by Diederich (1974), though with most analytic scales there are validity problems (Faigley *et al.* 1985, White 1993). Without clear specifications for grades given with each scale, it is not entirely clear whether the scales provide appropriate feedback or genuinely represent students' writing abilities. For example, a decision to give a grade of 80 per cent on a scale of vocabulary use may not provide either reliable or usable information for students (Hamp-Lyons 1991c). Nevertheless, such analytic scales for assessment are common (see examples in Fagan *et al.* 1985, Reid 1993).

One of the earliest and best-known scoring guides of this type for ESL is that developed by Jacobs *et al.* (1981; see also Hughey *et al.* 1983). Unlike the more typical analytic scales noted above, these scales are well supported by content and construct validity, they have been field tested, and they are designed specifically for classroom use rather than for large-scale assessment. They remain among the most popular analytic guidelines for L2 writing use; moreover, because of their specificity, they are also useful for in-class multiple-trait scoring procedures.

Non-quantitative assessment of student writing is an option that some teachers adopt because they do not feel the numerical

scoring of student writing provides a useful mechanism for feedback to students. Further, some teachers do not feel that such
scoring focuses the student's attention on the writing itself. A non-
quantitative orientation would focus on recommendations for
further changes to the student essays, and teacher assessment
would be in the form of prose responses to the essays. These
responses would highlight strong and weak points of the essays,
suggest areas in which the student could extend the writing, and
even indicate ways that the teacher might have written about the
same assignment. Non-quantitative assessment would also ask the
student to write reflective responses on the experience of writing
the essay, including the following:

- a review of the process
- particular problems that were difficult to resolve
- strong points of the writing
- other information that might have been included, and
- two or three points that will receive more attention during the
  next writing task.

Alternative approaches to writing assessment suggest relatively
uncommon options for assessing student performance that
extend to the writing process for a specific essay. All of the grading
approaches discussed above provide evaluative feedback at some
designated end-point (the product) in the student writing process
(Calfee 1992, Hiebert and Calfee 1992). Alternative assessment
approaches do not always have such a rigidly fixed evaluation
point (Pierce and O'Malley 1992).

One alternative that is becoming more common is the use of an
assessment conference. In this situation, student–teacher conferences
are set up to assess students' progress, to plan future goals for writing, to examine and assess a particular writing task or set of tasks,
and/or to discuss problems and strong points that have been
observed in the student's writing. This approach can also incorporate the notion of negotiated assessment. In this case, the student
and the teacher negotiate the assessment to be recorded for the
student's work, as well as plan future goals and decide how the
new goals should be assessed. The use of conferences for assessment purposes gives students some degree of ownership and
responsibility over the assessment process; it also allows for students' insights into the assessment process and permits them to
reflect on course goals and individual progress. This approach

may, however, be inappropriate for teachers who have reservations about students participating in their own assessment.

If assessment conferences are used, the goals should be set before the conference begins. Students should assemble relevant writing material and records of performance in the class. A guideline written by the teacher on assessment conference expectations may be useful to students; a form on which students list relevant material and writing assignments to be discussed during the conference is also a way to focus students and have well organized conferences. Students' letters of agreement and understanding also constitute useful follow-up to the conference.

A somewhat different version of student involvement in assessment occurs through the use of *self-assessment procedures*. Under this option, teachers ask students to work through a guideline form that asks the student to account for the work he or she has done to date. On such a form, each student reviews: his or her recent written work; his or her accomplishments in the class; strong performances or improvements that he or she wishes to claim as accomplishments; weaknesses that still give problems; and one or two areas that will represent further improvement if these areas are addressed appropriately in future work. Self-assessment procedures can also be used for specific essay assignments (Spandel and Stiggins 1990, White 1994). Students are asked to reflect on an essay recently completed, pointing out the strong and weak points of the essay and of the writing process. In this process, students should also point out their improvements reflected in this task over previous writing assignments. Based on this self-analysis, students assign themselves a grade for the essay. The teacher then tells the students how the teacher would evaluate the assignment in terms of improvement and grade. This pair of assessments can then be used to negotiate a grade and an agreed-upon report of student progress in the class. Alternatively, such a process can form only a percentage of the overall grade assigned to a paper.

Still another alternative type of assessment involves both a negotiated assessment and a self-assessment. At the beginning of the course, the teacher outlines possible *assessment contracts* from among which students can choose to fulfil the requirements for the course. Students are free to select different options and even to negotiate minor individual variations. These contracts are then used as the basis for assessing student writing progress during the course of the term. Such contracts will usually stipulate a certain quantity of writing, the types of assignments that will be completed, additional types of writing to be done, writing improvement goals for the student's progress, and the grade to be earned on the basis of a satisfactory completion of the contract. These contracts can also serve as the basis for self-assessment, negotiated assessment, and assessment conferences.

A more teacher-focused form of non-graded assessment is one based on *teacher observation*. Assessment in this format involves ongoing record keeping of teacher observations. Teachers regularly make notes of students' progress, of consistent weaknesses, of growing strengths. Teachers also make notes of students' writing assignments and their salient aspects. Additionally, teachers keep records of informal conferences and discussions with students. These records and observations then form the basis of student writing assessment. They may take the form of a set of grades, but more commonly they occur as written evaluations of student progress, focusing equally on strong points and perceived weaknesses. This approach is well suited for teachers who are obliged to report student progress but who do not put much faith in grades. Teacher observations can also be noted on guideline sheets that assist in principled observation. These sheets should provide space for all of the important concerns that an assessment of student writing might need to consider. Finally, such an ongoing assessment approach can be combined with a number of the other assessment options discussed above, including both conventional and alternative procedures.

A final approach to writing assessment is through *informal assessment*, in some respects a seeming contradiction in terms. Informal assessment involves teacher observation, and it stresses *non-grading discussion and negotiation* with students over their progress. This approach is partly predicated on the very optimistic assumption that students will bring strong self-motivations for working on their writing abilities. This approach is compatible with a curriculum that emphasizes engaging instructional activities and projects – providing a natural avenue for real or realistic writing (e.g. writing and presenting a play or a TV newscast, students reading their writing publicly to student audiences, discussion of various possible student journals and learning logs). It is well suited for whole-language classrooms and other elementary-level curricula which seek to encourage language skills development based on positive and meaningful learning experiences through language. It is perhaps a less viable assessment option for more advanced students and in institutional structures which require some formalized mechanism for student assessment of progress.

13.3.2.6 Problems with direct assessment

In most assessment situations, simpler assumptions about the development of writing tests have been replaced by the recognition of the many variables which are likely to have an impact on student performance: student backgrounds and interests, topics chosen, writing tasks used, prompt wordings, presence of visual resources in the prompt (e.g. tables, diagrams, charts, etc.), amount of time, and scoring procedures. Valid and reliable writing assessment will attempt to control a number of these variables, or at the least to be cognizant of their potential impact on assessment outcomes.

The rise of direct writing assessment, and in particular the single essay prompt that is holistically scored, has generated a number of criticisms, both in its early use and more recently, though for different reasons. Earlier criticism dealt primarily with the problems of establishing inter-rater reliability across essay raters. This criticism has been directly addressed by a number of studies and ongoing assessment programmes which have consistently demonstrated high inter-rater reliabilities (cf. Cherry and Meyer 1993).

Newer challenges to direct assessment of writing with holistic scoring have raised questions about the content and construct validity of such approaches. The questions concerning validity centre around the match between research on writing development and the writing assessment procedure. These concerns are particularly serious for large-scale assessment, since in-class contexts provide a number of responses to the difficulties with direct assessment of writing. Among the concerns typically discussed are the following:

1. Can assessment be achieved in a decontextualized one-time writing sample? (Is the format too artificial?)
2. Can a brief timed sample represent a student's ability to write in various contexts and for various purposes?
3. Can a single general rating reflect a student's writing ability? (Is a global measure possible?)

4. Can assessment of a writing product provide information about how the writing process has been carried out?
5. Can prompts be generalized across different topics?
6. Can an arbitrary task and topic generate equal interest and motivation across large groups of students?
7. Can a brief writing sample provide feedback and diagnostic information for student's later learning?
8. Can raters actually provide a holistic score or are they concentrating on specific parts of an essay?

As can be seen from the concerns above, the challenge to direct assessment is not that it requires a writing sample, but that the common practice of a single sample of a student's writing is insufficient for a valid assessment (Camp 1993, Hamp-Lyons 1991c, Horowitz 1991, White 1993, 1995, Williamson 1993). Many of these questions can be addressed in various ways, but they nevertheless pose real issues that must be considered by anyone choosing to employ direct assessment. One direction that has developed as a result of these questions is the movement towards portfolios for large-scale assessment.

13.3.3   *Portfolios*

A portfolio approach to writing assessment constitutes a major recent direction in assessment, both in large-scale and in classroom contexts. While there is not, as yet, an extensive research literature on this movement, there are a number of sources which describe several projects, their methods, and the assessment results to date (see, e.g., Belanoff and Dickson 1991, Tierney *et al.* 1991; cf. Hamp-Lyon and Condon 1993). The discussion to follow will first review a number of attempts to use portfolio assessment in large-scale assessment contexts.

13.3.3.1   Portfolios in large-scale assessment

The increasing exploration of portfolios for assessing the writing abilities of students beyond the classroom context has generated both excitement and a fair amount of scepticism. The excitement is due in part to the opportunity to break away from artificial 'objective' writing samples and in part to a number of interesting pilot efforts that have been reasonably successful in differing contexts. The scepticism is due to the emphatic and perhaps overzeal-ous claims made by portfolio proponents and to the recognition that assessment itself is a somewhat artificial undertaking and will always encounter limitations, irrespective of format and proce-dures (Dunbar *et al.* 1991, Messick 1994).

Perhaps the best-known example of portfolio use in advanced writing in the USA is the effort to develop portfolio assessment over the past decade at the State University of New York (SUNY) at Stonybrook. In the English Freshman Composition programme at SUNY, students must assemble a portfolio of their course writ-ing and receive a grade of C or better to pass. Every portfolio is graded by the classroom teacher and by one other instructor, and the outside reader must also give the portfolio a grade of C or higher for the portfolio to receive a passing grade. Student portfo-lios consist of three revised essays, one in-class essay, and cover sheets for each essay describing the process of the writing and the purpose of each essay. The three revised pieces include: (1) a nar-rative, descriptive, or expressive essay, (2) an academic essay, and (3) an essay that analyses and critiques another essay (Elbow and Belanoff 1991).

Raters are trained to give a 'pass' or 'no-pass' grade to the port-folios; individual teachers decide at a later point on higher grades for a passing portfolio. While the programme is effective in get-ting students to write more and perhaps write better, a number of problems have been noted with this approach. Teachers are asked to do more work in evaluating student writing; students may have more opportunities to cheat; some teachers feel that the portfolio overwhelms the course; and some teachers feel that repeated opportunities for revising constitute too lenient a system. Conversely, the strengths of this programme are that students must take the writing process seriously, that they must take account of audience as a realistic concern, that they must be responsible for a wider array of their writing and must reflect on this array, and that they are assessed on their real writing produc-tion for the course – not on a remote final essay (Elbow and Belanoff 1991).

A number of other universities have developed portfolio assess-ment programmes which operate almost similarly to the Stonybrook model. Minor variations involve the different uses of outside raters, different mid-term evaluations of the portfolios, various schemes for rating the portfolios, various options for types and numbers of essays included, various options for revising the submitted essays, and different types of cover information required from the students. Such programmes include those at the City University of New York, Christopher Newport College (Virginia), Kansas State University, the University of Michigan, Northern Arizona University, and Miami University of Ohio, among others (Hamp-Lyons and Condon 1993, Rosenberg 1991, Smit *et al.* 1991).

Portfolios have also been used as a university writing competency requirement in lieu of an upper-level writing proficiency exam. In these cases, universities typically decide on a subset of courses which would be used to generate writings that could be placed in the portfolio. For example, at the University of Alaska Southeast, portfolios are used during the junior year as an upper-level writing proficiency requirement instead of a writing examination (Wauters 1991). Students are expected to submit writing that covers expressive, explanatory, and persuasive modes as well as a cover letter explaining the pieces in the portfolio.

Another variation has been put in place at Southeastern Missouri State University (Holt and Baker 1991). In this case, students who fail an upper-division writing requirement, or who choose to opt for a portfolio alternative, must submit four papers from courses as well as a cover letter describing the papers. The papers submitted include a persuasive essay, a more general expository essay, and two other pieces of academic writing (letters, poetry, and short stories are not acceptable). These portfolios are then graded on a six-point scale. Three of the five pieces must receive a score of 4 or better for the portfolio to pass.

Portfolio assessment is also being examined as an assessment option for the NAEP programme (Gentile 1992). In a 1990 pilot study, NAEP collected approximately 2000 portfolios assembled by 4th and 8th graders. These portfolios included writing samples primarily of informative and narrative pieces and were rated on scales similar to those used for the NAEP writing prompts. Results of the pilot study indicated patterns of writing similar to the types elicited by the typical assessment prompts used by NAEP. In 1992, a more complete collection procedure was implemented but the results of this assessment of portfolios have not yet appeared publicly.

There are undoubtedly other uses of portfolios in various contexts around the world, and more reports of their use will appear in the coming years. In the USA, for example, a number of state Departments of Education are using portfolios for state-wide writing assessment. Vermont, in particular, has been the object of reports recently and, as might be expected with beginning efforts, is encountering a number of difficulties (Koretz 1993). Nevertheless, portfolios provide an approach which addresses many of the construct-validity problems noted with indirect and single-sample direct measures of writing ability. At the same time, portfolio assessment faces many of the same problems that confront direct measures of writing, and it also creates a few additional problems that will have to be addressed in the coming years (Camp 1993, Hamp-Lyon and Condon 1993, White 1994, 1995).

Among the limitations noted for large-scale portfolio assessment are the following:

1. Portfolios really refer to a means of writing collection rather than to a means of assessment.
2. The problems with establishing a single score or scale for essay prompts is even more complex for portfolios. How will a single score capture the variation in writing ability indicated in a portfolio?
3. There are serious problems with reliability. As more leeway is given to choice of writings in the portfolio, it becomes more difficult to establish grading equivalence.
4. Portfolios take more time to grade and thus are much costlier as an assessment option.
5. A system for portfolio assessment must also establish the authenticity of the writing. How will the portfolio raters know that the students actually wrote all the pieces in the portfolio, and when is editing and revising assistance from others too extensive to represent the student's own writing abilities?
6. A portfolio consisting of different writing tasks assigned by different teachers will lead to differences simply because some writing tasks are inherently more interesting and better constructed. How will such variations be controlled?

These and many other questions provide the challenges for the future of portfolio assessment in the coming decade.

While there are serious obstacles to portfolio assessment, just as there are to most other forms of large-scale assessment, there are also strengths to the portfolio approach which should not be overlooked:

1. It allows for assessment of multiple writing samples across a range of topics and task types.
2. It allows the possibility for students' reflection on their writing and their writing progress.
3. It assesses the best that a student is capable of producing.
4. It creates a more realistic audience for student writing.
5. It gives students responsibility for choosing the writing on which they want to be evaluated.
6. It provides for a strong link between instruction and assessment, a highly desirable quality for any assessment mechanism.

These potential benefits may make portfolios a powerful assessment approach in the years to come. The fact that there are serious issues to be addressed in making portfolio assessment work effectively does not detract from its potential as a strong alternative to single prompt writing evaluation.

13.3.3.2   Portfolios for in-class assessment

Portfolio uses in a classroom context permit many more options for assessment of student progress and have greater potential both for diagnostic uses and future placement uses. In a classroom context, a portfolio may be designed as a controlled format, rather like the way it is used in large-scale assessment, or it may become a larger ongoing collection that best represents a student's writing abilities and most successful writings. In this respect, portfolios follow directly from professional adult uses of portfolios as a way to sell one's skills and talents. In yet other contexts, portfolios are not merely a matter of students choosing their best work; rather, students include all of their major writing as well as much exploratory writing which may serve as a resource for future essays. Portfolios can also include writing resources such as instructional guidelines, semantic maps, readings, pictures, poems, and other possible items that might be associated with specific writing tasks and assignments.

One of the best qualities of portfolio assessment in in-class contexts lies in the fact that it allows for a combination of standard assessment approaches together with many alternative assessment options (as described in subsection 13.3.2.5 above). Portfolios, for example, constitute an ideal mechanism for conferencing with students. Students have in one place the important writings on which they are working, and the teacher and the student can both refer directly to various parts of those writings. The portfolio provides a natural agenda for the conference, and allows the student to do most of the talking about his or her writing. Not only can the portfolio allow both teacher and student to examine the strengths and weaknesses of writing in detail, but it can also allow the conference to range across the student's various efforts at revision and future plans for revision, identifying those pieces of writing that are likely to become part of his or her final portfolio assessment.

A second way that portfolios tie in with alternative assessment is that they provide a springboard for self-evaluation, whether as in-class practice or as part of any assessment conference. Tierney *et al.* (1991) offer a persuasive argument to the effect that portfolios assist self-evaluation because they emphasize a number of valued qualities for self-assessment approaches: student ownership, student centredness, non-competitiveness, individual customizing, a more objective (or reader's) view of the writing, student self-selection, and student involvement in establishing evaluation criteria.

In classes with younger students, portfolios can also become repositories of all the student's writings, including non-formal writing, writing across a range of subjects, and pre-writing notes, lists, semantic maps, charts, tables, etc. In a sense, such a portfolio becomes a knowledge resource for future writing activities as well as a record of past and ongoing writing tasks. Towards the end of the school year, portfolios can be examined to create a more focused representation of a student's writing progress through the year. At that point, the student and the teacher can work through choices for the portfolio, decisions on organizing the portfolio, explanations for items in the portfolio, and means for evaluating the portfolio. This process can also include sending the portfolio to parents so that they may see the student's progress together with what it represents from the teacher's perspective.

With older students, and in more advanced academic contexts, portfolios become a more personal documentation of student development. Portfolios become increasingly the student's responsibility, and the student and teacher typically work together to organize the material it contains. Students, however, write their own introductions to their portfolio material and explain the relevance of each piece they possess. While portfolios are a focal point for teacher–student negotiation and conferencing, students recognize that their portfolios for writing take on a larger assessment purpose for the course; portfolios become the means for students to represent themselves in the best possible light – the writing portfolio becomes more like the professional portfolio in this context.

Overall, the use of portfolios in classroom contexts appears to add important assessment dimensions that extend beyond the positive features noted for large-scale assessment:

1. Portfolios allow feedback into instruction and curriculum development, linking assessment and instruction.
2. They allow parents, administrators, and others to see accurate profiles of student abilities: their strengths, weaknesses, and progress.
3. They can be planned over the course of a curriculum cycle or academic year, well in advance of assessment time.
4. They allow for a collaborative approach to evaluation.
5. They base assessment on what students actually write in the classroom rather than on an artificially imposed external measure.
6. They allow for continuous, ever-expanding, and systematic assessment.
7. They position the teacher as the natural 'expert' evaluator. Teachers are called on to make important professional judgments.

(Drawn from Tierney *et al.* 1991)

With portfolio assessment, as with any approach, there is the danger of a myopic view, presenting only the positive aspects of a challenging and interesting assessment approach. Moreover, a procedure that emphasizes work over the extended course of time will be challenged by some who feel that assessment should value a student's proficiency level at the end-point rather than emphasize the ongoing process of writing and revising over time. Furthermore, the same dilemmas impact on portfolios as on other writing assessment. In many cases, students must receive grades, and ultimately portfolios are evaluated for the quality of writing more than for effort and student cooperation (White 1993).

13.4   The limitations of assessment

The greater emphasis on writing assessment in the past ten years, and the parallel increase in research, has made both researchers and teachers much more aware of the complexity involved in fair and appropriate assessment of student writing abilities. It is now well recognized that no approach to writing assessment is without problems. Recent research has also pointed out that different types of assessment are better suited to distinct instructional contexts, student abilities and goals, teacher preferences and purposes, and institutional expectations.

Writing assessment research and practice has certainly been confronting the limitations inherent in the evaluation of a complex advanced set of cognitive processes. Earlier exploration of writing skills was, perhaps, too confident that writing development could be readily assessed. The current discussion of assessment, and particularly of large-scale assessment, suggests a reasoned humility in the face of an extremely difficult task (assuming it is to be done fairly, appropriately, and reliably). Future work on writing assessment will continue to explore ways to meet teacher and institutional needs and, at the same time, to provide students with feedback and information that will instruct as well as assess (Camp 1993, White 1994).

Moreover, much practical assessment research now reflects recent changes in assessment theory. Construct validity is now seen by most assessment specialists as the driving force behind choices for appropriate assessment; that is, writing assessment should match its criteria to the writing that students are expected to carry out after they have completed writing courses, to reflect current notions of writing ability, and to do so in a socially responsible manner (Camp 1993, White 1993).

For issues surrounding the development and implementation of large-scale assessment, notions such as reliability, content validity, and concurrent validity are now seen as aspect of construct validity rather than as independent considerations (Camp 1993, Hamp-Lyons 1991c, Messick 1989). A number of consequences follow from this emphasis on construct validity: (1) there is a greater effort to investigate carefully the types of writing that are important for given groups of students; (2) there is greater interest in the attitudes of teachers towards types of writing skills; and (3) there is greater attention to the relations between writing instruction, writing assessment, and later uses of writing skills. Writing assessment must be seen not only as reflecting appropriate instructional goals but also as an active component in writing instruction and an integral part of the students' learning processes.

14

Conclusions: Writing in English

In the chapters which precede this authorial last gasp, we have tried to summarize at considerable length the various theoretical strands that have been explored by applied linguists and others in the recent past, and to draw these strands together into a coherent picture of where we have arrived in trying to understand the nature of a written text. Given this summary of what written text is and how it is created, we have tried to suggest ways in which writing might be taught that are consistent with what is known about the nature of text, the composing process, and the surrounding social context.

In a sense, we have not really dealt with the universal theory and practice of the teaching of writing; rather, we have looked at these issues in the context of the English language. We believe that what is true of the nature of text in English, and what applies to the teaching of writing in English, is probably also true in other languages, but we do not know that to be so, and therefore we make no claims for what we have said beyond the limits of English. We welcome commentary from scholars working in other languages to provide confirmation or disconfirmation of our findings and recommendations.

At this point, a final recapitulation of the volume would, we fear, tempt us to add yet another full chapter, so we shall refrain. We would like, however, to reaffirm a small set of conclusions which deserve special consideration. From our survey, we can claim that:

- the teaching of writing is separate and distinct from the teaching of syntactic accuracy and the teaching of various text conventions (e.g. spelling, punctuation);

- the learning of writing is more likely to succeed in conditions in which students find themselves wanting to communicate real messages to real audiences;
- the learning of writing is more likely to succeed in conditions in which extensive support is offered to the learner from prior text, in conditions in which there is peer involvement in the preparatory stages for writing, and in conditions in which there is also support from the teacher.

Teachers need not only offer the learner support and encouragement but must also serve as master craftsmen (and women) to whom the learner is apprenticed – the learner may then, over time, become a functioning member of a community in which the literate discourse function serves a real and viable purpose.

We have claimed that learners who come from communities which practise other sorts of discourse, or in which literate discourse served either no viable function or an entirely different real purpose, are at a disadvantage – not because they are ignorant or stupid, but rather because they have not realized or accepted the registers and purposes of discourse in the academic community. An important aspect of teaching such learners is simply to make them aware of the purposes served by academic discourse, but there is no guarantee that such awareness will make learners wish to participate in this particular type of literate discourse. At least, if learners choose not to participate, they will understand what they have chosen not to do and will be able to make an informed decision.

We have claimed that there are important differences within literate academic discourse practices between tasks which require learners to draw only upon their internal resources and tasks which require learners to go beyond themselves, to draw upon other text, and to use the writing process as a heuristic for the discovery of new meaning.

Having provided and supported these various research views, we have tried to develop a series of suggestions for ways in which the objectives deriving from theory can be put into practice in the classroom. We have divided this discussion into suggestions applicable to the beginning, intermediate, and advanced levels of writing instruction. We recognize that such a division is arbitrary and ultimately unsatisfactory; there are almost infinite sets of conditions that falsify such a division of the learning world. Indeed, we understand that, in a system that is age-graded, individuals may enter at any point at the proper age level but be entirely unprepared to benefit from instruction.

In another sense, the learning world can be divided into three other groupings: *kinesic, tactic,* and *legeric.* This separation, not based on age-grading, may help us to understand why certain individuals are not served by the system and may provide insights which will permit the system to adapt to the needs of misplaced individuals.

Kinesic learning involves physical coordination of various types, ranging from basic hand/eye coordination to the complex process involved in wrapping one's tongue around an unfamiliar phonology and the equally complex problem of manipulating some sort of writing implement to shape the graphemic symbols of an unknown orthographic system. Educational systems are relatively proficient at this sort of teaching.

Tactic learning can best be illustrated by an analogy. If one goes to a strange city and hires a taxi to go from the airport to a central hotel, one expects the taxi driver to go through a fairly complex navigational analysis, considering available routes, traffic patterns in relation to time of day, temporary obstacles (e.g. caused by construction) along the way, and one expects the driver to arrive at the hotel in an efficient and economical way. In working this navigational problem, the taxi driver functions within a closed system; there are, after all, a limited number of ways to move between the airport and the hotel, and there are limited choices with respect to traffic patterns and obstacles. In language, this compares to learning the syntactic system and the lexicon of a language. Educational systems are quite good at inculcating tactic learning.

Legeric learning, too, can best be illustrated by an analogy. If one goes to see a physician, complaining of some more or less localized pain, one expects the physician to diagnose the illness and to prescribe an appropriate treatment. In order to do so, the physician must function in an open-ended system in which the alternatives are virtually infinite. Employing laboratory tests, physical examinations, intuition, experience, and perhaps other skills, the physician can accomplish the objective and the patient can become well. In language, legeric learning implicates the mastery of the (educationally valued) rhetorical system – its discourses and its pragmatics. Educational systems are not very expert in teaching legeric skills; on the contrary, they tend to assume that students come fully equipped with such skills, or they do not even recognize the nature of such skills. As a result, students who are equipped with appropriate legeric skills tend to succeed while students who are not tend to fail, to be stigmatized by the system.

A society can be described in terms of the relative value it places on these three learning strands. Most educational systems begin paying attention to the kinesic skills at the earliest possible moment. It is assumed that all individuals within the normative ranges will easily acquire such skills. Except in the USA where professional athletes are outrageously rewarded, these skills are not normally highly valued, and it does not take long to acquire them – most elementary school students can be said to have mastered these skills. In most societies, tactic skills – the skills involved in driving a taxi – are not highly regarded, and it does not take long to acquire them. Taxi drivers are not too well compensated; indeed, they tend to fall towards the lower end of the socioeconomic scale. (This is not to say that there are no societies in which navigational skills are highly valued; in some Pacific Island societies, the navigator is among the most valued members of society.) On the other hand, in most societies, legeric skills are highly valued. Physicians take many years to acquire the licensure necessary to practise their trade and the skills requisite to the acquisition of a licence. They are among the most highly valued members of the society and are rewarded with handsome incomes. (This has not always been the case; in the seventeenth and eighteenth centuries, surgery in the USA was undertaken by barbers, and physicians did not have high social status. As the paradigms of medicine changed, as the disciplines of medicine redefined themselves, the social value of physicians increased.)

We would want to argue that the teaching of writing in many classrooms remains primarily focused on mastery at the kinesic and tactic levels; that is, instead of being assisted to acquire advanced skills involved in writing, students are taught the skills involved in producing the orthographic system (whether with a pen or with a word processor) and skills implicating surface structure features like grammar and spelling. Students are, in short, instructed essentially in the conventions associated with writing. We would want to argue further that the teaching of writing as we mean to discuss it implicates the legeric level – a level not well understood by researchers let alone by teachers. It is at the legeric level that experience and intuition combine, and the processes become a heuristic for the discovery of new knowledge.

To the extent that classes concerned with writing limit student performance to kinesic and tactic skills, and restrict students to operating within closed systems depending entirely on their internal resources, such classes are actually teaching a very limited form of writing. We have attempted in this volume to provide the rationale for moving the teaching of writing to the legeric level and then to provide the pedagogical means for doing so.

We understand that students begin at different stages; if a student enters the system with only kinesic skills, at whatever level, then the system has the responsibility to orient instruction sufficiently to permit that student to acquire tactic skills as part of acquiring legeric skills. Many students come equipped with tactic skills; after all, writers of graffiti, for example, are well equipped with tactic skills, but may be lacking legeric skills. In order for students to acquire legeric skills, they must want to do so, and they will want to do so only if they see that such skills have value in their society and their lives.

We understand further that the task we have undertaken is not complete. As our knowledge of the structure of written texts expands, and as our awareness of the means of inculcating legeric skills increases, the teaching of writing will change. To the best of our knowledge, we have provided a synthesis of where scholarship has arrived. We look forward to the next cycle of research which will expand or alter the underlying paradigms and will result in still more effective means for the teaching of writing. We understand that each generation of scholars stands on the shoulders of its parent generation and thus is able to see farther. We welcome this probability of greater insight through continued research on writing.

Seventy-five themes for writing instruction

This list is provided to facilitate easy access to a major part of this book.

Chapter 10: Teaching writing at beginning levels

Chapter 11: Teaching writing at intermediate levels

Chapter 12: Teaching writing at advanced levels

Bibliography

ABRAHAMSON, D. 1985. Creatures of invention. *National Wildlife* **23**, 2. 25–8.

ACKERMAN, J. 1993. The promise of writing to learn. *Written Communication* **10**, 334–70.

ADAMS, M. 1989. *Beginning to read: Thinking and learning about print.* London and Cambridge, MA: MIT Press.

ALDERSON, C. 1987. An overview of ESL/EFL testing in Britain. In C. ALDERSON, K. KRAHNKE and C. STANSFIELD (eds) *Reviews of English language proficiency tests.* Washington, DC: TESOL Publications. 3–4.

ALDERSON, C. 1993a. Judgments in language testing. In D. DOUGLAS and C. CHAPELLE (eds) *A new decade in language testing research.* Alexandria, VA: TESOL Publications. 46–57.

ALDERSON, C. 1993b. The relationship between grammar and reading in an English for academic purposes test battery. In D. DOUGLAS and C. CHAPELLE (eds) *A new decade in language testing research.* Alexandria, VA: TESOL Publications. 203–19.

ALDERSON, C. and G. BUCK. 1993. Standards in testing: A study of the practice of UK examination boards in EFL/EL testing. *Language Testing* **10**, 1–26.

ALDERSON, C., K. KRAHNKE and C. STANSFIELD (eds). 1987. *Reviews of English language proficiency tests.* Washington, DC: TESOL Publications.

ALLAEI, S. and U. CONNOR. 1991. Using performative assessment instruments with ESL student writers. In L. HAMP-LYONS (ed.) *Assessing second language writing in academic contexts.* Norwood, NJ: Ablex. 227–40.

ALLEN, R.V. 1976. *Language experiences in communication.* Boston: Houghton Mifflin.

AMNESTY INTERNATIONAL. 1984. Exiled South Korea leader calls for Amnesty's continued human rights support. *Amnesty International Newsletter.* (December, 1984) **1**.

ANDERSON, J. 1990. *Cognitive psychology and its implications,* 3rd edn. Oxford and New York: Freeman.

ANDERSON, P. 1985. What survey research tells us about writing at work. In L. ODELL and D. GOSWAMI (eds) *Writing in nonacademic settings.* New York: Guilford. 3–83.

431

ANSON, C. (ed.). 1989. *Writing and response: Theory, practice, and research.* Urbana, IL: National Council of Teachers of English.

APPLEBEE, A. 1981. *Writing in the secondary schools.* Urbana, IL: National Council of Teachers of English.

APPLEBEE, A. 1984. *Contexts for learning to write.* Norwood, NJ: Ablex.

APPLEBEE, A. 1986. Problems in process approaches: Toward a reconceptualization of process instruction. In A. PETROSKY and D. BARTHOLOMAE (eds) *The teaching of writing.* Chicago, IL: National Society of the Study of Education (University of Chicago Press). 95–113.

APPLEBEE, A., J. LANGER, L. JENKINS, I. MULLIS and M. FOERTSCH. 1990a. *Learning to write in our nation's schools: Instruction and achievement in 1988 at grades 4, 8, and 12.* Princeton, NJ: Educational Testing Service.

APPLEBEE, A., J. LANGER and I. MULLIS. 1986. *Writing: Trends across the decade, 1974–84.* Princeton, NJ: Educational Testing Service.

APPLEBEE, A., J. LANGER, I. MULLIS and L. JENKINS. 1990b. *The writing report card, 1984–88.* Princeton, NJ: Educational Testing Service.

APPLEBEE, A., J. LANGER, I. MULLIS, A. LATHAM and C. GENTILE. 1994. *NAEP 1992: Writing report card.* Washington, DC: Office of Educational Research and Improvement, US Department of Education. [Report #23-W01.]

ARMBRUSTER, B. 1991. Framing: A technique for improving learning from science texts. In C. SANTA and D. ALVERMANN (eds) *Science learning: Processes and applications.* Newark, DE: International Reading Association. 104–13.

ARMBRUSTER, B., T. ANDERSON and J. MEYER. 1991. Improving content area reading using instructional graphics. *Reading Research Quarterly* **26**, 393–416.

ARNOVE, R. and H. GRAFF (eds). 1987. *National Literacy campaigns.* London and New York: Plenum.

ARONSON, E., N. BLANEY, C. STEPHAN, J. SIKES and M. SNAPP. 1978. *The Jigsaw classroom,* Beverley Hills, CA/London: Sage.

ATKINSON, D. 1991. Discourse analysis and written discourse conventions. In W. GRABE *et al.* (eds) *Annual review of applied linguistics, 11.* Cambridge, England and New York: Cambridge University Press. 57–76.

ATKINSON, D. 1993. A historical discourse analysis of scientific research writing from 1675 to 1975: The case of the *Philosophical Transactions of the Royal Society of London.* Los Angeles: University of Southern California. Ph.D. diss.

AU, K., D. CROWELL, C. JORDAN, K. SLOAT, G. SPEIDEL, T. KLEIN and R. THARP. 1986. Development and implementation of the KEEP reading program. In J. ORASANU (ed.) *Reading comprehension: From research to practice.* Hove, Sussex and Hillsdale, NJ: L. Erlbaum. 235–52.

AU, K. and C. JORDAN. 1981. Teaching reading to Hawaiian children:

Finding a culturally appropriate solution. In H. TRUEBA, G. GUTHRIE, and K. AU (eds) *Culture and the bilingual classroom: Studies in classroom ethnography*. Rowley, MA: Newbury House. 139–52.

BACHMAN, L. 1990. *Fundamental considerations in language testing*. Oxford and New York: Oxford University Press.

BAKER, E., H. O'NEIL and R. LINN. 1993. Policy and validity prospects for performance-based assessment. *American Psychologist* **48**, 1210–18.

BAKHTIN, M. 1981. *The dialogic imagination*. (C. Emerson and M. Holquist, Trans.) Austin, TX: University of Texas Press.

BALDAUF, R. 1986. Linguistic constraints on participation in psychology. *American Psychologist* **41**, 220–4.

BALDAUF, R. and B. JERNUDD. 1983. Language of publications as a variable in scientific communication. *Australian Review of Applied Linguistics* **6**, 97–108.

BALDAUF, R. and B. JERNUDD. 1987. Academic communication in a foreign language: The example of Scandinavian psychology. *Australian Review of Applied Linguistics* **10**, 98–117.

BAMBERG, B. 1983. What makes a text coherent? *College Composition and Communication* **34**, 417–29.

BANGERT-DROWNS, R. 1993. The word processor as an instructional tool: A meta-analysis of word processing in writing instruction. *Review of Educational Research* **63**, 69–93.

BARBER, C. 1962/1985. Some measurable characteristics of modern science prose. In J. SWALES (ed.) *Episodes in ESP*. Hemel Hempsted and Englewood Cliffs, NJ: Prentice Hall. 1–14.

BARSALOU, L. 1992. *Cognitive psychology: An overview for cognitive scientists*. Hove, Sussex and Hillsdale, NJ: L. Erlbaum.

BARSALOU, L. 1993. Frames, concepts, and conceptual fields. In A. LEHRER and E. KITTAY (eds) *Frames, fields, and contrasts*. Hove, Sussex and Hillsdale, NJ: L. Erlbaum. 21–74.

BARTHOLOMAE, D. 1985. Inventing the university. *When a writer can't write*. New York: Guilford. 134–165.

BARTHOLOMAE, D. and A. PETROSKY. 1986. *Facts, artifacts and counterfacts: Theory and method for a reading and writing course*. Upper Montclair, NJ: Boynton/Cook.

BARTON, D. and R. IVANIC (eds). 1991. *Writing in the community*. London and Newbury Park, CA: Sage.

BASSO, K. 1974. The ethnography of writing. In R. BAUMAN and J. SHERZER (eds) *Explorations in the ethnography of speaking*. Cambridge, England and New York: Cambridge University Press. 425–32.

BATESON, G. 1979. *Mind and nature: A necessary unity*. London and New York: Bantam Books.

BAZERMAN, C. 1983. Scientific writing as a social act. In P ANDERSON, J. BROCKMAN and C. MILLER (eds) *New essays in technical writing and communication*. Farmingdale, NY: Baywood. 156–84.

BAZERMAN, C. 1985. Physicists writing physics: Schema-laden purposes and purpose-laden schema. *Written Communication* **2**, 3–23.

BAZERMAN, C. 1988. *Shaping written knowledge.* Madison, WI: University of Wisconsin Press.

BAZERMAN, C. 1991. Discourse analysis and social construction. In W. GRABE *et al.* (eds) *Annual review of applied linguistics, 11.* Cambridge, England and New York: Cambridge University Press. 77–83.

BAZERMAN, C. 1993. *Constructing experience.* Carbondale, IL: Southern Illinois University Press.

BEACH, R. 1989. Showing students how to assess: Demonstrating techniques for response in the writing conference. In C. ANSON (ed.) *Writing and response.* Urbana, IL: National Council of Teachers of English. 127–48.

DE BEAUGRANDE, R. 1980. *Text, discourse and process.* Norwood, NJ: Ablex.

DE BEAUGRANDE, R. 1982. Psychology and composition: Past, present, future. In M. NYSTRAND (ed.) *What writers know: The language, process, and structure of written composition.* London and New York: Academic Press. 211–67.

DE BEAUGRANDE, R. 1984. *Text production: Toward a science of composition.* Norwood, NJ: Ablex.

DE BEAUGRANDE, R. 1985. *Writing step by step.* London and New York: Harcourt Brace.

DE BEAUGRANDE, R. and W. DRESSLER. 1981. *Introduction to text linguistics.* London and New York: Longman.

BECK, I., M. McKEOWN, G. SINATRA and J. LOXTERMAN. 1991. Revising social studies text from a text-processing perspective: Evidence of improved comprehensibility. *Reading Research Quarterly* **26**, 251–76.

BELANOFF, P. and M. DICKSON (eds). 1991. *Portfolios: Process and product.* Portsmouth, NH: Boynton/Cook.

BENSON, J. and W. GREAVES (eds). 1985. *Systemic perspectives on discourse.* 2 Volumes. Norwood, NJ: Ablex.

BEREITER, C. 1990. Aspects of an educational learning theory. *Review of Educational Research* **60**, 603–24.

BEREITER, C. and M. SCARDAMALIA. 1985. Cognitive coping strategies and the problem of 'inert knowledge'. In S. CHIPMAN, J. SEGAL and R. GLASER (eds) *Thinking and learning skills: Volume 2. Research and open questions.* Hove, Sussex and Hillsdale, NJ: L. Erlbaum. 65–80.

BEREITER, C. and M. SCARDAMALIA. 1987. *The psychology of written composition.* Hillsdale, NJ: L. Erlbaum.

BEREITER, C. and M. SCARDAMALIA. 1989. Intentional learning as a goal of instruction. In L. RESNICK (ed.) *Knowing, learning, and instruction: Essays in honor of Robert Glaser.* Hillsdale, NJ: L. Erlbaum. 361–91.

BEREITER, C. and M. SCARDAMALIA. 1993. *Surpassing ourselves: An inquiry into the nature and complications of expertise.* Chicago: Open Court Press.

BERKENKOTTER, C. and T. HUCKIN. 1993. Rethinking genre from a sociocognitive perspective. *Written Communication* **10**, 475–509.

BERKENKOTTER, C. and T. HUCKIN. 1995. *Genre knowledge in disciplinary communication.* Hillsdale, NJ: L. Erlbaum.

BERLIN, J. 1984. *Writing instruction in nineteenth century American colleges.* Carbondale, IL: Southern Illinois University Press.

BERLIN, J. 1987. *Rhetoric and reality: Writing instruction in American colleges, 1900–1985.* Carbondale, IL: Southern Illinois University Press.

BERMAN, R. and D. SLOBIN. 1994. *Relating events in narratives: A crosslinguistic and developmental study.* Hove, Sussex and Hillsdale, NJ: L. Erlbaum.

BERNHARDT, E. 1994. A content analysis of reading methods texts: What are we told about the nonnative speaker of English? *Journal of Reading Behavior* 26, 159–89.

BERNSTEIN, B. 1972a. Social class, language and socialization. In P.P. GIGLIOLI (ed.) *Language and social context.* Harmondsworth, England: Penguin. 157–78.

BERNSTEIN, B. 1972b. A critique of the concept of compensatory education. In C. CAZDEN, V. JOHN and D. HYMES (eds) *Functions of language in the classroom.* New York: Teachers College Press. 135–51.

BERNSTEIN, B. 1990. *Class, codes and control 4: The structuring of pedagogic discourse.* London and New York: Routledge.

BERTHOFF, A. 1981. *The making of meaning.* Upper Montclair, NJ: Boynton/Cook.

BESNIER, N. 1988. The linguistic relationships of spoken and written Nukulaelae registers. *Language* 64, 707–36.

BHATIA, V.K. 1993. *Analysing Genre: Language use in professional settings.* London and New York: Longman.

BIBER, D. 1988. *Variation across speech and writing.* Cambridge, England and New York: Cambridge University Press.

BIBER, D. 1989. A typology of English texts. *Linguistics* 27, 3–43.

BIBER, D. 1992. On the complexity of discourse complexity: A multidimensional analysis. *Discourse Processes* 15, 133–63.

BIBER, D. 1994. An analytic framework for register studies. In D. BIBER and E. FINEGAN (eds) *Sociolinguistic perspectives on register.* Oxford and New York: Oxford University Press. 31–56.

BIBER, D. 1995. *Cross-linguistic patterns of register variation: A multi-dimensional comparison of English, Tuvaluan, Korean, and Somali.* Cambridge, England and New York: Cambridge University Press.

BIBER, D. and E. FINEGAN. 1988. Adverbial stance types in English. *Discourse Processes* 11, 1–34.

BIBER, D. and E. FINEGAN. 1989. Styles of stance in English: Lexical and grammatical markings of evidentiality and affect. *Text* 9, 93–124.

BICKNER, R. and P. PEYASANTIWONG. 1988. Cultural variation in reflective writing. In A. PURVES (ed.) *Writing across languages and cultures.* London and Newbury Park, CA: Sage. 160–74.

BISSEX, G. 1980. *Gnys at work: A child learns to read and write.* Cambridge, MA: Harvard University Press.

BIZZELL, P. 1982. College composition: Initiation into the academic discourse community. *Curriculum Inquiry* **12**, 191–207.

BIZZELL, P. 1986a. What happens when the basic writer comes to college? *College Composition and Communication* 37, 294–310.

BIZZELL, P. 1986b. Foundationalism and anti-foundationalism in composition studies. *Pre/Text* **7**, 37–56.

BIZZELL, P. 1993. *Academic discourse and critical consciousness.* Pittsburgh: University of Pittsburgh Press.

BLAIR, H. 1783/1965. *Lectures on rhetoric and belles lettres* (H. Harding, ed.). Carbondale, IL: Southern Illinois University Press.

BLOK, H. and K. DE GLOPPER. 1992. Large scale writing assessment. In L. VERHOEVEN and J.H.A.L. DE JONG (eds) *The construct of language proficiency.* Philadelphia: J. Benjamins. 101–11.

BLOOME, D. and J. GREEN. 1992. Educational contexts of literacy. In W. GRABE *et al.* (eds) *Annual review of applied linguistics, 12. Literacy.* Cambridge, England and New York: Cambridge University Press. 49–70.

BOGGS, S. 1985. *Speaking, relating and learning.* Norwood, NJ: Ablex.

BONK. W. 1990. A synthesis of social cognition and writing research. *Written Communication* **7**, 136–63.

BOOMER, G. 1985. *Fair dinkum teaching and learning: Reflections on literacy and power.* Upper Montclair, NJ: Boynton/Cook.

BRACEY, G. 1995. The assessor assessed: A 'revisionist' looks at a critique of the Sandia report. *Journal of Educational Research* **88**, 136–44.

BRELAND, H., R. CAMP, R. JONES, M. MORRIS and D. ROCK. 1987. *Assessing writing skill.* New York: College Entrance Examination Board. [Research Monograph #11.]

BRINTON, D., M.A. SNOW and M. WESCHE (eds). 1989. *Content-based second language instruction.* New York: Newbury House.

BRITTON, B. and J. BLACK. 1985a. Understanding expository text: From structure to process and world knowledge. In B. BRITTON and J. BLACK (eds) *Understanding expository text.* Hove, Sussex and Hillsdale, NJ: L. Erlbaum. 1–9.

BRITTON, B. and J. BLACK (eds). 1985b. *Understanding expository text.* Hove, Sussex and Hillsdale, NJ: L. Erlbaum.

BRITTON, B. and S. GULGOZ. 1991. Using Kintsch's computational model to improve instructional text: Effects of repairing inference calls on recall and cognitive structures. *Journal of Educational Psychology* **83**, 329–45.

BRITTON, B., A. WOODWARD and M. BINKLEY (eds). 1993. *Learning from textbooks: Theory and practice.* Hove, Sussex and Hillsdale, NJ: L. Erlbaum.

BRITTON, J. 1983. Shaping at the point of utterance. In A. FREEDMAN, I. PRINGLE and J. YALDEN (eds) *Learning to write: First language/second language.* London and New York: Longman. 13–19.

BRITTON, J., T. BURGESS, N. MARTIN, A. MCLEOD, and H. ROSEN. 1975. *The development of writing ability (11–18).* London: Macmillan.

BROWN, A. 1994. The advancement of learning. *Educational Researcher* **23**, 4–12.

BROWN, A. and J. CAMPIONE. 1994. Guided discovery in a community of learners. In K. MCGILLY (ed.) *Classroom lessons: Integrating cognitive theories.* Cambridge, MA: MIT Press. 229–70.

BROWN, A. and A. PALINCSAR. 1989. Guided, cooperative learning and individual knowledge acquisition. In L. RESNICK (ed.) *Knowing, learning, and instruction: Essays in honor of Robert Glaser.* Hove, Sussex and Hillsdale, NJ: L. Erlbaum. 393–451.

BROWN, G. and G. YULE. 1983. *Discourse analysis.* Cambridge, England and New York: Cambridge University Press.

BRUCE, B., J.K. PEYTON, and T. BATESON (eds.). 1993 *Network-based classrooms: Promises and realities.* Cambridge and New York: Cambridge University Press.

BRUCE, B. and A. RUBIN. 1993. *Electronic quills: A situated evaluation of using computers for writing in classrooms.* Hove, Sussex and Hillsdale, NJ: L. Erlbaum.

BRUFFEE, J. 1986. Social construction, language, and the authority of knowledge: A bibliographic essay. *College English* **48**, 773–90.

BRUNER, J. 1983. *Child's talk: learning to use language.* Oxford: Oxford University Press.

BRUTHIAUX, P. 1993. *Child's talk: learning to use language.* Oxford: Oxford Univesity Press.

BRYSON, M. and M. SCARDAMALIA. 1991. Teaching writing to students at risk for academic failure. In B. MEANS, C. CHELEMER and M. KNAPP (eds) *Teaching advanced skills to at-risk students.* San Francisco: Jossey-Bass. 141–67.

BULLOCK COMMITTEE. 1975. *A language for life.* London: Department of Education and Science, Her Majesty's Stationery Office.

CALFEE, R. 1992. Authentic assessment of reading and writing in the elementary classroom. In M. DREHER and W. SLATER (eds) *Elementary school literacy: Critical issues.* Norwood, MA: Christopher Gordon. 211–39.

CALKINS, L. 1983. *Lessons from a child.* London and Portsmouth, NH: Heinemann.

CALKINS, L. 1986. *The art of teaching writing.* London and Portsmouth, NH: Heinemann.

CAMP, R. 1993. Changing the model for the direct assessment of writing. In M. WILLIAMSON and B. HUOT (eds) *Validating holistic scoring for writing assessment.* Cresskill, NJ: Hampton Press. 45–78.

CAMPBELL, C. 1990. Writing with others' words: Using background reading text in academic compositions. In B. KROLL (ed.) *Second language writing.* Cambridge and New York: Cambridge University Press. 211–230.

CAMPBELL, G. 1776/1963. *The philosophy of rhetoric* (L. Bitzer, ed.). Carbondale, IL: Southern Illinois University Press.

CANALE, M. 1983. From communicative competence to communicative language pedagogy. In J. RICHARDS and R. SCHMIDT (eds) *Language and communication.* London and New York: Longman.

CANALE, M., M. BELANGER and N. FRENETTE. 1988. Evaluation of minority student writing in first and second languages. In J. FINE (ed.) *Second language discourse: A textbook of current research.* Norwood, NJ: Ablex. 147–65.

CANALE, M. and M. SWAIN. 1980. Theoretical bases of communicative approaches to second language teaching and testing. *Applied Linguistics* **1**, 1–47.

CANTONI, G. 1987. *Content-area language instruction.* Wokingham, England and Reading, MA: Addison-Wesley.

CARLISLE, R. 1989. The writing of Anglo and Hispanic elementary school students in bilingual, submersion, and regular programs. *Studies in Second Language Acquisition* **11**, 257–80.

CARLSON, S. 1988. Cultural differences in writing and reasoning skills. In A. Purves (ed.) *Writing across languages and cultures.* London and Newbury Park, CA: Sage. 227–60

CARLSON, S., B. BRIDGEMAN, R. CAMP and J. WAANDERS. 1985. *Relationships of admission test scores to writing performance of native and nonnative speakers of English.* Princeton, NJ: Educational Testing Service. [TOEFL Research Report #19.]

CARNICELLI, T. 1980. The writing conference: A one-on-one conversation. In T. DONOVAN and B. MCCLELLAND (eds) *Eight approaches to teaching composition.* Urbana, IL: National Council of Teachers of English. 101–31.

CARRELL, P. 1982. Cohesion is not coherence. *TESOL Quarterly* **16**, 479–88.

CARRELL, P. 1987. Text as interaction: Some implications of text analysis and reading research for ESL composition. In U. CONNOR and R.B. KAPLAN (eds) *Writing across languages: Analysis of L2 text.* Wokingham, England and Reading, MA: Addison-Wesley. 47–56.

CARSON, J. 1992. Becoming biliterate: First language influences. *Journal of Second Language Writing* **1**, 37–60.

CARSON, J., P. CARRELL, S. SILBERSTEIN, B. KROLL and P. KUEHN. 1990. Reading-writing relationships in first and second language. *TESOL Quarterly* **24**, 245–66.

CARSON, J. and G. NELSON. 1994. Writing groups: Cross-cultural issues. *Journal of Second Language Writing* **3**, 17–30.

CARTER, M. 1990. The idea of expertise: An exploration of cognitive and social dimensions of writing. *College Composition and Communication* **41**, 265–86.

CARTER, R. 1990. When is a report not a report? Observations from academic and nonacademic settings. In W. NASH (ed.) *The writing scholar: Studies in academic discourse.* London and Newbury Park: Sage. 171–91.

CAZDEN, C. 1988. *Classroom discourse: The language of teaching and learning.* Oxford and Portsmouth, NH: Heinemann.

CAZDEN, C. and B. GRAY. 1992. Australian approaches to genre-based writing instruction. Paper presented at the 27th Annual TESOL Convention, Vancouver, BC, March 1992.

CELCE-MURCIA, M., Z. DORNYEI and S. THURELL. 1994. Communicative competence: A pedagogically motivated framework. Paper presented at 1994 Arizona Round Table on Language. Tucson, AZ, February 1994.

CERNIGLIA, C., K. MEDSKER and U. CONNOR. 1990. Improving coherence using computer-assisted instruction. In U. CONNOR and A. JOHNS (eds) *Coherence in writing.* Washington, DC: TESOL Publications. 229–41.

CHAFE, W. 1982. Integration and involvement in speaking, writing, and oral literature. In D. TANNEN (ed.) *Spoken and written language.* Norwood, NJ: Ablex. 35–54.

CHAFE, W. 1985. Linguistic differences produced by differences between speaking and writing. In D. OLSON, N. TORRANCE and A. HILYARD (eds) *Literacy, language, and learning.* Cambridge, England and New York: Cambridge University Press. 105–23.

CHAFE, W. and J. NICHOLS (eds). 1986. *Evidentiality: The linguistic coding of epistemology.* Norwood, NJ: Ablex.

CHAPELLE, C., W. GRABE and M. BERNS. 1993. *Communicative language proficiency: Definitions and implications for TOEFL 2000.* [ETS Internal Report.] Princeton, NJ: Educational Testing Service.

CHARNEY, D. and R. CARLSON. 1995. Learning to write in a genre: What student writers take from model texts. *Research in the Teaching of English* **29**, 88–125.

CHENG, P. 1985. An analysis of contrastive rhetoric: English and Chinese expository prose, pedagogical implications, and strategies for the ESL teacher in a ninth grade curriculum. Unpublished Ph.D. diss., The Pennsylvania State University.

CHERRY, R. and P. MEYER. 1993. Reliability issues in holistic assessment. In M. WILLIAMSON and B. HUOT (eds) *Validating holistic scoring for writing assessment.* Cresskill, NJ: Hampton Press. 109–41.

CHOI, S. and M. BOWERMAN. 1991. Learning to express motion events in English and Korean: The influence of language-specific lexicalization patterns. *Cognition* **44**, 83–121.

CHRISTIE, F. 1985. Some current issues in first language writing development. *Australian Review of Applied Linguistics* **8**, 27–54.

CHRISTIE, F. 1989. Language development in education. In R. HASAN and J. MARTIN (eds) *Language development: Language learning, learning culture.* Norwood, NJ: Ablex. 152–98.

CHRISTIE, F. 1992. Literacy in Australia. In W. GRABE *et al.* (eds) *Annual review of applied linguistics, 12. Literacy.* Cambridge, England and New York: Cambridge University Press. 142–55.

CHRISTIE, F. (ed.). 1990. *Literacy for a changing world.* Hawthorn, Victoria: Australian Council for Educational Research.

CHRISTIE, F. *et al.* 1991. *Language as a resource for meaning. Report booklets 1–4 and teacher manual.* Sydney: Harcourt Brace Jovanovich.

CHRISTIE, F. *et al.* (eds). 1989. *Writing in schools: Study guide.* Geelong, Victoria: Deakin University Press.

CLANCY, P. 1986. The acquisition of communicative style in Japanese. In B. SCHIEFFELIN and E. OCHS (eds) *Language socialization across cultures.* London and New York: Cambridge University Press. 213–50.

CLAPHAM, C. 1993. Is ESP testing justified? In D. DOUGLAS and C. CHAPELLE (eds) *A new decade in language testing research.* Alexandria, VA: TESOL Publications. 257–71.

CLAY, M. 1975. *What did I write: Beginning writing behavior.* Oxford and Auckland, New Zealand: Heinemann Educational Books.

CLIFFORD, J. 1981. Composing in stages: The effects of a collaborative pedagogy. *Research in the Teaching of English* 15, 37–53.

CLYNE, M. 1981. Culture and discourse structure. *Journal of Pragmatics* 5, 61–6.

CLYNE, M. 1983. Linguistics and written discourse in particular languages: Contrastive studies: English and German. In R.B. KAPLAN *et al.* (eds) *Annual review of applied linguistics, 3.* Cambridge, England and New York: Cambridge University Press. 38–49.

CLYNE, M. 1985. *Language and society in the German-speaking countries.* Cambridge, England and New York: Cambridge University Press.

CLYNE, M. 1987. Cultural differences in the organization of academic texts: English and German. *Journal of Pragmatics* 11, 211–47.

CLYNE, M. 1991. The sociocultural dimension: The dilemma of the German-speaking scholar. In H. SCHRODER (ed.) *Subject-oriented texts.* New York: Walter deGruyter. 49–67.

COCHRAN-SMITH, M. 1991. Word processing and writing in elementary classrooms: A critical review of related literature. *Review of Educational Research* 61, 107–55.

COE, R. 1986. Teaching writing: The process approach, humanism, and the context of 'crisis.' In S. DeCASTELL, A. LUKE and K. EGAN (eds) *Literacy, society and schooling: A reader.* Cambridge, England and New York: Cambridge University Press. 270–312.

COE, R. 1994. 'An arousing and fulfillment of desires': The rhetoric of genre in the process era – and beyond. In A, FREEDMAN and P. MEDWAY (eds) *Genre and the new rhetoric.* London and New York: Taylor & Francis. 181–90.

COHEN, A. 1990. *Language learning.* New York: Newbury House.

COHEN, A. and M. Cavalcanti. 1990. Feedback on composition: Teacher and student verbal reports. In B. KROLL (ed.) *Second language writing.* Cambridge, England and New York: Cambridge University Press. 155–77.

COHEN, G. 1983. *The psychology of cognition,* 2nd edn. London and New York: Academic Press.

COLLERSON, J. (ed.). 1990. *Writing for life.* Rozelle, NSW: Primary English Teaching Association.

COLLINS, A., J.S. BROWN and S. NEWMAN. 1989. Cognitive apprenticeship: Teaching the craft of reading, writing, and mathematics. In L. RESNICK (ed.) *Knowing, learning, and instruction: Essays in honor of Robert Glazer.* Hove, Sussex and Hillsdale, NJ: L. Erlbaum. 453–94.

COLLINS, H. 1985. *Changing order: Replication and induction in scientific practice.* London and Beverly Hills, CA: Sage.

COLLINS, J. and M. WILLIAMSON. 1984. Assigned rhetorical context and semantic abbreviation in writing. In R. BEACH and L. BRIDWELL (eds) *New directions in composition research.* New York: Guilford. 285–96.

COMPRONE, J. 1987. Literary theory and composition. In G. TATE (ed.) *Teaching composition.* Fort Worth, TX: Texas Christian University Press. 291–330.

CONLEY, J. and W. O'BARR. 1990. *Rules versus relationships: The ethnography of legal discourse.* Chicago: University of Chicago Press.

CONNOR, U. 1987. Research frontiers in writing analysis. *TESOL Quarterly* **21**, 677–96.

CONNOR, U. 1995. *Contrastive rhetoric: Cross-cultural aspects of second language writing.* Cambridge, England and New York: Cambridge University Press.

CONNOR, U. and K. ASENAVAGE. 1994. Peer response groups in ESL writing classes: How much impact on revision. *Journal of Second Language Writing* **3**, 257–76.

CONNOR, U. and M. FARMER. 1990. The teaching of topical structure analysis as a revision strategy for ESL writers. In B. KROLL (ed.) *Second language writing.* Cambridge, England and New York: Cambridge University Press. 126–39.

CONNOR, U. and J. LAUER. 1988. Cross-cultural variation in persuasive student writing. In A. PURVES (ed.) *Writing across languages and cultures.* London and Newbury Park, CA: Sage. 138–59.

CONNOR, U. and P. McCAGG. 1987. A contrastive study of English expository prose paraphrases. In U. CONNOR and R.B. KAPLAN (eds) *Writing across languages: Analysis of L2 text.* Wokingham, England and Reading, MA: Addison-Wesley. 73–86.

COOK-GUMPERZ, J. (ed.). 1986. *The social construction of literacy.* Cambridge, England and New York: Cambridge University Press.

COOPER, C. and S. GREENBAUM (eds). 1986. *Studying writing: Linguistic approaches.* London and Beverly Hills, CA: Sage.

COOPER, C. and A. MATSUHASHI. 1983. A theory of the writing process. In M. MARTLEW (ed.) *The psychology of written language: A developmental approach.* Chichester, Sussex and New York: John Wiley. 3–39.

COOPER, M. 1986. The ecology of writing. *College English* **48**, 364–75.

COOPER, M. 1989. Why are we talking about discourse communities? Or, foundationalism rears its ugly head once more. In M. COOPER and M. HOLZMAN (eds) *Writing as social practice.* Portsmouth, NH: Boynton/Cook. 202–20.

COOPER, R. 1979. Language planning, language spread, and language change. In J. ALATIS and G.R. TUCKER (eds) *Language in public life*. Georgetown University Round Table on Languages and Linguistics 1979. Washington, DC: Georgetown University Press. 23–50.

COPE, B. and M. KALANTZIS (eds). 1993. *The powers of literacy: A genre approach to teaching writing*. Pittsburgh: University of Pittsburgh Press.

COPELAND, J. and E. LOMAX. 1988. Building effective student writing groups. In J. GOLUB (ed.) *Focus on collaborative learning*. Urbana, IL: National Council of Teachers of English. 99–104.

CORBETT, E. 1971. (1) *Classical rhetoric for the modern student*, 2nd edn. Oxford and New York. Oxford University Press.

COULTHARD, M. (ed.). 1994. *Advances in written text analysis*. London and New York: Routledge.

COUTURE, B. (ed.). 1986. *Functional approaches to writing: Research perspectives*. Norwood, NJ: Ablex.

COUTURE, B. and J. RYMER. 1993. Situational exigence: Composing processes on the job by writer's role and task value. In R. SPILKA (ed.) *Writing in the workplace*. Carbondale, IL: Southern Illinois University Press. 4–20.

COX, B., T. SHANAHAN and E. SULSBY. 1990. Good and poor elementary readers' use of cohesion in writing. *Reading Research Quarterly* **25**, 47–65.

COX, B., T. SHANAHAN and M. TINZMANN. 1991. Children's knowledge of organization, cohesion, and voice in written exposition. *Research in the Teaching of English* **25**, 179–218.

CRANDALL, J. 1993. Content-centered learning in the United States. In W. GRABE *et al.* (eds) *Annual review of applied linguistics, 13. Issues in second language teaching and learning*. Cambridge, England and New York: Cambridge University Press. 111–26.

CRESSY, D. 1980. *Literacy and the social order*. Cambridge and New York: Cambridge University Press.

CROWHURST, M. 1987. Cohesion in argument and narration at three grade levels. *Research in the Teaching of English* **21**, 185–201.

CROWHURST, M. 1990. The development of persuasive/argumentative writing. In R. BEACH and S. HYNDS (eds) *Developing discourse practices in adolescence and adulthood*. Norwood, NJ: Ablex. 200–23.

CROWLEY, S. 1989. *An introduction to deconstruction*. Urbana, IL: National Council of Teachers of English.

CROWLEY, S. 1990. *The methodical memory*. Carbondale, IL: Southern Illinois University Press.

CROWLEY, S. 1995. Composition's ethic of service, the universal of requirement, and the discourse of student need. *Journal of Advanced Composition* **15**, 227–39.

CUMMING, A. 1989. Writing expertise and second language proficiency. *Language Learning* **39**, 81–141.

CUMMING, A. 1990a. Expertise in evaluating second language compositions. *Language Testing* 7, 31–51.

CUMMING, A. 1990b. Metalinguistic and ideational thinking in second language composing. *Written Communication* 7, 482–511.

CZUBAROFF, J. 1989. The deliberative character of strategic discourse debates. In H. SIMONS (ed.) *Rhetoric in the human sciences.* London and Newbury Park, CA: Sage. 28–47.

DAIKER, D., A. KEREK and M. MORENBERG (eds). 1985. *Sentence combining: A rhetorical perspective.* Carbondale. IL: Southern Illinois University Press.

DANEŠ, F. 1974. Functional sentence perspective and the organization of text. In F. DANEŠ (ed.) *Papers on functional sentence perspective.* The Hague: Mouton. 106–28.

D'ANGELO, F. 1975. *A conceptual theory of rhetoric.* Cambridge, MA: Winthrop.

D'ANGELO, F. 1987. Aims, modes, and forms of discourse. In G. TATE (ed.) *Teaching composition.* Fort Worth, TX: Texas Christian University Press. 131–54.

DANTAS-WHITNEY, M. and W. GRABE. 1989. English and Brazilian Portuguese editorial prose. Paper presented at the 24th Annual TESOL Convention, San Antonio, TX, April 1989.

DAVIS, A., M. CLARKE and L. RHODES. 1994. Extended text and the writing proficiency of students in urban elementary schools. *Journal of Educational Psychology* 86, 556–66.

DEGENHART, R.E. (ed.). 1987. *Assessment of student writing in an international context.* Jyväskylä: Institute for Educational Research, University of Jyväskylä.

DEMAURO, G. 1992. *An investigation of the appropriateness of the TOEFL test as a matching variable to equate TWE topics.* Princeton, NJ: Educational Testing Service. [TOEFL Research Reports #37.]

DEMUTH, K. 1990. Maturation and the acquisition of the Sesotho passive. *Language* 65, 56–81.

DEREWIANKA, B. 1990. *Exploring how texts work.* Rozelle, NSW: Primary English Teaching Association (dist. by Heinemann, Portsmouth, NH).

DIEDERICH, P. 1974. *Measuring growth in English.* Urbana, IL: National Council of Teachers of English.

DILLON, G. 1981. *Constructing texts.* Bloomington, IN: Indiana University Press.

DILLON, G. 1983. Interpersonal functions of textual analysis. Lecture presented at the University of Southern California. March, 1983.

DIPARDO, A. and S. FREEDMAN. 1988. Peer response groups in the writing classroom: Theoretical foundations and new directions. *Review of Educational Research* 58, 119–49.

DIXON, C. and D. NESSEL. 1983. *Language experience approach to reading (and writing).* Hayward, CA: Alemany Press.

DOBRIN, D. 1986. Protocols once more. *College English* 48, 713–25.

DOBRIN, D. 1989. *Writing and technique.* Urbana, IL: National Council of Teachers of English.

DOHENY-FARINA, S. 1986. Writing in an emerging organization: An ethnographic study. *Written Communication* 3, 158–85.

DUDLEY-EVANS, T. 1989. An outline of the value of genre analysis in LSP work. In C. LAUREN and M. NORDMAN (eds) *Special language.* Clevedon, England and Philadelphia: Multilingual Matters. 72–9.

DUNBAR, S., D. KORETZ and H. HOOVER. 1991. Quality control in the development and use of performance assessments. *Applied Measurement in Education* 4, 289–303

DYSON, A. 1989. *Multiple worlds of child writers: Friends learning to write.* New York: Teachers College Press.

DYSON, A. 1993. *Social worlds of children learning to write.* New York: Teachers College Press.

EAGLETON, T. 1983. *Literary theory: An introduction.* Minneapolis: University of Minnesota Press.

EDE, L. and A. LUNSFORD. 1984. Audience addressed/audience invoked: The role of audience in composition theory and pedagogy. *College Composition and Communication* 35, 155–71.

EDELSKY, C. 1982. Writing in a bilingual program: The relation of L1 and L2 texts. *TESOL Quarterly* 16, 211–28.

EDELSKY, C. 1986. *Writing in a bilingual program: Habia una vez.* Norwood, NJ: Ablex.

EDELSKY, C., B. ALTWERGER and B. FLORES. 1991. *Whole language: What's the difference?* Oxford and Portsmouth, NH: Heinemann.

EGGINGTON, W. 1987. Written academic discourse in Korean: Implications for effective communication. In U. CONNOR and R.B. KAPLAN (eds) *Writing across languages: Analysis of L2 text.* Wokingham, England and Reading, MA: Addison-Wesley. 153–68.

EISENSTEIN, M. 1979. *The printing press as an agent of change, communications, and cultural transformations in early modern Europe.* 2 Volumes. Cambridge, England and New York: Cambridge University Press.

EISENSTEIN, M. 1985. On the printing press as an agent of change. In D. OLSON, N. TORRANCE and A. HILYARD (eds) *Literacy, language and learning.* Cambridge, England and New York: Cambridge University Press. 19–33.

ELBOW, P. 1973. *Writing without teachers.* Oxford and New York: Oxford University Press.

ELBOW, P. 1981. *Writing with power.* Oxford and New York: Oxford University Press.

ELBOW, P. and P. BELANOFF. 1989. *Sharing and responding.* London and New York: Random House.

ELBOW, P. and P. BELANOFF. 1991. State University of New York at Stonybrook portfolio-based evaluation program. In P. BELANOFF and M. DICKSON (eds) *Portfolios: process and product.* Portsmouth, NH: Boynton/Cook. 3–16.

EMIG, J. 1971. *The composing processes of twelfth graders.* Urbana, IL: National Council of Teachers of English.

EMIG, J. 1983. *The web of meaning.* Upper Montclair, NJ: Boynton/Cook.

EMPSON, W. 1961. *Seven types of ambiguity.* Harmondsworth: Penguin.

ENRIGHT, D.S. and M. MCCLOSKEY. 1988. *Integrating English.* Wokingham, England and Reading, MA: Addison-Wesley.

ERICSSON, K. and H. SIMON. 1984. *Protocol analysis: Verbal reports as data.* Cambridge, England and Cambridge, MA: MIT Press.

EVENSON, L. 1990. Pointers to superstructure in standard writing. In U. CONNOR and A. JOHNS (eds) *Coherence in writing.* Washington, DC: TESOL Publications. 169–83.

FAGAN, W., J. JENSEN and C. COOPER. 1985. *Measures for research and evaluation in the English language arts,* Vol. 2. Urbana, IL: National Council of Teachers of English.

FAIGLEY, L. 1979. Problems in analyzing maturity in college and adult writing. In D. DAIKER, A. KEREK and M. MORENBERG (eds) *Sentence combining and the teaching of writing.* Akron, OH: L&S Books. 94–100.

FAIGLEY, L. 1985. Nonacademic writing: The social perspective. In L. ODELL and D. GOSWAMI (eds) *Writing in nonacademic settings.* New York: Guilford Press. 231–48.

FAIGLEY, L. 1986. Competing theories of process: A critique and a proposal. *College Composition and Communication* **48**, 527–42.

FAIGLEY, L., R. CHERRY, D. JOLIFFE and A. SKINNER. 1985. *Assessing writers' knowledge and processes of composing.* Norwood, NJ: Ablex.

FAIRCLOUGH, N. 1992a. Discourse and text: Linguistic and intertextual analysis within discourse analysis. *Language and Society* **3**, 193–217.

FAIRCLOUGH, N. (ed.). 1992b. *Critical language awareness.* London and New York: Longman.

FALTIS, C. 1992. *Joinfostering: Adapting teaching strategies for the multilingual classroom.* New York: Merrill.

FATHMAN, A. and C. KESSLER. 1993. Cooperative language learning in school contexts. In W. GRABE *et al.* (eds) *Annual review of applied linguistics, 13. Issues in second language teaching and learning.* Cambridge, England and New York: Cambridge University Press. 127–40.

FATHMAN, A. and E. WHALLEY. 1990. Teacher response to student writing: Focus on form versus content. In B. KROLL (ed.) *Second language writing.* Cambridge, England and New York: Cambridge University Press. 178–90.

FEITELSON, D. 1988. *Facts and fads in beginning reading.* Norwood, NJ: Ablex.

FERRIS, D. 1994. Rhetorical strategies in student persuasive writing: Differences between native and non-native English speakers. *Research in the Teaching of English* **28**, 45–65.

FERRIS, D. 1995. Student reactions to teacher response in multiple-draft composition studies. *TESOL Quarterly* **29**, 33–53.

FIRBAS, J. 1986. On the dynamics of written communication in light of the theory of functional sentence perspective. In C. COOPER and S. GREENBAUM (eds) *Studying writing: Linguistic approaches.* Beverly Hills, CA: Sage. 40–71.

FLECK, L. 1935. *Genesis and development of a scientific fact.* (trans. F. Bradley and J. Trenn). Chicago: University of Chicago Press.

FLOWER, L. 1979. Writer-based prose: A cognitive basis for problems in writing. *College English* 41, 19–37.

FLOWER, L. 1988. The construction of purpose in writing and reading. *College English* 50, 528–50.

FLOWER, L. 1989. Cognition, context, and theory building. *College Composition and Communication* 40, 282–311.

FLOWER, L. 1994. *The construction of negotiated meaning: A social cognitive theory of writing.* Carbondale, IL: Southern Illinois University Press.

FLOWER, L. and J. HAYES. 1977. Problem-solving strategies and the writing process. *College English* 39, 449–61.

FLOWER, L. and J. HAYES. 1980a. The cognition of discovery: Defining a rhetorical problem. *College Composition and Communication* 31, 21–32.

FLOWER, L. and J. HAYES. 1980b. The dynamics of composing: Making plans and juggling constraints. In L. GREGG and E. STEINBERG (eds) *Cognitive processes in writing.* Hove, Sussex and Hillsdale, NJ: L. Erlbaum. 31–50.

FLOWER, L. and J. HAYES. 1981a. A cognitive process theory of writing. *College Composition and Communication* 32, 365–87.

FLOWER, L. and J. HAYES. 1981b. Plans that guide the composing process. In C. FREDRIKSEN and J. DOMINIC (eds) *Writing: The nature, development, and teaching of written communication*, Vol. 2. Hove, Sussex and Hillsdale, NJ: L. Erlbaum. 39–58.

FLOWER, L. and J. HAYES. 1984. Images, plans and prose: The representation of meaning in writing. *Written Communication* 1, 120–60.

FLOWER, L., V. STEIN, J. ACKERMAN, M. KANTZ, K. McCORMICK and W. PECK. 1990. *Reading-to-write: Exploring a cognitive and social process.* Oxford and New York: Oxford University Press.

FLYNN, T. and M. KING (eds). 1993. *Dynamics of the writing conference.* Urbana, IL: National Council of Teachers of English.

FOTOS, S. 1991. The cloze test as an integrative measure of EFL proficiency: A substitute for essays on college entrance examinations? *Language Learning* 41, 313–36.

FOWLER, R. 1986. *Linguistic criticism.* Oxford and New York: Oxford University Press.

FRANK, M. 1979. *If you're trying to teach kids how to write, you've gotta have this book!* Nashville, TN: Incentive Publications.

FRAWLEY, W. 1993. *Linguistic semantics.* Hove, Sussex and Hillsdale, NJ: L. Erlbaum.

FREEBODY, P. and A. WELCH (eds). 1993. *Knowledge, culture & power:*

International perspectives on literacy as policy and practice. Pittsburgh: University of Pittsburgh Press.

FREEDMAN, A. 1993. Show and tell? The role of explicit teaching in the learning of new genres. *Research in the Teaching of English* **27**, 222–51.

FREEDMAN, A. and P. MEDWAY (eds). 1994. *Genre and the new rhetoric.* Bristol, PA: Taylor & Francis.

FREEDMAN, S. (ed.). 1985. *The acquisition of written language: Response and revision.* Norwood, NJ: Ablex.

FREEDMAN, S. 1987. *Response to student writing.* Urbana, IL: National Council of teachers of English. [NCTE Research Report No. 23.]

FREEDMAN, S. and M. SPERLING. 1985. Written language acquisition: The role of response and the writing conference. In S. FREEDMAN (ed.) *Acquisition of written language: Response and revision.* Norwood, NJ: Ablex. 106–30.

FREEMAN, Y. and D. FREEMAN. 1992. *Whole language for second language learners.* Oxford and Portsmouth, NH: Heinemann.

FREIDLANDER, A. 1990. Composing in English: Effects of a first language on writing in English as a second language. In B. KROLL (ed.) *Second language writing.* Cambridge, England and New York: Cambridge University Press. 109–25.

FREIRE, P. 1985. *The politics of education.* South Hadley, MA: Bergin & Garvey.

FREIRE, P. 1994. *Pedagogy of hope.* New York: Continuum.

FREIRE, P. and D. MACEDO. 1987. *Literacy: Reading the word and the world.* South Hadley, MA: Bergin & Garvey.

FRIES, P. 1994. On theme, rheme and discourse goals. In M. COULTHARD (ed.) *Advances in written text analysis.* Oxford and New York: Routledge. 229–49.

GAIES, S. 1980. T-unit analysis in second language research: Applications, problems and limitations. *TESOL Quarterly* **14**, 53–60.

GARDNER, H. 1985. *The mind's new science: A history of the cognitive revolution.* New York: Basic Books.

GARNHAM, A. 1985. *Psycholinguistics: Central topics.* London and Baltimore, MD: Edward Arnold.

GASKILL, W. 1986. Revising in Spanish and English as a second language: A process oriented study of composition. Los Angeles: UCLA. Ph.D. diss.

GASKINS, I. 1994. Creating optimum learning environments: Is membership in the whole language community necessary? In F. LEHR and J. OSBORN (eds) *Reading, language, and literacy.* Hove, Sussex and Hillsdale, NJ: L. Erlbaum. 115–30.

GEE, J. 1986. Orality and literacy: From the *Savage mind* to *Ways with words.* *TESOL Quarterly* **20**, 717–46.

GEE, J. 1990. *Social linguistics and literacies.* New York: Falmer Press.

GEERTZ, C. 1973. *The interpretation of cultures.* New York: Basic Books.

GEERTZ, C. 1983. *Local knowledge.* New York: Basic Books.

GEISLER, C. 1994. *Academic literacy and the nature of expertise.* Hove, Sussex and Hillsdale, NJ: L. Erlbaum.

GENESEE, F. 1994. Some holes in whole language. *TESOL Matters.* 4.3. 3.

GENTILE, C. 1992. *Exploring new methods for collecting students' school-based writing: NAEP's portfolio study.* Princeton, NJ: Educational Testing Service.

GEORGE, D. 1984. Working with peer groups in the composition classroom. *College Composition and Communication* 35, 320–6.

GERE, A. 1987. *Writing groups: History, theory and implication.* Carbondale, IL: Southern Illinois University Press.

GILBERT, G. and M. MULKAY. 1984. *Opening Pandora's box: A sociological analysis of scientists' discourse.* Cambridge, England and New York: Cambridge University Press.

GIROUX, H. 1988. *Schooling and the struggle for public life.* Minneapolis: University of Minnesota Press.

GIVÓN, T. (ed.). 1983. *Topic continuity in discourse.* Philadelphia: John Benjamin.

GIVÓN, T. 1985. *Quantified studies in discourse.* [Special issues of *Text.* 5. 1/2.]

GOLDBERG, A. 1985. Groves, philharmonic at Chandler Pavilion. *Los Angeles Times.* (March 16, 1995) IV.1.

GOLDMAN, S. and H. TRUEBA (eds). 1987. *Becoming literate in English as a second language.* Norwood, NJ: Ablex.

GOLDSTEIN, L. and S. CONRAD. 1990. Student input and negotiation of meaning in ESL writing conferences. *TESOL Quarterly* 24, 443–60.

GOLUB, J. (ed.). 1988. *Focus on collaborative learning.* Urbana, IL: National Council of Teachers of English.

GOLUB-SMITH, M., C. REESE and K. STEINHAUS. 1993. *Topic and topic type comparability on the test of written English.* Princeton, NJ: Educational Testing Service. [TOEFL Research Reports #42.]

GOODMAN, K. 1986. *What's whole in whole language.* Oxford and Portsmouth, NH: Heinemann.

GOODMAN, Y. 1985. Kidwatching: Observing children in the classroom. In A. JAGGER and M.T. SMITH-BURKE (eds) *Observing the language learner.* Newark, DE: International Reading Association. 9–18.

GOODY, J. 1977. *The domestication of the savage mind.* Cambridge, England and New York: Cambridge University Press.

GOODY, J. 1987. *The interface between the written and the oral.* Cambridge, England and New York: Cambridge University Press.

GOODY, J. and I. WATT. 1963. The consequences of literacy. *Comparative Studies in History and Society* 5, 304–45.

GORMAN, T.P., A. PURVES and R.E. DEGENHART (eds). 1988. *The international writing tasks and scoring scales. International study of achievement in writing: Vol. 5.* Oxford: Pergamon Press.

GOUGH, K. 1968. Implications of literacy in traditional China and India. In J. GOODY (ed.) *Literacy in traditional societies.* Cambridge, England and New York: Cambridge University Press. 69–84.

GRABE, W. 1987. Contrastive rhetoric and text-type research. In U. CONNOR and R.B. KAPLAN (eds) *Writing across languages: Analysis of L2 text.* Wokingham, England and Reading, MA: Addison-Wesley. 115–35.

GRABE, W. 1988a. Assessing the term 'interactive'. In P. CARRELL, J. DEVINE and D. ESKEY (eds) *Interactive approaches to second language reading.* Cambridge, England and New York: Cambridge University Press. 56–70.

GRABE, W. 1988b. English, information access, and technology transfer: A rationale for English as an international language. *World Englishes* **7**, 63–72.

GRABE, W. 1990. Current developments in written discourse analysis. *Lenguas Modernas* **17**, 35–56.

GRABE, W. 1992. Applied linguistics and linguistics. In W. GRABE and R.B. KAPLAN (eds) *Introduction to applied linguistics.* Wokingham, England and Reading, MA: Addison-Wesley. 35–58.

GRABE, W. and D. BIBER. 1987. Freshman student writing and the contrastive rhetoric hypothesis. Paper presented at the 7th SLRF Conference. Los Angeles, February 1987.

GRABE, W. and C. CHAPELLE. 1995. Communicative competence, strategic competence, and procedural competence. Paper presented at the annual meeting of the American Association for Applied Linguistics. Long Beach, CA, March 1995.

GRABE, W. and R.B. KAPLAN 1986. Science, technology, language and information: Implications for language- and language-in-education planning. *International Journal of the Sociology of Language* **59**, 41–79.

GRABE, W. and R.B. KAPLAN. 1989. Writing in a second language: Contrastive rhetoric. In D. JOHNSON and D. ROEN (eds) *Richness in writing.* London and New York: Longman. 263–83.

GRAFF, H. 1987. *The legacies of literacy.* Bloomington, IN: University of Indiana Press.

GRAVES, D. 1983. *Writing: Teachers and children at work.* London and Portsmouth, NH: Heinemann.

GRAVES, D. 1984. *A researcher learns to write.* London and Portsmouth, NH: Heinemann.

GRAVES, R. 1993. Composition in Canadian universities. *Written Communication* **10**, 72–105.

GRAY, B. 1990. Natural language learning in aboriginal classrooms: Reflections on teaching and learning. In C. WALTON and W. EGGINGTON (eds) *Language: Maintenance, power and education in Australian Aboriginal contexts.* Darwin: Northern Territories University Press. 105–39.

GREENBERG, K. 1988. Review of *Assessing Writing Skills. College Composition and Communication* **39**, 478–9.

HAAS, C. and L. FLOWER. 1988. Rhetorical reading strategies and the construction of meaning. *College Composition and Communication* **39**, 167–83.

HAIRSTON, M. 1982. Winds of change: Thomas Kuhn and the revolution in the teaching of writing. *College Composition and Communication* **33**, 76–88.

HALE, G. 1992. *Effects of amount of time allowed on the test of written English.* Princeton, NJ: Educational Testing Service. [TOEFL Research Reports #39.]

HALLIDAY, M.A.K. 1973. *Explorations in the functions of language.* London and Boston: Edward Arnold.

HALLIDAY, M.A.K. 1975. *Learning how to mean: Explorations in the development of language.* London and Boston: Edward Arnold.

HALLIDAY, M.A.K. 1978. *Language as a social semiotic: The social interpretation of language and meaning.* London and Boston: Edward Arnold.

HALLIDAY, M.A.K. 1985. *An introduction to functional grammar.* London and Boston: Edward Arnold.

HALLIDAY, M.A.K. 1989. *Spoken and written language.* Oxford and New York: Oxford University Press.

HALLIDAY, M.A.K. 1993a. *Language in a changing world.* Deakin, AUS: Applied Linguistics Association of Australia. [Occasional Paper #13.]

HALLIDAY, M.A.K. 1993b. Toward a language-based theory of learning. *Linguistics and Education* **5**, 93–116.

HALLIDAY, M.A.K. 1994. The construction of knowledge and value in the grammar of scientific discourse, with reference to Charles Darwin's *The origin of species.* In M. COULTHARD (ed.) *Advances in written text analysis.* London and New York: Routledge. 136–56.

HALLIDAY, M.A.K. and R. HASAN. 1976. *Cohesion in English.* London and New York: Longman.

HALLIDAY, M.A.K. and R. HASAN. 1989. *Language, context, and text: Aspects of language in a social semiotic perspective.* Oxford and New York: Oxford University Press.

HALLIDAY, M.A.K. and J. MARTIN. 1993. *Writing science: Literacy and discursive power.* Pittsburgh: University of Pittsburgh Press.

HAMP-LYONS, L. 1990. Second language writing: Assessment issues. In B. KROLL (ed.) *Second language writing.* Cambridge, England and New York: Cambridge University Press. 69–87.

HAMP-LYONS, L. 1991a. Issues and directions in assessing second language writing in academic contexts. In L. HAMP-LYONS (ed.) *Assessing second language writing in academic contexts.* Norwood, NJ: Ablex. 323–9.

HAMP-LYONS, L. 1991b. Pre-text: Task related influences on the writer. In L. HAMP-LYONS (ed.) *Assessing second language writing in academic contexts.* Norwood, NJ: Ablex. 87–107.

HAMP-LYONS, L. 1991c. Scoring procedures for ESL contexts. In L. HAMP-LYONS (ed.) *Assessing second language writing in academic contexts.* Norwood, NJ: Ablex. 241–76.

HAMP-LYONS, L. (ed.). 1991d. *Assessing second language writing in academic contexts.* Norwood, NJ: Ablex.

HAMP-LYONS, L. and W. CONDON. 1993. Questioning assumptions about portfolio-based assessment. *College Composition and Communication* **44**, 176–90.

HAMP-LYONS, L. and G. HENNING. 1991. Communicative writing profiles: An investigation of the transferability of a multiple-trait scoring instrument across ESL writing assessment contexts. *Language Learning* **41**, 337–73.

HANANIA, E. and M. SHIKHANI. 1986. Interrelationships among three tests of language proficiency: Standardized ESL, cloze and writing. *TESOL Quarterly* **20**, 97–109.

HARLEY, B., P. ALLEN, J. CUMMINS and M. SWAIN (eds). 1990. *The development of second language proficiency.* Cambridge, England and New York: Cambridge University Press.

HARRIS, D. 1990. The use of 'organizing sentences' in the structure of paragraphs in science textbooks. In U. CONNOR and A. JOHNS (eds) *Coherence in writing.* Alexandria, VA: TESOL Publications. 69–86.

HARRIS, M. 1992. Collaboration is not collaboration is not collaboration: Writing center tutorials vs. peer-response groups. *College Composition and Communication* **43**, 369–83.

HARSTE, J., V. WOODWARD and C. BURKE. 1984. *Language stories and literacy lessons.* London and Portsmouth, NH: Heinemann.

HASAN, R. 1989. Semantic variation and sociolinguistics. *Australian Journal of Linguistics* **9**, 221–75.

HASAN, R. and J. MARTIN (eds). 1989. *Language development: Learning language, learning culture.* Norwood, NJ: Ablex.

HATIM, B. 1991. The pragmatics of argumentation in Arabic: The rise and fall of a text type. *Text* **11**, 189–99.

HAVELOCK, E. 1976. *The origins of western literacy.* Toronto: Ontario Institute for Studies in Education.

HAYES, J. and L. FLOWER. 1983. Uncovering cognitive processes in writing: An introduction to protocol analysis. In P. MOSENTHAL, L. TAMOR and S. WALMSLEY (eds) *Research in writing: Principles and methods.* London and New York: Longman. 206–19.

HAYES, J., L. FLOWER, K. SCHRIVER, J. STRATMAN, and L. CAREY. 1987. Cognitive processes in revision. In S. Rosenberg (ed.) *Advances in applied psycholinguistics: Vol 2. Reading, writing, and language learning.* Cambridge, England and New York: Cambridge University Press. 176–240.

HEATH, S.B. 1982. What no bedtime story means: Narrative skills at home and in school. *Language in Society* **11**, 49–76.

HEATH, S.B. 1983. *Ways with words.* Cambridge, England and New York: Cambridge University Press.

HEATH, S.B. 1985. Literacy or literate skills? Considerations for ESL/EFL learners. In P. LARSEN, E. JUDD, and D. MESSERSCHMITT (eds) *On TESOL '84.* Washington, DC: TESOL Publications. 15–28.

HEATH, S.B. 1986a. Critical factors in literacy development. In S. DeCASTELL, A. LUKE and K. EGAN (eds) *Literacy, society and schooling: A reader.* Cambridge, England and New York: Cambridge University Press. 209–29.

HEATH, S.B. 1986b. Sociocultural contexts of language development. In CALIFORNIA OFFICE OF BILINGUAL EDUCATION, *Beyond language: Social and cultural factors in schooling language minority children.* Los Angeles, CA: Evaluation, Dissemination and Assessment Center, California State University, Los Angeles. 143–86.

HEATH, S.B. 1993. Inner city life through drama: Imagining the language classroom. *TESOL Quarterly* **27**, 177–92.

HEATH, S.B. and A. BRANDSCOMBE. 1985. Intelligent writing in an audience community: Teacher, students, and researcher. In S. FREEDMAN (ed.) *The acquisition of written language: Response and revision.* Norwood, NJ: Ablex. 3–32.

HEATH, S.B. and L. MANGIOLA. 1991. *Children of promise: Literate activity in linguistically and culturally diverse classrooms.* Washington, DC: National Education Association.

HEDGE, T. 1988. *Writing.* Oxford and New York: Oxford University Press.

HEIMLICH, J. and S. PITTELMAN 1986. *Semantic mapping: Classroom applications.* Newark, DE: International Reading Association.

HENNING, G. 1992. *Scalar analysis of the test of written English.* Princeton, NJ: Educational Testing Service. [TOEFL Research Report #38.]

HIEBERT, F. and R. CALFEE 1992. Assessment of literacy: From standardized tests to performance and portfolios. In A. FARSTRUP and S.J. SAMUELS (eds) *What research has to say about reading instruction.* Newark, DE: International Reading Association. 70–100.

HILGERS, T. and J. MARSELLA. 1992. *Making your writing program work: A guide to good practices.* London and Newbury Park, CA: Sage.

HILLOCKS, G. 1986. *Research on written composition.* Urbana, IL: National Council of Research in English.

HINDS, J. 1983a. Linguistics and written discourse in particular languages: Contrastive studies: English and Japanese. In R.B. KAPLAN *et al.* (eds) *Annual review of applied linguistics, 3.* Cambridge, England and New York: Cambridge University Press. 78–84.

HINDS, J. 1983b. Contrastive rhetoric: English and Japanese. *Text* **3**, 183–95.

HINDS, J. 1987. Reader vs. writer responsibility: A new typology. In U. CONNOR and R.B. KAPLAN (eds) *Writing across languages: Analysis of L2 text.* Wokingham, England and Reading, MA: Addison-Wesley. 141–52.

HINDS, J. 1990. Inductive, deductive, quasi-inductive: Expository writing in Japanese, Korean, Chinese, and Thai. In U. CONNOR and A. JOHNS (eds) *Coherence in writing.* Washington, DC: TESOL Publications. 87–109.

HIRSCH, E.D. 1987. *Cultural literacy.* Boston: Houghton Mifflin.

HOEY, M. 1983. *On the surface of discourse.* London: Allen & Unwin.

HOEY, M. 1986. Overlapping patterns of discourse organization and their implications for clause relational analysis of problem-solution texts. In C. COOPER and S. GREENBAUM (eds) *Studying writing: Linguistics approaches.* London and Beverly Hills, CA: Sage. 187–214.

HOEY, M. 1991. *Patterns of lexis in text.* Oxford and New York: Oxford University Press.

HOEY, M. 1994. Signalling in discourse: A functional analysis of a common discourse pattern in written and spoken English. In M. COULTHARD (ed.) *Advances in written text analysis.* London and New York: Routledge. 26–45.

HOLT, D. and N. BAKER. 1991. Portfolios as a follow-up option in a proficiency-testing program. In. P. BELANOFF and M. DICKSON (eds) *Portfolios: Process and product.* Portsmouth, NH: Boynton/Cook. 37–45.

HOLT, M. 1992. The value of written peer criticism. *College Composition and Communication* **43**, 384–392.

HORNER, W. (ed.). 1983. *The present state of scholarship in historical and contemporary rhetoric.* Columbia, MO: University of Missouri Press.

HOROWITZ, D. 1991. ESL writing assessments: Contradictions and resolutions. In L. HAMP-LYONS (ed.) *Assessing second language writing in academic contexts.* Norwood, NJ: Ablex. 71–85.

HOUSTON, R. 1988. *Literacy in early modern Europe.* London and New York: Longman.

HUDELSON, S. 1984. 'Kan yu ret an rayt en ingles': Children become literate in English as a second language. *TESOL Quarterly* **18**, 221–38.

HUDELSON, S. 1989a. Writing in a second language. In R.B. KAPLAN *et al.* (eds) *Annual review of applied linguistics, 9.* Cambridge, England and New York: Cambridge University Press. 210–22.

HUDELSON, S. 1989b. *Write on: Children writing in ESL.* Englewood Cliffs, NJ: Prentice Hall.

HUDSON, R. 1980. Sociolinguistics. Cambridge and New York: Cambridge University Press.

HUGHEY, J., D. WORMUTH, V.F. HARTFIEL and H. JACOBS. 1983. *Teaching ESL composition: Principles and techniques.* Rowley, MA: Newbury House.

HUNT, E. and F. AGNOLI. 1991. The Whorfian hypothesis: A cognitive psychological perspective. *Psychological Review* **98**, 377–389.

HUNT, K. 1965. *Grammatical structures written at three grade levels.* Urbana, IL: National Council of Teachers of English.

HUNT, K. 1983. Sentence combining and the teaching of writing. In M. MARTLEW (ed.) *The psychology of written language: A developmental approach.* New York: J. Wiley. 99–125.

HUTCHINSON, T. and A. WATERS. 1987. *English for specific purposes: A learning centered approach.* Cambridge, England and New York: Cambridge University Press.

HYMES, D. 1972. On communicative competence. In J. PRIDE and

454   *Bibliography*

A. HOLMES (eds) *Sociolinguistics.* Harmsworth and New York: Penguin.
269–93.

IELTS HANDBOOK. 1995. Cambridge: University of Cambridge Local
Examination Syndicate.

INDRASUTRA, C. 1988. Narrative styles in the writing of Thai and American
students. In A. PURVES (ed.) *Writing across languages and cultures.*
Newbury Park, CA: Sage. 206–26.

INGRAM, D. 1990. The Australian second language proficiency ratings
(ASLPR). In J.H.A.L. De Jong (ed.) *Standardization in language testing.*
Amsterdam: Free University Press. 46–61. [*AILA Review,* 7]

INGRAM, D. and E. WYLIE. 1984. *Australian second language proficiency
ratings.* Canberra: Australian Government Publishing Service.

JACKENDOFF, R. 1972. *Semantic interpretation in generative grammar.*
Cambridge, MA: MIT Press.

JACOBS, H., S. ZINGRAF, D. WORMUTH, V. HARTFIEL and J. HUGHEY. 1981.
Testing ESL composition: A practical approach. Rowley, MA: Newbury
House.

JAGGER, A. and M.T. SMITH-BURKE (eds.). 1985. *Observing the language
learner.* Neward, DE: International Reading Association.

JENKINS, S. and J. HINDS. 1987. Business letter writing: English, French
and Japanese. *TESOL Quarterly* **21**, 327–49.

JOHNS, A. 1986. Coherence and academic writing: Some definitions and
suggestions for teaching. *TESOL Quarterly* **20**, 247–65.

JOHNS, A. 1990. L1 composition theories: Implications for developing theories of L2 composition. In B. KROLL (ed.) *Second language writing.*
Cambridge, England and New York: Cambridge University Press.
24–36.

JOHNS, A. and T. DUDLEY-EVANS. 1991. English for specific purposes:
International in scope, specific in purpose. *TESOL Quarterly* **25**,
297–314.

JOHNSON, D. and D. ROEN (eds). 1989. *Richness in writing: Empowering ESL
students.* London and New York: Longman.

JOHNSON, D.W. and R. JOHNSON. 1991. *Learning together and alone:
Cooperative, competitive, and individualistic learning.* Edina, MN:
Interaction Book Company.

JOHNSON-LAIRD, P. 1983. *Mental Models.* Cambridge, MA: Harvard
University Press.

JONES, S. 1985. Problems with monitor use in second language composing. In M. ROSE (ed.) *When a writer can't write.* New York: Guilford.
96–118.

JONES, S. and J. TETROE. 1987. Composing in a second language. In
A. MATSUHASHI (ed.) *Writing in real time.* Norwood, NJ: Ablex. 34–57.

JONZ, J. 1990. Another turn in the conversation: What does cloze
measure? *TESOL Quarterly* **24**, 61–83.

JOOS, M. 1967. *The five clocks.* London and New York: Harcourt Brace
Jovanovich.

JUST, M. and P. CARPENTER. 1992. A capacity theory of comprehension: Individual differences in working memory. *Psychological Review* **99**, 122–49.

KACHRU, B. 1985. Institutionalized second language varieties. In S. GREENBAUM (ed.) *The English language today.* Oxford and New York: Oxford University Press. 211–26.

KACHRU, B. 1992. Why applied linguistics leaks. Plenary address presented at the annual meeting of the American Association for Applied Linguistics. Seattle, WA, February, 1992.

KACHRU, Y. 1983. Linguistics and written discourse in particular languages: Contrastive studies: English and Hindi. In R.B. KAPLAN *et al.* (eds) *Annual review of applied linguistics, 3.* Cambridge, England and New York: Cambridge University Press. 50–77.

KACHRU, Y. 1987. Cross-cultural texts, discourse strategies and discourse interpretation. In L. SMITH (ed.) *Discourse across cultures: Strategies in world Englishes.* Englewood Cliffs, NJ: Prentice Hall. 87–100.

KACHRU, Y. 1988. Writers in Hindi and English. In A. PURVES (ed.) *Writing across languages and cultures.* London and Newbury Park, CA: Sage. 109–37.

KAESTLE, C., H. DAMON-MOORE, L. STEDMAN, K. TINSLEY and W. TROLLINGER. 1991. *Literacy in the United States.* New Haven, CT: Yale University Press.

KAGAN, S. 1992. *Cooperative learning.* San Juan Capistrano, CA: Resources for Teachers.

KAPLAN, R.B. 1966. Cultural thought patterns in intercultural education. *Language Learning* **16**, 1–20.

KAPLAN, R.B. 1972. *The anatomy of rhetoric: Prolegomena to a functional theory of rhetoric.* Philadelphia: Center for Curriculum Development (distributed by Heinle & Heinle, New York).

KAPLAN, R.B. 1983. An introduction to the study of written texts: The 'discourse compact.' In R.B. KAPLAN *et al.* (eds) *Annual review of applied linguistics, 3.* Cambridge, England and New York: Cambridge University Press. 138–51.

KAPLAN, R.B. 1987. Cultural thought patterns revisited. In U. CONNOR and R.B. KAPLAN (eds) *Writing across languages: Analysis of L2 text.* Wokingham, England and Reading, MA: Addison-Wesley. 9–22.

KAPLAN, R.B. 1988. Contrastive rhetoric and second language learning: Notes toward a theory of contrastive rhetoric. In A. PURVES (ed.) *Writing across languages and cultures.* London and Newbury Park, CA: Sage. 275–304.

KAPLAN, R.B. 1991. Concluding essay: On applied linguistics and discourse analysis. In W. GRABE *et al.* (eds) *Annual Review of Applied Linguistics,* **11**. Cambridge, England and New York: Cambridge University Press. 199–204.

KAPLAN, R.B. 1992. Applied linguistics and language policy and planning.

In W. GRABE and R.B. KAPLAN (eds.) *Introduction to applied linguistics.* Wokingham, England and Reading, MA: Addison-Wesley. 143–165.

KAPLAN, R.B. 1993. The hegemony of English in science and technology. *Journal of Multilingual and Multicultural Development* **14**, 151–72.

KAPLAN, R.B. (ed.). 1995. *The teaching of writing around the Pacific Basin.* [Special issue of *Journal of Asian Pacific Communication.* 6]

KAPLAN, R.B. and W. GRABE. 1991. The fiction in science writing. In H. SCHRODER (ed.) *Subject-oriented texts: Language for special purposes and text theory.* New York: Walter De Gruyter. 199–217.

KAPLAN, R.B. and P. SHAW. 1983. *Exploring academic English.* Rowley, MA: Newbury House.

KAPLAN, R.B. *et al.* (eds). 1983. *Annual review of applied linguistics, 3.* Rowley, MA: Newbury House.

KAUFER, D. and R. YOUNG. 1993. Writing in the content areas: Some theoretical complexities. In L. ODELL (ed.) *Theory and practice in the teaching of writing: Rethinking the discipline.* Carbondale, IL: Southern Illinois University Press. 71–104.

KELLOGG, R. 1994. *The psychology of writing.* Oxford and New York: Oxford University Press.

KINNEAVY, J. 1971. *A theory of discourse: The aims of discourse.* Englewood Cliffs, NJ: Prentice Hall.

KINNEAVY, J. 1983. A pluralistic synthesis of four contemporary models for teaching composition. In A. FREEDMAN, I. PRINGLE and J. YALDEN (eds) *Learning to write: First language/second language.* London and New York: Longman. 121–38.

KINNEAVY, J. 1987. Writing across the curriculum. In G. TATE (ed.) *Teaching composition.* Fort Worth, TX: Texas Christian University Press. 353–77.

KINTSCH, W. and T. VAN DIJK. 1978. Toward a model of text comprehension and production. *Psychological Review* **85**, 363–94.

KIRSCH, G. and D. ROEN (eds). 1990. *A sense of audience in written communication.* London and Newbury Park, CA: Sage.

KORETZ, D. 1993. New report on Vermont portfolio project documents challenges. *National Council on Measurement in Education Quarterly Newsletter.* 1.4. 1–2.

KRAPELS, A. 1990. An overview of second language writing process research. In B. KROLL (ed.) *Second language writing.* Cambridge, England and New York: Cambridge University Press. 37–56.

KRASHEN, S. 1984. *Writing: Research, theory and applications.* Oxford and New York: Pergamon Press.

KRESS, G. 1989. *Linguistic processes in sociocultural practice.* Oxford and New York: Oxford University Press.

KRESS, G. 1991. Critical discourse analysis. In W. GRABE *et al.* (eds) *Annual review of applied linguistics, 11.* Cambridge, England and New York: Cambridge University Press. 84–99.

KRESS, G. 1994. *Learning to write.* 2nd ed. London: Routledge.

KRUEGER, M. and F. RYAN (eds). 1993. *Language and content: Discipline and content-based approaches to language study.* Lexington, MA: D.C. Heath.

KROLL, BARBARA. (ed.). 1990. *Second language writing.* Cambridge, England and New York: Cambridge University Press.

KROLL, BARBARA and J. REID. 1994. Guidelines for designing writing prompts: Clarifications, caveats, and cautions. *Journal of Second Language Writing* **3**, 231–55.

KROLL, BARRY. 1981. Developmental relationships between speaking and writing. In B KROLL and R. VANN (eds) *Exploring speaking-writing relationships.* Urbana, IL: National Council of Teachers of English. 32–54.

KROLL, BARRY. 1984. Writing for readers: Three perspectives on audience. *College Composition and Communication* **35**, 172–85.

KUHN, T. 1970. *The structure of scientific revolutions,* 2nd edn. Chicago: University of Chicago Press.

KUTZ, E., S. GROGAN and V. ZAMEL. 1993. *The discovery of competence: Teaching and learning with diverse student writers.* London and Portsmouth, NH: Heinemann.

LACKSTROM, J., L. SELINKER and L. TRIMBLE. 1973. Technical rhetorical principles and grammatical choice. *TESOL Quarterly* **7**, 127–36.

LADUSAW, W. 1988. Semantic theory. In F. NEWMEYER (ed.) *Linguistics: The Cambridge survey,* Vol. 1. Cambridge, England and New York: Cambridge University Press. 89–112.

LANGACKER, R. 1995. Raising and transparency. *Language.* 1–62.

LANGER, J. 1987. A sociocognitive perspective on literacy. In J. LANGER (ed.) *Language, literacy, and culture: Issues of society and schooling.* Norwood, NJ: Ablex. 1–20.

LAPONCE, J. 1987. *Languages and their territories.* Toronto: Univesity of Toronto Press.

LAREAU, A. 1989. *Home advantage.* New York: Falmer Press.

LARGE, J.A. 1983. *The foreign language barrier: Problems in scientific communication.* London: Andre Deutsch.

LARSEN-FREEMAN, D. 1978. An ESL index of development. *TESOL Quarterly* **12**, 439–48.

LATOUR, B. 1987. *Science in action.* Cambridge, England and New York: Cambridge University Press.

LATOUR, B. and S. WOOLGAR. 1979. *Laboratory life: The social construction of scientific fact.* London and Beverly Hills, CA: Sage.

LAUER, J. and J. ASHER. 1988. *Composition research: Empirical designs.* Oxford and New York: Oxford University Press.

LAUTAMATTI, L. 1987. Observations on the development of the topic of simplified discourse. In U. CONNOR and R.B. KAPLAN (eds) *Writing across languages: Analysis of L2 text.* Wokingham, England and Reading, MA: Addison-Wesley. 87–114.

LAWSON, B., S. RYAN and R. WINTEROWD (eds). 1989. *Encountering student texts.* Urbana, IL: National Council of Teachers of English.

LAY, N. 1982. Composing processes of adult ESL learners: A case study. *TESOL Quarterly* **16**, 406.

LEKI, I. 1990. Coaching from the margins: Issues in written response. In B. KROLL (ed.) *Second language writing*. Cambridge, England and New York: Cambridge University Press. 57–68.

LEKI, I. 1991. Twenty-five years of contrastive rhetoric: Text analysis and writing pedagogies. *TESOL Quarterly* **25**, 123–43.

LEKI, I. 1992. *Understanding ESL writers: A guide for teachers*. London and Portsmouth, NH: Heinemann.

LEMKE, J. 1995. *Textual politics: Discourse and social dynamics*. New York: Taylor & Francis.

LEY, C., B. SCHAIR and B. DISMUKES. 1994. Longitudinal study of the reading attitudes and behaviors of middle school students. *Reading Psychology* **15**, 11–38.

LIBERMAN, Y. and I. LIBERMAN. 1990. Whole language vs. code emphasis: Underlying assumptions and their implications for reading instructions. *Annals of Dyslexia* **40**, 51–76.

LINDEMANN, E. 1987. *A rhetoric for writing teachers*. Oxford and New York: Oxford University Press.

LINDEN, M. and A. WHIMBEY. 1990. *Why Johnny can't write: How to improve writing skills*. Hove, Sussex and Hillsdale, NJ: L. Erlbaum.

LOBAN, W. 1976. *Language development: Kindergarten through grade twelve*. Urbana, IL: National Council of Teachers of English.

LONG, R. 1990. The writer's audience: Fact or fiction? In G. KIRSCH and D. ROEN (eds) *A sense of audience in written communication*. London and Newbury Park, CA: Sage. 73–84.

LUCY, J. 1992. *Language diversity and thought: A reformulation of the linguistic relativity hypothesis*. Cambridge, England and New York: Cambridge University Press.

LUX, P. 1991. Discourse styles of Anglo and Latin American college student writers. Tempe, AZ; Arizona State University. Ph.D. diss.

LUX, P. and W. GRABE. 1991. Multivariate approaches to contrastive rhetoric. *Lenguas Modernas* **18**, 133–60.

LYNCH, M. 1985. *Art and artifact in laboratory science: A study of shop work and shop talk at a research laboratory*. London and Boston: Routledge & Kegan Paul.

MACKINNON, J. 1993. Becoming a rhetor: Developing writing ability in a mature, writing-intensive organization. In R. SPILKA (ed.) *Writing in the workplace*. Carbondale, IL: Southern Illinois University Press. 41–55.

MACLEAN, R. 1989. Composing processes. In F. CHRISTIE *et al.* (eds) *Writing in schools: Study guide*. Geelong, Victoria: Deakin University Press. 131–49.

MACRORIE, K. 1970. *Uptaught*. Rochelle Park, NJ: Hayden.

MACRORIE, K. 1980. *Searching writing*. Upper Montclair, NJ: Boynton/ Cook.

MAHER, J. 1987. The role of English as the international language of medicine. *Applied Linguistics* **7**, 206–18.

MAHER, J. and D. ROKOSZ. 1992. Language use and the professions. In
W. GRABE and R.B. KAPLAN (eds) *Introduction to applied linguistics.*
Wokingham, England and Reading, MA: Addison-Wesley. 231–53.

MANN, W. and S. THOMPSON. 1988. Rhetorical structure theory. *Text* 8,
243–81.

MANN, W. and S. THOMPSON (eds). 1992. *Discourse description: Diverse
linguistic analyses of a fund-raising text.* Philadelphia: J. Benjamin.

MANNING, M., G. MANNING and R. LONG. 1994. *Theme immersion: Inquiry-
based curriculum in elementary and middle schools.* London and
Portsmouth, NH: Heinemann.

MARLAND, M. 1977. *Language across the curriculum.* London: Heinemann.

MARTIN, J. 1985. Process and text: Two aspects of semiosis. In J. BENSON
and W. GREAVES (eds) *Systemic perspectives in discourse.* Vol. 1. Norwood,
NJ: Ablex. 248–74.

MARTIN, J. 1989. *Factual writing: Exploring and challenging social reality.*
Oxford and New York: Oxford University Press.

MARTIN, J. 1992. *English text: System and structure.* Philadelphia: J.
Benjamin.

MARTIN, J. 1993. Genre and literacy – Modeling context in educational
linguistics. In W. GRABE *et al.* (eds) *Annual review of applied linguistics, 13.
Issues in second language teaching and learning.* Cambridge, England and
New York: Cambridge University Press. 141–72.

MARTIN, J. and J. ROTHERY. 1986. What a functional approach to the writing task can show teachers about 'good writing'. In B. COUTURE (ed.)
Functional approaches to writing: Research perspectives. Norwood, NJ: Ablex.
241–65.

MATALENE, C. 1985. Contrastive rhetoric: An American writing teacher in
China. *College English* 47, 789–807.

MATALENE, C. 1995. Of the people, by the people, for the people: Texts in
public contexts. In J. REYNOLDS, C. MATALENE, J. MAGNOTTO, D. SAMSON,
JR. and L. SADLER (eds) *Professional writing in context: Lessons from teaching
and consulting in worlds of work.* Hove, Sussex and Hillsdale, NJ: L.
Erlbaum. 33–67.

MCGINLEY, W. and R. TIERNEY. 1989. Traversing the topical landscape.
Written Communication 6, 243–69.

MCKENNA, M., R. ROBINSON and J. MILLER. 1993. Whole language and
research: The case for caution. In D. LEU *et al.* (eds) *Examining central
issues in literacy research, theory, and practice.* 42nd Yearbook of the
National Reading Conference. Chicago, IL: National Reading
Conference. 141–52.

MCKENNA, M., S. STAHL and D. REINKING. 1994. A critical commentary on
research, politics, and whole language. *Journal of Reading Behavior* 26,
211–33.

MCLEOD, S. and M. DOVEN (eds). 1992. *Writing across the curriculum: A
guide to developing programs.* London and Newbury Park, CA: Sage.

MECH, D. 1985. How delicate is the balance of nature? *National Wildlife* **23**, 2. 54–8.

MEDGYES, P. and R.B. KAPLAN. 1992. Discourse in a foreign language: The example of Hungarian scholars. *International Journal of the Sociology of Language* **98**, 67–100.

MEINBACH, A., L. ROTHLEIN and A. FREDERICKS. 1995. *The complete guide to thematic units: Creating the integrated curriculum.* Norwood, MA: Christopher-Gordon.

MERTON, R. 1973. *The sociology of science.* Chicago: University of Chicago Press.

MESSICK, S. 1989. Validity. In R. LINN (ed.) *Educational measurement,* 3rd edn. London and New York: Macmillan. 13–104.

MESSICK, S. 1994. The interplay of evidence and consequences in the validation of performance assessments. *Educational Researcher* **23**, 13–24.

MEYER, B. 1975. *The organization of prose and its effects on memory.* Amsterdam: North-Holland.

MEYER, B. 1984. Organizational aspects of text: Effects on reading comprehension and applications for the classroom. In J. FLOOD and D. LAPP (eds) *Promoting reading comprehension.* Newark, DE: International Reading Association. 113–38.

MEYER, B. 1985. Prose analysis: Purposes, procedures, and problems. In B. BRITTON and J. BLACK (eds) *Understanding expository text.* Hove, Sussex and Hillsdale, NJ: L. Erlbaum. 11–64.

MEYER, B. 1987. Following the author's top-level organization: An important skill for reading comprehension. In R. TIERNEY, P. ANDERS and J. MITCHELL (eds) *Understanding readers' understanding: Theory and practice.* Hillsdale, NJ: L. Erlbaum. 59–76.

MILANOVIC, M. 1987. Large-scale language testing. In R. LORD and H. CHENG (eds) *Language education Hong Kong.* Hong Kong: The Chinese University Press. 123–32.

MILLER, C. 1984. Genre as social action. *Quarterly Journal of Speech* **70**, 151–67.

MILLER, T. (ed.). 1995. *Functional approaches to written texts: Classroom applications.* Paris: TESOL France.

MOFFETT, J. 1968. *Teaching the universe of discourse.* Boston: Houghton Mifflin.

MOHAN, B. 1986. *Language and content.* Wokingham, England and Reading, MA: Addison-Wesley.

MOHAN, B. 1990. LEP students and the integration of language and content: Knowledge structures and tasks. In C. SIMICH-DUDGEON (ed.) *Proceedings of the first research symposium on limited English proficient student issues.* Washington, DC: Office of Bilingual Education and Minority Language Affairs. 113–60.

MOLL, L. (ed.). 1990. *Vygotsky and education: Instructional implications and applications of socio-historical psychology.* Cambridge, England and New York: Cambridge University Press.

MONTAÑO-HARMON, M. 1988. Discourse features in the compositions of Mexican English as a second language, Mexican–American, Chicano and Anglo high school students: Considerations for the formulation of educational policy. Los Angeles: University of Southern California. Ph.D. diss.

MONTAÑO-HARMON, M. 1991. Discourse features of written Mexican Spanish: Current research in contrastive rhetoric and its implications. *Hispania* **74**, 417–25.

MOSENTHAL, P. and R. TIERNEY. 1984. Cohesion: problems with talking about text. *Reading Research Quarterly* **19**, 240–4.

MUCHIRI, M., N. MULAMBA, G. MYERS and D. NDOLOI. 1995. Importing composition. *College Composition and Communication* **46**, 175–98.

MULKAY, M. 1979. *Science and the sociology of knowledge.* London: Unwin & Allen.

MULLEN, K. 1987. Test of ability to subordinate. In C. ALDERSON, K. KRAHNKE and C. STANSFIELD (eds) *Reviews of English language proficiency tests.* Washington, DC: TESOL Publications. 73–6.

MURRAY, D. 1968. *A writer teaches writing.* Boston: Houghton Mifflin.

MURRAY, D. 1980. Writing as process: How writing finds its own meaning. In T. DONOVAN and B. MCCLELLAND (eds) *Eight approaches to teaching composition.* Urbana, IL: National Council of Teachers of English. 3–20.

MURRAY, D. 1985. *A writer teaches writing,* 2nd edn. Boston: Houghton Mifflin.

MYERS, G. 1985. The social construction of two biologists' proposals. *Written Communication* **2**, 219–45.

MYERS, G. 1986. Writing research and the sociology of scientific knowledge: A review of three new books. *College English* **48**, 595–610.

MYERS, G. 1989. The pragmatics of politeness in scientific articles. *Applied Linguistics* **10**, 1–35.

MYERS, G. 1990. *Writing biology: Texts in the social construction of knowledge.* Madison, WI: University of Wisconsin Press.

NAGY, W. 1988. *Teaching vocabulary to improve reading comprehension.* Urbana, IL: National Council of teachers of English.

NATIONAL COUNCIL OF TEACHERS OF ENGLISH (NCTE) (eds). 1983. *Idea exchange for English teachers.* Urbana, IL: National Council of teachers of English.

NEEDELS, M. and M. KNAPP. 1994. Teaching writing to children who are underserved. *Journal of Educational Psychology* **86**, 339–49.

NEEL, J. 1988. *Plato, Derrida, and writing.* Carbondale, IL: Southern Illinois University Press.

NELSON, G. and J. MURPHY. 1992. An L2 writing group: Task and social dimensions. *Journal of Second Language Writing* **1**, 171–93.

NELSON, G. and J. MURPHY. 1993. Peer response groups: Do L2 writers use peer comments in revising their drafts? *TESOL Quarterly* **27**, 135–42.

NEWELL, A. and H. SIMON. 1972. *Human problem solving.* Englewood Cliffs, NJ: Prentice Hall.

NEWKIRK, T. 1987. *More than stories.* London and Portsmouth, NH: Heinemann.

NEWKIRK, T. (ed.). 1993. *Nuts and bolts: A practical guide to teaching college composition.* London and Portsmouth, NH: Heinemann.

NEWMAN, D., P. GRIFFIN and M. COLE. 1989. *The construction zone.* Cambridge, England and New York: Cambridge University Press.

NOLD, E. and S. FREEDMAN. 1977. An analysis of readers' responses to essays. *Research in the Teaching of English* **11**, 164–77.

NORTH, S. 1987. *The making of knowledge in composition.* London and Portsmouth, NH: Heinemann.

NYSTRAND, M. 1986. *The structure of written communication: Studies in reciprocity between writers and readers.* London and New York: Academic Press.

NYSTRAND, M. 1989. A social-interactive model of writing. *Written Communication* **6**, 66–85.

NYSTRAND, M. 1990. Sharing words: The effects of readers on developing writers. *Written Communication* **7**, 3–24.

NYSTRAND, M. and D. BRANDT. 1989. Response to writing as a context for learning to write. In C. ANSON (ed.) *Writing and response.* Urbana, IL: National Council of Teachers of English. 209–30.

OAKHILL, J. and A. GARNHAM. 1988. *Becoming a skilled reader.* Oxford and New York: Basil Blackwell.

O'BARR, W. 1982. *Linguistic evidence: Language, power, and strategy in the courtroom.* London and New York: Academic Press.

OCHS, E. 1979. Planned and unplanned discourse. In T. GIVÓN (ed.) *Discourse and syntax.* [Syntax and Semantics 12.] London and New York: Academic Press. 51–80.

OCHS, E. 1988. *Language and cultural development.* Cambridge, England and New York: Cambridge University Press.

ODELL, L. 1985. Beyond the text: Relations between writing and social context. In L. ODELL and D. GOSWAMI (eds) *Writing in nonacademic settings.* New York: Guilford. 249–80.

ODELL, L. and D. GOSWAMI (eds). 1985. *Writing in nonacademic settings.* New York: Guilford Press.

O'HARE, F. 1973. *Sentence combining: Improving student writing without formal grammar instruction.* Urbana, IL: National Council of Teachers of English.

OLLER, J., JR. 1983. Evidence for a general language proficiency factor: An expectancy grammar. In J. OLLER (ed.) *Issues in language testing research.* Rowley, MA: Newbury House. 3–10.

OLLER, J., JR. and J. JONZ (eds). 1994. *Cloze and coherence.* Lewisburg, PA: Bucknell University Press.

OLSEN, L. 1993. Research on discourse communities: An overview. In

R. SPILKA (ed.) *Writing in the workplace.* Carbondale, IL: Southern Illinois University Press. 181–94.

OLSON, D. 1977. From utterance to text: The bias of language in speech and writing. *Harvard Educational Review* 47, 257–81.

OLSON, D. 1991. Literacy as metalinguistics. In D. OLSON and N. TORRANCE (eds) *Literacy and orality.* Cambridge, England and New York: Cambridge University Press. 251–70.

OLSON, D. 1994. *The world on paper.* Cambridge, England and New York: Cambridge University Press.

ONG, W. 1982. *Orality and literacy: The technologizing of the word.* London: Methuen.

OSTLER, S. 1987. English in parallels: A comparison of English and Arabic prose. In U. CONNOR and R.B. KAPLAN (eds) *Writing across languages: Analysis of L2 text.* Wokingham, England and Reading, MA: Addison-Wesley. 169–85.

PAINTER, C. 1989. Learning language: A functional view of language development. In R. HASAN and J. MARTIN (eds) *Language development: Learning language, learning culture.* Norwood, NJ: Ablex. 18–65.

PAIVIO, A. 1986. *Mental representations.* Oxford and New York: Oxford University Press.

PALINCSAR, A. and A. BROWN. 1984. Reciprocal teaching of comprehension-fostering and monitoring activities. *Cognition and Instruction* 1, 117–75.

PALINCSAR, A. and L. KLENK. 1991. Dialogues promoting reading comprehension. In B. MEANS, C. CHELEMER and M. KNAPP (eds) *Teaching advanced skills to at-risk students.* San Francisco: Jossey Bass. 112–30.

PANDHARIPANDE, R. 1983. Linguistics and written discourse in particular languages: Contrastive studies: English and Marathi. In R.B. KAPLAN *et al.* (eds) *Annual review of applied linguistics,* 3. Rowley, MA: Newbury House. 118–38.

PARADIS, J. 1991. Text and Action: The operator's manual in context and in court. In C. BAZERMAN and J. PARADIS (eds) *Textual dynamics of the professions.* Madison, WI: University of Wisconsin Press. 256–78.

PARADIS, J., D. DOBRIN and R. MILLER. 1985. Writing at Exxon ITD: Notes on the writing environment of an R&D organization. In L. ODELL and D. GOSWAMI (eds) *Writing in nonacademic settings.* New York: Guilford. 281–307.

PARK, D. 1982. The meaning of audience. *College English.* 44, 247–57.

PEARSON, P.D. and L. FIELDING. 1991. Comprehension instruction. In R. Barr *et al.* (eds) *Handbook of reading research.* Vol. 2. London and New York: Longman. 815–60.

PENNINGTON, M. 1993. A critical examination of word processing effects in relation to L2 writers. *Journal of Second Language Writing* 2, 227–55.

PEREGOY, S. and O. BOLYE. 1993. *Reading, writing, and learning in ESL: A resource book for K-8 teachers.* London and New York: Longman.

PERERA, K. 1984. *Children's writing and reading: Analysing classroom language.* Oxford and New York: Basil Blackwell.

PERFETTI, C. and D. McCUTCHEN. 1987. Schooled language competence: Linguistic abilities in reading and writing. In S. ROSENBERG (ed.) *Advances in applied psycholinguistics: Volume 2. Reading, writing, and language learning.* Cambridge, England and New York: Cambridge University Press. 105–41.

PERKINS, K. 1983. On the use of composition scoring techniques, objective measures, and objective test to evaluate ESL writing ability. *TESOL Quarterly* **17**, 651–71.

PERL, S. 1979. The composing processes of unskilled college writers. *Research in the Teaching of English* **13**, 317–36.

PEYTON, J.K. (ed.). 1990. *Students and teachers writing together.* Washington, DC: TESOL Publications.

PEYTON, J.K., J. STATON, G. RICHARDSON and W. WOLFRAM. 1990. The influence of writing task on ESL students' written production. *Research in the Teaching of English* **24**, 142–71.

PHELPS, L. 1988. *Composition as a human science.* Oxford and New York: Oxford University Press.

PHILIPS, S. 1983. *The invisible culture: Communication in classroom and community on the Warm Springs indian reservation.* London and New York: Longman.

PHILLIPSON, R. 1992. *Linguistic imperialism.* Oxford and New York: Oxford University Press.

PIERCE, L. and M. O'MALLEY. 1992. *Performance and portfolio assessment for language minority students.* Washington, DC: National Clearinghouse for Bilingual Education. [NCBE Program Information Guide Series #9.]

POGNER, K.-H. (ed.). 1994. *More on writing.* Odense, Denmark: Institute of Language and Communication. [Odense Working Papers in Language and Communication #6.]

POOLE, D. 1991. Discourse analysis in ethnographic research. In W. GRABE *et al.* (eds) *Annual review of applied linguistics,* **11**. Cambridge, England and New York: Cambridge University Press. 42–56.

PRELLY, L. 1989. The rhetorical construction of scientific ethos. In H. SIMONS (ed.) *Rhetoric in the human sciences.* London and Newbury Park, CA: Sage. 48–68.

PRESSLEY, M. *et al.* 1989. Strategies that improve memory and comprehension of what is read. *Elementary School Journal* **90**, 3–32.

PRESSLEY, M. *et al.* 1991. Teaching literacy strategies across the curriculum: A case study at benchmark school. In J. ZUTELL and S. McCORMICK (eds) *Learner factors/teacher factors: Issues in literacy research and instruction.* 40th Yearbook of the National Reading Conference. Chicago, IL: National Reading Conference. 219–28.

PRESSLEY, M. *et al.* 1992. Beyond direct explanation: Transactional instruction in reading comprehension strategies. *Elementary School Journal* **92**, 513–55.

PRESSLEY, M. *et al.* 1994. Transactional instruction of comprehension strategies: The Montgomery County, Maryland, SAIL program. *Reading & Writing Quarterly* **10**, 5–20.

PRIESTLEY, J. 1777/1965. *A course of lectures on oratory and criticism.* [ed. V.M. Bevilacqua and R. Murphy.] Carbondale, IL: Southern Illinois University Press.

PRINCE, E. 1981. Toward a taxonomy of given-new information. In P. COLE (ed.) *Radical pragmatics.* London and New York: Academic Press. 223–55.

PRINCE, E. 1992. The ZPG letter: Subjects, definiteness, and information status. In W. MANN and S. THOMPSON (eds) *Discourse description: Diverse linguistic analyses of a fund-raising text.* Philadelphia: J. Benjamins. 295–325.

PURVES, A. 1984. In search of an internationally-valid scheme for scoring compositions. *College Composition and Communication* **35**, 426–38.

PURVES, A. 1991. *The scribal society.* London and New York: Longman.

PURVES, A. (ed.). 1988. *Writing across languages and culture.* London and Newbury Park, CA: Sage.

PURVES, A. and G. HAWISHER. 1990. Writers, judges, and text models. In R. BEACH and S. HYNDS (eds) *Developing discourse practices in adolescence and adulthood.* Norwood, NJ: Ablex. 183–99.

PURVES, A. and W. PURVES. 1986. Culture, text models, and the activity of writing. *Research in the Teaching of English* **20**, 174–97.

PURVES, A., A. SOTER, S. TAKALA and A. VAHAPASSI. 1984. Toward a domain-referenced system for classifying composition assignments. *Research on the Teaching of English* **18**, 385–416.

PURVES, A. and S. TAKALA (eds). 1982. *An international perspective on the evaluation of written composition: Evaluation in education: An international review series*, Vol. 3, No. 5. Oxford: Pergamon.

QUIRK, R. *et al.* 1985. *A comprehensive grammar of English.* London and New York: Longman.

RABIN, C. 1986. The discourse status of commentary. In C. COOPER and S. GREENBAUM (eds) *Studying writing: Linguistic approaches.* London and Beverly Hills, CA: Sage. 215–25.

RADECKI, P. and J. SWALES. 1988. ESL student reaction to written comments on their written work. *System* **16**, 355–65.

RAFOTH, B. 1988. Discourse community: Where writers, readers, and texts come together. In B. RAFOTH and D. RUBIN (eds) *The social construction of written communication.* Norwood, NJ: Ablex. 131–46.

RAFOTH, B. 1990. The concept of discourse community: Descriptive and explanatory adequacy. In G. KIRSCH and D. ROEN (eds) *A sense of audience in written communication.* London and Newbury Park, CA: Sage. 140–52.

RAIMES, A. 1983a. Anguish as a second language? Remedies for composition teachers. In A. FREEDMAN, I. PRINGLE and J. YALDEN (eds) *Learning to write: First language/second language.* London and New York: Longman. 258–72.

RAIMES, A. 1983b. Tradition and revolution in ESL teaching. *TESOL Quarterly* **17**, 535–52.

RAIMES, A. 1983c. *Techniques in teaching writing.* Oxford and New York: Oxford University Press.

RAIMES, A. 1985. What unskilled ESL students do as they write: A classroom study of composing. *TESOL Quarterly* **19**, 229–58.

RAIMES, A. 1987. Language proficiency, writing ability and composing strategies: A study of ESL college student writers. *Language Learning* **37**, 439–68.

RAIMES, A. 1991. Out of the woods: Emerging traditions in the teaching of writing. *TESOL Quarterly* **25**, 407–30.

RAIMES, A. 1992. *Exploring through writing: A process approach to ESL composition,* 2nd edn. New York: St Martins Press.

RAYNER, K. and A. POLLATSEK. 1989. *The psychology of reading.* Hemel Hempstead and Englewood Cliffs, NJ: Prentice-Hall.

READANCE, J., T. BEAN and R.S. BALDWIN. 1989. *Content area reading: An integrated approach,* 3rd edn. Dubuque, IA: Kendall Hunt.

REID, J. 1988. Quantitative differences in English prose written by Arabic, Chinese, Spanish, and English students. Ft Collins, CO: Colorado State University. Ph.D. diss.

REID, J. 1993. *Teaching ESL writing.* Englewood Cliffs, NJ: Regents Prentice Hall.

REID, J. and B. KROLL. 1995. Designing and assessing effective classroom writing assignments for NES and ESL students. *Journal of Second Language Writing* **4**, 17–41.

REITHER, J. 1985. Writing and knowing: Toward redefining the writing process. *College English* **47**, 620–8.

REITHER, J. 1993. Bridging the gap: Scenic motives for collaborative writing in workplace and school. In R. SPILKA (ed.) *Writing in the workplace.* Carbondale, IL: Southern Illinois University Press. 195–206.

REPPEN, R. 1995a. Variation in elementary student language: A multidimensional perspective. Flagstaff, A2: Northern Arizona University. Ph.D. diss.

REPPEN, R. 1995b. A genre-based approach to content writing instruction. *TESOL Journal* **4**, 2. 32–5.

REPPEN, R. and W. GRABE. 1993. Spanish transfer effects in the English writing of elementary school students. *Lenguas Modernas* **20**, 113–28.

RESNICK, D. and L. RESNICK. 1977. The nature of literacy: A historical explanation. *Harvard Educational Review* **47**, 370–85.

REYNOLDS, J., C. MATALENE, J. MAGNOTTO, D, SAMSOM, JR. and L. SADLER. 1995. *Professional writing in context: Lessons from teaching and consulting.* Hove, Sussex and Hillsdale, NJ: L. Erlbaum.

RICHARDS, J. 1990. From meaning into words: Writing in a second or foreign language. In J. RICHARDS, *The language teaching matrix*. Cambridge, England and New York: Cambridge University Press. 100–17.

RICHGELS, D., L. McGEE, R. LOMAX and C. SHEARD. 1987. Awareness of four text structures: Effects on recall of expository prose. *Reading Research Quarterly* **22**, 177–96.

RIEBEN, L. and C. PERFETTI (eds). 1991. *Learning to read*. Hove, Sussex and Hillsdale, NJ: L. Erlbaum.

ROBB, T., S. ROSS and I. SHORTREED. 1986. Salience of feedback on error and its effect on ESL writing quality. *TESOL Quarterly* **20**, 83–93.

ROBINSON, G. 1992. *ESP today*. Hemel Hempsted and Englewood Cliffs, NJ: Prentice Hall.

ROGOFF, B. 1990. *Apprenticeship in thinking*. Oxford and New York: Oxford University Press.

RORTY, R. 1979. *Philosophy and the mirror of nature*. Princeton, NJ: Princeton University Press.

ROSENBERG, R. 1991. Using the portfolio to meet state-mandated assessment: A case study. In P. BELANOFF and M. DICKSON (eds) *Portfolios: Process and product*. Portsmouth, NH: Boynton/Cook. 69–79.

ROTHERY, J. 1989. Learning about language. In R. HASAN and J. MARTIN (eds) *Language development: Learning language, learning culture*. Norwood, NJ: Ablex. 199–256.

SA'ADEDDIN, M. 1989. Text development and Arabic-English negative interference. *Applied Linguistics* **10**, 36–51.

SANTA, C. and D. ALVERMANN (eds). 1991. *Science learning: Processes and applications*. Newark, DE: International Reading Association.

SCARDAMALIA, M. and C. BEREITER. 1986. Research on written composition. In M. WITTROCK (ed.) *Handbook of research on teaching*, 3rd edn. New York: Macmillan Education Ltd. 778–803.

SCARDAMALIA, M. and C. BEREITER. 1987. Knowledge telling and knowledge transforming in written composition. In S. ROSENBERG (ed.) *Advances in applied psycholinguistics, Volume 2: Reading, writing, and language learning*. Cambridge, England and New York: Cambridge University Press. 142–75.

SCARDAMALIA, M. and C. BEREITER. 1991. Literate expertise. In K.A. ERICSSON and J. SMITH (eds) *Toward a general theory of expertise*. Cambridge, England and New York: Cambridge University Press. 172–94.

SCHIEFFELIN, B. and E. OCHS (eds). 1986. *Language socialization across cultures*. Cambridge, England and New York: Cambridge University Press.

SCHIFFRIN, D. 1987. *Discourse markers*. Cambridge, England and New York: Cambridge University Press.

SCHIFFRIN, D. 1991. Conversational analysis. In W. GRABE *et al.* (eds) *Annual review of applied linguistics, 11. Discourse analysis*. Cambridge, England and New York: Cambridge University Press. 3–16.

SCHIFFRIN, D. 1994. *Approaches to discourse*. Oxford and New York: Blackwell.

SCHOLES, R. (ed.). 1993. *Literacy and language analysis.* Hove, Sussex and Hillsdale, NJ: L. Erlbaum.

SCHRIVER, K. 1992. Teaching writers to anticipate readers' needs: A classroom-evaluated pedagogy. *Written Communication* **9**, 179–208.

SCHRODER, H. (ed.). 1991. *Subject-oriented texts: Language for special purposes and text theory.* New York: Walter de Gruyter.

SCOLLON, R. 1991. Eight legs and one elbow: Stance and structure in Chinese–English compositions. Paper presented at the International Reading Association, Second North American Conference on Adult and Adolescent Literacy. Banff, Canada, March 1991.

SCOLLON, R. and S. SCOLLON. 1981. *Narrative, literacy and face in interethnic communication.* Norwood, NJ: Ablex.

SCOLLON, R. and S. SCOLLON. 1983. Face in interethnic communication. In J. RICHARDS and R. SCHMIDT (eds) *Language and communication.* London and New York: Longman. 156–88.

SCRIBNER, S. and M. COLE. 1981. *The psychology of literacy.* Cambridge, MA: Harvard University Press.

SELFE, C. 1981. The composing processes of four high and four low writing apprehensives: A case study. Austin, TX: University of Texas. Ph.D. diss.

SELFE, C. 1984. The predrafting processes of four high- and four low-apprehensive writers. *Research in the Teaching of English* **18**, 45–64.

SELFE, C. and S. HILLIGOSS (eds). 1994. *Literacy and computers: The complications of teaching and learning with technology.* New York: The Modern Language Association.

SHAPIRO, M. 1987. Language and Politics. In R.B. KAPLAN *et al.* (eds) *Annual review of applied linguistics,* 7. Cambridge, England and New York: Cambridge University Press. 74–85.

SHARAN, Y. and S. SHARAN. 1992. *Expanding cooperative learning through group investigation.* New York: Teachers College Press.

SHAUGHNESSY, M. 1977. *Errors and expectations: A guide for the teacher of basic writing.* Oxford and New York: Oxford University Press.

SHIH, M. 1986. Content-based approaches to teaching academic writing. *TESOL Quarterly* **20**, 617–48.

SHOR, I. (ed.). 1987. *Freire for the classroom.* Portsmouth, NH: Boynton/Cook.

SHORT, D. 1991. *How to integrate language and content instruction.* Washington, DC: Center for Applied Linguistics.

SHORT, D. 1994. Expanding middle school horizons: Integrating language, culture, and social studies. *TESOL Quarterly* **28**, 581–608.

SHUCHMAN, H. 1981. *Information transfer in engineering.* Washington, DC: Futures Group.

SHUY, R. 1987. Language and the law. In R.B. KAPLAn *et al.* (eds) *Annual review of applied linguistics,* 7. Cambridge, England and New York: Cambridge University Press. 50–63.

SHUY, R. 1991. *Language crimes.* Oxford and Cambridge, MA: Blackwell.

SILVA, T. 1990. Second language composition instruction: Developments, issues, and directions in ESL. In B. KROLL (ed.) *Second language writing.* Cambridge, England and New York: Cambridge University Press. 11–23.

SILVA, T. 1992. Research agendas for ESL writing: Differences in ESL and NES writing. Paper presented at the 27th Annual TESOL Convention. Vancouver, BC, March.

SILVA, T. 1993. Toward an understanding of the distinct nature of L2 writing: The ESL research and its implications. *TESOL Quarterly* **27**, 657–77.

SINCLAIR, J. 1991. *Corpus, concordance, collocation.* Oxford and New York: Oxford University Press.

SINCLAIR, J. 1994. Trust the text. In M. COULTHARD (ed.) *Advances in written text analysis.* London and New York: Routledge. 12–25.

SINGER, M. 1990. *Psychology of language: An introduction to sentence and discourse processes.* Hove, Sussex and Hillsdale, NJ: L. Erlbaum.

SLAVIN, R. 1990. *Cooperative learning: Theory, research, and practice.* London and Englewood Cliffs, NJ: Prentice Hall.

SLOBIN, D. 1990. The development from child speaker to native speaker. In J. STIGLER, R. SHWEDER and G. HERDT (eds) *Cultural psychology: Essays on comparative human development.* Cambridge, England and New York: Cambridge University Press. 233–56.

SLOBIN, D. and A. BOCAZ. 1988. Learning to talk about movement through time and space: The development of narrative abilities in Spanish and English. *Lenguas Modernas* **15**, 5–24.

SMAGORINSKY, P. 1992. How reading model essays affects writers. In J. IRWIN and M. DOYLE (eds) *Reading/writing connections: Learning from research.* Newark, DE: International Reading Association. 160–76.

SMAGORINSKY, P. (ed.). 1994. *Speaking about writing: Reflections of research methodology.* London and Thousand Oaks, CA: Sage.

SMIT, D., P. KOLONSKY and K. SELTZER. 1991. Implementing a portfolio system. In P. BELANOFF and M. DICKSON (eds) *Portfolios: Process and product.* Portsmouth, NH: Boynton/Cook. 46–56.

SMITH, N. 1989. *The twitter machine.* Oxford and New York: Blackwell.

SNOW, C., W. BARNES, J. CHANDLER, I. GOODMAN and L. HEMPHILL. 1991. *Unfulfilled expectations: Home and school influences on literacy.* Cambridge, MA: Harvard University Press.

SNYDER, I. 1993. Writing with word processors: A research overview. *Educational Research* **35**, 49–68.

SOKMEN, A. 1988. Taking advantage of conference-centered writing. *TESOL Newsletter* **22**, 1, 5.

SOMMER, N. 1980. Revision strategies of student writers and experienced adult writers. *College Composition and Communication* **31**, 378–88.

SOTER, A. 1988. The second language learner and cultural transfer in narration. In A. PURVES (ed.) *Writing across languages and cultures.* London and Newbury Park, CA: Sage. 177–205.

SPACK, R. 1988. Initiating ESL students into the academic discourse community: How far should we go. *TESOL Quarterly* **22**, 29–51.

SPANDEL, V. and R. STIGGINS. 1990. *Creating writers: Linking assessment and writing instruction.* London and New York: Longman.

SPEAR, K. 1988. *Sharing writing: Peer response groups in English classes.* Portsmouth, NH: Boynton/Cook.

SPEAR, K. (ed.). 1993. *Peer response groups in action: Writing together in secondary schools.* Portsmouth, NH: Boynton/Cook.

SPERBER, D. and D. WILSON. 1986. *Relevance.* Oxford: Blackwell Publishers and Cambridge, MA: Harvard University Press.

SPIEGEL, D. and J. FITZGERALD. 1991. Textual cohesion and coherence in children's writing revisited. *Research in the Teaching of English* **24**, 48–66.

SPILKA, R. 1993a. Influencing workplace practice: A challenge to professional writing specialists in academia. In R. SPILKA (ed.) *Writing in the workplace.* Carbondale, IL: Southern Illinois University Press. 207–19.

SPILKA, R. (ed.). 1993b. *Writing in the workplace.* Carbondale, IL: Southern Illinois University Press.

SPINDLER, G. and L. SPINDLER. 1987a. Teaching and learning how to do the ethnography of education. In G. SPINDLER and L. SPINDLER (eds) *Interpretive ethnography of education.* Hove, Sussex and Hillsdale, NJ: L. Erlbaum. 17–33.

SPINDLER, G. and L. SPINDLER (eds). 1987b. *Interpretive ethnography of education.* Hove, Sussex and Hillsdale, NJ: L. Erlbaum.

SPIRO, R. and B. TAYLOR. 1987. On investigating children's transition from narrative to expository discourse: The multidimensional nature of psychological text classification. In R. TIERNEY, P. ANDERS and J. MITCHELL (eds) *Understanding readers' understanding.* Hove, Sussex and Hillsdale, NJ: L. Erlbaum. 77–93.

SPIRO, R., W. VISPOEL, J. SCHMITZ, A. SAMARAPUNGAVAN and A.E. BOERGER. 1987. Knowledge acquisition for application: Cognitive flexibility and transfer in complex content domains. In B. BRITTON and S. GLYNN (eds) *Executive control processes in reading.* Hove, Sussex and Hillsdale, NJ: L. Erlbaum. 177–99.

SRIDHAR, S.N. 1994. A reality check for SLA theories. *TESOL Quarterly* **28**, 800–5.

STAHL, R. (ed.). 1994. *Cooperative learning in social studies.* Wokingham, England and Reading, MA: Addison-Wesley.

STAHL, S. 1994. Whole language in kindergarten and first grade: Separating the rhetoric from the effects. In F. LEHR and J. OSBORN (eds) *Reading, language, and literacy.* Hove, Sussex and Hillsdale, NJ: L. Erlbaum. 101–14.

STAHL, S. and P. MILLER. 1989. Whole language and language experience approaches for beginning reading: A quantitative research synthesis. *Review of Educational Research* **59**, 87–116.

STANLEY, J. 1992. Coaching student writers to be effective peer evaluators. *Journal of Second Language Writing* 1, 217–33.

STANOVICH, K. 1980. Toward an interactive-compensatory model of individual differences in the development of reading fluency. *Reading Research Quarterly* 16, 32–71.

STANOVICH, K. 1986. Matthew effects in reading: Some consequences of individual differences in the acquisition of literacy. *Reading Research Quarterly* 21, 360–407.

STANOVICH, K. 1992. The psychology of reading: Evolutionary and revolutionary developments. In W. GRABE *et al.* (eds) *Annual review of applied linguistics, 12. Literacy.* Cambridge, England and New York: Cambridge University Press. 3–30.

STANSFIELD, C. 1986. A history of the Test of Written English: The developmental years. *Language Testing* 3, 224–34.

STANSFIELD, C and J. ROSS. 1988. A long-term research agenda for the Test of Written English. *Language Testing* 5, 160–86.

STATON, J., R. SHUY, J.K. PEYTON and L. REED. 1988. *Dialogue journal communication: Classroom, linguistic, social and cognitive views.* Norwood, NJ: Ablex.

STEDMAN, L. 1994. The Sandia report and U.S. achievement: An assessment. *Journal of Educational Research* 87, 133–146.

STEDMAN, L. and C. KAESTLE. 1987. Literacy and reading performance in the United Stated from 1880 to the present. *Reading Research Quarterly* 22, 8–46.

STEINER, G. 1978. *On difficulty and other essays.* Oxford and New York: Oxford University Press.

STEWART, M.F. and C. GROBE. 1979. Syntactic maturity, mechanics of writing, and teachers' quality ratings. *Research in the Teaching of Writing* 13, 207–15.

STOLAREK, E. 1994. Prose modeling and metacogition: The effect of modeling on developing a metacognitive stance toward writing. *Research in the Teaching of Writing* 28, 154–74.

STREET, B. 1984. *Literacy in theory and practice.* Cambridge, England and New York: Cambridge University Press.

STREET, B. (ed.). 1993. *Cross-cultural approaches to literacy.* Cambridge, England and New York: Cambridge University Press.

STUBBS, M. 1980. *Language and literacy: The sociolinguistics of reading and writing.* London and Boston: Routledge & Kegan Paul.

STYGALL, G. 1991. Texts in oral context: The 'transmission' of jury instructions in an Indiana trial. In C. BAZERMAN and J. PARADIS (eds) *Textual dynamics of the professions.* Madison, WI: University of Wisconsin Press. 234–253.

SWALES, J. 1981. *Aspects of article introductions.* Birmingham: Language Studies Unit, University of Aston. [Aston ESP Research Reports 1.]

SWALES, J. (ed.). 1985. *Episodes in ESP.* Oxford: Pergamon.

SWALES, J. 1990. *Genre analysis: English in academic and research settings.* Cambridge, England and New York: Cambridge University Press.

SWALES, J. 1991. Discourse analysis in professional contexts. In W. GRABE *et al.* (eds) *Annual review of applied linguistics, 11.* Cambridge, England and New York: Cambridge University Press. 103–14.

SWALES, J. 1993. Genre and engagement. *Revue Belge de Philologie et d'Histoire* 71, 687–98.

SWALES, J. and H. NAJJAR. 1987. The writing of research article introductions. *Written Communication* 4, 175–91.

TADROS, A. 1994. Predictive categories in expository text. In M. COULTHARD (ed.) *Advances in written text analysis.* London and New York: Routledge. 69–82.

TANG, G. 1992. The effects of graphic representation of knowledge structures on ESL reading comprehension. *Studies in Second Language Acquisition* 14, 177–95.

TANNEN, D. 1982. Oral and literate strategies in spoken and written narratives. *Language* 58, 1–21.

TANNEN, D. 1985. Relative focus on involvement in oral and written discourse. In D. OLSON, N. TORRANCE and A. HILYARD (eds) *Literacy, language, and learning: The nature and consequence of reading and writing.* Cambridge, England and New York: Cambridge University Press. 124–47.

TANNEN, D. 1987. The orality of literature and the literacy of conversation. In J. LANGER (ed.) *Language, literacy and culture: Issues in society and schooling.* Norwood, NJ: Ablex. 67–88.

TANNEN, D. 1989. *Talking voices.* Cambridge, England and New York: Cambridge University Press.

TARONE, E., S. DWYER, S, GILLETTE and V. ICKE. 1981. On the use of the passive in two astrophysics journal papers. *ESP Journal* 1, 123–40.

TATE, G. (ed.). 1987. *Teaching composition.* Fort Worth, TX: Texas Christian University Press.

TAYLOR, D. 1993. A counseling approach to writing conferences. In T. FLYNN and M. KING (eds) *Dynamics of the writing conference.* Urbana, IL: National Council of Teachers of English. 24–33.

TAYLOR G. and T. CHEN. 1991. Linguistic, cultural, and subcultural issues in contrastive discourse analysis: Anglo-American and Chinese scientific texts. *Applied Linguistics* 12, 319–36.

TCHUDI, S. and M. HUERTA. 1983. *Teaching writing in the content areas: Middle school/junior high.* Washington, DC: National Education Association.

TEST OF WRITTEN ENGLISH (TWE) GUIDE. 1992. Princeton, NJ: Educational Testing Service.

THARP, R. and R. GALLIMORE. 1988. *Rousing minds to life.* Cambridge, England and New York: Cambridge University Press.

TIERNEY, R., M. CARTER and L. DESAI. 1991. *Portfolio assessment in the reading–writing classroom.* Norwood, MA: Christopher Gordon.

TIERNEY, R. and P. MOSENTHAL. 1983. Cohesion and textual coherence. *Research in the Teaching of English* 17, 215–29.

TIERNEY, R. and P.D. PEARSON. 1983. Toward a composing model of reading. *Language Arts* 60, 568–80.

TIERNEY, R., J. READANCE and E. DISHNER. 1990. *Reading strategies and practices: A compendium.* 3rd edn. Boston: Allyn & Bacon.

TOMPKINS, G. 1990. *Teaching writing: Balancing process and product.* New York: Merrill.

TRIMBLE, L. 1985. *English for science and technology.* Rowley, MA: Newbury House.

TSAO, F. 1983. Linguistics and written discourse in particular languages: Contrastive studies: English and Chinese. In R.B. KAPLAN *et al.* (eds) *Annual review of applied linguistics, 3.* Rowley, MA: Newbury House. 99–117.

TUMAN, M. (ed.). 1992. *Literacy online.* Pittsburgh, PA: University of Pittsburgh Press.

UNIVERSITY OF SOUTHERN CALIFORNIA (USC), UCC.USM. 1985. University of Southern California, University Computer Center, Users Manual, AAO2. page 8.

URZUA, C. 1987. 'You stopped too soon': Second language children composing and revising. *TESOL Quarterly* 21, 279–304.

VACHEK, J. 1966. *The linguistic school of Prague.* Bloomington, IN: University of Indiana Press.

VAHAPASSI, A. 1988. The problem of selection of writing tasks in cross-cultural study. In A. PURVES (ed.) *Writing across languages and cultures.* London and Newbury Park; CA: Sage. 51–78.

VANDE KOPPLE, W. 1982. The given-new strategy of comprehension and some natural expository paragraphs. *Journal of Psycholinguistic Research* 11, 501–20.

VANDE KOPPLE, W. 1983. Something old, something new: Functional sentence perspective. *Research in the Teaching of English* 17, 85–99.

VANDE KOPPLE, W. 1986. Given and new information and some aspects of the structures, semantics, and pragmatics of written texts. In C. COOPER and S. GREENBAUM (eds) *Studying writing: Linguistic approaches.* London and Newbury Park, CA: Sage. 72–111.

VANDE KOPPLE, W. 1990. Themes, thematic progressions, and some implications for understanding discourse. *Written Communication* 8, 311–47.

VAN DIJK, T. 1985. *Handbook of discourse analysis,* 4 Vols. London and New York: Academic Press.

VAN DIJK, T. 1988. *News as discourse.* Hillsdale, NJ: L. Erlbaum.

VAN DIJK, T. and W. KINTSCH. 1983. *Strategies of discourse comprehension.* London and New York: Academic Press.

VAN NAERRSEN, M. and R.B. KAPLAN. 1987. Language and science. In R.B. KAPLAN *et al.* (eds) *Annual review of applied linguistics, 7.* Cambridge, England and New York: Cambridge University Press. 86–104.

VENTOLA, E. and A. MAURANEN. 1991. Non-native and native revising of scientific articles. In E. VENTOLA (ed.) *Functional and systemic linguistics: Approaches and uses.* Berlin: Mouton de Gruyter. 457–92.

VYGOTSKY, L. 1962. *Thought and language* (E. Haufmann and G. Vadar, eds and trans.). Cambridge, MA: MIT Press.

VYGOTSKY, L. 1978. *Mind in society* (M. Cole *et al.* eds and trans.). Cambridge, MA: Harvard University Press.

VYGOTSKY, L. 1983. The prehistory of written language. In M. MARTLEW (ed.) *The psychology of written composition.* New York: J. Wiley. 279–91.

WALD, B. 1987. The development of writing skills among Hispanic high school students. In S. GOLDMAN and H. TRUEBA (eds) *Becoming literate in English as a second language.* Norwood, NJ: Ablex. 155–185.

WALKER, C. and D. ELIAS. 1987. Writing conference talk: Factors associated with high- and low-rated writing conferences. *Research in the Teaching of English* **21**, 266–85.

WALSHE, R. 1981a. *Every child can write!* Victoria, NSW: Primary English Teacher's Association.

WALSHE, R. 1981b. *Donald Graves in Australia: Children want to write ...* Victoria, NSW: Primary English Teacher's Association.

WALSMLEY, S. 1994. *Children exploring their world: Theme teaching in elementary school.* London and Portsmouth, NH: Heinemann.

WALVOORD, B. and L. MCCARTHY. 1991. *Thinking and writing in college: A naturalistic study of students in four disciplines.* Urbana, IL: National Council of Teachers of English.

WASIK, B. and R. SLAVIN. 1993. Preventing early reading failure with one-to-one tutoring: A review of five programs. *Reading Research Quarterly* **28**, 179–200.

WAUTERS, J. 1991. Evaluation for empowerment: A portfolio proposal for Alaska. In P. BELANOFF and M. DICKSON (eds) *Portfolios: Process and product.* Portsmouth, NH: Boynton/Cook. 57–68.

WEASENFORTH, D. 1995. Rhetorical abstration as a facet of expected response: A structural equation modeling analysis. Los Angeles: University of Southern California. Ph.D. diss.

WELLS, G. 1986. *The meaning makers: Children learning language and using language to learn.* London and Portsmouth, NH: Heinemann.

WELLS, G. 1994. The complementary contributions of Halliday and Vygotsky to a 'language-based theory of learning'. *Linguistics and Education* **6**, 41–91.

WELLS, G. and G. CHANG-WELLS. 1992. *Constructing knowledge together.* London and Portsmouth, NH: Heinemann.

WERTSCH, J. (ed.). 1985. *Culture, communication and cognition.* Cambridge and New York: Cambridge University Press.

WERTSCH, J. 1991. Voices of the mind: A sociocultural approach to mediated action. Cambridge, MA: Harvard University Press.

WHITE, E. 1993. Holistic scoring: Past triumphs, future challenges. In M. WILLIAMSON and B. HUOT (eds) *Validating holistic scoring for writing assessment.* Cresskill, NJ: Hampton Press. 79–108.

WHITE, E. 1994. *Teaching and assessing writing*, 2nd edn. San Francisco: Jossey Bass.

WHITE, E. 1995. An apologia for the timed impromptu essay test. *College Composition and Communication* **46**, 30–45.

WHITE, R. and V. ARNDT. 1991. *Process writing*. London and New York: Longman.

WHITWORTH, R. 1988. Collaborative learning and other disasters. In J. GOLUB (ed.) *Focus on collaborative learning*. Urbana, IL: National Council of teachers of English. 13–20.

WHORF, B.L. 1941. Grammatical categories. *Language* **21**, 1–11.

WIDDOWSON, H.G. 1978. *Language teaching as communication*. Oxford and New York: Oxford University Press.

WIDDOWSON, H.G. 1979. *Explorations in applied linguistics*. Oxford and New York: Oxford University Press.

WIDDOWSON, H.G. 1980. Conceptual and communicative functions in written discourse. *Applied Linguistics* **1**, 234–43.

WIDDOWSON, H.G. 1983. *Learning purpose and language use*. Oxford and New York: Oxford University Press.

WILD, A. 1985. Performance review. *L.A. Times*. (March 16, 1985) V.1.

WILLEY, R. 1990. Pre-classical roots of the addressed/invoked dichotomy of audience. In G. KIRSCH and D. ROEN (eds) *A sense of audience in written communication*. London and Newbury Park, CA: Sage. 25–39.

WILLIAMS, F. 1976. *Explorations of the linguistic attitudes of teachers*. Rowley, MA: Newbury House.

WILLIAMSON, M. 1993. An introduction to holistic scoring: The social, historical, and theoretical context for writing assessment. In M. WILLIAMSON and B. HUOT (eds) *Validating holistic scoring for writing assessment*. Cresskill, NJ: Hampton Press. 1–43.

WINSOR, D. 1990. Engineering writing/writing engineering. *College Composition and Communication* **41**, 58–70.

WITTE, S. 1983a. Topical structure and revision: An exploratory study. *College Composition and Communication* **34**, 313–41.

WITTE, S. 1983b. Topical structure and writing quality: Some possible text-based explanations for readers' judgments of student writing. *Visible Language* **17**, 177–205.

WITTE, S. 1992. Context, text, intertext: Toward a constructivist semiotic of writing. *Written Communication* **9**, 237–308.

WITTE, S. and R. CHERRY. 1986. Writing processes and written products in composition research. In C. COOPER and S. GREENBAUM (eds) *Studying writing: Linguistics approaches*. London and Newbury Park, CA: Sage. 112–53.

WITTE, S. and L. FAIGLEY. 1981. Coherence, cohesion, and writing quality. *College Composition and Communication* **32**, 189–204.

WODAK, R. 1989. Topic development, syntax, and social class. *Discourse Processes* **11**, 267–86.

WODAK, R. 1990. Discourse analysis: Problems, findings, perspectives. *Text* **10**, 125–32.

WOLFSON, N. 1989. *Perspectives: Sociolinguistics and TESOL.* New York: Newbury House.

YOUNG, R. 1987. Recent developments in rhetorical invention. In G. TATE (ed.) *Teaching composition.* Fort Worth, TX: Texas Christian University Press. 1–38.

YOUNG, R., A. BECKER and K. PIKE. 1970. *Rhetoric: Discovery and change.* London and New York: Harcourt, Brace and World.

ZAMEL, V. 1982. Writing: The process of discovering meaning. *TESOL Quarterly* **16**, 195–209.

ZAMEL, V. 1983. The composing processes of advanced ESL students: Six case studies. *TESOL Quarterly* **17**, 165–87.

ZAMEL, V. 1985. Responding to student writing. *TESOL Quarterly* **19**, 79–101.

ZAMEL, V. 1987. Recent research on writing pedagogy. *TESOL Quarterly* **21**, 697–715.

ZAMEL, V. 1992. Writing one's way into reading. *TESOL Quarterly* **26**, 463–85.

ZELLERMEYER, M. 1988. An analysis of oral and literate texts: Two types of reader–writer relationships in Hebrew and English. In B. RAFOTH and D. RUBIN (eds) *The social construction of written communication.* Norwood, NJ: Ablex. 287–303.

ZHU, W. 1994. Effects of training for peer revision in college freshman composition classes. Flagstaff, AZ: Northern Arizona University. Ph.D. diss.

Subject Index

Author Index